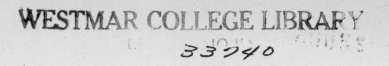

Bureau of International Research
Harvard University and Radcliffe College

THE RELATIVITY OF WAR AND PEACE

A STUDY IN LAW, HISTORY, AND POLITICS

THE RELATIVITY

OF

WAR AND PEACE

A Study in Law, History, and Politics

BY

FRITZ GROB

Professor of Political Science at Olivet College

Foreword by Roscoe Pound

33740

NEW HAVEN

YALE UNIVERSITY PRESS

LONDON · GEOFFREY CUMBERLEGE · OXFORD UNIVERSITY PRESS

1949

*The Bureau of International Research has aided the author in
carrying on research and in publishing the results. The Bureau
assumes no responsibility for the statements or views expressed.*

To

MAX HUBER

and

ROSCOE POUND

Foreword

There is a story of a clergyman who was surprised to find on the table in a lawyer's study a book entitled *A Treatise on Election, Conversion, and Redemption.* He was even more surprised to find it was a treatise on three technical doctrines of Anglo-American equity. Each of the three words has more than one meaning, which must be drawn from the context in which it is used. Election means one thing in political science, another in the lawyer's books on equity, and another in theology. Conversion has one meaning at common law, another in equity, and another in theology. Redemption means one thing in the common law as to pledges, another in equity as to mortgages, and still another in theology. Aristotle thought not of one word with a number of meanings but of a number of meanings expressed by only one word. He compared this with the case of one meaning with more than one word to express it. For the former he used the term homonym; for the latter his term synonym is still in familiar use. A prime reason for homonyms is that we seek to understand the unknown on the analogy of the known; the new by referring it to the old. Thus even technical terms easily acquire many meanings. Moreover, certain terms of ethical import, such as law, right, duty, acquire what we call a good will which makes those who have causes to advocate eager to get the advantage of them in argument. Other terms may have acquired connotations which make the advocate of a cause reluctant to admit that they are applicable and so lead him to specious qualifications of them. If a dubious proposition can be put in terms of a word which has acquired good will it may find acceptance which it could not otherwise command. Analogical use of a solving term and qualification of inconvenient apparently applicable terms are especially useful to statesmen and diplomats. Escape from awkward constitutional provisions or evasion of awkward legal limitations may often be effected by resort to a convenient homonym or invoking a distinction or qualification which conceals the reality of a situation. Such terms and such qualifications leading to pseudo-terms have to be scrutinized with respect to the situations for which they are invoked. Unhappily, they tempt jurists to seek to reach absolute definitions which will embrace all the applications, ignoring the special conditions of fact for which they were devised.

A distinction must be made between legal conceptions and juristic conceptions. Legal conceptions, e.g., Bailment, Sale, Trust, are defined by law. They are legally defined categories. When a state of facts comes within one of these categories certain rules, principles, and standards become applicable. Juristic conceptions are not defined by law. Such ideas as a right, a duty, a liberty, or a privilege are not legal conceptions. They are worked out by jurists for purposes of understanding, teaching, and applying the law. Hence while lawyers know what a bailment or a trust is (although use of a trust as a means of effecting restraint of trade has led to a popular meaning of the term with reference to the purpose instead of the means) there is endless discussion among jurists as to what a right is, and the practicing lawyer is much confused among the six or more meanings which the word has acquired. We must inquire not as to the word but as to particular meanings in particular connections; whether there is a legal conception or one or more juristic conceptions which the word seeks to cover, and whether the meanings in the several connections can be unified or cannot be brought under any useful broad definition. To take an example from everyday private law, terms which have a clear definite meaning in judicial opinions or in the textbooks may be used in a loose popular sense in statutes with the result that interpretation and application become difficult. Thus the word "custody" has a settled technical use in the common law as to larceny. It is used otherwise as to children in divorce proceedings, and has been used to mean possession in statutes as to the duties of a person with whom a will has been deposited for safe keeping to await the testator's death. Here, however, the lawyer is helped by the narrow choice of materials which make up the form of law. The Anglo-American lawyer need look only at statutes and authoritative reported judicial decisions and can judge of treatises by them. The Continental lawyer has the codes, the statutes, and the Roman and modern Roman law books in which to find legal conceptions defined and by which to judge of juristic conceptions.

When one inquires as to the technical definition of war in international law his task is more complicated. For one thing it is complicated by a difficulty as to the meaning of "law" in inter-

national law. The writers on international law, agreeing with
Continental jurists, think of *droit, Recht,* right-and-law, a wider
term than our word "law." Also the forms of international law
are by no means so clearly defined as those of municipal private
law. Hence one must go over the literature of politics, diplomacy,
ethics of foreign relations, as well as treaties and customarily received texts. Even if one were to approach the subject from the
narrowly limited point of view of Anglo-American analytical
jurists, the task would still be complicated by the requirement
that the courts take the facts as to existence or nonexistence of
war from the political departments of government. Use of the
term war in political discussions is so obviously dictated by national economic self-interest or zeal for acquisition or exercise of
power or in internal politics by the exigencies of party strife
that nothing can be made of such discussions for legal purposes.

In my lecture on Philosophical Theory and International Law
(Visscher Lecture at Leyden, 1922) I showed how Grotius made
his theory of international law to the pattern of international
relations in the seventeenth-century era of absolute monarchies
and how inapplicable his theory was to the facts of international
society of today. Dr. Grob shows how inapplicable to those facts
are the philosophical and natural-law definitions of war. Moreover, "war in the legal sense" or "war in the sense of international
law," if capable of definition, cannot be defined with assurance
so long as we can't define international law and ascertain its
authoritative forms with assurance. Arguments drawn from
French discussions of the French constitutional provision as to
war without a vote of both houses of Parliament are of no worth
because French constitutional provisions are not law in the analytical sense. They are hortatory, ignored or interpreted to order to
the exigencies of partisan politics. When from the books on politics we turn to "customary international law" the difficult and
much debated question as to the nature of law still embarrasses us.
"War" in international law does not necessarily mean the same as
"war" in the sense of Article I, Section 8, paragraph 11 of the
Constitution of the United States. But is the latter text like the
provision of Article V of the Federal Bill of Rights that "no person shall be held for a capital or otherwise infamous crime unless
on a presentment or indictment of a grand jury"? As to the Federal Bill of Rights, if one is prosecuted in derogation of the con-

stitutional prohibition the courts will simply refuse to entertain the unconstitutional prosecution. But who can enforce against the executive a constitutional provision that only the legislative department of government can declare war? This must be considered especially where what is war is held to be a political question as to which the courts must be governed by the pronouncements of the political organs for the case in hand. Hence we can work out a legal theory for the prohibition in the American Bill of Rights while we have to struggle with inconsistencies of political manipulation for the other case.

Even in municipal private law, however, there is often difficulty in framing a general definition or general theory where one legal term is used in application of different rules and has only an appearance of unity of meaning to admit of absolute defining. Thus "possession" has to be understood for Roman law with reference to acquisition by adverse possession (acquisitive prescription) on the one hand, and the possessory interdicts on the other hand, and theories which attempt a universal definition with reference to both have often fallen down between them. Again, in American law definitions of possession with reference to the common-law refinements as to larceny and use of the term in recent statutes as to possession of narcotics at one's peril, which cannot be reconciled by any analytical formula, have to be given up. We have to recognize that we can't make one abstract theory or one definition to fit "possession" in every case in which it is used in the books. In the same way the term "war" must be understood with reference to particular rules of international law which happen to be under consideration.

Use of terms other than "war" or "peace," e.g., "state of war," "hostilities," "belligerency," "state of peace," "expeditionary force," "intervention," "reprisals," "pacific blockade," in order to evade difficulties arising from prohibitions or mandatory directions in constitutions or bodies of fundamental precepts has not lightened the difficulties of the subject. The settled practice of Turkey up to the middle of the eighteenth century not to make treaties of peace but only to accede to armistices because the Koran forbade treaties of peace with the infidel seems childish. But it has its parallel in French waging of what in all effect and common sense was war with China in the eighties of the last century under names used to evade a requirement of the French constitution. The exigencies of like prohibitions or directions in constitutions are behind much of the phenomena which have perplexed jurists who have sought to define war. "Pacific blockade" in particular has been a convenient term to enable a government to by-pass a constitutional prohibition.

To go back to the story of the clergyman and the law book, the point may be carried even further. If we are thinking of rules of law as to wrongful assertion of dominion over another's chattel, "conversion" means one thing. If we are thinking of rules of succession to land directed to be sold and disposition of the money, or to money directed to be invested in the purchase of land, "conversion" means something very different. If we are thinking of a *quo warranto* proceeding and of the rules as to the means by which one of the parties asserts title to an office he holds, "election" means one thing. If we are thinking of the rules applicable where a widow, entitled to a legacy under her husband's will, is also entitled under a statute to share in his estate, "election" has a very different meaning. If we are thinking of the rules of law as to the effect of open, notorious, continuous, exclusive adverse possession of a chattel, "possession" means one thing. If the question is one of interpretation and application to the chauffeur and porter operating a hotel bus of a statute against possession and transportation of intoxicating liquor in a dry area, the term "possession" may mean something else. The precept element of the law is defined in authoritative forms. The terminology is the work of jurists and teachers and doctrinal writers. It must be understood with reference to the precepts in connection with which the terms are employed.

All law has to reckon with such things. But international law is embarrassed further by pretended legal categories in long use, which include too much or too little such as "partial state of war," and others above referred to, and by artificialities of official dates of beginning and of termination of war, fixed for particular political or economic purposes, and as a rule turning out to be inapplicable to or confusing in application to particular rules as to war. How the term "war," regarded as a legal term with a fixed context for all purposes, may darken counsel is brought out in a recent case in the Supreme Court of the United States decided by five judges, four dissenting, in which Mr. Justice Frankfurter said: "War does not cease with a cease fire order. . . . 'The state of war' may be terminated by treaty or legislation or Presidential proclamation. Whatever the mode, its termination is a political act."* The question was really one of interpretation of an act of Congress. Did the act mean to confer an emergency power in derogation of liberty for so long as the administration chose to consider the war continuing or did it mean to confer the power for the duration of the emergency created by the exigencies of actual fighting? Because war may be considered a political condition of which for general purposes the political departments of the government must be the judge, it does not follow that those departments are, under our constitutional polity, the final interpreters of statutes conferring emergency powers of deprivation of liberty on the executive.

Some of the situations arising from a general idea that war begins on the date of a declaration and can only be ended by a formal treaty of peace or political act, so that Liechtenstein is still "technically at war" with Prussia, San Marino with Turkey, Berwick-upon-Tweed with Russia, and the Tuscarora Indians with Germany, are more worthy of a Gilbert and Sullivan opera or of Lewis Carroll's professors than of legal treatises.

A famous pronouncement of Javolenus in Justinian's Digest tells us that all definition is perilous. Even if, as some have thought, *definitio* here means maxim, as it seems to have meant to Cicero, in which case the proposition is eminently sound, it is no less true of proposed definitions of legal terms which seek to include all manner of many diverse applications, often used to cover up meanings rather than to impart them. Thus the problem to which Dr. Grob has addressed himself is one of law and of the science of law generally. It is not confined to international law. Dr. Grob has made a real contribution to analytical jurisprudence.

ROSCOE POUND

* *Ludecke* v. *Watkins*, 335 U.S. 160 (1948).

Contents

Foreword by Roscoe Pound   vii

Author's Introduction   xv

PART I. HISTORICAL

Chapter I. Terms in Connection with the Ideas of War and Peace as Such   3

Chapter II. Terms in Connection with the Ideas of Operations Short of War and of War Part Way   15

Chapter III. War or Peace?   37

     Section 1. American Naval Operations against France, 1798–1800, and against Germany and Italy, 1941   37

     Section 2. The Boxer Expedition, 1900–1901   64

     Section 3. German Military Operations against Italy, 1915–1916   79

Chapter IV. Battles in "Peace"   82

     Section 1. The Battle off Navarino, 1827, and Other Operations Accompanied by Protestations of Peace   82

     Section 2. French Operations against Annam, 1882–1884, and against China, 1883–1885   97

     Section 3. The Manchurian Conflict, 1931–1933, and the Sino-Japanese "Incident," 1937–1941   140

PART II. THEORETICAL

Chapter V. Of Rules of Law on War   161

     1. In General   161

     2. International Law   162

     3. Municipal Law   170

Chapter VI. "The" Legal Definition of War   173

Chapter VII. The Relativity of War and Peace   189
    Section 1. General Considerations   189
    Section 2. Armed Intervention   224
    Section 3. Armed Reprisals   237
    Section 4. Pacific Blockades   247
    Section 5. On the Parties to War   267
    Section 6. Authorized and Unauthorized Operations   273
    Section 7. War and Diplomatic Relations   275
    Section 8. War with and without Clash of Arms   279
    Section 9. On Declarations of War   283
    Section 10. On the Duration of War   302
    Section 11. Observations Regarding War and Peace
        under the Charter of the United Nations   324

Bibliography   333

Cases Quoted   349

Notes   351

Indexes:
    Authors   389
    Other Persons   391
    States   395
    Subjects   397

Cartoon: The Conflict in the Far East Presents a Problem for Uncle Sam. From the *Philadelphia Inquirer*.   155

Author's Introduction

This book, as is indicated by its subtitle, is primarily a study in *law*, both international and municipal. What are war and peace from the point of view of the law? It is to answer this question that the book has been written. It would not have been advisable to clarify these concepts through legal considerations alone, without regard for anything else. Legal considerations had to be frequently supplemented by considerations of a historical or political nature. This book, in order to serve its purpose, had to be a study in law, *history*, and *politics*.

It will hardly be necessary to explain at length why this study was made. It was undertaken on account of a well-known fact. The question of what legally constitutes war and, for that matter, peace has time and again baffled governments, courts, and international bodies. According to a study entitled *The Attempt to Define War* (published in 1933 by the Carnegie Endowment for International Peace), "war" is "a word which seems to paralyze thought." Indeed, there is, to give a famous example, no better way to embarrass an American international lawyer than to ask him: When was the United States for the first time legally at war? Was it from 1798 to 1800 against France? Or was it from 1812 to 1814 against Great Britain? Many equally embarrassing questions regarding the border line between war and peace could be posed in connection with operations that have taken place in the nineteenth and twentieth centuries. In quite a number of cases the official reaction to the question whether operations constituted war seemed to be paradoxical. In 1931 and 1932 the Japanese, to give a recent example, invaded and virtually annexed Manchuria. Did these operations constitute a "resort to war?" Not according to the League of Nations, which refrained from reacting with sanctions. In 1937 the Japanese started their operations against China proper, operations which were to last for more than eight years. Did these operations constitute a "state of war?" Not according to the chairman of the Senate through an exchange of letters across the Atlantic, by the late Dr. Walther Burckhardt, Professor of Law at the University of Bern. The author, furthermore, is much indebted to Professor Edwin Borchard of the Yale University Law School for reading the manuscript. It ought to be added that the author hails from Switzerland and that he remembers with gratitude the devotion with which American friends have read parts of the manuscript and made suggestions for improvements in point of language. Thanks for such assistance are due to Dr. Eleanor Wyllys Allen of Cambridge, Mass., to Miss Eleanor and Mr. Allen Hyde of Hartford, Conn., and to Mr. Richard F. Koch, Professor in the Department of Modern Languages of the Massachusetts Institute of Technology.

F. G.

PART I

HISTORICAL

CHAPTER I

Terms in Connection with the Ideas of
War and Peace as Such

It is a matter of common knowledge that almost all American municipal law applies in peace and in war alike. A few scattered rules apply in peace only, and a relatively small number apply only in war. The same is true of other municipal law systems.

International law offers a different picture. Rules that apply in peace and in war alike are scarce. The bulk of international law falls into two main divisions; the rules of one refer to peace, the rules of the other to war. Many treatises on international law are divided into two parts of approximately equal size, one devoted to peace, and one to war.

In a word, the antithesis of peace and war, rarely presenting itself in municipal law, is ever present in international law.

Innumerable rules of law refer to peace pure and simple. Innumerable rules of law, on the other hand, refer to war pure and simple. One and the same rule may refer to both peace and war. One hundred and fifty-seven years ago the Bill of Rights became a part of the Constitution of the United States. The bill says in Article III: "No soldier shall, in time of peace, be quartered in any home without the consent of the owner, nor in time of war but in a manner to be prescribed by law."

The task of distinguishing peace and war would be much facilitated if legal language confined itself to the terms "peace" and "war." Unfortunately legal language is not so simple as that. It was not so simple as that in the days when the first Congress drafted the Bill of Rights, and it is considerably less so today.

There are rules of law which refer to a "state of war," to a "state of peace," to an "act of war." To these must be added other terms generally regarded as belonging to the legal vocabulary. They are to be found in court proceedings, parliamentary debates, diplomatic papers, speeches, and other official statements made by statesmen and in works of legal writers. Such terms are: de jure war, de facto war, belligerency, and nonbelligerency.

The term "state of war" rather frequently occurs in both municipal and international law. The operation of certain provisions of the Neutrality Act of 1935 depended upon "war" among foreign states being proclaimed by the President of the United States. The succeeding Neutrality Acts of 1936, 1937, and 1939 enjoined the President to proclaim the existence not of war but of a "state of war" among foreign states.[1] In the past, declarations of war were often but not always to the effect that X considered itself from such and such a date to be in a "state of war" with Y.[2] On December 11, 1941, at 9:30 A.M., the German chargé d'affaires in Washington, Dr. Hans Thomsen, handed to Mr. Ray Atherton, Chief of the European Division of the State Department, the German declaration of war. It concluded by stating that Germany from that day on considered itself as being in a "state of war" with the United States of America.[3] At about the same hour the Italian Foreign Minister, Count Ciano, informed the American chargé d'affaires in Rome, Mr. George Wadsworth, that Italy considered itself "at war" with the United States.[4] What reason is there to speak not only of war pure and simple but, in addition, of a "state of war"?

And what legal reason is there for the term "state of peace," a term which occurs seldom in comparison with the term "state of war"? After the long, deadly feud between Communist Russia and National Socialist Germany there was, to give an example, a peculiar flutter of dove's wings over the German-Russian Nonaggression Pact of August 23, 1939, in which both parties were "moved by a desire to strengthen the state of peace existing between them." [5]

The terms "de jure war" and "de facto war" are met chiefly in works of legal writers but are likewise to be heard in court proceedings, parliamentary debates, and statements made by statesmen. On June 10, 1941, almost exactly half a year before Italy's declaration of war against the United States, Premier

Mussolini spoke to the Italian nation before the Chamber of Fasces and Corporations on Italy's war policy. He characterized the "situation" then existing between the United States and Italy as amounting already to a "war de facto if not de jure." [6] What exactly is the idea that Mussolini was trying to put across?

On the face of it, the terms "de jure war" and "de facto war" would seem to be less perplexing than "state of war." "De jure war" is evidently only another way of saying "war according to its legal definition," or "war in the technical sense," or "war in the legal sense." Some say more specifically "war in the sense of international law." All these terms are well known to the student of international law. They point to what international lawyers say is their all-important yardstick for the determination of the existence of war. It will be argued that "de facto war," on the other hand, must obviously be war according to such a legal definition but which, for one reason or another, is not recognized as such. It is all too clear that this gives no final answer as to the meaning of the term "de facto war." If the much-talked-of legal definition of war holds water, well and good. If it does not, the meaning of both "de jure war" and "de facto war" is left hanging in the air.

The declaration of war made by the United States in 1917 against Germany refers to "repeated *acts of war*" committed by the Imperial German Government against the government and the people of the United States.[7] The German declaration of war against the United States of December 11, 1941, accuses the United States of "open acts of war" committed against Germany.[8] In the two years preceding the German declaration of war the student of American foreign policy was repeatedly confronted with the term "act of war." Expressions of opinion in Congress and elsewhere were marked by disagreement and even uncertainty as to what constitutes an "act of war."

On September 3, 1940, President Roosevelt informed Congress of the agreement with the British Government under which the United States was to transfer to Great Britain fifty over-age destroyers and obtain from Great Britain ninety-nine-year leases for sea and air bases at eight strategic continental and island points stretching from Newfoundland to British Guiana. The President in his message to Congress emphasized that the deal did not represent a "threat to any nation" and that it was not inconsistent "in any sense with our status of peace." [9] The deal took Congress by surprise. Amid widespread approval and applause for the agreement, some criticism was voiced. Senator Clark, Democrat, of Idaho, Representatives Miller of Connecticut, Oliver of Maine, Rogers of Massachusetts, Short of Missouri, and Smith of Ohio attacked the transfer of the destroyers as an "act of war." Congressional reaction included the comment by Representative Fish, Republican, of New York: "It usurps the power of Congress. It violates the Constitution and international law. It is virtually an act of war." [10] On January 7, 1941, the President indirectly referred to such criticism in a passage of his message to Congress on the state of the Union. The President said:

Let us say to the democracies: "We Americans are vitally concerned in your defense of freedom. We are putting forth our energies, our resources and our organizing powers to give you the strength to regain and maintain a free world. We shall send you, in ever-increasing numbers, ships, planes, tanks, guns. That is our purpose and our pledge."

In fulfillment of this purpose we will not be intimidated by the threats of dictators that they will regard as a breach of international law or as an *act of war* our aid to the democracies which dare to resist their aggression. Such aid is not an *act of war*, even if a dictator should unilaterally proclaim it so to be.

When the dictators, if the dictators are ready to make war upon us, they will not wait for an *act of war* on our part.

They did not wait for Norway or Belgium or the Netherlands to commit an act of war. [11]

What exactly constitutes an "act of war"? Two recent incidents that occurred in the Senate Committee on Military Affairs and on the floor of the Senate tend to demonstrate that the answer is not easy.

On June 18, 1940, Henry L. Stimson, one of America's most distinguished lawyers, delivered at the Yale Commencement an address in which he listed seven points of policy that the United States, in his opinion, should follow. Taking as his theme the value of the British fleet to the United States, Mr. Stimson proposed that "we should throw open all our ports to the British and French naval and merchant marine for all repairs and refueling and other naval services." [12] Two days later President Roosevelt nominated Mr. Stimson to be Secretary of War. On July 2 the Committee on Military Affairs of the Senate met in the presence of Mr. Stimson to consider the nomination. In the course of the hearing Senator Vandenberg remarked that the one specific thing that disturbed him was the second point in Mr. Stimson's speech at Yale. "Would that not be an *act of war?*" he asked.

"My impression is, no," Mr. Stimson replied. "I do not think it would."

Senator Vandenberg then asked how it could be anything else than an *act of war*.

Mr. Stimson replied: "It is certainly an act of non-neutrality; but whether it is an act of belligerency, I would withhold statement. . . . If it should become necessary for the security of the United States I should regard it as an act of legitimate self-defense which the United States should take regardless of what before the arrival of the present emergency was called neutrality and international law."

Senator Vandenberg once more came back to his point, asking, "Would it or would it not be an *act of war* to open our ports to British and French belligerent fleets?"

"I cannot answer that," Mr. Stimson replied.[13]

The incident which occurred on the floor of the Senate had as its background the dramatic rendezvous between President Roosevelt and Prime Minister Churchill held early in August, 1941, on the Atlantic off the North American coast. The meeting resulted in the declaration of American and British policy which has become known to the world as the Atlantic Charter, and occurred, it will be remembered, on board the

British battleship *Prince of Wales*, which soon afterward sank beneath the waves at Singapore. On August 19 Senator Clark, Missouri Democrat, asked Senator Barkley, majority leader, the following question:

When the President and his two sons, together with the Chief of Staff of the Army and the Chief of Staff of Naval Operations, were on a belligerent ship, a battleship of a nation engaged in war on the high seas, if unfortunately that ship had been bombed by a belligerent aircraft, which thank God it was not, and disaster had ensued, does the Senator think that would have been an *act of war* against the United States?

Senator Barkley confined himself to replying that this "of course might have created a situation that would have excited the American people and involved some difficulty with the enemy power."[14]

The term "belligerency" sometimes serves as a substitute for the term "war." In the course of the hearing reported above before the Senate Committee on Military Affairs, Secretary of War Stimson thus said "act of belligerency" instead of "act of war." "Belligerency" thus plainly partakes of the lack of certainty surrounding the term "war." The term "belligerency," instead of "war," though, is most frequently applied to a civil war. Recognition of "belligerency" means acting toward the parties in a civil war either wholly or in part as though a war among states existed. It means granting the parties rights which flow from international neutrality, such as that of visiting and searching merchantmen for contraband of war and establishing a blockade of the enemy coast or part of it. In addition, it may mean the application of the provisions of a domestic neutrality law. President Grant, in his seventh annual message to Congress, on December 7, 1875, argued against recognition on the part of the United States of "belligerency" in the first Cuban insurrection which was then nine years old.[15] President McKinley, in his first annual message to Congress, December 6, 1897, opposed recognition of "belligerency" in the second Cuban insurrection.[16] On June 23, 1937, during the Spanish civil war, Foreign Secretary Eden told the House of Commons that he had received a communication from General Franco containing a reasoned claim for recognition of "belligerency." This communication was being examined, he said.[17]

The term *"nonbelligerency,"* unlike "belligerency," is brand new.

It made its first official appearance in a communiqué issued on December 8, 1939, by the Fascist Grand Council, Italy's highest deliberative and advisory body.[18]

It reappeared on February 1, 1940, in a declaration of Shukru Saracoglu, Turkish Foreign Minister, and on November 1, 1940, in a speech by President Ismet Inonu to the Turkish National Assembly.[19]

On December 19, 1941, the Spanish Government announced that Spain, in view of the extension of the second World War, would maintain, as in the earlier phase of the conflict, her "position of nonbelligerency." After the collapse of Italian fascism, however, Spanish foreign policy changed. On October 1, 1943, Generalissimo Franco announced that Spain had abandoned her policy of "nonbelligerency" in favor of a policy of "vigilant neutrality." [20]

After the outbreak of the war between the United States and Japan, Argentina announced a policy of "nonbelligerency." In Article XV of the final act negotiated in Havana from July 21 to 30, 1940, among the twenty-one American republics, the parties declared that any attempt on the part of a non-American state against the integrity or inviolability of the territory, the sovereignty, or the political independence of an American state shall be considered as an act of aggression against the states which sign this declaration. The signatory nations furthermore agreed to consult among themselves in the event of such aggression in order to agree upon the measures it might be advisable to take. They also envisaged complementary agreements to organize cooperation for defense and assistance.[21] On December 9, 1941, two days after the Japanese attack on Pearl Harbor, the Argentine Cabinet announced a

decree whereby Argentina would not treat the United States
as a belligerent. Argentina, in other words, did not assume
toward the United States all those duties that international law
requires neutral nations to assume.[22] In practice, this meant
that United States warships were permitted to use Argentine
ports without time limit. In the course of the conference of the
twenty-one American republics at Rio de Janeiro in January,
1942, Foreign Minister Enrique Ruiz Guinazu of Argentina
referred to his country's "non-belligerency in accord with Article XV of the Act of Havana." [23]

What does "nonbelligerency" mean?

It would be premature to try to state with finality what the
new expression implies. It is not too early, however, to state
what it seems to imply. The meaning of the term would seem
to vary.

"Nonbelligerency," as first displayed in the communiqué
of the Fascist Grand Council of December 8, 1939, looked
somewhat perplexing in view of the fact that Italy, in September, 1939, had issued no declaration of neutrality. Clarification
came soon, however, in a speech made on December 16 to the
Chamber of Fasces and Corporations by Italy's Foreign Minister Count Ciano and in official German comment thereon.[24]
"Nonbelligerency," in the case of Italy, seemed to connote a
wait-and-see attitude of neutrality maintained with Germany's consent, and, at the same time, to reaffirm the German-
Italian Pact of Friendship and Alliance of May 22, 1939, commonly known as the Rome-Berlin Axis.[25] This interpretation
is confirmed by the recently published diaries of Count Ciano.
The Rome-Berlin Axis, according to Count Ciano, had a clause
that for three or four years neither Italy nor Germany would
raise questions that might disturb European peace.[26] When in
August, 1939, Hitler nevertheless prepared for war against
Poland, Mussolini alternated between neutrality and participation in the war,[27] but finally became convinced of the necessity
of temporary neutrality [28] in consideration of Italy's unpreparedness.[29] "He does not want to say the word 'neutrality,'
but it is this frame of mind that he has definitely reached,"

wrote Count Ciano on August 27, 1939.[30] Mussolini did not
want to utter the word "neutrality" because the position of a
neutral humiliated him. "The Italians," he said on October 9,
1939, "after having heard my warlike propaganda for eighteen
years, cannot understand how I can become the herald of
peace, now that Europe is in flames. There is no other explanation except the military unpreparedness of the country, but
even for this I am made responsible—me, mind you—who
have always proclaimed the power of our armed forces." [31] It
was under these circumstances that the term "nonbelligerency" originated at the start of World War II, in the Italian
Foreign Office, if not with Mussolini himself.

In the case of Turkey the meaning of "nonbelligerency" appears to have changed with the progress of the war. In the declaration of Foreign Minister Shukru Saracoglu of February 1,
1940, five months or so before Italy's entry into the war, "nonbelligerency" apparently pointed to the "benevolent" neutrality toward France and the United Kingdom envisaged for the
situation then existing in Article IV of the Anglo-Franco-
Turkish Treaty of Mutual Assistance of October 19, 1939.[32]
"Nonbelligerency" seems to have been quite different from
neutrality. "Turkey is not neutral but a non-belligerent," said
Shukru Saracoglu in his declaration. In the speech made by
President Ismet Inonu to the National Assembly on November 1, 1940, four and a half months after the fall of France,
"nonbelligerency" would seem to signify little more than a
pious reference to the remaining alliance with the United
Kingdom. The London Cabinet by this time had released
Turkey from the letter of her pledges on the understanding
that she would try to live up to the treaty of 1939 according
to her capabilities.[33] Turkey's attitude toward all belligerents,
as outlined in President Inonu's speech, was characterized by
impartiality and abstention. Turkey, while sticking to the expression "nonbelligerency" out of deference for the United
Kingdom, apparently had returned to classical neutrality.

The Spanish Government, it seems, meant one thing when
it spoke of "nonbelligerency" in relation to the Western Euro-

pean theater of war, and another in relation to the Russian theater.

Spain, on September 4, 1939, issued a proclamation of neutrality enjoining all Spanish subjects to observe "the strictest neutrality" in conformity with Spanish municipal law and with international law.[34] On June 12, 1940, two days after Italy's entry into the war, the Spanish Government, however, suddenly adopted an attitude of "nonbelligerency." For this change Sir Samuel Hoare, now Viscount Templewood, wartime British Ambassador to Spain, requested an explanation. Generalissimo Franco's ambiguous answer was that "as the war has now come to the Mediterranean, it was necessary for Spain to show its direct interest in what had happened and to be prepared for all emergencies." The change, he added, did not mean that the Spanish Government had departed from its "general policy of abstention" from the war.[35] It is established, however, that Spain, in disregard of the rules of neutrality, was taking sides in favor of the Axis Powers. As early as June, 1940, Sir Samuel Hoare found the Germans and Italians deeply entrenched in every department of the government.[36] In the fall of 1942, again according to Sir Samuel Hoare, Axis night observation, radio transmission stations, and sabotage organizations were operating in the Straits of Gibraltar with the undeniable connivance of the local Spanish authorities.[37] In August, 1943, the British Ambassador was instructed to call on Generalissimo Franco to protest against such decidedly unneutral acts as the relaying by Spanish authorities of reports to the enemy of the passage of Allied convoys through the Straits of Gibraltar and the crossing of Spanish territory by German bombers to attack Allied shipping in the Atlantic.[38]

The Spanish Government, in speaking of Spain's "nonbelligerency," certainly had no intention of advertising its unneutral conduct in the Western European theater of war. It had, on the contrary, every interest to declare officially that it had not departed from its "general policy of abstention" from the war. Spain, accordingly, performed her unneutral acts in secrecy. When, for example, in December, 1940, the Spaniards agreed to supply German tankers with fuel for German destroyers engaged in operations in the Bay of Biscay, the Spanish Foreign Minister "vigorously requested observing greatest caution in carrying out the measure." These tankers were to take on fuel at night in out-of-the-way bays along the Spanish coast.[39]

The term "nonbelligerency" in the case of Spain and in relation to the Western European theater of war was, it seems, calculated to serve the purpose of emphasizing Franco's reiterated but unkept promises given to Hitler and Mussolini to enter the war against the enemies of the Axis at a favorable moment for Spain and the Axis.[40] Such a promise was first given to Hitler in June, 1940.[41] The captured German, Italian, and Spanish documents recently published by the United States State Department reveal that the Spanish dictator refrained from keeping his promises because of cowardice, unpreparedness, and failure to obtain approval of his demands for economic and military assistance and postwar territorial aggrandizement in North Africa at the expense of France.[42]

In relation to the Russian theater of war, the term "nonbelligerency" no doubt served the purpose of openly admitting and stressing what was a matter of common knowledge, namely, Spain's breach of neutrality. Spain was, since March, 1939, a party to the so-called Anti-Comintern Pact,[43] and Spanish military forces, especially the Blue Division of so-called "volunteers," fought at Germany's side against the U.S.S.R. until the spring of 1944.[44]

Little needs to be said about Argentina's "nonbelligerency." It meant partiality pure and simple, contrary to Argentina's obligations as a neutral. It is a well-known fact that Argentina's foreign policy changed almost immediately after the Pan-American Conference at Rio de Janeiro in January, 1942. There the Argentine Government subscribed to a series of resolutions that committed the American republics to anti-Axis measures, including the immediate breaking of diplomatic, financial, and commercial relations. Argentina, instead of carrying out these obligations, adopted a policy which in

many respects gave aid and comfort to the enemies of the
Allied Nations. Captured German documents prove beyond
reasonable doubt that the Costello, Ramirez, and Farrell-Peron
governments of Argentina were active partners of the Axis
during the war.[45]

The term "nonbelligerency," as it was used by the governments of Italy, Turkey, Spain, and Argentina, surely is not a
legal but a diplomatic term. These governments, while proclaiming "nonbelligerency," were not referring to some rule
of law providing for an attitude of "nonbelligerency." The
final act of Havana of July 21 to 30, 1940, for instance, does
not refer to "nonbelligerency," in spite of the fact that in
January, 1942, Foreign Minister Enrique Ruiz Guinazu spoke
at Rio de Janeiro of Argentina's "nonbelligerency in accord
with Article XV of the Act of Havana." The meaning of the
expression "nonbelligerency" in the instances referred to
above varies from neutrality pro tem in the case of Italy to
downright partiality, contrary to the rules of law on neutrality, in the case of Argentina.

There have occurred in recent history other instances of
states announcing their "nonbelligerency." In trying to find
out, then, what this newfangled and rather awkward expression means, one should beware of the assumption that there is
any such thing as a definition of "nonbelligerency." Each case
must be looked into specifically and be assessed on its own
merits.[46]

To say that rules of law nowhere refer to "nonbelligerency"
would be to make a statement of the most sweeping kind and
one presupposing an encyclopedic knowledge of law possessed
by none. Yet it is probably fair to say so of American municipal and international law. "Nonbelligerency," to that extent
at least, does not seem to be a legal term at all. The term thus
may henceforth be discarded from a study concerned with the
clarification of legal terms. We do not need to worry about
"nonbelligerency," but we do have to worry about "war,"
"state of war," "de jure war," "de facto war," "belligerency,"
"act of war," "peace," and "state of peace."

Terms in Connection with the Ideas of Operations Short of War and of War Part Way

It has often been said that states are either at war or at peace. To put it in other terms, nations proceed from peace straight into war. Hugo Grotius quotes Cicero to the effect that there is no middle ground between war and peace.[1] In *Janson* v. *Driefontein, Consolidated Mines, Ltd.*, decided by the House of Lords shortly after the Boer War, Lord Macnaghten says: "I think the learned counsel for the respondent was right in saying that the law recognizes a state of peace and a state of war, but that it knows nothing of an intermediate state which is neither one thing nor the other—neither peace nor war." [2] Many a noted lawyer might be quoted to the same effect.

The proposition according to which states are either at war or at peace, however, does not stand unchallenged. There are to be found in court proceedings, parliamentary debates, speeches and other official statements made by statesmen, and in works of legal writers, terms, presumably legal, which suggest, first, that after all there may be operations short of war, a twilight zone of war, so to speak, and, secondly, that states, instead of being at war pure and simple, may be at war only to a limited extent.

Terms suggestive of operations short of war are "intermediate state," "state of hostilities," and, last but not least, "measures short of war." Terms suggesting that states may be at war not purely and simply but only part way are: "imperfect war," "limited war," "partial war," "incomplete war," and "quasi war."

The expression "intermediate state," it seems, originated in the House of Lords at the start of the Crimean War. Emperor Nicholas I of Russia started military operations in the Crimean War in July, 1853, by causing a Russian army corps to pass the Pruth and to lay hold of the two Romanian principalities,

Moldavia and Wallachia, then under the suzerainty of the Ottoman Porte. The Sultan held back until September 29. On that day he issued a proclamation to the effect that the Ottoman Empire had entered upon a "state of war" with Russia. The cause of the war lay in Emperor Nicholas I's policy of Pan-Slavic expansion toward Constantinople, outlined for him in the legendary will of Peter the Great. This policy was sharply opposed by Great Britain and France. The Cabinet of Lord Aberdeen and Napoleon III were resolved to stand up for Turkey's territorial integrity. On November 30 an Ottoman fleet was caught unawares by a Russian squadron off Sinope, on the coast of the Black Sea, and completely destroyed. To cut the maritime communications of Russia with her Asiatic provinces, the Western Powers, at the beginning of 1854, moved their Mediterranean fleets into the Black Sea and, through their naval commanders, "invited" the Russian naval commanders in those waters to proceed to Sebastopol and other Russian ports and to remain there. Russia severed her diplomatic relations with both Great Britain and France on February 4, 1854. In consequence, the British and French Ambassadors were recalled from St. Petersburg. Great Britain and France joined the Sultan in his war against Russia when Russia, on March 18, 1854, refused to answer an ultimatum demanding the evacuation of the Danubian principalities before April 30.[3]

When the British Parliament met on January 31, 1854, great interest was manifested among its members as to the exact relation of Great Britain and Russia. In the course of the debates several members demanded information regarding the plans of the government, and, in particular, asked whether Great Britain then was at peace or at war with Russia. In reply to such inquiries, the Secretary of State for Foreign Affairs, Lord Clarendon, declared in the House of Lords on February 14, 1854, in phrases that have gone down in history:

I come now to the more important part of the speech of my noble friend . . . I mean the question whether we are at peace or at war.

My Lords, that is a most important question; but your Lordships must be aware that a distinct answer cannot be given at the present moment. We are not at war, because war is not declared —we are not strictly at peace with Russia.

Here the Foreign Secretary was interrupted by one of their Lordships laughing aloud. He continued:

My noble friend may laugh; but he must know perfectly well that I am correct in saying that we are not at war with Russia, although diplomatic relations with that country are suspended. . . . I consider that we are in the *intermediate state;* that our desire for peace is just as sincere as ever, but then I must say our hopes of maintaining it are gradually dwindling away and that we are drifting towards war.[4]

The Earl of Derby replied:

The noble Earl, the Secretary of State for Foreign Affairs, is too cautious in his language in this respect to tell us whether we are at war or at peace . . . I want to know what is the state of the country when we are neither at peace nor at war nor neutral. My noble friend has given us a new phrase in parliamentary or diplomatic language.[5]

The expression "state of hostilities," like "state of war," has a highly technical ring. Americans today are still puzzling over the question whether or not, from 1798 to 1800, the United States was at war with France. In Section 1 of Chapter III it will be seen that the problem is by no means an academic one. It had, and curiously enough today still has, its practical implications. Sir William Scott (later Lord Stowell), judge of the British High Court of Admiralty, in a judgment rendered on December 7, 1798, refers to "the present state of hostilities (if so it may be called) between America and France." It ought to be added that the famed judge gave no reasons for his assertion that a "state of hostilities" existed.[6]

Other examples of a "state of hostilities" have been heard of since. In February, 1940, when the Japanese-Chinese "incident" was about two-and-one-half years old, Renzo Sawada, the Japanese Ambassador in Paris, submitted to the French

Foreign Office a memorandum seeking to obtain recognition by the French Government of the fact that "a state of hostilities on a large scale exists in China." No substantiation was given for the contention that a "state of hostilities" existed. The purpose of the Japanese request, however, was clear. The Japanese move was part of a plan to induce France to stoop to a "hands off" policy much more far-reaching than the conduct of abstention provided for by the laws of neutrality in case of war. Japan had insisted for more than two years that ammunition and military supplies were reaching Generalissimo Chiang Kai-shek from French Indo-China. What Japan wanted was a formal French statement indicating that France would permit no traffic over the French-controlled railway between Indo-China and China that would be of assistance to China.[7]

He who seeks advice on the meaning of the term "state of hostilities" might be inclined to turn for guidance to what legal writers have to say on "measures short of war." No such advice, however, is to be obtained from legal writers. One might consult any of the more recent textbooks on international law and find that not one of them deals with a "state of hostilities." We are informed instead, by and large, that there are three kinds of measures short of war: *armed reprisals, armed intervention,* and *pacific blockade.* The "measures short of war" being thus divided into three categories at first sight appear to be neatly in metes and bounds. It would be a serious mistake, however, to assume that such in fact is the case. The wobbling concept of war causes the whole structure of the "measures short of war" to wobble. The frontier line between war and "measures short of war" is in dispute, and there are endless disputes as to the boundaries of the three categories.

The term "measures short of war" came upon the stage of history in the course of the nineteenth century. Napoleon surely never had heard of "measures short of war." To identify the judge, parliamentarian, statesman, or legal writer who fathered the expression would be a troublesome task and one hardly worth while. The term was for decades unknown to the man in the street. In 1939, however, public attention was suddenly focused upon this expression by the annual message which President Franklin D. Roosevelt delivered in person to a joint session of Congress on January 4.

We have learned that God-fearing democracies of the world which observe the sanctity of treaties and good faith in their dealings with other nations cannot safely be indifferent to international lawlessness anywhere. They cannot forever let pass, without effective protest, acts of aggression against sister nations—acts which automatically undermine all of us.

Obviously they must proceed along practical peaceful lines. But the mere fact that we rightly decline to intervene with arms to prevent acts of aggression does not mean that we must act as if there were no aggression at all. Words may be futile, but *war is not the only means of commanding* a decent respect for the opinions of mankind. There are *many methods short of war*, but stronger and more effective than mere words, of bringing home to aggressor governments the aggregate sentiments of our own people.[8]

The words "we rightly decline to intervene with arms" make it clear that the President was not referring to "measures short of war" in any of the "technical" senses attributed to the expression by the various writers on international law. In all its "technical" meanings, the term implies the use of armed force. As spoken by the President the words were interpreted throughout Washington as indicating the purpose of the Government of the United States to apply economic sanctions against nations with which it might be at odds, or which might be threatening the peace of the world.[9]

So much for terms suggestive of a twilight zone of war. Now a consideration of terms suggesting that states may be at war only *part way*.

It is rather late for the terms "imperfect war," "limited war," "partial war," and "incomplete war." These terms nowadays sound strangely remote. Locating them in court proceedings, parliamentary debates, or statements made by statesmen is almost like digging dead words out of their graves.

It is little known, even in America, that the first extensive operations of the United States Navy, subsequent to the adoption of the Constitution, are said to have been an "imperfect," "limited," or "partial war." The "state of hostilities" which, according to Sir William Scott, existed between the United States and France at the close of the eighteenth and at the threshold of the nineteenth century,[10] had its origin in extensive and continued depredations committed on American seaborne commerce by French ships of war and privateers operating in the great naval war that had started between France and Great Britain in 1793 and was to end only after Waterloo. As the temper of the American people rose in resentment against accumulated wrongs, there were many who thought that a declaration of war, followed by all-out military and naval operations against France, would best suit the interests as well as the honor of the United States. Public feeling in the United States, however, never became ripe for a declaration of war against the homeland of Lafayette, De Grasse, and Rochambeau. Under those circumstances, Congress in the main confined itself to directing American ships of war and authorizing American private armed vessels to attack and to capture *armed* vessels sailing under the French flag on the high seas and to retake American merchantmen which might have been captured by French vessels. There occurred in consequence a great many engagements between American and French armed vessels. No order or authority was given for retaking friendly vessels, British vessels for instance, for operating against French armed vessels in French territorial waters, or for operating against unarmed French vessels anywhere. Nor did the army of the United States have orders to operate against the French on land. No "A.E.F." was provided for.

On April 21, 1799, Capt. Thomas Tingy, commanding the U.S.S. *Ganges*, recaptured from a French privateer the ship *Eliza*, John Bas, master. Ship and cargo belonged to citizens of the United States. Captain Tingy, in consequence, filed a libel in the district court of Pennsylvania against the *Eliza* and her cargo. The libel prayed for salvage in conformity with an Act of Congress of March 2, 1799, which declared that for ships and goods belonging to citizens of the United States, if retaken from "the enemy" after more than four days, the owners were to allow one half of the whole value for salvage. The facts being admitted by the answer of the respondents, the district court decreed to the libelant one half of the whole value of ship and cargo. This decree was affirmed in the Circuit Court for the District of Pennsylvania without argument, and by consent of the parties, in order to expedite a final decision by the Supreme Court.

The case was argued before the Supreme Court, with only four justices in attendance, during its August term of 1800,[11] the last term held in the city of Philadelphia. The argument turned chiefly upon the question whether France was an "enemy" of the United States. This seems to have caused a great controversy at the bar. The Court knew that in December, 1798, this very question had "embarrassed" Sir William Scott and that he had spoken of "the present state of hostilities (if so it may be called) between America and France." Justice Moore thought that "our situation is so extraordinary that I doubt whether a parallel case can be traced in the history of nations." The Supreme Court, after lengthy deliberations, found that France was an "enemy" according to the intent of the Act of March 2, 1799.

This, one might think, should have been reason enough to affirm the decree of the Circuit Court. However, it did not seem enough to Justices Washington, Chase, and Paterson. Justice Washington, appointed to the Supreme Court in 1798 by President John Adams, by the way, was a nephew of General Washington.[12] The three justices contended that the United States and France were, to a certain extent at least, at war, and that accordingly France, from that angle too and apart from any legislative interpretation, was an "enemy" of the United States. There existed between the United States and France an "imperfect war" according to Justices Washington and Paterson, and a "limited" or "partial war" according to Justice Chase. This sounds reasonable enough in view of what the United States was doing and of what it might have done. There were, as has been pointed out, only restricted naval operations, and on land no operations at all. There can be no doubt that the terms used by the three justices would have been in good stead in any discussion on strategy. Justices Washington, Paterson, and Chase, however, meant to discuss not strategy but a legal issue. Justice Washington said in so many words that "in law" and "technically speaking" the United States and France were engaged in an "imperfect war" and that France was therefore an "enemy according to the technical understanding of the word."

As against this it ought to be said that terms like "imperfect" or "limited" or "partial war," in order to make sense in a *legal* discussion, as a matter of course, must rest on *legal* considerations. Operations, military or naval or both, in other words, cannot "technically" be called "imperfect" or "limited" or "partial war" unless they appear so to be when measured with the yardstick of some rule of law on war. It is here that the troubles with the opinions of the three justices start. If one tries to relate their findings to some rule of law on war, one loses the guidance of authority. The three opinions to that extent lack a neat, straight line of argument. They are hard to follow and by their lack of lucidity offer a partial explanation of why posterity has cared so little about *Bas* v. *Tingy*.

It ought to be added that Justice Washington referred to a *definition* of war in which he "believed." He offered it with the time-honored phrase "it may, I believe, be safely laid down," a phrase so often used by jurists who find themselves in a blind alley. "War is every contention by force between two nations in external matters under the authority of their respective governments." It cannot be seen where "in law" this definition came from. The definition as far as the law is concerned remained floating in the air.

The terms "imperfect," "partial," and "limited" war thus echo from the City of Brotherly Love as mere words with no legal reasoning behind them. This is not enough. Words alone will not do.

In Section 1 of Chapter III it will be seen that the legal nature of the American naval operations of 1798 to 1801 became in 1886 the object of the most delightful forensic foil play before the Court of Claims. What was a "state of hostilities" according to Sir William Scott and an "imperfect" or "partial" or "limited" war according to the Supreme Court was no war at all in the eyes of the Court of Claims. Between 1935 and 1938 the Office of Naval Records and Library, at the instance of President Roosevelt, published the documentary material relating to this period.[13] With the Supreme Court and the Court of Claims seemingly at cross purposes, the Office of Naval Records and Library apparently did not know which way to turn when it came to giving their publication a title. Yet an expert was found to light the path out of the wilderness of perplexity. The expert opinion overruled both the decision of the Supreme Court of 1800 and the decision of the Court of Claims of 1886. The seven volumes carry the title *Quasi War with France*. Mark this, for it is unique. The profusion of material contained in the seven volumes is amazing. Page 152 of the first volume, for instance, reveals how water, rum, and grog were doled out on board the U.S. Frigate *Constellation*. The volumes are singularly silent, however, on the question of how the young navy of the United States happened to fight a "Quasi War."

In the following paragraphs attention will briefly be drawn to what one of the most prominent European historians and statesmen of the nineteenth century has called an "incomplete war." The historian and statesman was François P. G. Guizot, from 1840 to 1848, in the latter part of the July monarchy, master spirit of France through his offices as Minister of Foreign Affairs and Prime Minister.

During the winter of 1837 to 1838, the French vice-consul in Buenos Aires addressed to the government of the province of that name, which was then in charge of the foreign relations of the Argentine Confederacy, a series of claims concerning the naturalization, service in the militia, extraordinary taxation of and alleged denial of justice to some Frenchmen living in the Argentine territory. Gen. Don Juan Manuel de Rosas, dictator of the Argentine Confederacy, refused to discuss the French claims except with a regularly accredited diplomatic representative.[14] On March 28, 1838, Rear Admiral Leblanc, commander of the French naval forces in South American waters, on orders from the government of King Louis Philippe, in consequence informed the Argentine Government of the establishment of a "strict" blockade against the port of Buenos Aires and the whole Argentine coast. The French admiral declared that this blockade was to be maintained until the grounds of complaint upon which it was established should be removed. The French did not mean to prevent the ingress and egress of Argentine vessels only. Under penalty of confiscation of ship and cargo for captured blockade-runners, they interdicted all intercourse by sea between the world at large and Argentina. Rear Admiral Leblanc accordingly sent a notification of the "strict" blockade to the foreign ministers and consuls in Buenos Aires and the French Minister of Foreign Affairs notified the foreign diplomatic representatives in Paris.[15]

It is important to note that the French for more than six months confined themselves to cutting off the coast of Argentina from intercourse with the outside world. Until October 10, 1838, no military operations took place on shore. On that day, 265 French marines and 150 Uruguayan insurgents stormed and captured with insignificant losses the weakly fortified island of Martín García. This is the small Argentine island which in 1940 was to attract attention as the place of internment of the officers of the scuttled German pocket battleship *Admiral Graf Spee*.[16] The capture of Martín García manifestly was not a genuine operation on land. The island commands a navigable passage in the estuary of the Río de la Plata. Its capture simply served to complement and to facilitate the existing blockade. In September, 1839, almost a year and a half after the beginning of the blockade, Rear Admiral Leblanc sent 400 marines ashore to man the defenses of Montevideo in a war then existing between the Oriental Republic of Uruguay and the Argentine Confederacy. France thus participated in a foreign war. At about the same time France began to participate also in a civil war then existing within the Argentine Confederacy by actively supporting General Lavalle, former President of the Argentine Republic and then leader of an insurrectionist army formed by Argentine immigrants in Montevideo. This support consisted chiefly in transporting Lavalle's small army from Martín García up the Uruguayan River into the province of Entre Rios and in protecting it during the winter of 1839–40 from the Paraná River while it was holding the Argentine province of Corrientes. When on July 15, 1840, the insurrectionist army was driven from the field, it again found protection under the guns of the French fleet on the Paraná River. A few days later, the French loaded the entire army of 3,300 men and their six cannon on board transports, conveyed them under the fire of the batteries of Rosario with but few losses [17] down the river, and disembarked them in the province of Buenos Aires.

The French forces on the Rio de la Plata in the fall of 1840 amounted to 36 vessels and about 6,000 officers and men. The blockade had caused serious interruption to the commercial intercourse of all nations. It had been especially detrimental to the commerce of England. The trade of England with the port of Buenos Aires amounted to no less than one million pounds annually and, if the export returns were included, two million pounds.[18] Widespread unemployment followed the suspension of commerce in Buenos Aires. The finances of the province collapsed, and all schools, hospitals, and other public institutions were closed. Yet after two years and a half the French had not succeeded in forcing Rosas to grant their demands. In October, 1840, Admiral Mackau proposed negotiations, and on October 29, 1840, the two parties signed a treaty settling their differences.[19]

A hundred years ago there was not the slightest doubt anywhere that a blockade interdicting and penalizing all intercourse by sea between the world at large and a certain coast was a belligerent right and a belligerent right only. Such interference with the recognized principle of the freedom of the seas with its detrimental consequences for the trade of third states was conditioned upon the existence of war. On this all writers on international law agreed. On this the practice of states was uniform. Such practice was evidenced by a great many treaty provisions regulating blockades as a means of warfare.[20] The blockade by the French of the Argentine Confederacy from 1838–40 occupies a unique place in the history of international law. With no genuine operations on land being undertaken for a period of a year and a half, the French Government would have been hard put to it to claim that France was at war with the Argentine Confederacy. The French Government as a matter of fact for at least that period did not claim that war existed. On the contrary, it considered itself at peace with Rosas. It looked with misgivings at the operation which Admiral Leblanc, without authorization from Paris, had undertaken on October 10, 1838, against the island of Martín García. Such an operation, in their opinion, came pretty close to war. In instructions sent on March 6, 1839, to the French representative in Montevideo, the Cabinet of Prime Minister Molé approved of the operation against Martín García provided that it had been necessary to complement the blockade, but warned at the same time that the measures employed against the Argentine Confederacy should by no means assume a character scarcely distinguishable from war. Nothing was more contrary to the intentions of the government than a "state of war," the instructions said.[21] The French blockade of the Argentine Confederacy was unique because it had never happened before that a government had notified third states of a strict blockade while claiming to be at peace with the blockaded state. For France, the blockade no doubt was most advantageous. France, at the expense of third states, succeeded in cutting off all sea-borne trade from Argentina without at the same time undergoing the expenses and hazards involved in sending an expeditionary corps across the Atlantic. The blockade conformed to the following principle said to have been laid down by King Louis Philippe for the adjustment of disputes with transatlantic states: "Resort often to diplomatic notes; seldom to blockades; never to the expedition of *pantalons rouges*" [French infantry].

As to third states, one would expect that they would categorically refuse to recognize the legality of a blockade established in the absence of war. Yet nothing of the sort happened, at least not as far as the two states most interested, namely, the United States of America and Great Britain, were concerned. The administration of President Van Buren displayed a surprising indifference with regard to the legality of the French activities in Argentine waters. On February 11, 1839, the House of Representatives requested the President of the United States to inform that body what explanations, if any, the King of the French had tendered to the United States in relation to the recent blockade of the Rio de la Plata and the treatment of vessels of the United States, public and private, by the blockading squadron. In response to such requests President Van Buren submitted to the House of Representatives a collection of documents which left the vital question of the legality of the blockade completely untouched. The Attorney General, in an advisory opinion, instead of denouncing the capture by the French of American merchantmen as entirely illegal, surprisingly informed the President of the United States that, in the absence of rules in relation to blockades in time of peace, such a novel blockade as that established by the French could be treated only according to the rules which refer to the traditional blockade in time of war.[22] It was not until July 7, 1840, that international law and American foreign traders found in Congress an advocate in Caleb Cushing, prominent statesman and diplomatist and a Massachusetts member of the House of Representatives. On that day Caleb Cushing stated before the House that the blockade of Argentina, in the absence of war, was illegal and should never have been acquiesced in by the silence of third states.[23] In Great Britain similar views were voiced in the House of Commons and the House of Lords. Upward of three hundred merchants, traders, and shipowners memorialized the British Government, urging it to put an end to the blockade. In spite of this the British Government never questioned the legality of the blockade as such. The British Government probably was handicapped by the fact that early in 1837 Adm. Sir Peter Halkett had established a similar blockade against the coast of New Granada (Colombia). The British admiral had been authorized to enforce against the Government of New Granada certain demands of the British Government "in any way that may be deemed most advisable." Palmerston, after the event, had approved of the blockade. This strict blockade established against New Granada in time of peace, though, had lasted only twelve days. In addition all the ships seized had been promptly released without being proceeded against when the blockade was raised.[24] When Sir Stratford Canning requested the Foreign Secretary in the House of Commons on June 5, 1839, to inform the House of the general grounds and principles upon which the French Government founded its right to institute the blockade against Argentina, Viscount Palmerston did not feel himself at liberty to express an opinion, either one way or the other. An entirely different verdict was given by the Prime Minister in the House of Lords on January 27, 1840. Lord Melbourne, by a surprising twist of logic, came around to the opinion that the French blockade after all was founded upon the existence of war and was therefore legal, since the blockade itself amounted to war. Thus what could only be the legal consequence of war was declared to be war itself! [25]

On October 29, 1841, the very day on which the Mackau convention was signed, Guizot became Minister of Foreign Affairs in a new French Cabinet headed by Marshal Soult. Guizot advocated ratification of the Mackau convention before the Chamber of Peers and before the Chamber of Deputies on February 9 and 20, 1841, respectively. In his speech before the Chamber of Peers, Guizot characterized the memorable blockade as it existed from March, 1838, till September, 1839, that is, the period before France began to participate in the war of Uruguay and in the civil war led by Lavalle, as an "incomplete war." [26] There was for this period, it will be remembered, no war at all in the view of the Cabinet headed by Prime Minister Molé. Did Guizot, as did the justices of the American Supreme Court in the case of *Bas* v. *Tingy*, mean to say that such halfway war existed "in law" or "technically speaking"? Did Guizot, in other words, take up the cue so generously tendered by Prime Minister Melbourne, repudiating thereby the view held by the Molé Cabinet and attempting to establish for the blockade ex post facto some legal justification? Or did Guizot mean to talk simply common sense? No definite answer seems to be possible. Guizot surely had no reason to defend the legality of the blockade before the French Parliament; it had never been questioned in either House. Guizot, on the other hand, told the Chamber of Deputies on February 20, 1841, that the blockade had caused incessant complaints on the part of the United States, Great Britain, and all the other maritime states trading with Buenos Aires. With the exception of the United States and Great Britain, such complaints might well have been based upon the contention that the blockade had been established in time of peace. The Hanse towns had thus protested against the legality of a similar blockade which the Molé Cabinet had established at almost the same time against the coast of Mexico.[27] The term "incomplete war," under those circumstances, might have been meant to be "technical" and calculated as a parliamentary answer to diplomatic complaints. If Guizot, in fact, meant to say incomplete war "technically speaking" or "in law," he twisted logic as badly as did Lord Melbourne before the House of Lords on January 27, 1840. He tried to justify the blockade by the blockade itself. Nor can it be seen for what legal reasons Guizot, as distinguished from Lord Melbourne, called the blockade an "incomplete" war, or why an "incomplete" war should have had any legal consequences at all. Guizot, in short, was distressingly enigmatic if he intended to be "technical." The chances are that the illustrious historian did not mean to be "technical" at all, but simply intended to use common language. Guizot's parliamentary speeches are ennobled by that simplicity and lucidity which carried his reputation as a historian to the crest of fame. There can be no objection whatever against the term "incomplete war," if such term in common parlance is applied to a blockade not supplemented by military operations on land.

The term "incomplete war" as an allegedly technical term needs checking, whatever the idea that Guizot was trying to put across. In addition to the sneaking uncertainties of "imperfect war," "limited war," "partial war," "incomplete war," and "quasi war," the student of law may encounter the terms "imperfect state of war," "limited state of war," "partial state of war," "incomplete state of war," and "quasi state of war." In the following paragraphs attention will be given to what an American appellate court has termed an "incomplete state of war." The case has the advantage of being well within the memory of living men.

In the contest between Carranza, Villa, and Zapata for supremacy in Mexico that started upon the overthrow of Huerta in July, 1914, Carranza's superiority had become undoubted by the autumn of 1915. On October 19, 1915, the United States extended recognition to the de facto government of which the Citizen First Chief of the Constitutionalist Army General Carranza was the head.[28] President Wilson, in his message on the state of the nation to the joint session of Congress on December 8, 1915, affirmed that the United States "now hopefully awaits the rebirth of the troubled republic."[29] Those expectations came to nought. In the closing months of 1915 and during the first part of 1916 Mexican bandits committed frequent depredations and murders not only on American property and lives on Mexican soil but on American territory along the lower Rio Grande. Ranches were raided and trains were wrecked and plundered. American garrisons were attacked at night, equipment and horses were stolen, and American soldiers killed. General Carranza was unable or possibly considered it inadvisable to apprehend and punish the perpetrators.[30]

A particularly grave incident occurred on March 9, 1916.

On that day, before dawn, Villa with about 400 of his men crossed into New Mexico and attacked the town of Columbus in Indian fashion. The raiders set fire to the principal buildings, killed 18 persons, 9 civilians and 9 cavalry men, and then escaped into Mexican territory. Villa was reported to have a total of from 2,000 to 3,000 men. General Gavira, in charge of the Mexican district opposite Columbus, frankly admitted that the Carranza government could do but little in running down the Villa band.[31]

Under these circumstances, President Wilson at once directed that an adequate force be sent into Mexico in hot pursuit of the Columbus raiders. A force of at least 5,000 picked cavalry, with field-gun detachments and several companies of infantry, was organized at Columbus. On March 16 it crossed the Mexican border under the command of Gen. John J. Pershing and headed southward through the Chihuahua Desert in the hope of taking the raiders in their camp beyond Casas Grandes. The American Government, though without notice to or the specific consent of the Carranza government, acted in accordance with a practice concerning the pursuit of marauding Indians that had been adopted by the two countries in the latter part of the nineteenth century.[32] President Wilson, the Department of State, and Congress were most explicit as to the instructions given to General Pershing. General Pershing's force was officially styled a "punitive expedition" with the single object of capturing Villa and putting a stop to his forays. The slogan of the day, it will be remembered, was "Villa dead or alive!" Any intention of acting against the Mexican Government, let alone an intention of waging war against it, was emphatically disclaimed.[33] The Carranza government, in spite of this, at once adopted an ambiguous attitude. On the one hand, it protested against the presence of American troops on Mexican soil; on the other, it promised that the Carranza troops would cooperate in the effort to capture Villa.[34] Such cooperation was in fact forthcoming for a short while, but soon gave way to obstruction.[35] From April to June the situation grew steadily worse. Mexican bandits renewed their depredations on American property and lives on both sides of the boundary line.[36] Scarcely a month after the Pershing expedition had begun its vain search for Villa, the Mexican Government began to ask for its withdrawal, although its presence was the only efficient means of protecting American homes and lives. On May 22 it informed the Government of the United States "that in case of a refusal to retire these troops, there is no further recourse than to defend its territory by appeal to arms." On June 16 General Trevino, commanding the Mexican forces in the state of Chihuahua, informed General Pershing that he had orders from Carranza to prevent the Pershing expedition by the use of arms from moving in any direction except back toward the United States. General Pershing promptly replied that he would use his own judgment as to when and in what direction he would move his forces in the pursuit of bandits.[37] The expedition into Mexico was about to turn into an expedition against Mexico when, on Sunday, June 18, 1916, President Wilson called out substantially all the state militia of the United States, totaling about 100,000 men, with a view to sending them to the Mexican border.[38] The tension reached its climax when, on June 21, in consequence of Carranza's instructions to General Trevino, two troops of American cavalry clashed with several hundred Carranza soldiers at Carrizal in the state of Chihuahua. The Mexicans were said to have lost 46 killed and 39 wounded. Twelve American soldiers were killed and 24 captured and imprisoned in the penitentiary of Chihuahua. President Wilson at once demanded that the prisoners be released. On June 28 Carranza gave proof of his desire for peace by releasing the prisoners and sending them back to the United States. The interchange of amicable notes that ensued paved the way for a peaceful settlement of the crisis which had brought the two countries to the verge of war. The Pershing expedition withdrew from Mexican territory in February, 1917.[39]

There is one incident in the so-called Pershing expedition which merits special attention. On June 16, 1916, the press reported that early on the morning of the 15th a party of a hundred or more Mexican "bandits" had crossed the Rio Grande and attacked two troops of United States cavalry encamped near the little settlement of San Ignazio, south of Laredo, Texas. After the firing had lasted half an hour the Mexicans escaped to the south. Three American soldiers were killed and six wounded. The Mexican toll was reported as eight known dead, a number wounded, and "several" captured.[40]

The captured "bandits," four in all, were placed on trial before the State District Court of Webb County, Texas, for the murder of Oberlies, a corporal in one of the above-mentioned troops of the United States cavalry, and, being convicted, were given death sentences. On April 17, 1918, upon motion for a new trial, the Court of Criminal Appeals of the state of Texas reversed the judgment and remanded the case. The presiding judge decided that the four defendants were not "bandits," but members of a force of seventy-five belonging to the Constitutionalist Army of Mexico, and that at the time of the "battle" of San Ignazio they were commanded by their officers. On the other hand, it was not established, and it does not seem at all likely, that the commanding officers were in turn invading Texas under instructions from the Carranza government. In point of law the court held that a soldier fighting and killing in compliance with orders ought not to be convicted of murder. Hence the decision to reverse. The court further held that the defendants, provided they had committed any offense at all, had done so in a "war" or rather in an "incomplete state of war" existing at the time of the "battle" of San Ignazio between the United States and Mexico, and that if they were to be dealt with under those circumstances it should be done by the United States Government and not by the Texas courts. Hence the decision to remand.

The statement of the court that the United States and Mexico were at "war" or rather in an "incomplete state of war" is perplexing, in view of the fact that the two governments at no time during the whole course of the Pershing expedition considered themselves as being at war. The court left no doubt that it meant "war" or rather an "incomplete state of war" technically speaking or "in law." Hence the court should have made known the rule or rules "in law," either municipal or international, which caused it to assert the existence of "war" or rather of an "incomplete state of war." Yet, as in the case of *Bas* v. *Tingy*, the rationale of the decision in that respect is singularly irrational. The court, instead of pointing out the law, cited two Supreme Court decisions that lack any connection whatever with the "battle" of San Ignazio. In addition, it quoted two definitions of war. One definition might be considered enough. The first definition is that "laid down" by Mr. Justice Washington in the case of *Bas* v. *Tingy*. As was pointed out above, Justice Washington "believed" in it as though it were gospel truth. The second definition is taken from Vattel's famous *Le Droit des Gens ou Principes de la Loi Naturelle*, published for the first time in 1758. War, according to Vattel, is the "state in which nations, under the authority of their respective governments prosecute their rights by force." [41] It is not necessary to discuss here Vattel's definition. Whatever its value, it does not fit the "battle" of San Ignazio. The "battle" of San Ignazio, as far as Mexico is concerned, in all likelihood was not fought under the authority of the Carranza government. Apart from a vague hint at unidentified "authorities," no explanation whatever is offered for the "incomplete state of war." The court in short completely failed to make out its case with regard either to "war" or "incomplete state of war." The rationale of the decision, to that extent at least, is an almost incredibly muddled and inconsistent piece of reasoning. It defies understanding. It leaves the reader puzzled and amazed.[42] It is only fair to say that any court anywhere might have bungled this case too. Judges decide such cases to a large extent according to the enlightenment shed upon them by the textbooks on international law. These, it will be seen, are not exactly a help when it comes to preparing the future practitioner for decisions involving the momentous problem of the existence of war or peace.

There seems to be something "phony" about the terms which indicate that in law states may be at war to some extent only. "Imperfect war," "limited war," and "partial war" do not make sense in the case of *Bas* v. *Tingy*. "Incomplete war" sounds mystically vague in Guizot's speech, provided always that Guizot meant to be "technical." The "incomplete state of war" in the case of *Arce et al.* v. *the State of Texas* defies understanding. Such repeated obscurity, it will be seen, is not a mere coincidence.

The list of what seem to be basic terms in a legal study on war and peace has by now grown uncomfortably long. Still it is not complete. When it comes to the world's number one problem, the marvels of legal or presumably legal terminology know no end. This is particularly true with respect to the kind of terms pointed out in the present chapter. Every once in a while a "situation" crops up that is deemed to be not quite black and not quite white, but so particularly within the gray twilight zone of war as to call for a new designation. Every once in a while some halfway war is said to exist and to be so extraordinary and without parallel in the history of nations as to call for a new and bigger and better appellation.

Suffice it to give one example. At the close of 1902 Germany, Great Britain, and Italy had established against Venezuela a strict blockade which reminds one of the earlier period of the French blockade of the Argentine coast in 1838–40 in that no military operations were performed on shore. This blockade, however, was supplemented by the seizure of Venezuelan ships, public and private, not only for breach of the blockade, but wherever found. E. T. Holland, Professor of International Law at Oxford University, considered the steps taken by Germany and Great Britain as anomalous "from the point of view of international law." "The true nature of things," he said, called for the expression "war *sub modo*." This startling discovery seems to have charmed several writers on international law. Yet it is easy enough to rebut it from the very "point of view of international law." Holland simply "supposed" that war existed. He failed to point out the international rule of law on war according to which the German-British measures could be considered to constitute war at all.

Much less did he show the legal reasons which would justify the qualification of "sub modo." The expression "war sub modo" is worse than useless. It adds confusion to confusion.[43]

A few additional terms will be pointed out in subsequent chapters.

A fairly complete list of what look like basic terms for a legal study on war and peace runs about as follows: (1) Terms in connection with the idea of war or peace as such: state of war, de jure war, de facto war, belligerency, act of war, state of peace. (2) Terms in connection with the idea of operations short of war: intermediate state, state of hostilities, measures short of war, armed intervention, armed reprisals, pacific blockade. (3) Terms in connection with the idea of war part way: imperfect war, imperfect state of war, limited war, limited state of war, partial war, partial state of war, incomplete war, incomplete state of war, quasi war, quasi state of war.

This avalanche of terms is puzzling and amazing. It produces a sense of paralyzing confusion, of not knowing what it is all about. What legal reality lies behind, where is the truth in this welter of words? It is proposed to see this thing through here.

What is the legal meaning of the two central, all-important terms "war" and "peace"? This cardinal question ought not to be approached before attention has been given to two captivating sets of cases. Chapter III will deal with delicate cases in which the authorities disagree as to whether operations occurred in war or in peace. Chapter IV will be devoted to the sensational and tricky phenomenon of battles allegedly fought in peace.

CHAPTER III

War or Peace?

It would be easy to record in this chapter numerous sets of operations in regard to which there has been disagreement either in theory or in practice, or in both, as to whether they constituted war legally or were performed in peace. The present chapter is confined to reporting three carefully chosen cases:

(1). The American naval operations against France from 1798 to 1800. These will be shortly compared with the naval operations which the United States, following the "shoot-on-sight" order of President Roosevelt, conducted against Germany and Italy in the period from September 11 to December 11, 1941.

(2). The Boxer Expedition in 1900 and 1901.

(3). The German military operations against Italy in the period from May 24, 1915, to August 28, 1916, which attracted little attention in the over-all picture of World War I, but which are nevertheless instructive for the problem as to what constitutes war.

The first case, that of the American naval operations against France from 1798 to 1800, no doubt, is the most interesting of the three. The question as to whether these operations constituted war has never been satisfactorily answered. The right answer to this question, moreover, is still a practical issue almost 150 years after the event.

SECTION 1. THE AMERICAN NAVAL OPERATIONS AGAINST
FRANCE, 1798–1800, AND AGAINST GERMANY AND
ITALY, 1941

The naval operations which the United States conducted against France at the end of the eighteenth century have already been briefly dealt with in the preceding chapter. In August, 1800, their legal nature was examined by the Supreme Court in the case of *Bas* v. *Tingy*. It is now necessary to enter into full particulars.[1]

This calls for an examination of the relations between the United States and France from the American struggle for independence up to 1801. Such examination, as far as Americans are concerned, involves points of familiar history.

The American struggle for independence started on April 19, 1775, with engagements between British soldiers and American colonists at Lexington and Concord, Massachusetts. On July 4, 1776, the second Continental Congress of the thirteen American Colonies meeting in Philadelphia adopted the immortal Declaration of Independence. At the close of 1777 Howe, the Commander in Chief of the British forces in America, had been driven from New Jersey, and, after the drawn battle of Germantown, was immobilized in Philadelphia. A British army from Canada under the command of Burgoyne had capitulated to General Gates at Saratoga, New York. Yet at the end of a successful campaign the American cause was in dire straits. Gates had broken with Washington. Washington's army of less than 9,000 men was lying at Valley Forge, unable to prosecute a winter campaign. As Washington wrote to Congress, the army was so reduced by starvation and cold that unless some capital change took place it must "starve, dissolve or disperse." Nearly 3,000 men were unfit for duty because they were without shoes and adequate clothing. Discontent and jealousy were prevalent in the highest ranks. Congress did practically nothing to remedy the breakdown of supplies. The physical condition of the army was in harmony with the financial condition of the thirteen states. The issue of paper money had caused a sharp depreciation in the value of the currency and necessarily impaired the credit of the government.[2]

Relief was to come from France. In France, which was still smarting under the loss of Canada, popular sentiment was with the thirteen states. Benjamin Franklin had early established relations with the Court of Louis XVI through his friend

Dumas, a Swiss man of letters who was a devoted adherent of the American cause and who had long advised an alliance between the thirteen states and France. Early in December, 1777, the news of Burgoyne's capitulation at Saratoga reached Paris, where Dumas, Franklin, and other American agents pressed the Department of Foreign Affairs for the assistance of France, dangling before the eyes of Comte de Vergennes, the Minister of Foreign Affairs, the bait of a practical monopoly of American commerce. Burgoyne's capitulation appeared to turn the tide of events. The want and suffering at Valley Forge were still unknown to the French. Louis XVI decided to acknowledge and to support by every means in his power the independence of the revolting British colonies. By the middle of December the American agents and the French Government agreed to enter upon a treaty of alliance and a treaty of amity and commerce. France in consequence fully assisted the thirteen states with troops, munitions, and money. The total cost of the American Revolutionary War to France is estimated to have been $2,300,000,000.[3] This enormous expenditure undoubtedly hastened the catastrophe toward which the Bourbon monarchy was heading. With the strong assistance of France, the War of Independence was prosecuted to a successful close. The surrender of Cornwallis, Commander of the southern British Army, at Yorktown on October 19, 1783, was made under the guns of the powerful French fleet of Admiral De Grasse to the combined American and French Armies of Washington and Rochambeau. The surrender of Cornwallis virtually terminated the Revolutionary War.[4]

The *Treaty of Alliance of February 6, 1778* and the *Treaty of Amity and Commerce* of the same date between the Most Christian King and the Thirteen United States of North America are of particular interest because they are the first of all the treaties entered into by the United States. They were both signed on behalf of the United States by Benjamin Franklin, Silas Deane, and Arthur Lee, and were ratified by Congress on May 4, 1778.[5]

By the eleventh article of the Treaty of Alliance, momentous guaranties, out of which afterward arose most serious complications, were given by each party to the other. The United States guaranteed to his Most Christian Majesty "forever, against all other powers," the possessions of the crown of France in America. The possessions of France in America at this date were the islands of St. Pierre and Miquelon off Newfoundland; the West Indian islands of San Domingo, Martinique, Guadeloupe, Santa Lucia, St. Vincent, Tobago, Desirade, Marie Galante, Granada; and, on the mainland, Cayenne, each and all of which the United States guaranteed to France *forever*. His Most Christian Majesty, on the other hand, guaranteed to the United States their political independence and the integrity of their territorial possessions as fixed by the future treaty of peace between the United States and Great Britain.

The elaborate Treaty of Amity and Commerce contained the following "perpetual" stipulations covering a maritime war in which one party was belligerent and the other neutral:

A merchant vessel belonging to one of the parties, even if laden wholly or in part with enemy property, was to be allowed to sail without any opposition to and from a port belonging to an enemy of the other party. Goods of the nature of contraband, of which a limited list, not including foodstuffs, was agreed upon, however, were excepted. In other words: free ships were to make free goods.[6]

Ships of war or privateers [7] of either party meeting a merchantman of the other party were to remain beyond cannon shot and to send two or three men only in a boat to board the merchantman. To these the master or commander of the merchantman was to exhibit his passport or sea letter concerning the ownership of the vessel and certificates containing the particulars of the cargo, so that it could be known whether any contraband goods were on board.[8] In case the certificates disclosed the existence of contraband goods, the captors were strictly forbidden to break up the hatches or otherwise to disturb the cargo by search. They were peaceably to take the vessel to port for adjudication in the respective prize courts. The presence of contraband goods on board was not to be considered as "infecting" the vessel or the noncontraband residue of the cargo. In case of confiscation of contraband goods, the vessel, with the residue of her cargo, was to be permitted to proceed upon the voyage.[9]

Whatever goods laden by the subjects of either party were to be found on any ship belonging to the enemy or enemy subjects, whether of the nature of contraband or not, were liable to confiscation in the same manner as if they belonged to the enemy. In other words: unfree ships were to make unfree goods.[10]

The vessels of war or privateers of either ally were entitled freely to enter and leave the ports of the other with goods taken from an enemy. On the contrary, no shelter was to be given in port to vessels of war or privateers of an enemy of either ally, which had made prize of the property of either of the allies. Permission to enter the ports of either ally was to be given to such vessels of war or privateers only when they were forced by stress of weather or the dangers of the sea, and they were obliged to depart therefrom as soon as possible. Privateers commissioned by the enemy of one party, even if bringing no prizes, were not to be allowed to refit their ships in the ports of the other ally, nor to sell their merchandise, nor even to purchase victuals, except such as were necessary to reach the nearest home port.[11]

Such, briefly, were the chief engagements made by the United States with France in the American struggle for independence. So long as France remained at peace, these engagements slept unnoticed, but they were ready to spring into life at the first blast of war, particularly with Great Britain. Soon enough, the blast sounded a crusade of monarchical Europe against republican France.

In 1789 the French Revolution began. In 1793 France outraged the feelings of the British people by the execution of Louis XVI, by the conquest of Belgium, and by threats against the Netherlands. In February of that year Great Britain joined the coalition against France as the result of a settled policy never willingly to acquiesce in the annexation of Belgium or the Netherlands by a Continental power. Thus began the great war between Great Britain and France which was to last almost continuously for twenty-two years until it ended with Waterloo.[12] In little more than a month, Great Britain, being the almost undisputed mistress of the seas, took from France all her possessions in the West Indies.[13] The obligation of the United States to guarantee the French possessions in America, according to the eleventh article of the Treaty of Alliance of 1778, had sprung into life.

To have made good its obligation would have involved the United States in a second war with Great Britain. For such a war the United States, at that time a little republic of some two and one-half million inhabitants, was utterly unprepared. It was financially poor and exhausted by seven years of warfare for its independence.[14] The situation was greatly relieved by the fact that France never asked for compliance with the Treaty of Alliance, thinking doubtless that the food supplies which the United States could carry under its neutral flag would be more valuable than any naval or military aid which it could give. This, however, was not a renunciation of the guaranty, nor was it so regarded by the United States. Jefferson, Secretary of State in the Cabinet of President Washington, said he had no doubt that the United States would "interpose at the proper time."[15] On April 22, 1793, Washington, under those circumstances, issued what was in substance though not in name a brief proclamation of neutrality. It is interesting to note that Washington side-stepped the word "neutrality" in conformity with a compromise arrived at in the Cabinet. The proclamation, after pointing to the war existing between Austria, Prussia, Sardinia, Great Britain, and the United Netherlands on the one hand and France on the other, stated that "the duty and interest of the United States require that they should with sincerity and good faith adopt and pursue a conduct friendly and impartial toward the belligerent powers."[16]

The war between France and her enemies at once assumed

such bitterness, particularly as to Great Britain, that neutral rights were disregarded by both parties. Each party tried to starve the other into submission by depriving it of the benefits of neutral trade. Captures were not limited to contraband of war and vessels and cargoes destined for blockaded ports. As early as May 9, 1793, the French National Convention declared that "the flags of the neutral powers are not respected by the enemies of France" and that, under those circumstances, France in turn could not fulfill any longer her obligations toward neutral states. It therefore decreed that French vessels of war and privateers arrest and bring into the ports of the Republic for adjudication (1) all neutral vessels laden with goods belonging to nationals of neutral states, regardless of whether they were of the nature of contraband or not, if bound for an enemy port, and (2) all neutral vessels laden with enemy merchandise wherever bound. The neutral vessels, after unloading, were to be released. Provisions belonging to nationals of neutral states were to be paid for. Enemy property was to be declared good prize and confiscated to the profit of the captors. Thus began the "French spoliations," which involved a manifest violation of the principle of "free ships, free goods" as laid down in Article XXV of the Treaty of Amity and Commerce of February 6, 1778.[17]

Soon after depredations on American trade by British vessels, authorized by British Orders in Council, brought the United States to the verge of war with Great Britain. In order to avert the impending crisis, Washington decided to send Chief Justice Jay as Envoy Extraordinary to London. Jay was particularly instructed to press for compensation for the spoliations sustained, and, if possible, to negotiate a commercial treaty including the principle that in the event of a naval war free ships were to make free goods, a definition of contraband excluding foodstuffs, and other liberal stipulations. In any case, no treaty was to be negotiated contrary to the engagements of the United States with France. The Treaty of Amity, Commerce, and Navigation, signed at London on November 19, 1794,[18] however, failed to fulfill this condition.

It was consented to by the Senate on June 24, 1795, by a bare two-thirds majority, and ratified by Washington only after long hesitation, there being no other practical course to pursue. It specifically provided for the seizure of enemy property in neutral ships and for the pre-emption of foodstuffs (Arts. XVII, XVIII). Furthermore, it granted to the vessels of war and privateers of each party the same "exclusive" port privileges as had been accorded in Articles XIX and XXIV of the previous treaty between France and the United States of February 6, 1778. The exclusive port privileges of France in the United States were thus openly extended to her enemy, Great Britain.[19]

The Jay Treaty naturally caused deep offense to France. The Executive Directory by a succession of retaliatory decrees incited both ships of war and privateers to further spoliations on American commerce. On July 2, 1796, it informed the neutral powers that the French would apply to neutral vessels, in matters of search, capture, and confiscation, the same rules that their governments permitted the English to enforce.[20] The indefinite terms of this communication gave scope for an almost unlimited vexation of neutral commerce. Among the many other decrees of the Executive Directory, that of March 2, 1797, was particularly hard on American trade. It declared that Americans holding a commission for privateering against French commerce should be treated as pirates, and that every American ship which did not have on board a crew list or *rôle d'équipage*, besides her passport and certificates describing the cargo, should be good prize.[21] It is probable that, when this decree was issued, there was not one American ship afloat with the required crew list, and it is equally probable that the French Government knew this to be a fact.[22] Captures without number ensued. They are disclosed in a vivid report which Pickering, Secretary of State, communicated to the House of Representatives on June 22, 1797.[23] The single circumstance of an American vessel being destined to a British port; or the want of, or informality in, a sea letter or a bill of lading; or the destruction of a paper of any kind whatsoever; or the supercargo's being a foreigner by birth, although by naturalization a citizen of the United States, was considered sufficient to warrant a condemnation of American property. Such property, even if bound for a neutral or French port, or when lying in a French port, was seized without any pretense. In the West Indies—after their recapture from the British— the judges of the prize courts were themselves often the owners of the privateers upon the legality of whose seizures they had to decide and thus participated in the fruits of their own decrees of condemnation.[24] Vessels and cargoes were condemned in mock trials without permitting the owners or their agents to make any defense. American citizens, in addition, were beaten and imprisoned and American vessels were plundered, fired at, and burned. The Secretary of State reported to Congress on January 21, 1799, that the French depredations on American commerce had occasioned a total loss of property of probably more than twenty million dollars.[25] This was an immense sum for those days. It was greater than the entire annual revenue of the United States. The American vessels despoiled by France from 1793 to the middle of 1801 numbered 2,090.[26]

The American citizens thus deprived of their property claimed the protection of their government. The United States uniformly insisted upon the illegality of the conduct of France from the point of view both of the Treaty of Amity and Commerce of 1778 and the generally recognized rules of civilized naval warfare. It persisted in demanding redress. France, on the other hand, freely admitted the principle of the American contention.[27] A study of the diplomatic correspondence of these years, however, shows that James Monroe, the American Minister in Paris, was constantly hampered in his endeavors to adjust the spoliation claims by amicable negotiations through the French Government's insistence upon the fulfillment of the American guaranty regarding the French West Indies and the incompatibility of the Jay Treaty with the Treaty of Amity and Commerce of 1778.[28] The claims of France were thus set up against those advanced by the United States on behalf of its despoiled citizens.

On October 7, 1796, the Executive Directory gave notice that it was recalling its Minister Plenipotentiary to the United States. In December, 1796, it refused to accept the credentials of Charles Cotesworth Pinckney, successor to Monroe, and declared that it would "no longer recognize or receive a minister plenipotentiary of the United States, until after reparation of the grievances demanded of the American Government, which reparation the French Republic has a right to expect." [29] Pinckney was thereupon ordered to leave France. Diplomatic relations with the United States were thus broken off.

In the United States many Federalists now demanded war but President Washington, John Adams, and Alexander Hamilton realized that the country was unprepared, while the Anti-Federalists or Republicans insisted that there was no ground for war and that the strained relations were due to the mismanagement of the Federalists.[30]

The President was determined to re-establish diplomatic relations, and on July 13, 1797, commissioned Charles Cotesworth Pinckney, John Marshall, and Elbridge Gerry to proceed to France. They were instructed, among other things, to secure an adjustment of the claims for spoliations of citizens of the United States. On October 4, 1797, immediately after their arrival in Paris, the commissioners informed Talleyrand of their presence and requested an interview. Instead of granting their request, the Foreign Minister sent three gentlemen, who have become known in history as X Y and Z, to wait upon them. As a preliminary to the opening of negotiations, the three gentlemen demanded the payment of £50,000 as a *douceur* to Talleyrand and his associates and a loan to France of 32,000,000 Dutch florins. This the commissioners emphatically turned down. It was not until March 2, 1798, that Talleyrand received them. Being unable to renew the relations, the envoys left Paris. When the "X Y Z" dispatches were received in Philadelphia, the President announced to Congress that he would never send another minister to France without assurance that he would "be received, respected and honored as the representative of a great, free, powerful and independent nation." "Millions for defense, but not one cent for tribute" became the watchword of the day.[31]

The statutes of the United States reveal the impression which the dispatches from Paris made upon Congress. "An Act to provide an additional armament for the further protection of the trade of the United States; and for other purposes" of April 27, 1798,[32] authorizing the President to procure and fit out a number of armed vessels, not exceeding twelve, was the first of a series of enactments envisaging recourse to armed force against France. It was passed in the House amid great excitement. Edward Livingston, who closed the debate on the part of the opposition, said he considered "the country now in a state of war; and let no man flatter himself that the vote which has been given is not a declaration of war." [33] Three days later this act was followed by "An Act to establish an Executive Department, to be nominated The Department of the Navy." [34] The very existence of the Navy Department and of a Secretary of the Navy thus date from this eventful period of American history. On May 28, 1798, Congress passed a short "Act more effectually to protect the commerce and the coasts of the United States." [35] This act authorized the commanders of the armed vessels belonging to the United States to seize and to bring into port for adjudication any *armed* vessel of France which *off the coasts* had committed, or which should be found hovering *off the coasts* for the purpose of committing depredations, and also to retake any merchantman which might have been captured by any such *armed* French vessel. Most important of all the enactments was "An Act further to protect the commerce of the United States" of July 9, 1798.[36] It authorized the commanders of ships of war and of commissioned private armed vessels, under instructions from the President, to subdue, capture, and bring into port for adjudication any *armed* French vessel within the jurisdictional limits of the United States *or elsewhere on the high seas,* and to recapture American vessels, goods, and effects.

The army too was enlarged and prepared for action. On July 7, 1798, Washington, in his retirement at Mount Vernon, was appointed "Lieutenant General and Commander-in-Chief of all the armies raised or to be raised for the service of the United States." [37] "An Act to augment the Army of the United States, and for other purposes" of July 16, 1798, dealt with the armies to be organized. It authorized the President of the United States to raise, in addition to the then existing military establishment, twelve regiments of infantry and six troops of light dragoons, to be enlisted for and during "the continuance of the existing *differences*" between the United States and France.[38] Ten days later President John Adams nominated Alexander Hamilton to be Inspector General of the Army, with the rank of Major General.[39]

On July 7, an act of Congress had declared that the treaties between the United States and France had been repeatedly violated by the French Government, that the just claims of the United States for reparation of the injuries so sustained had been refused, and that, under the authority of the French Government, there was pursued against the United States "*a system of predatory violence.*" [40] Hence the treaties theretofore concluded with France were declared to be no longer binding on the United States. As a consequence thereof and of an act passed on June 13, 1798, suspending commercial intercourse between the United States and France,[41] President John Adams, on July 13, 1798, revoked the *exequaturs* of the French consul general, consuls, and vice-consuls.[42]

Following the close of the Congressional session, the Attorney General gave to the Secretary of State an opinion of great importance. The Attorney General, considering both the conduct of the French Republic relative to the United States and the laws enacted by Congress at its preceding session, advised the Secretary of State on August 21, 1798, that there existed a maritime war between the two nations and that, consequently, persons commissioned by France and aiding that nation in her naval operations should be treated as enemies and confined as prisoners of war.[43]

At its next session in 1799 and 1800, Congress passed additional acts directed against France. Three acts dealt with the army. "An Act giving eventual authority to the President of the United States to augment the army" of March 2, 1799, authorized the President to raise, in addition to the other military forces of the United States, twenty-four regiments of infantry and other additional forces, *"in case war shall break out* between the United States and a foreign European power, or in case of an imminent danger of invasion by any such power." [44] Another act passed the next day, March 3, entitled "An Act for the better organizing of the Troops of the United States, and for other purposes," provided that certain troops should be raised only if *"war shall break out* between the United States and some European prince, potentate or state." [45] Ultimately, an Act of February 20, 1800, suspended all further enlistments under the Act of July 16, 1798, unless in the recess of Congress and during the continuance of "the existing *differences"* with France, *"war shall break out* between the United States and the French Republic." [46]

The army, as already has been pointed out, never saw action. American activities against France consisted in naval operations only, and these were confined to attacking and capturing *armed* vessels of France in American home waters and on the high seas and to recapturing American vessels. These naval operations—the first extensive ones subsequent to the adoption of the Constitution—are described in detail in the above-mentioned seven volumes of *Naval Documents, Quasi War with France.* The force of armed public vessels originally comprised only three frigates, the *United States,* the *Constitution,* and the *Constellation.* The *Constitution* and the *Constellation,* by the way, were restored to the active list as a tribute to naval traditions on August 24, 1940. The *Constellation,* in consequence, served as a part-time flagship of Adm. Ernest J. King, Commander in Chief of the Atlantic Fleet, before his appointment, on March 9, 1942, to the post of Chief of Naval Operations and Commander in Chief, United States Fleet.[47] Gradually the small force grew to a total of 54 vessels, which operated off the Atlantic coast and in the West Indies, with occasional cruises to Europe. In the entire period, probably upward of a thousand armed merchantmen supplemented the naval efforts against the French.[48]

The most notable among the engagements were two fought in the West Indies by the *Constellation*, of 38 guns and 316 men, under Captain Truxtun. Her opponent on the first occasion, February 9, 1799, was the French national frigate, *L'Insurgente*, of 40 guns and 400 men; and on the second, on February 1, 1800, the French national frigate, *La Vengeance*, of 54 guns and 320 men. *L'Insurgente*, after a spirited action lasting an hour and a quarter, with 29 men killed and 41 wounded, struck her colors to the *Constellation*. *La Vengeance*, after a general action which continued incessantly for five hours, made off in the darkness of the night. The *Constellation*, on the latter occasion, had 40 men killed and 25 wounded.[49] There were other engagements on the part of the United States armed public vessels, and many spirited actions between American and French private armed vessels. About 85 prizes were taken by the United States vessels, not counting small boats and recaptured vessels.[50]

The captured *L'Insurgente* with her decks encumbered with wreckage and the bodies of wounded and dead men "resembled a slaughter house." Yet Captain Truxtun and Captain Barreaut, captured commander of *L'Insurgente*, wrangled over the question whether the United States and France were at war or at peace.[51] It is important to note that, in any event, the captured crews of the armed French vessels were treated in accordance with the opinion of the Attorney General of August 21, 1798. They were treated as prisoners of war: confined; hospitalized if necessary; liberated on parole, if they were officers; or exchanged in accordance with agreements (cartels) negotiated between the two parties.[52]

Meantime, Talleyrand, with the diplomatic relations between the two countries interrupted, communicated with the American Cabinet through Murray, the American Minister at The Hague. He sent word that whatever plenipotentiary the Government of the United States might send to France in order to terminate the existing differences between the two countries would undoubtedly be received "with the respect due to the representative of a free, independent and powerful nation." President John Adams seized the opportunity of this overture and dispatched Chief Justice Ellsworth, Mr. Davie, and Mr. Murray as a second plenipotentiary triumvirate to France.[53]

The elaborate instruction of the Secretary of State, Pickering, dated October 16, 1799, after reciting "the unexampled aggressions, depredations and hostilities, authorized and sanctioned by the French Republic against the commerce and citizens of the United States" and the uncourteous reception given to the mission of Pinckney, Marshall, and Gerry, proceeded to declare:

This conduct of the French Republic would well have justified an immediate declaration of war on the part of the United States, but desirous of maintaining *peace*, and still willing to leave open the door of reconciliation with France, the United States contented themselves with preparations for defense, and measures calculated to protect their commerce.[54]

The instructions required the envoys first of all to secure for the citizens of the United States full compensation for all losses and damages which they had sustained by reason of illegal captures and condemnations, the claims to be heard and determined by a mixed claims commission. In accordance with the Act of Congress of July 7, 1798, the former treaties with France, in particular Article XI of the Treaty of Alliance of February 6, 1778, guaranteeing to France her present possessions in America, were to be considered as no longer binding on the United States.[55]

When these envoys arrived in France they found that the Executive Directory had been overthrown. They had to deal

with Bonaparte as First Consul, who was then about to leave
Paris for that great campaign which, beginning with the passage of the Alps, was to end at Marengo. Joseph Bonaparte, his
elder brother, afterward King of Spain, headed the commission of negotiators on behalf of France.[56] Their instructions
made the acknowledgment of the continuing existence of the
former treaties with the United States the basis of negotiations
and the condition of compensation for the spoliations. The
French negotiators, therefore, strenuously denied the right of
the American Government to annul these treaties by a simple
act of Congress. Upon this rock the negotiations split.[57] The
American envoys finally agreed to recognize the continued
existence of the treaties, including the right of France to the
guaranty of her possessions in America and the exclusive port
privileges accorded by Articles XIX and XXIV of the Treaty
of Amity and Commerce of February 6, 1778.[58] No agreement, however, could be reached either for freeing the United
States from these obligations, or for the payment of indemnity
on the part of France. On September 30, 1800, after months
of weary discussions, the parties signed a convention, Article
II of which ran as follows:

The Ministers Plenipotentiary of the two Parties, not being able
to agree at present, respecting the Treaty of Alliance of 6th February, 1778, the Treaty of Amity and Commerce of the same
date, and . . . the indemnities mutually due, or claimed, the
Parties will negotiate further on these subjects at a convenient
time, and until they may have agreed upon these points, the said
Treaties . . . shall have no operation.[59]

The settlement of the difficulties growing out of the Treaty
of Alliance and the Treaty of Amity and Commerce of 1778,
with their entangling engagements for the United States, and
of the claims of the despoiled American citizens, was thus ad-
journed. On February 18, 1801, President John Adams, by
and with the advice and consent of the Senate, ratified this
convention, provided that the second article be expunged. The
First Consul, on July 31, 1801, ratified the convention thus

modified, *provided* that by the retrenchment of the second article the two states renounce the respective pretensions which were the object of the article. On December 19, 1801, the Senate, on again being asked for its advice and consent by President Jefferson, consented to ratify the convention with the *proviso* of the First Consul, and returned it to the President for the usual promulgation.[60]

Thus was completed what Madison, Secretary of State under President Jefferson, in a letter of February 6, 1804, to the United States Minister in Madrid, called "the bargain," [61] by which the United States waived the spoliation claims in consideration of release from all obligations founded upon the treaties of 1778, especially the burdensome guaranty of the French territories in America. The rights of American ship-owners were traded away in return for a great national advantage.

The assumption by the United States Government of the original obligations of France to American citizens, and its complete substitution for France as the responsible debtor, appeared to many a prominent contemporary as the necessary legal and equitable consequence of this set-off and mutual release. The Fifth Amendment of the Constitution, which forbids taking of private property for public use without just compensation, was especially pointed out. John M. Clayton reported in the Senate in 1846 of John Marshall, by common consent the greatest of the chief justices and, with the exception of the late Justice Holmes the greatest of the justices, "that having been connected with the events of that period, and conversant with the circumstances under which the claims arose, he was, from his own knowledge, satisfied that there was the strongest obligation on the Government to compensate the sufferers by the French spoliations." [62] The original sufferers, their widows and heirs, executors, administrators, and assigns, residing chiefly in the large seaports from which the despoiled vessels originally sailed, presented to Congress, between 1802 and 1864, 3,293 memorials and petitions requesting just compensation. There were also resolutions in favor of these claims, some of which were repeated and accompanied by elaborate arguments, by the thirteen original states. The question of compensation, in the same period, moreover, was the subject of no less than 42 reports in the Senate and the House. The validity of the claims was recognized by Edward Everett, Daniel Webster, Caleb Cushing, Rufus Choate, Charles Sumner, and other distinguished statesmen. Eminent opponents were Calhoun, Silas Wright, and Benton. A bill passed by Congress for the relief of the claimants was vetoed by President Polk on August 8, 1846. President Pierce vetoed a similar measure on February 17, 1855.[63]

At last an act of Congress, approved January 20, 1885, by President Arthur, entitled "An Act to provide for the ascertainment of claims of American citizens for spoliations committed by the French prior to the 31st day of July, 1801," [64] referred the claims to the Court of Claims. The act provided that within two years from its passage, such citizens of the United States, or their legal representatives, as had valid claims of a specified class to indemnity upon the French Government arising out of spoliations prior to July 31, 1801, might apply by petition to the Court of Claims. The court was to examine and determine the validity and amount of these claims according to the rules of law, municipal and international, and, without entering judgment, report to Congress such conclusions of fact and law as in their opinion affected the liability of the United States.[65] Their conclusions thus were mere advisory opinions for future actions. Notice of all petitions presented under this act was to be served upon the Attorney General of the United States, who was authorized to be heard by the court and was to resist the claims by all proper legal defenses.[66]

The Act of January 20, 1885, resulted in the filing of petitions embracing nearly 3,000 vessels, involving between 5,000 and 6,000 cases. Opinions were obtained after bitter fighting, the government succeeding in about 75 per cent of the cases. The amounts claimed were greatly reduced by the court on account of the inability of the claimants to obtain the needed documentary evidence, much of which had been lost or destroyed in the lapse of years. It was not until December 6, 1915, that the Attorney General, in his Annual Report, announced the final disposition of all French spoliation claims remaining on the docket of the Court of Claims. It appears that Congress, from 1891 to 1905, made four appropriations totaling $3,910,-860.61 in accordance with reports of the Court of Claims. There has been no appropriation to pay such awards since 1905. President Taft in his message of December 21, 1911, President Coolidge, in his message of December 3, 1924, and Secretary of State Hughes, in a letter to the chairman of the Senate Committee on Claims, expressed the hope that the last remaining awards would finally be paid. Those still before Congress and unpaid amount to $3,240,019.34. By the way, $2,491,000 in round figures concern claims that have been paid by insurance companies or private underwriters. The insurance companies and the heirs and assignees, etc., of private underwriters received favorable awards under the principle of subrogation. The remaining awards have been before Congress several times since 1905, but never passed both Houses in the same session. On May 8, 1940, a hearing was held before the Senate Committee on Claims on a bill introduced by Senator Walsh of Massachusetts for the allowance of these unpaid awards. Shortly thereafter the committee voted to postpone consideration indefinitely. On June 22, 1940, Senator Brown of Michigan advised the Senate of this action. During World War II Congress took no further action on the French spoliation claims. The mills of democracy sometimes grind exceeding slow.[67]

The opinions in the initial cases before the Court of Claims were written by Judge John Davis. They are highly interesting, not only on account of the origin and the extraordinary age of the claims, but also for the light they shed on the problem of the existence of war. In this respect the principal defense of the United States amounted to a complete abandonment of the views held by the Cabinets of both Washington and John Adams and by the Government of the French Republic. The United States contended that, during the period of the alleged spoliations, war existed with France, and, as the United States could have no claim against France for indiscriminate capture, condemnation, and confiscation of the private property of its citizens in time of war, neither could the claimants have any resulting claims against them.[68] It therefore became of great importance to determine whether there had actually been a war between the two countries. In May, 1886, this question was extensively argued and examined in the case of *Gray, Administrator*, v. *United States*. In December, 1886, it was rehearsed in the case of *Cushing, Administrator*, v. *United States*. Additional arguments are to be found in the many reports on the French spoliations submitted either to the House of Representatives or the Senate. The gist of these arguments is embodied in the great report made by Charles Sumner to the Senate on April 4, 1864, which, in turn, was incorporated *in extenso* by Broadhead in his report to the House on May 7, 1884, preceding the passage of the Act of January 20, 1885. The following exposition will consider indiscriminately the arguments submitted to Congress and those examined by the Court of Claims.

The United States substantiated its contention that there existed between 1798 and 1800 a war with France by advancing the following points:

(1) Battles were fought and blood shed on the high seas.[69]

(2) Prisoners were taken by each government from the other and dealt with as prisoners of war according to the laws and customs of war.[70]

(3) Diplomatic and consular intercourse were interrupted.[71]

(4) The determination as to whether war exists and is justifiable belongs in the United States to the political department of the government, and its determination is conclusive upon the judiciary. The political department of the government enacted such laws as authorized the forcible capture of French armed vessels and their condemnation as booty. This was a conclusive determination of the government that war existed between the United States and France.[72]

(5) The Convention concluded on September 30, 1800, between the French Republic and the United States was a Treaty of Peace.[73]

(6) The Supreme Court of the United States in the case of *Bas* v. *Tingy* established that there existed from 1798 to 1800 between the United States and France an imperfect, limited, or partial war. That settles the question as to the existence of war "in all its bearings." [74]

The arguments advanced on the other side are no less thought provoking:

(1) It may be admitted that battles were fought and blood shed on the high seas, that prisoners were taken by each government from the other and dealt with as prisoners of war according to the laws and customs of war, and that diplomatic and consular intercourse were interrupted. These facts constitute very strong evidence of the existence of war, but they are not conclusive.[75]

(2) *Congress* did not consider war as existing. The opinion of Congress at the time can best be gleaned from the laws which it passed. This legislation shows that war was imminent but did not in fact exist. On May 28, 1798, was passed the important statute entitled "An Act more effectively to protect the commerce and the coasts of the United States." Certainly there was nothing warlike in this title. Nor was anything said about war in its text. The Act of July 7, 1798, abrogating the treaties with France, does not speak of war either, but of a *"system of predatory violence."* The Act of July 16, 1798, authorized an augmentation of the army for and during the continuance of "the existing *differences*" between the United States and France. As late as February 20, 1800, while the negotiations in Paris were proceeding, an act was passed which provided for the suspension of further enlistments, unless, in the recess of Congress and during the continuance of "the existing *differences* between the United States and France," *"war shall break out"* between the two countries. Other enactments likewise looked toward war in the future. Such was the case with the Acts of March 2 and March 3, 1799. Why, if war did

exist, should the President, as late as March 2, 1799, be empowered to increase the army upon one of two conditions, viz., that *war should break out* or an invasion be imminent? None of these measures either refer to war at all, or, if they do, they refer to it, not as actually existing, but only as a possible future contingency. The above synopsis of the testimony of Congressional legislation is proof positive that throughout this whole period of trouble Congress did not consider war as existing. Is it not impossible to assert that, according to the understanding of the government, war actually existed? [76]

(3) In *diplomatic documents* the events of 1798 to 1800 are not referred to as "war." The instructions mentioned above of October 16, 1799, to Ellsworth, Davie, and Murray, did not recognize a state of war as existing or as having existed. They said that the conduct of France would have justified a declaration of war, but that the United States, "desirous of maintaining *peace*," contented themselves with preparations for defense and with measures calculated to protect their commerce. Furthermore, the American envoys declared to the French plenipotentiaries on April 11, 1800, that the acts of Congress, *"far from contemplating a co-operation with the enemies of the Republic,* did not even authorize reprisals upon her merchantmen. . . ." Again in the instructions to the United States Minister to Great Britain of September 20, 1800, the Secretary of State, who was none other than John Marshall, referred to war only as a probable event, not as an actual event already arrived at. The Secretary of State said: "The aggressions, sometimes of one and sometimes of another, belligerent Power, have forced us *to contemplate and to prepare for war, as a probable event.*"

On the side of France the diplomatic documents are equally explicit. Talleyrand, as Minister of Foreign Affairs, wrote on August 28, 1798: "France, *in fine,* has a double motive, as a nation and as a republic, not to expose to any hazard the present existence of the United States. . . . Therefore it never *thought of making war against them.* . . . Every contrary supposition is an insult to common sense." Joseph Bonaparte and the other negotiators for France, in a formal communication to the American plenipotentiaries of August 11, 1800, declared "that the state of misunderstanding, which has existed for some time between France and the United States, by the act of some agents, rather than by the will of the respective governments, has *not been a state of war*, at least not on the side of France." The same plenipotentiaries, under date of December 12, 1801, contented themselves with characterizing the relations between the two powers at this period as an "almost hostile state." [77]

(4) The events of 1798 to 1800 have been characterized as not amounting to war in both Congress and the French Parliament.

Edward Livingston, in the House of Representatives, like the Attorney General in 1798, it is true, very strongly sustained the opposite position.[78] It is, however, not possible to agree that this extreme position was justified. The year 1798 was a time of great excitement. Between danger of international conflict and the heat of internal partisan contest, statesmen could not look at the situation with the calmness possessed by their successors. Those successors, with some exceptions to be sure, regarded the relations between the countries as not amounting to war.

On May 24, 1828, Mr. Chambers reported to the Senate:

The relations which existed between the two nations, in the interval between the passage of the several Acts of Congress before referred to and the convention of 1800, were *very peculiar*, but, in the opinion of the Committee, *cannot be considered as placing the two nations in the attitude of a war*, which would destroy the obligations of previously existing treaties.[79]

Mr. Everett, from Massachusetts, in a report submitted to the House of Representatives on February 21, 1835, said:

The extreme violence of the measures of the French government and the accumulated injuries heaped upon our citizens, would have amply justified the government of the United States in a recourse to war. But *peaceful remedies* and *measures of defense* were preferred. These vigorous acts of defense and preparation, evincing that, if necessary, the United States were determined *to proceed still further and go to war* for the protection of their citizens, had the happy effect of precluding a resort to that extreme measure of redress.[80]

When the report on the convention of September 30, 1800, was laid before the legislative assembly of France, one of the French plenipotentiaries, charged with its vindication, announced that it had terminated the *misunderstanding* between France and the United States.[81]

These legislative documents fitly characterize the international relations to which they refer. The harmony of the two nations was ruffled but war did not exist.[82]

(5) In order to put the United States into a state of war, a positive declaration on the part of Congress is required, for Article I, Section 8, of the Constitution provides that Congress alone shall have power to declare war. Congress never made a declaration of war against France. There was, consequently, no war between France and the United States.[83]

(6) It has been urged that the Convention concluded on September 30, 1800, between the French Republic and the United States was a *treaty of peace*, but it is not possible to agree with this contention. Although, beginning in Article I with a declaration that there shall be "a firm, inviolable and universal peace," borrowed in precise terms from the Jay Treaty with Great Britain of 1794, the Convention did not purport to be a treaty of peace.

The caption of that treaty has been pointed to. But, curiously enough, neither of the originals—that supposed to be in the custody of France nor that supposed to be in the Department of State—is obtainable. That belonging to the United States Government has long since disappeared; a like fate has befallen the French copy. We are, therefore, forced to turn to the copies to be found in print in various compilations of treaties in order to find out what information can be obtained from a careful comparison of them. No material difference appears anywhere in the texts, but there are differences in the caption, and there, indeed, we should be prepared to find them, as the caption is not considered to be part of the treaty, and is sometimes drawn to suit the taste of the editor.

In Clercq's collection of French treaties, the caption, it is true, runs as follows: *"Traité de paix, d'amitié et de commerce conclu à Paris le 8 vendémiaire an IX (30 septembre 1800) entre la France et les Etats-Unis d'Amérique."* The editor does not say whether he had a copy of the original treaty or whether he relied upon another publication.[84] The caption in J. C. Bancroft Davis' edition of treaties entitled the compact "Convention between the French Republic and the United States of America." [85] The same caption is to be found in Volume VIII of the Statutes at Large prepared in 1846.[86] It should be noticed, as to this copy, that the letter from the Joint Committee of Congress found at the beginning of this volume states: "We learn that every law and treaty has been carefully collated with the originals in the Department of State." In President John Adams' message dated December 15, 1800, transmitting the treaty for consideration and decision to the Senate, the head note is exactly as in the Statutes at Large.[87] The inference that the convention is a treaty of peace, therefore, cannot possibly be drawn from the caption. Consequently, the nature of the treaty must be gleaned from its contents. If it concludes a war, that fact will necessarily appear in some form, as it does in the treaties of 1783 and 1814 with Great Britain, and in the treaty of 1848 with Mexico. Yet in the twenty-seven articles which cover the many different subjects at that time usually found in a treaty of amity and commerce, there is nowhere the slightest indication that, in the opinion of the parties, there had been a war and that they were making a treaty of peace. In the preamble, the object of the treaty is stated to be a termination of the "differences" between the two countries, not of the "war" nor even of the "hostilities" alleged to have existed between them.

The treaty itself, which is not concerned with the termination of a war and therefore is not a treaty of peace, is strong proof that there was no war between France and the United States.[88]

(7) War, according to Vattel, is the state in which nations, under the authority of their respective governments, prosecute their rights by force. In such a state, according to Vattel, *every* citizen of one nation becomes the enemy of *every* citizen of the other.[89] From 1798 to 1800, not every French citizen was an enemy of every American citizen, nor was every American citizen an enemy of every French citizen. In the legislation of the United States of those days, permission was given only for the seizure of *armed* French vessels. Unarmed French merchantmen were to pursue their voyages unmolested. Unarmed French vessels in distress because of weather or in want of provisions were even allowed to refit and provision in United States ports. It might be added that throughout the whole duration of the troubles the tribunals of each country were open to the citizens of the other. A Frenchman was not an "enemy alien" in the courts of the United States.[90]

Here ends the most spirited debate as to the existence of war which has taken place in American legal history up to this time. No similar debate can be found in the published court reports of the British Empire, France, Germany, Italy, and of other states. The Court of Claims arrived at, and in later decisions [91] constantly adhered to, the conclusion that there had been no war between France and the United States, that hence the spoliation claims were founded on valid obligations of France to the United States, that the United States had surrendered those claims to France for a valuable consideration benefiting the nation, and that this use of the claims raised an obligation on the part of the United States to compensate the individual claimants.[92]

The lines of reasoning for and against the existence of war are not for discussion in this chapter. The soundness of the pros and cons will be considered in the theoretical part of this study. It should be noted, though, forthwith, that there are signs indicating that neither side succeeded in making out its case. Captains Truxtun and Barreaut argued the question whether the United States and France were at war or at peace on board the *Constellation* in 1799. The same argument, in fact, is still going on today, almost one hundred and fifty years after the event. President Franklin D. Roosevelt, in his press conference of March 7, 1939, referred to the "*quasi* war" with France of 1798–1800 as an example of how difficult it may be to make out what war is. A definition of what war is, he said, is "an extremely difficult thing." [93] On January 27, 1941, the *Boston Evening Transcript* recalled the events of 1798–1800 in an editorial entitled "Was It War?" The question is not yet decided, the editorial said.[94] This verdict, we shall see, is correct.

In 1941 history was to repeat itself. The "shoot on sight" order, issued by the President on September 11, 1941,[95] in his capacity as Chief Executive and Commander in Chief of the Army and Navy, like the act of Congress of July 9, 1798, provided for limited naval operations. In addition, it provided for limited aerial operations. American naval vessels and American planes were ordered to attack Axis submarines and Axis surface raiders in waters deemed vital to American defense. Prior to the German and Italian declarations of war of December 11, 1941, it seems that no order was given for attacking German or Italian vessels outside American "defense waters," or for operating against German or Italian merchantmen anywhere. During the night of October 20–21 the United States lost its first warship in the battle of the Atlantic, when the destroyer *Reuben James* was torpedoed and sunk west of Iceland. On December 21 the Secretary of the Navy, Frank Knox, announced that the Navy had probably sunk or damaged fourteen enemy submarines in the Atlantic. The statement did not reveal whether these blows had been struck before or after the German declaration of war, or were the total of the attacks since the issuance of the order to "shoot on sight." [96]

Was the United States already at war with Germany and Italy during the period from September 11 to December 11? The answers given to that question were diverse and confusing. Senator Aiken, Republican from Vermont,[97] and quite a few members in both houses of Congress were of the opinion that the President, by issuing the "shoot on sight" order, had intruded on the province of Congress, to which the Constitution intrusted the right to declare war.[98] Other members of Congress, like Senator Wheeler, Democrat of Montana,[99] and Senator Taft, Republican of Ohio,[100] did not think that war existed. It was a measure of the confused state of opinions that Herbert Hoover expressly refused to commit himself on the issue. In a speech broadcast nationally by the Columbia Broadcasting System on November 19, the former President said he did not know whether the nation was at war, for that depended on the way one defined war.[101]

Section 2. The Boxer Expedition, 1900–1901

At the close of the nineteenth century, irritation against foreigners in China was widespread.[1] The defeat by Japan in the war of 1894–95; the self-arrogation, by Roman Catholic missionaries, of prerogatives of officials of the Empire; interference on the part of missionaries of all denominations with the corrupt administration of justice; the "lease" in 1898 of Tsingtao and Kiaochow Bay to Germany, of Port Arthur, Dairen and its hinterland, and of Kwangtung Province to Russia, of the Bay of Kwangchow to France, and of Weihaiwei to Great Britain; the granting of railway and mining concessions; fear of total partition of the Empire—all these contributed to hatred of the Chinese people for foreigners.

In the northeast the local militia, "Righteous Harmony Fists," or "Boxers" as the English called them, adopted the slogan "Protect the country and destroy the foreigners!" In 1899 the Boxers began to molest Westerners. By June, 1900, the situation in the metropolitan province of Chihli (Hopeh Province since the Chinese Revolution of 1911) had become acute. Native Christians were being massacred and aliens were in danger.

At the beginning of the disorders, the court proceeded against the rioters in words if not in deeds. Yet rioting gradually acquired a national character and finally reached the point where the Chinese Government could not have subdued it even if it had so wished. With the growth of the uprising in magnitude and power the court altered its policy. It finally organized, financed, and directed what is usually called the "Boxer uprising."

To protect American property and lives, Rear Admiral Kempf, commanding all United States war vessels of the Asiatic fleet north of Hongkong, on orders from President McKinley, joined an international fleet at Taku, at the mouth of the Peiho, on May 28.[2] On the same day, at a hurriedly called meeting of the diplomatic corps at Peking, it was decided to call legation guards from Taku. These, consisting of 21 officers and 429 men of American, Austrian, British, French, German, Japanese, Italian, and Russian troops, arrived in the course of the next day.[3] Ten days later the foreign representatives in Peking sent messages to the fleets at Taku asking for additional guards. The senior naval officer commanding the British fleet at once sent a combined force from the various warships, which, by that time, numbered 25. The expedition was commanded by the British Vice-Admiral Seymour and consisted of 2,056 officers and men. On June 11, at a point about three miles from Langfang, the first of four troop trains repulsed an attack by the Boxers. The railway beyond Langfang had been badly damaged and was in need of repair. Other skirmishes with the Boxers followed on the 14th at the Langfang and Lofa stations. On June 16 the railroad to Taku was found to be damaged. The relief force was thus cut off from its base. The opposition met by the expedition had so delayed its advance that provisions and munitions were running low. On June 17 and 18 the four trains withdrew to Yangtsun, about halfway between Langfang and Tientsin. The last train was unexpectedly attacked by a force estimated at 5,000 men, including cavalry, large numbers of whom were armed with magazine rifles of the latest pattern. Captured banners indicated that they belonged to the army of Gen. Tung Fu Hsing, in command of the Chinese troops in the hunting park outside Peking. These showed that Chinese Imperial troops were being employed to defeat the expedition. Between June 19 and 22 the expedition withdrew afoot under continuous fighting down the Peiho to the imperial arsenal near Hsiku, where, on June 25, they were succored by an international relief column. Next day the combined force, after destroying the arsenal with its immense stores of war material, arrived at Tientsin without further incident. Admiral Seymour turned in a casualty list of 62 killed and 228 wounded. The expedition had failed in its main object, the rescue of the diplomatic representatives at Peking.[4]

Meantime heavy fighting had occurred both at Taku and at Tientsin.

On June 15 the naval commanders at the mouth of the Peiho learned that the forts at Taku were being provisioned and re-enforced by the Chinese, whereupon they notified the viceroy of Chihli at Tientsin that, in view of the danger to the Allied troops marching to Peking and to a small force stationed at Tientsin, they would occupy these forts at 2:00 A.M. of the 17th. The several naval commanders arranged that, if not surrendered, the forts would be bombarded at 4:00 A.M., but at 12:50 A.M. the Chinese anticipated the action of the Allies by opening fire simultaneously from every gun in the forts that could be trained on the ships. The fire from the forts was quickly returned by British, French, German, and Russian gunboats and continued for several hours. The forts then were stormed by a land attack and occupied. The English torpedo-boat destroyers *Fame* and *Whiting* captured four Imperial Chinese destroyers lying at the dockyard between Taku and Tongku. The casualties among the Allied land and naval forces amounted to about 28 killed and 80 wounded. The bodies of 450 Chinese were found in the northwest fort, and a prisoner stated that about 50 bodies had been thrown into the moat.[5]

In Tientsin the Boxers had obtained entire control in the native walled city by June 15. The European troops in the British, French, and German concessions, then numbering about 2,500 men, mostly Russians, were kept busy guarding the settlement from the depredations of numerous roving bands of Boxers. On June 17 the bombardment of the foreign settlement began, accompanied by attacks on a large scale. The Allies at Tientsin fought for their lives until June 23, when the relief force, on its way to succor the Seymour expedition near Hsiku, pushed through to their rescue. On the 26th, the numbers of the Europeans were increased by the return of the Seymour expedition, and fears for the safety of the garrison were allayed, although the Boxers and Chinese troops continued to shell and attack the settlement. Re-enforcements continued to arrive, making the Allied strength on July 11 about 12,000. On July 13 and 14 the Allies, after severe fighting, took the native walled city and drove the enemy from all their strongholds. As described by various correspondents, the conditions in the walled city when the Allies entered exemplified in a most striking manner the horrors of war: hundreds of Chinese dead lay about in the streets or were piled along the walls; others, wounded, lay as if dead when approached, fearing to be killed, as doubtless many were. The looting and pillage of the city, mostly by natives but joined in by many European soldiers, was entirely unrestricted on the first day. Later the Allied commanders, as soon as attention could be given to it, adopted severe repressive measures to put a stop to it, and the scandal was soon discontinued. The Japanese, on account of the perfect discipline under which they were held in those days, are said to have been the least involved in this orgy of thieving and outrage.[6]

The relief of the legations in Peking, temporarily obscured by the events at Tientsin, was now organized again. On August 3 the Allied commanders at Taku arranged to begin the advance on the following day with approximately 20,000 men, made up, like the first and second relief expeditions, of American, Austrian, British, French, German, Italian, Japanese, and Russian troops. The Allies, after severe fighting, captured Peitsang on the 5th and Yangtsung on the 6th. Americans, English, Japanese, and Russians forced their way into Peking and relieved the legations on August 14, and, on the succeeding two days, completed their work of clearing out the enemy.[7] Then, as in Tientsin a month earlier, looting and pillage began. Immense and quite incalculable damage to private property was done during the following three days of authorized plundering. Each contingent accorded the palm to some other in respect to the art of remorseless plundering, but the fact remains that every one of them went in hot and strong for plunder. There was open trafficking in looted goods, and whole cargoes of objects of art and other valuables were sent to Europe and America. The looting was carried out in the crudest fashion by the Russians, who accompanied it with vandalic demolitions. Except for the Thirty Years' War and the plundering campaigns under the Most Christian King Louis XIV, there had been nothing like it in modern times. Unfortunately it was attended by other excesses: wanton acts of incendiarism, outrages on women, murder, barbarities of all descriptions.[8]

The following are the chief events that had occurred in the meantime in Peking. On June 20 the German Minister, Baron von Ketteler, while on his way to the Tsungli Yamen (the Chinese Foreign Office), had been fatally shot by a Chinese soldier. On the same day Chinese troops, under the Grand Secretary Yung Lu, Commander in Chief of the Imperial Army, surrounded the whole quarter of the city in which the legations were situated and opened fire on all sides. For four weeks there was scarcely an hour without fire upon some of the lines of the legation guards or into some legation, varying from a single shot to a general and continuous attack. The legation guards were commanded by Sir Claude MacDonald, the British Minister. The Austrian, Belgian, Dutch, Italian, and most of the French legation buildings were burned. The British legation, a veritable fortress with bomb-proof cellars, withstood all attacks. After July 14 negotiations between the legations and the Tsungli Yamen for a time greatly lessened the rifle firing and brought about a cessation of Chinese artillery activity. The legation guards, during the whole siege, had altogether 65 killed and 135 wounded. The occupation of Peking by the international forces was immediately followed by the flight of the Imperial Court to Sianfu, capital of Shensi Province.[9]

The military operations of the Allies in China had been conducted so far without any commander in chief. Each national force had been operating under the separate command of its senior officer. By the middle of July the Russian Government suggested the concentration of the general command in one single hand.[10] On August 6 Czar Nicholas II agreed with Kaiser Wilhelm II upon the nomination of Field Marshal Count von Waldersee, from 1888 to 1891 Chief of Staff of the German Army, to that post.[11] This was ultimately subscribed to by the other powers.[12] On September 25, forty days after the relief of Peking, the Commander in Chief arrived at Taku.[13]

Affairs in China were far from tranquil for a long time after the legations had been relieved. The Allied forces were then in possession of Peking together with a line of communications running to Tientsin and the coast. The rest of the province of Chihli and the other northern provinces in which the "Righteous Harmony Fists" had gained a foothold were still dominated by them. Complete "pacification" of those areas, by a series of small expeditions, was not achieved until April, 1901. The most prominent of those expeditions was that directed against Paotingfu, capital of Chihli, by the Commander in Chief, in October, 1900. The Allied troops occupied Paotingfu on October 18 without meeting with resistance. Some expeditions were sent only for the purpose of keeping the troops active; others were organized merely to suppress bands of brigands. After February, 1901, only German troops made expeditions; all other contingents remained completely passive, as there was no longer any reason for more extensive operations.[14] On June 4, 1901, Count von Waldersee laid down his command of the Allied forces.[15]

The negotiations at Peking between the plenipotentiaries of the powers and those of the Chinese Government lasted till September 7, 1901. On that day the plenipotentiaries of Austria-Hungary, Belgium, France, Germany, Great Britain, Italy, Japan, the Netherlands, Russia, the United States, and China, signed a treaty for the purpose of ending the situation which had been created by the disorders of the summer of 1900. This treaty is termed a "Final Protocol," not a "treaty of peace." None of its twelve articles refers to "war." According to Article XII, the remaining international troops, with the exception of the legation guards, were to evacuate the city of Peking completely by September 17, 1901, and, except for the forces which were to be left at Tientsin and at other points between Peking and the sea, the province of Chihli was to be evacuated by September 22.[16]

The American forces set in motion in July, 1900, for the anticipated campaign in China totaled 435 officers and about 15,000 enlisted men. Between 5,000 and 6,000 arrived in China before the capture of Peking, being part of an independent command, known as the China Relief Expedition, under Maj. Gen. Adna R. Chaffee. After the fall of Peking, the United States Government considered the object of the China Relief Expedition as accomplished. Orders were cabled diverting the remaining troops en route for China. General Chaffee was instructed to take no further aggressive action unless it should be necessary for defensive purposes and, on September 25, to send to Manila all the American troops in China, with the exception of a legation guard to consist of a regiment of infantry, a squadron of cavalry, and one light battery.[17] During the following seven months, the duties of American troops in China were practically such as were usual for them in garrison or camp with this difference: four companies of infantry and two troops of cavalry were charged with the duty of maintaining order in certain sections of Peking. General Chaffee's instructions were to withdraw his troops—except a legation guard of 150 men—as soon after May 1, 1901, as practicable. On May 19, the China Relief Expedition was officially disbanded. The American casualties for the whole expedition amounted to 33 killed in action and 29 dead of wounds.[18]

The military operations following upon the Boxer uprising and usually known as the "Boxer Expedition" are characterized by many peculiar features.

The Empress Dowager, in a decree published in the *Peking Gazette* of June 21, 1900, said, it is true: "With tears we have announced the war in the ancestral shrines," [19] but no declaration of war was ever made either on the part of China or of the powers.

The Chinese diplomatic representatives accredited to the powers and those of the powers accredited to the Chinese Government were not recalled. An Imperial edict, dated June 29, expressly directed the Chinese representatives abroad to remain at their posts.[20]

Barring a few scattered skirmishes, the military operations were confined to the capture of Taku and Tientsin, the two relief expeditions, the defense of the legations, the capture of Peking, and the various expeditions in the neighborhood of the above places. They were practically limited to the province of Chihli, one of the eighteen provinces of China, and within this comparatively small area had relatively few objectives. In regions south of the Tientsin-Paotingfu line, French and Chinese troops camped peacefully together.[21] On January 6, 1901, Count von Waldersee noted in his diary:

We are not at war with the viceroys of Shantung, Nanking and Wuchang. The three gentlemen cleverly try to steer a middle course between the Emperor and the Powers and thus represent a force to be taken into account by both sides. Whence arise the most amazing situations. Since summer the bulk of the fleets of the allied Powers lies at the mouth of the Yangtze. It is so close to the strongly armed fort of Woosung that from the sea the cannon of the ramparts and the troops drilling behind them are clearly visible. We are constantly prepared for a fight. The admirals and the viceroys nevertheless call on each other. In Shantung the viceroy acts as though he were our best friend. He sent me a telegram wishing me "A happy new year"!!! [22]

The military operations were not supplemented by naval operations, with the exception of the capture of the four imperial destroyers by the English torpedo-boat destroyers, the *Whiting* and the *Fame*, between Taku and Tongfu on June 17, 1900. The men-of-war of the Allied Powers neither attacked the Chinese vessels of war nor captured Chinese merchantmen, and vice versa.

Third powers were not requested to assume an attitude of neutrality, nor was their commerce molested on grounds of contraband or blockade of any portion of the Chinese coast.

In the leading French spoliation cases, the United States tried to substantiate its contention that from 1798 to 1800 war existed between the United States and France by advancing the argument, among others, that captured combatants were mutually dealt with as prisoners of war according to the "laws and customs" of war. Now there can be no doubt that in China quarter was seldom given. The one prisoner referred to above in the description of the capture of the Taku forts is a lonely figure. The records of the campaign, by and large, are silent about prisoners of war.[23] Other leading principles of the "laws and customs" of war—the prohibition of pillage and the duty to respect noncombatants—were likewise set aside, as was evidenced by the scandals following upon the capture of Tientsin and Peking. The commanders of the Allied forces, on the other hand, did not hesitate to take over the police, the judicial power, and the civil service in the occupied territory, according to the "laws and customs" in relation to the authority of belligerents in occupied enemy territory. The Commander in Chief held that leaving public order and safety and the civil service in the hands of the mandarins would amount to a downright monstrosity. The military administration thus established was known under the name of "Provisional Government." [24] The "laws and customs" of war on land, in a word, were indifferently observed: they were applied in some respects but not in others.

The Court of Claims drew its conclusion that there had been no war between France and the United States from 1798 to 1800 partly from the fact that the diplomatic documents of this period did not refer to "war." It is interesting, therefore, to pay attention to the diplomatic language applied to the military operations in China in 1900 and 1901. They are called "war," [25] "actual warfare," [26] *de facto* state of war," [27] "warlike acts," [28] "intervention," [29] "armed intervention," [30] "hostilities," [31] "military action," [32] "military operations," [33] "military measures," [34] "expedition," [35] and "punitive expedition." [36] The diplomatic documents, furthermore, refer to "war expenses," [37] "claims for war expenses," [38] "war indemnities," [39] "peace negotiations," [40] "conditions of peace," [41] and "the conclusion of peace." [42] The Chinese are referred to as "the enemy." [43] Seemingly paradoxical and perplexing expressions occur in a letter dated July 19, 1900, in which the Emperor of China requested the good offices of the President of the United States (McKinley). It refers to the existing "friendly relations" between China and the United States and, at the same time, expresses hopes for "the restoration of order and peace." [44] A similar communication was addressed to the German Emperor.[45] A letter which the Emperor of China on the same day sent to the President of the French Republic (Émile Loubet) goes so far as to speak of "the most cordial relations" existing between China and France.[46] The diplomatic correspondence, in a word, reveals the greatest variety of terms running from "war" to "most cordial relations." To try, as did the Court of Claims, to determine the legal nature of naval or military operations by pointing to the language employed in diplomatic correspondence is a procedure to which the mind hesitates to subscribe, but for the present we may let it pass again. In any event, it is evident that in the case of the Boxer Expedition, an attempt to answer the question as to the existence of war by referring to the language used in the diplomatic correspondence will, from the outset, come to nought.

A further perusal of the diplomatic correspondence reveals that certain statesmen expressly gave their views as to the existence or nonexistence of war. These were very much divided. The Russian Minister of Foreign Affairs, Count Lamsdorff, in July, 1900, and also in later stages of the Boxer Expedition, held that there was no war between Russia and China.[47] The German Ambassador in St. Petersburg, Prince Radolin, called such an opinion a "queer fiction." [48] John Hay, American Secretary of State, on June 23, 1900, declared that the United States Government, all the facts not being known, did not think that a state of war "necessarily" exists.[49] The Marquis de Montebello, French Ambassador to St. Petersburg, in a dispatch to Delcassé, French Minister of Foreign Affairs, on the contrary, held that war with China, though undeclared, existed in fact.[50] Delcassé himself, in the course of July, 1900, changed his way of thinking. On July 7 he told Prince Münster, the German Ambassador in Paris, that he decidedly was of the opinion that the Allied Powers, though they ought not to declare war, were already waging war against China.[51] Yet a fortnight later he wrote to the Minister of the Navy: "Finally there is no reason to conceal that the situation created by the rebellion and anarchy in China, *may* oblige the powers, contrary to their wishes, to state the impossibility of not recognizing a state of war with all its consequences." [52]

There are, besides these unsubstantiated opinions, more interesting ones in which reasons are given for the contention that there was or was not a war in China. On June 22, 1900, the Chinese Minister in London, in an interview with the Prime Minister, the Marquess of Salisbury, wished to know whether, notwithstanding the fact that the Taku forts had fired on the international forces without orders from the government at Peking, the powers considered themselves at war with China. The Prime Minister replied that if the forts at Taku had fired without such orders, and the attacks on the international troops (Seymour's relief expedition) likewise were without authority, there was no reason to consider that a "state of war" existed.[53]

In July news reached Berlin and other European capitals to the effect that the legations in Peking had been stormed and that the diplomatic representatives had been killed.[54] At the same time it seems greatly exaggerated rumors were being circulated as to the casualties suffered by the Allied forces. On July 6, the German Secretary of State for Foreign Affairs, Count von Bülow, reported to Kaiser Wilhelm II that the Russian Government was loath to declare war. The comment on this report in a marginal note by Kaiser Wilhelm II runs as follows: "It's all humbug! What more is wanted there? The ministers dead, hundreds of soldiers and marines dead and wounded, the admirals in distress, and this no war!?"[55]

In a telegram of August 23 the Kaiser reported to Count von Bülow: "Lascelles [Sir Frank Cavendish, British Ambassador in Berlin] asked me: 'Are we at war with China?' Answer: 'Is it customary to storm, burn down and sack the capital of other powers in time of peace?' "[56]

In the same dispatch, in a subsequent marginal note, the Kaiser reveals that he derived his contention that war existed from the fact that the Russian Government spoke of "peace" negotiations. It was highly illogical to his way of thinking to deny that war existed and at the same time to talk about "peace" negotiations. "In Germany no self-respecting Secretary of a Legation would get himself into such a hodge-podge."[57]

The Russian Minister of Foreign Affairs, on the contrary, pointed to the Czar's assurance that Russia would evacuate Chinese territory immediately upon the restoration of orderly conditions, and declared this to be "the best proof" for his contention that there was no war between Russia and China.[58] Count Lamsdorff, in an interview with the German Ambassador in St. Petersburg on September 7, 1900, emphasized the word "negotiations," since in the absence of war there could indeed be no question of "peace" negotiations.[59]

The question whether the Boxer Expedition constituted a

a war or not ultimately became a judicial issue in both the United States and Germany.

The fifty-eighth article of war, according to the Revised Statutes of the United States of 1873–74, prescribes that:

In time of war . . . murder . . . shall be punishable by the sentence of a general court-martial, when committed by persons in the military service of the United States, and the punishment in any such case shall not be less than the punishment provided, for the like offense, by the laws of the State, Territory or District in which such offense may have been committed.[60]

It has been pointed out above that from October, 1900, to May, 1901, four companies of infantry and two troops of cavalry of the United States Army were charged with the duty of maintaining order in certain sections of Peking. On December 23, 1900, Fred Hamilton was a private in Troop K, Sixth Cavalry Regiment, United States Army, stationed at Camp Reilly, Peking.[61] At that time and place he shot and killed one Corp. Charley Cooper of the same regiment, and for this offense was, on February 4, 1901, tried by a general court-martial convened and sitting at Peking. The charge read: "Murder in violation of the fifty-eighth article of war." The trial resulted in a judgment of conviction. The court sentenced the accused "to be dishonorably discharged from the service of the United States, forfeiting all pay and allowances due him, and to be confined at hard labor in such penitentiary as the reviewing authority may direct for the period of his natural life."

The reviewing authority approved the proceedings, the findings, and the sentence. It was of the opinion, however, that the accused had labored under some provocation and hence reduced the term of his confinement to a period of twenty years. The United States penitentiary at Fort Leavenworth, Kansas, was designated as the place for his confinement.

In 1905 Hamilton filed an application for a writ of habeas corpus with the Circuit Court for the District of Kansas. It was the insistence of counsel for the petitioner that at the time of the homicide no war existed as was required by the article of war above quoted to confer jurisdiction upon a general court-martial to try the petitioner for the offense charged against him, and that, therefore, the military court was without jurisdiction in the premises and its judgment void.

Counsel for the respondent in his briefs and arguments, on the contrary, contended that at the time of the homicide war existed in China, in which the United States Government was a participant, and that, therefore, the punishment of one in the military service of the United States, then in that country, for the commission of the crimes enumerated in the fifty-eighth article of war was authorized.

The court termed the question thus presented for determination as "one of first instance and large importance." As shown by the record, during the military occupation of China by the troops of the United States, no less than 271 trials by general court-martial had been held, resulting in 244 convictions.

In approaching the question the court, like the United States in *Gray, Administrator,* v. *United States,* stated it to be the well-settled law of the United States that the existence of war must be determined by the political department of the government and that the courts take judicial notice of such determination and are bound thereby.[62] The court then went on to point out that, by Act of Congress, the pay of officers and men in the military service of the United States during the time they were occupied in China was increased to the amount paid in time of war. This the court held to be a recognition of the existence of war on the part of the Congress of the United States.

The court furthermore recalled that Justice Grier, adopting Vattel's definition of war, while delivering his opinion in the prize cases [63] had said: "War has been well defined to be that state in which a nation prosecutes its right by force." Itself adopting this definition approved by the Supreme Court of the United States, the court held that, at the time of the homicide in question, the United States Government was asserting in China its right of protection over its citizens and accredited representatives and their property by force of arms and that, consequently, there prevailed a war in China.

The opinion concluded that the essential and requisite jurisdictional fact authorizing a trial of the petitioner by a general court-martial under the fifty-eighth article of war, did, and must "of necessity" be held to have existed, and that the judgment of that court must be upheld and enforced and the writ of habeas corpus denied.

It is interesting to compare this decision of an American court with a decision rendered on June 24, 1904, by the highest court of the German Reich. The pay of the German officers and men participating in the military operations in China, like that of the officers and men forming the American "Chinese Relief Expedition," had been increased to the amount paid in time of war.[64] The German *Reichsgericht*, regardless of this fact, in an obiter dictum, declared that the German expeditionary corps was not waging a "war in the sense of international law." [65] The Reichsgericht thus adopted a view which was at variance with that entertained by the Kaiser and supreme war lord, but was shared by the German Foreign Office. In a meeting of the commission on the budget of the Reichstag, held either late in 1900 or at the beginning of 1901, there had occurred a debate as to the question whether, after all, Germany and China were in a state of war or not. The answer given by the representative of the German Foreign Office was decidedly "no." Germany and China were not at war "in the sense of international law," the representative of the Foreign Office said.[66]

The preceding paragraphs show that courts of different states and high officials even within one and the same state manifestly disagree as to what war is. In fact, they do not seem to know. One is reminded of what Finley Peter Dunne, alias Mr. Doolly, the great American humorist and philosopher reported about the second Hague Peace Conference.

Th' dillygate fr'm Chiny arose, an' says he: "I'd like to know what war is. What is war anyhow?" "The Lord knows, we don't," says th' chairman. "We're all profissors iv colledges or lawyers whin we're home," he says. . . . "Well," says old Wow Chow, "I'd like to go back home an' tell thim what war really is. A few years back ye sint a lot iv young men over to our part iv th' worruld an' without sayin' with ye'er leave or by ye'er leave they shot us an' hung us up by our psyche knots, an' they burned down our little bamboo houses. Thin they wint up to Pekin, set fire to th' town an' stole ivrything in sight. I just go out iv th' back dure in time to escape a jab in th' spine fr'm a German that I never see befure. . . . Was that war, or wasn't it?" he says. "It was an expedition," says th' dillygate fr'm England, "to serve th' high moral jooties iv Christian civvylization." "Thin," says th' dilly-gate fr'm Chiny, puttin' on his hat, "I'm f'r war," he says. "It aint so rough," he says. An' he wint home.[67]

SECTION 3. GERMAN MILITARY OPERATIONS AGAINST ITALY, 1915–1916

During the period of World War I doubts occurred in several instances as to whether certain countries were at peace or at war. Such was the case for a time with Germany and Italy.

Italy declared war on Austria-Hungary on May 24, 1915.[1] It was not until August 27, 1916, however, that the Italian Government asked the Swiss Federal Council to inform the German Government that, as of the next day, August 28, 1916, Italy considered itself in a "state of war" with Germany.[2]

The following are the main features of the situation existing between Germany and Italy during the intervening fifteen months:

The German Ambassador and the Bavarian Minister in Rome, on the one hand, and the Italian diplomatic representatives in Berlin and Munich, on the other, requested their passports at the start of the war between Austria-Hungary and Italy. A few days later the German and the Italian Governments recalled their consuls. Diplomatic intercourse between Germany and Italy thereafter was achieved through the medium of the Swiss Federal Council, which also assumed the protection of Italian interests in Germany and of German interests in Italy.

Direct railway, postal, and telegraphic connections were likewise suspended; indirect connections to a certain extent, with the tacit consent of both governments and with the aid of the Swiss Administration, however, continued for several months.[3]

The armed forces which Austria-Hungary was able to oppose to the Italian attack were so insufficient that the Austro-Hungarian High Command had to request German assistance as early as May, 1915. According to an understanding arrived at on May 18, 1915, between the chiefs of the general staffs of the Austro-Hungarian and the German Armies (von Hötzendorf and von Falkenhayn), Germany was to assist Austria-Hungary at the outbreak of the war to the extent of three divisions.[4] When its ambassador left Rome, the German Government informed the Italian Government that the Italian troops, in their operations against Austria-Hungary, would encounter German troops also. Thus during the period under consideration, Austrian and German soldiers fought in common on the Italian front. German assistance was of great importance. The Italian declaration of war against Germany stated that it was German assistance that had enabled the Austro-Hungarian High Command to launch its great offensive operations against Italy in the summer of 1916.

In spite of this fact, it is important to note that neither Germany nor Italy requested third states to declare themselves neutral. Nor did any third state of its own accord declare its neutrality. The Swiss declaration of neutrality toward Germany and Italy, for instance, was made upon receipt by the Swiss Government of the Italian declaration of war.[5]

It appears that "in law," or "technically speaking," the Italian Government considered Germany and Italy as being at peace up to August 28, 1916. The Italian declaration of war, as mentioned above, dates the beginning of the "state of war" with Germany as of that date. Such technical peace in the eyes of the Italian Government, it is true, sharply contrasted with the military operations conducted by German troops against Italy.[6] As in the case of the Boxer Expedition, it so happened that the respective governments disagreed as to what it was all about. In a speech delivered before the Reichstag on September 28, 1916, the German Chancellor briefly outlined the policy which the German Government had adopted toward Italy after May 24, 1915. Herr von Bethmann-Hollweg referred to the military operations conducted by German troops and declared that there existed between the two countries in fact a state of war, though war had not been declared.[7]

The Italian journal of international law, the *Rivista di Diritto Internazionale*, in an editorial of September, 1916, puts the question: "How should one term the *relations* (*rapporti*) which existed between Italy and Germany in the period from May 24, 1915 to August 27 of this year? What was the character of and what definition exactly covers the *condition of things* (*condizione di cose*) prevailing during this long period of time between the two countries?"[8] The editor, though expatiating on his question at considerable length, finds no answer. He concludes by suggesting that the legal significance of the very terms "war" and "peace" may not be clearly established and hence ought to be investigated.[9] In this suggestion the editor, it will be seen, was absolutely right.

CHAPTER IV

Battles in "Peace"

The above title, no doubt, is disturbing to common sense. It sounds like a contradiction in terms. Yet it would be easy enough to produce a long list of battles of which it has officially been said that they did not amount to war. The present chapter, on the whole, is confined to three carefully chosen cases.

Section 1 deals with the famous battle off Navarino of 1827, a battle which was accompanied by assertions of peace, especially on the part of the British Government. These assertions of peace will be briefly compared with assertions of peace made by other governments in connection with other operations.

In Section 2 is reported an episode of modern French history. This section deals with the operations which France conducted against Annam in 1883–84, and against China in 1883–85, operations which accompanied the establishment of the French protectorate over Annam and Tongking.

Section 3 is devoted to two sets of operations taken from recent history: the operations which Japan conducted in "peace" against China from 1931 to 1933 during the so-called Manchurian conflict and from 1937 to 1941 during the so-called "incident."

It will be seen that from the point of view of the law there is a difference between the various battles in "peace." Section 1 deals with a genuine battle in peace, Sections 2 and 3 concern battles in "peace" which were merely political and diplomatic fabrications.

SECTION 1. THE BATTLE OFF NAVARINO, 1827, AND OTHER OPERATIONS ACCOMPANIED BY PROTESTATIONS OF PEACE

In the course of the eighteenth century, the Ottoman Empire crumbled rapidly. Among the causes of the decline were the first stirrings of the idea "one nation, one state," which was destined to play such an important part in the fall and rise of states in the Balkans, Italy, Germany, and Austria. In 1774, during a war between Turkey and Russia, the Greeks of the Morea, urged on by promises of Russian help, rose against the Sultan, but lost out when it suited the policy of the Empress Catherine to make peace with the Porte. Yet the spirit of national independence among the Greeks survived and developed. In the spring of 1821 the Greeks in the Morea rose anew. By the close of the year the revolution had spread beyond the Isthmus of Corinth, throughout continental Greece, and over the mountain passes into Thessaly and Macedonia. Turkish troops were unable to restore the authority of the Sultan. In the summer of 1824, however, Pasha Mehemet Ali of Egypt turned the tide of the civil war at sea with his fleet. In the following year Ibrahim, his son, turned the fortunes of war with his army on land. Ibrahim set to work with a brutality that seemed aimed at nothing less than the extermination of the entire Greek nation. In 1826 the end, indeed, seemed approaching. It was the time when all Europe watched with breathless interest the defense of the little town of Missolonghi behind the ramparts of which the forlorn hope of Greece was making a last heroic stand.[1]

The powers at first committed themselves to a policy of leaving the Greek Revolution to burn itself out. This policy of nonintervention, however, was frustrated by the refusal of the Western nations to follow the lead of their governments. In Europe at large the news of the "resurrection of Greece" had been received with an outburst of unbounded enthusiasm. Philhellenic societies, which had sprung up all over Western Europe, were providing money and volunteers for the assistance of the Greeks.[2]

It was during the siege of Missolonghi that Canning took the initiative and suggested a joint intervention of the powers. In January, 1826, after the death of Czar Alexander I, who had long urged the necessity of intervention, the Duke of Wellington was sent as a special envoy to St. Petersburg to congratulate Nicholas I on his accession, and, at the same time, to reach an understanding as to common action.[3]

On April 4, 1826, the British and Russian plenipotentiaries signed the treaty known as the Protocol of St. Petersburg. According to this instrument, Great Britain was empowered to propose to the Ottoman Porte a settlement of the Greek question based upon the establishment of Greece as an autonomous though tributary dependency of the Ottoman Empire.[4]

The Porte, in a manifesto published on June 9, 1827, declared that the revolution in Greece was a matter which could brook no interference and categorically rejected, as irreconcilable with the Koran, the proffered mediation between it and a "handful of brigands."[5] No other attitude could well have been expected in view of the Turkish successes.

France now agreed to act in conjunction with Great Britain and Russia and on July 6, 1827, "in the name of the Most Holy and Undivided Trinity," the three powers signed a "Treaty for the Pacification of Greece."[6] The three signatory powers engaged, by means of a joint declaration to be signed by their diplomatic representatives at Constantinople, *collectively* to offer mediation to the Ottoman Porte with a view to settling the Greek question along the lines of the Protocol of St. Petersburg. At the same time an immediate armistice was to be insisted on as a preliminary to and indispensable condition of any negotiation. By additional secret articles, it was agreed that the powers were jointly to exert all their efforts to bring about such armistice "without, however, taking any part in the hostilities between the two contending parties."[7]

The three governments transmitted instructions to this effect to the admirals commanding their respective squadrons in the seas of The Levant. Refusal of the Porte to consent to an armistice was anticipated. In such contingency the admirals of the three powers were instructed to unite their squadrons and to intercept every supply sent by sea either from Turkey or Egypt to the Turkish forces in Greece. The instructions emphasized that the powers intended to mediate between the two parties, and that, hence, any use of armed force against the

Turks should be avoided. "You are aware that you ought to be most particularly careful that the measures which you may adopt against the Ottoman Navy do not degenerate into hostilities." The united naval forces were to use force only if the Turks persisted in forcing the lines of communications which were to be intercepted.[7]

On August 16, 1827, the ambassadors of the three Allied courts at Constantinople presented to the Porte the joint declaration in conformity with the treaty of July 6. They offered their mediation between the Porte and the provisional government of Greece. They further proposed an armistice. Finally they demanded an answer within fifteen days. On August 30 the three ambassadors, through their dragomans, demanded the answer of the Turkish Government. The Reis Effendi, Minister of Foreign Affairs, referred to the manifesto of June 9 as containing the deliberate and firm determination of the Porte, and added: "My positive, absolute, definitive, invariable and eternal answer, is that the Sublime Porte does not accept any proposition regarding the Greeks, that it will persist in its will for ever and ever and until the day of the last judgment." The ambassadors then presented an additional note, informing the Porte that, in consequence of this refusal, the Allied courts would take the necessary measures to enforce an armistice, but without in any manner interrupting the friendly relations between them and the Turkish Government.[8]

The ambassadors of the three Allied courts immediately informed the commanders of their respective naval squadrons in The Levant that they were now called upon to proceed to the execution of their instructions.[9]

In the meantime a powerful new Egyptian fleet, with reinforcements which Ibrahim had long been anxiously expecting, had sailed from Alexandria in the beginning of August, and succeeded on September 9 in joining the Turkish fleet in the harbor of Navarino. Vice-Adm. Sir Edward Codrington, with the British squadron, arrived off Navarino two days later and decided to remain in a situation which would enable him to watch the further proceedings of the Turkish-Egyptian fleet.

On the 19th, he informed the Turkish admiral of his instructions to prevent the transfer of Turkish and Egyptian supplies to the Turkish forces in Greece and if necessary, to employ force. When, despite this warning, part of the Turkish fleet ventured out from Navarino, the English prepared for battle. The tense situation culminated in the dramatic appearance of Rear Admiral De Rigny with the French squadron to the windward of the Turkish vessels. In face of the two squadrons, the Ottoman ships all returned to the harbor of Navarino.[10]

On September 25, Ibrahim met the English and French admirals in a conference at which a sort of armistice in the Greek Revolution was arranged for about twenty days. Ibrahim, pending the arrival by couriers of new instructions requested by him from Constantinople and Alexandria, undertook to suspend all naval and military operations. Upon this the Allied squadrons sailed away to revictual, leaving but a couple of guardships to watch the Ottoman fleet.[11]

As soon as the coast was clear, Ibrahim, on September 30, long before there was time for any answer to have arrived to his request of the 25th for new instructions, ventured out to sea again with a squadron with a view to provisioning Patras. Warned by one of the guardships, Codrington intercepted Ibrahim at the entrance of the Gulf of Lepanto and turned him back, sending several 32-pound shots across the bows of Turkish ships that were slow in heaving to. The Turkish squadron returned to the harbor of Navarino. Thus, it is interesting to note, Codrington twice succeeded in imposing terms on Ibrahim by the mere threat of force. On October 13, near Zante, Codrington fell in with the Russian squadron under Rear Admiral Heyden. Next day both arrived off Navarino, where, on the 17th, they were joined by De Rigny with the French squadron.[12]

Disappointed in his attempt at naval operations, Ibrahim proceeded to put down the revolution on land with fire and sword. Clouds of fire and smoke rising all around the Gulf of Coron bore testimony to the work of devastation going on.[13]

The situation at Constantinople during the previous weeks had been tense. The ambassadors of the three Allied Powers foresaw the possibility of a collision between the Allied and the Turkish-Egyptian fleets. "We are waiting in hourly expectation of some decisive intelligence, probably of a gunpowder description, from the Archipelago," wrote Stratford Canning, the British Ambassador, a cousin of Prime Minister George Canning, on October 1.[14]

Lord Dudley, British Secretary of State for Foreign Affairs, had misgivings too. In a dispatch to Codrington on October 16, he said: "The principle I should recommend you to bear in mind as the key to any difficulties that may still present themselves to you, is that we are not at war—that we do not desire to be at war—but that what we aim at is to part the combatants." [15]

This warning did not reach Codrington until it was too late. The telegraph was as yet unknown, and the imperfect postal arrangements were still dependent on sailing vessels,[16] with the single exception of a steamboat between Corfu and Zante.

On October 18, the three admirals met in a conference. Their precise instructions, as pointed out above, were to prevent supplies being brought from Turkey or Egypt to the seat of war, and not to use force unless the Turks persisted in forcing the passages which were to be intercepted. Yet the three commanders, as has so often happened in military and naval history, now began to act on their own account. They envisaged three possible courses to effect an *armistice* between the Turks and the Greeks. First, to maintain a blockade off Navarino throughout the winter; this they ruled out as being "expensive," and perhaps useless, since a storm might disperse the squadrons and give Ibrahim an opportunity to escape. Second, to secure the inactivity of the Ottoman fleet by assembling the Allied squadrons in the Bay of Navarino; this they also ruled out, as inadequate to cause the Porte to give in and consent to an armistice. Third, to assemble the Allied squadrons in the Bay of Navarino, and at the same time to propose an armistice. This last plan the Allied admirals unanimously adopted. It just meant that the three admirals would demand an armistice and that if Ibrahim refused, they would attack his fleet.[17]

As Ibrahim's refusal was a foregone conclusion, the admirals had not seriously considered making their demand for an armistice, but meant to fight on the flimsiest pretext. On October 18, the very day on which the three admirals met in conference, Codrington issued instructions to the combined fleet, according to which, unless a shot was fired first from any of the Turkish ships, they were to open fire upon a signal being given for that purpose.[18] Next day he wrote to his wife: "Well, this day has gone by with all preparations and no fight . . . my own squadron appears to be so perfectly up to the mark, that they will think it a pity if all end in smoke." The Russian admiral, Heyden, was "ready, perhaps too ready, to go all lengths." [19]

The Turco-Egyptian fleet was moored in the form of a compact horseshoe at the entrance portion of the harbor. Its strength, strange to say, is a matter of some doubt. It consisted probably of 65 sail with 2,240 guns and about 40 transports. The Allied fleet numbered 27 ships and 1,276 guns.[20]

In the early afternoon of Friday, October 20, 1827, the combined squadrons stood toward Navarino, the British and French forming the weather, or starboard, and the Russians the leeward line. At about 2:00 P.M. they cleared for action, and, unmolested, passed the Turkish batteries at the entrance of the harbor and began to take up anchorage. When some British corvettes and brigs were sent to Turkish fireships with the high-handed and provocative request that these craft should move further away from the station taken up by the Allies, the Turks, according to Codrington, supposing that force was about to be employed, opened musketry fire and killed several Britishers. The action quickly became general. The bloody and destructive battle was continued with unabated fury for four hours. So thick was the smoke in the bay that the Russian ships, as they entered, had great difficulty in finding their way and in distinguishing friend from foe. Codrington, himself a prominent participant in the battle of Trafalgar, reports that the scene of wreck and devastation which presented itself at the end of the battle was "such as had been seldom before witnessed." The Turks behaved with the utmost bravery, but having allowed the Allies to enter the bay, instead of opening fire from every gun on land and water that would bear, their fate was sealed. Their lack of decision cost them 60 ships and probably 4,000 men, without causing any proportionate degree of damage to the Allies. Several ships of the Allies were badly damaged, but none lost. The number of their killed amounted to 181; 390 were wounded.[21] Each side took captives from the other.

Vague intelligence of the battle off Navarino reached the ambassadors at Constantinople on the 29th. It was forwarded to Stratford Canning by the captain of an English merchantman from Smyrna on "a shabby bit of paper, like a note picked up in the street."[22] Next day the ambassadors through their dragomans conveyed to the Reis Effendi "the expression of the sincere desire of the High Powers for the *continuance of peace* between them and the Sublime Porte" and anxiously inquired whether it regarded "what had happened between its fleet and the fleet of the three Great Powers as establishing a state of war between them." The Reis Effendi replied that he was unaware of what had happened at Navarino and gave no answer.[23] There was again no answer to the above inquiry forthcoming when on November 2, the ambassadors, while "deploring the melancholy results of the necessity which compelled their squadrons to oppose force to force," officially informed the Reis Effendi that the Ottoman fleet had been destroyed as a consequence of aggression perpetrated on the Allied squadrons.[24] In order "to convince the Sublime Porte of the sincerity of the *pacific dispositions* of the High Powers, from which the High Powers earnestly desire never to have to depart" the three representatives, on the 4th reiterated to the Reis Effendi through their dragomans "the invitation, forthwith to inform them whether the Sublime Porte is animated by similar feelings."[25]

The sarcastic answer of the Reis Effendi of November 4, 1827, has gone down in history.

What answer would you have to give me to a question quite contradictory in itself? . . . I have no answer to give to your Ministers. Their conduct is an instance of extreme contrariety. The case is actually as if in breaking a man's head, I, at the same time, assured him of my friendship. Would not such a proceeding be absurd? [26]

As it was, in spite of the disastrous battle off Navarino, "the sick man at the Bosphorus" did not resort to war against the Allies, and their ambassadors remained for the time being at Constantinople.

The news of the victory, dispatched by Codrington and depicting the Turks as the aggressor, reached London on November 10, twenty days after the event.[27] On the 13th there appeared in the *London Gazette* the notice that King George IV had been pleased to nominate and appoint Vice-Adm. Sir Edward Codrington to be a Knight Grand Cross of the Most Honorable Military Order of the Bath. When at the end of January, 1828, the House of Commons met, the dispatch sent by Codrington was still their only source of information respecting Navarino. There were many panegyrics bestowed upon the gallantry of Codrington. It was asserted that no deed of arms related in British history could exceed the gallant affair of Navarino.[28] Lord John Russell—who three decades later became so well known to Americans as diplomatic antagonist of William H. Seward, Secretary of State under President Lincoln—believed the battle off Navarino to have been a "glorious victory" and "as honest a victory as had ever been gained since the beginning of the world." [29] Yet there were signs indicating that all might not be so well. From the beginning the Cabinet thought that Codrington might have been precipitate.[30] To a large body of public opinion throughout the country, the affair of Navarino had caused dismay and astonishment.[31] The vice-admiral's behavior was believed to be and was condemned as rash, useless, and impolitic.[32] In the speech from the Throne at the opening of Parliament, January

29, 1828, the battle off Navarino was referred to as "a collision wholly unexpected" and as an "untoward event." The Sultan was designated as "an ancient ally." [33]

On February 14, Mr. Hobhouse, a close friend of Byron and one of the most active members of the Greek Committee in London,[34] moved that the thanks of the House of Commons be given to Vice-Adm. Sir Edward Codrington for his able and gallant conduct in the successful and decisive action with the Turkish fleet in the Bay of Navarino.[35] The motion was objected to by the Cabinet of the Duke of Wellington, formed in January, 1828, after Canning's death. It was ultimately withdrawn. Huskisson, Colonial Secretary, and Peel, Home Secretary and leader of the House of Commons, spoke on behalf of the Cabinet. Their chief reasons advanced against the motion were the following: According to a rule established by precedents the thanks of Parliament are voted to officers for triumphs achieved through their zeal, skill, and gallantry in *war*. When the battle off Navarino occurred, "there was nothing but peace" between Great Britain and Turkey. There was peace because the battle had not been planned and directed by the respective governments. It was a sheer "accident." It was an event which in private life would be styled a "chance-medley." In Huskisson's speech, the possibility of insubordination on the part of the three admirals was discreetly hinted at. Huskisson called them the "authors" of an accident which "perhaps" could not have been avoided. In view of the fact that in addition to Codrington a French and a Russian admiral were involved in the "accident" the language of the Cabinet had need to be restrained.[36] Codrington, by the way, was recalled in May, 1828, on account of "an unfortunate misconception of the views and intentions of Her Majesty's Government." [37]

It so happened that both the representatives of the three allied courts at Constantinople and the Cabinet of the Duke of Wellington took the prima facie amazing view that the bloody and "glorious victory" off Navarino, one of the most outstanding achievements in the naval annals of Great Britain,

France, and Russia, was wrested from a friendly power in time of peace.

The view taken by the London Cabinet, odd though it seems at first thought, yielded a legal result the soundness of which stands to reason. It would have been absurd to vote the thanks of Parliament for a victory which was the outcome of sheer quarter-deck diplomacy and insubordination.

The protestations of uninterrupted peace made by the three ambassadors at Constantinople likewise make sense, despite the sarcastic comments of the Reis Effendi. Stratford Canning and his French and Russian colleagues knew what they were talking about. Their protestations of uninterrupted peace were in harmony with the pacific policy agreed upon by the three powers in the Treaty of July 6, 1827. Nothing was further from the intentions of the British Government, at any rate, than a war with Turkey. To Great Britain, anxious for her trade routes to India, the preservation of the Ottoman Empire as essential to the balance of power in Europe, had long been a political axiom.[38] Prime Minister George Canning wrote to his cousin Stratford Canning on September 5, 1826, that no minister of England in his senses would dream of incurring a war against Turkey "out of reverence either to Aristides or St. Paul." [39]

The protestations of uninterrupted peace made by the three ambassadors were, no doubt, also for the purpose of appeasing the Sultan. By the sudden destruction of the Turco-Egyptian fleet, the sentiments of the Sultan were naturally roused to the highest pitch. His first impulse was to hold the ambassadors personally responsible. When General Ribeaupierre, the French Ambassador, read the "shabby bit of paper," the color left his face, and Stratford Canning knew that the message perhaps meant "three heads in one basket." Fortunately the Sultan was brought to milder counsels by an old statesman. Half a century earlier residence in the Seven Towers or something worse, would have been the inescapable lot of the foreign representatives.[40]

The assertions of peace made by the Cabinet in London

manifestly differed in character from those made by the diplomatic representatives in Constantinople. The former had juridical significance. They were made in relation to the rule that the British Parliament votes thanks to officers for victories gained in war. The latter were unrelated to any rule of law on war, either municipal or international. They were motivated by political considerations and by misgivings entertained by the ambassadors for their personal safety.

What was said in London on the one hand and in Constantinople on the other well illustrates a general truth. Any assertion of peace, or, for that matter, of war, either may be related to some rule of law on war, municipal or international, or may have a purely political or some other meaning. It is fallacious, therefore, to jump blindly from such assertions, particularly if made by diplomats, to the conclusion that from a legal point of view either peace or war exists.

Protestations of peace, friendship, lack of enmity on the part of a state invading and using armed force against another state are not infrequent.

In 1660 Louis XIV of France married the Spanish Infanta, Maria Teresa. On the death of his father-in-law, Philip IV, he unsuccessfully claimed, in the name of his consort, certain districts of the Spanish Netherlands (Belgium). In 1667 he invaded Flanders with an army of 50,000 men and fought against the Spanish governor the so-called Queen's War. In a manifesto sent to all the princes of Europe, Louis protested that he was not breaking the peace. This was a *political* move to induce Europe to believe that he was not a conqueror, but simply taking possession of what belonged as of right [41] to his queen.

On May 31, 1853, Emperor Nicholas I of Russia sent an ultimatum to the Ottoman Porte intimating that, if certain demands were not granted without qualification within eight days, Russian troops would cross the Pruth and, "by force, but without war," occupy the Danubian principalities. The assertion that no war was intended was made for the *political* purpose of appeasing Great Britain, France, Austria, and Prussia.[42]

In April, 1914, attention of the American public was focused upon the conflict which, in consequence of the Tampico
incident, had arisen between the Government of the United
States and the usurper General Huerta, who then was in control of Mexico City and of a large portion of Mexico. On April
21 this conflict took a sudden turn for the worse. In the small
hours of the morning Secretary of State Bryan learned that
the German steamer *Ypiranga* was about to arrive at Vera
Cruz with 200 machine guns and 15,000,000 cartridges. President Wilson at once directed Rear Admiral Fletcher, commanding a detached squadron of the United States Atlantic
fleet, to seize the customhouse at Vera Cruz so as to prevent
the cargo from falling into the hands of Huerta and his followers. Several hours later marines and bluejackets landed
under the fire of snipers and occupied the customhouse and
other public buildings. After severe fighting for several days
with snipers and Huertista soldiers the landing force took possession of the whole city. No further action took place thereafter. American casualties amounted to 19 killed and 56
wounded.[43] On April 22 the Congress of the United States
declared in a joint resolution "that the United States disclaims
any hostility to the Mexican people or any purpose to make
war upon them." This undoubtedly expressed President Wilson's *policy* toward Mexico which solely aimed at unseating
"that scoundrel Huerta" and at replacing "government by
murder" with a popular government. Of the intention of the
United States Government to respect the political independence and territorial integrity of Mexico there could be no
question.[44] In point of law, it is interesting to note that President Wilson did not send troops into Mexico upon his own
authority as Commander in Chief of the Army and of the
Navy. In a special message, dated April 20, 1914,[45] he requested the authorization by Congress, in which, under Article I, Section 8, Paragraph 11 of the Constitution, is vested
the power to engage the United States in war. The Congress
granted such authorization in the above-mentioned joint resolution of April 22, 1914, in which the United States at the

same time disclaimed "any hostility to the Mexican people or any purpose to make war upon them."

On August 25, 1941, Russian and British troops began to move into Iran and to occupy strategic points for the purpose of guarding the Iranian oil fields and securing the communication lines from Britain to Russia. Engagements with the Iranian Army, Navy and Air Force occurred during a period of about three days. On August 26 the Russian Foreign Office announced that the U.S.S.R. still regarded Iran as a traditional "friend," despite the joint Soviet and British invasion, and that they would take no steps to break off diplomatic relations with the Teheran Government.[46] This protestation of friendship, no doubt, had no legal but did have *political* significance. Respecting rules of law on war, suffice it to point out that both Iran and the U.S.S.R. were parties to the Hague Convention (II) of 1899 Respecting the Laws and Customs of War on Land.[47] It goes without saying that these rules of law on war applied to the Russian and Iranian military operations. The two countries thus were legally insofar at war in spite of the Russian protestation of friendship. The political purpose of calling Iran in the midst of operations a "friend," it would seem, was to project a *rapprochement* between Iran and the United Nations. On January 31, 1942, Great Britain and the U.S.S.R. concluded with Iran a treaty of alliance, and on May 2 President Roosevelt announced that the United States lend-lease aid would be extended to Iran.[48] In 1943 Iran entered into World War II as an enemy of Germany.

There are still other instances of invasions and engagements accompanied by assertions of peace, friendship, or lack of enmity. Some might be quoted that belong to the realm of historical myth. Suffice it to mention a mystic report regarding the *Risorgimento*. After the conquest of Sicily, Garibaldi with his redshirts started the invasion of Southern Italy in early August, 1860. On October 15 King Victor Emmanuel II of Sardinia, proceeding south from the Papal States, crossed the Neapolitan border at the head of his troops. On September 6 King Francis II of the Two Sicilies had left Naples and sailed for Gaeta where he stayed until shortly before the capitulation of this place to a Piedmontese army on February 13, 1861. Calvo and other writers of international law report that the Sardinian Minister, having accompanied King Francis to Gaeta, assured him "day after day" of the friendship of King Victor Emmanuel.[49] This just isn't so. It is a fact that the Sardinian Minister remained in Naples and there bid his adieu to the last King of the Two Sicilies.[50]

In this connection attention ought to be drawn to the other side of the picture, to assertions of a purely political character made by a state to the effect that it is at war. The "state of war" which the Lithuanian Government from 1920 to 1927 asserted to exist between Lithuania and Poland is a case in point.

On October 9, 1920, a Polish division under the "rebel" General Zeligowski captured the city and territory of Vilna. Zeligowski, by his coup, broke the agreement made at Suvalki two days earlier, whereby Poland and Lithuania recognized a temporary line of demarcation which left Vilna and Vilna territory with Lithuania. On March 15, 1923, the Conference of Ambassadors assigned both the city and territory of Vilna definitely to Poland. Lithuania, however, refused to recognize the decision and, as it had done since 1920, continued to protest against the Polish occupation.[51] It refused to establish diplomatic relations with its neighbor, or to allow any traffic between Lithuania and Poland. No train crossed the Lithuanian-Polish frontier. The highways leading from Lithuania into Poland were overgrown with weeds and the telephone and telegraph wires were down. It was not until March 19, 1938, that Lithuania gave in to a Polish ultimatum, the principal items of which were demands for the establishment of diplomatic relations, the opening of the frontiers to road and railway traffic, and the resumption of telephone and telegraph connections.[52]

After the coup of General Zeligowski, successive Lithuanian governments, for a period of about seven years, while publicly acknowledging that military operations for the purpose of recapturing the city and region of Vilna were "out of the question," maintained that a "state of war" existed with Poland. In the meeting of the Council of the League of Nations of December 7, 1927, the Lithuanian delegate, Voldemaras, explained what Lithuania meant by this "state of war," and consented to avoid using the term in the future. "State of war" was not intended to have any legal meaning. The term was chosen, instead, for the sake of emphasizing "the absence of normal relations between the two countries," and for the *political purpose* of bringing into focus Lithuania's claim to the city and region of Vilna.[53]

SECTION 2. FRENCH OPERATIONS AGAINST ANNAM, 1882–1884, AND AGAINST CHINA, 1883–1885

In the middle of the last century, the Empire of Annam comprised three geographically distinct parts. In the north, *Tongking*, with the delta of the Red River; in the center, *Annam proper*, the long strip of territory between the Cordillera of Annam and the China Sea; in the south, *Cochin-China*, with the delta of the Mekong.[1]

The emperors of Annam had been for two hundred years vassals of the Emperor of China. They paid a periodic tribute to the Son of Heaven and, in return, received from him their investiture and protection.[2]

Between 1858 and 1867 the French conquered Cochin-China, which became a French colony. The kingdom of Cambodia, to the north of Cochin-China, became a French protectorate in 1863, Annam and Tongking in 1874, and Laos, to the west of Annam proper and of Tongking, in 1893. Cochin-China, Cambodia, Annam proper, Tongking, and Laos had after 1896 a common administration known as *"le gouvernement général de l'Indochine française."* [3]

The establishment of the French protectorate over Annam proper and Tongking was the result of military and naval operations which stand out for their duration, the number of men engaged, and the losses sustained. In the French colonial history of the last century they are second only to the Algerian campaigns under Louis Philippe from 1830 to 1847.[4] These military and naval operations furnish one of the most illuminating examples of battles fought in times of "peace."

At the beginning of 1874, the governor of the colony of Cochin-China, after long negotiations, managed to overcome the patriotic inhibitions of two Annamite ambassadors, and finally bullied them into signing a treaty with France. This was in fact a treaty establishing a French protectorate over Annam, although the word "protectorate" had been crossed out at the last moment. More sugar coating is apparent in the fact that the Court of Hue, about to be put under international guardianship, was dubbed an "allied" government. The treaty was distinguished by the title of "Traité Politique." It bore the date of March 15, 1874. On April 13, 1875,[5] the ratifications of this treaty, and those of an elaborate treaty of commerce were exchanged with much pomp in Hue.

The pledges exchanged in the treaty of protectorate which were the most instrumental in shaping future events were the following:

In Article 2 the President of the French Republic, in obvious disregard of the suzerainty of China, recognized the entire independence of the Emperor of Annam from any foreign power. He promised furthermore that upon request of the Emperor he would lend without charge the support necessary to suppress the piracy which was desolating the coast of the Empire, to maintain law and order within the Annamite States, and to defend them against any aggression from without.

In Article 3, a guardianship was provided which was far from being total. The Emperor of Annam simply promised to conduct his foreign affairs in conformity with the French foreign policy.

In Article 11, the government of Annam undertook to open to trade the city of Hanoi, capital of Tongking, and the two ports of Haiphong and Quin-Nhon on the coast of Tongking and Annam. Article 11 also granted to all nations free passage on the Red River from the gulf of Tongking as far as the Chinese province of Yunnan.

On May 24, 1874, the French chargé d'affaires in Peking handed to Prince Kong, President of the Tsungli Yamen, i.e., Council of Foreign Affairs of the Celestial Empire, a copy of the Traité Politique of March 15, 1874. At the same time he asked for the recall of the Chinese troops, which, in accordance with a request of Emperor Tu-Duc, had been garrisoned in Tongking for several years for the protection of law and order.[6] Prince Kong's answer of June 15 was evasive and noncommittal as to Chinese suzerainty over Annam. Regarding the Chinese troops in Tongking, he observed that they had already been withdrawn, as their presence was no longer necessary. In other words, the Chinese Government, while not protesting against the French protectorate over Annam, avoided recognizing it either directly or indirectly.[7]

In 1876 Tu-Duc, in spite of his "entire independence" of any foreign power, sent the customary embassy with the periodic tribute to the Court of Peking.[8] When, two years later, Chinese insurgents numbering about 10,000 invaded the Northern provinces of Tongking, the Court of Hue appealed to both the French and the Chinese for help. The Governor of Cochin-China confined himself to dispatching one company with orders to look out for the safety of the French concessions. The Chinese Government, on the other hand, took its part as protector much more seriously. It sent a whole army corps to cooperate with the Annamite troops. After the insurgents had been routed, an imperial decree published in the official *Peking Gazette* of December 11, 1879, stated: "The laws of China still remain in force. At one stroke, calmness has been restored among those whom our investiture establishes as our vassals." [9]

The French protectorate in Tongking scarcely existed except on paper. At the beginning of 1880 the main body of the Chinese army corps, sent into Tongking in 1878, was recalled. The rear guard, however, was left in the region situated between the Red River and the Chinese frontier. The Red River was far from being open to commerce. Yellow Flags and Black Flags [10] impeded navigation to the detriment of the French

33740

concessions, and in defiance of Article 11 of the Traité Politique. Pirates continued to ravage the coasts of Tongking. In
the absence of French cruisers, Chinese junks of war policed
the gulf of Tongking, and proceeded to summary executions.[11]

The French Government resolved to get rid of the Black
Flags and of the pirates on the coast and thus to secure its right
of way to the interior of China by way of the Red River. The
Cabinet, headed by Jules Ferry, expressed its belief, in a message to Parliament, that this purpose might "perhaps" be at-
tained by increasing the French naval forces at the mouths of
the Red River and on the various river courses leading into
Tongking. Accordingly, in July, 1881, the Cabinet asked for
and obtained from Parliament an appropriation amounting to
about two and a half million francs for the purpose of fitting
out one sloop, two gunboats, and three shallow-draught river
boats.[12]

The instructions which the Minister of the Navy sent to
the Governor of Cochin-China in September were explicit
enough. Any kind of "military action" was definitely ruled
out. Driving the Black Flags from the Red River was looked
upon merely as a police measure against "pirates," though
these soldiers belonged to an Annamite fief and were in the
pay of Tu-Duc.[13]

The Governor of Cochin-China gave clear orders to Commander Rivière, chief of the French naval division off Cochin-
China. In the improbable case that Rivière should meet with
Annamite or Chinese troops, themselves commissioned to police the Red River, or with the Chinese then being stationed
near the Chinese frontier, a conflict was to be carefully
avoided. Only the Black Flags were to be attacked.[14]

On April 25, 1882, Rivière, completely disregarding the instructions of the Minister of the Navy of September, 1881,
bombarded and captured the citadel of Hanoi with a force of
about 1,500 officers and men, consisting of artillery, marines,
and infantry. The French had four men wounded. The Annamite casualties amounted to forty dead and at least twenty

wounded.[15] Nothing was done to purge the Red River of the Black Flags about whose misdeeds there had been so much talk and so little concrete evidence. Indeed, there seemed to be no longer any cause for complaints against them. On July 5, 1882, the Foreign Minister of Annam wrote the Governor of Cochin-China that for more than a year the Black Flags had left the river traffic entirely unmolested.[16]

As soon as news of the bombardment and capture of the citadel of Hanoi reached Europe, the Marquess Tseng, Chinese Minister in Paris, protested against what he justly considered to be a violation of Chinese suzerainty over Annam. In Peking, the members of the Tsungli Yamen entered a protest with Mr. Bourée, French Minister to the Court of the Celestial Empire. They met with the same kind of demurrer as did the Marquess Tseng in Paris. Toward the end of November, 1882, however, with military operations looming between China and France, Bourée on his own responsibility performed a diplomatic *volte-face*. He negotiated an agreement in Tientsin with Li Hung Chang, Viceroy of Chihli Province, acting on behalf of the Tsungli Yamen, which, subject to the consent of their respective governments, was intended to form the basis of a convention destined to eliminate the dangers of an armed conflict between China and France. This agreement provided for the opening of Yunnan Province to foreign trade and for the delimitation within the region situated between the Red River and the Chinese frontier of two parts, a northern one to be policed by China and a southern one to be policed by France. Eugène Duclerc, Premier and Minister of Foreign Affairs, expressed his satisfaction with the terms Bourée had secured. Had Duclerc remained in office, the history of French consolidation in Annam would probably soon have been brought to a close as far as China was concerned.[17]

But Duclerc and his Cabinet resigned on January 29, 1883. There followed a short-lived Cabinet headed by Armand Fallières. Fallières was succeeded by Jules Ferry, titular leader of the Republican majority since the death of Léon Gambetta on New Year's Eve, 1882.[18] Ferry was destined to remain at the helm for over two years and to become the most outstanding figure in the whole history of modern French colonial policy. He was recalled to office and promised to put an end to parliamentary chaos, to protect the democratic Republic from its internal enemies—meaning the monarchist-clerical opposition on the right—and to conduct a foreign policy of peace, though not one of inaction. It is important to note the foreign-policy plank in the ministerial declaration read by Ferry on February 22 to both the Chamber of Deputies and the Senate:

Gentlemen, the foreign policy of this Cabinet, like that pursued for eleven years by its predecessors, can be only a policy of peace. Peace is the first need and the deep-seated instinct of every great democracy. Yet a pacific policy is not necessarily a policy of inactivity. Everywhere, in all questions in which our interests and our honor are engaged, we desire and must preserve for France the rank to which she is justly entitled.[19]

One of the first things Ferry did in putting into practice his policy of peace was to repudiate Bourée's agreement with Li Hung Chang. The agreement entailed concessions for the benefit of China to which he felt he was unable to subscribe. On March 5, Challemel-Lacour, the new Minister of Foreign Affairs, "in order to indicate his sentiment clearly on this point," abruptly recalled Bourée.[20]

Soon afterward Rivière, although the instructions of September, 1881, ruling out any kind of "military action" were still in force, occupied the Bay of Hongay [21] and prepared to conquer the whole delta of the Red River.[22] On March 27 Rivière, after a battle which he called "classical," occupied the city of Nam-Dinh and then returned to Hanoi, only to find the capital beleaguered by Annamite troops.[23] On May 19 Rivière, three officers, and twenty-six men were killed in a sharp engagement that developed near Hanoi. Hanoi was pillaged and about half its dwellings burned. The French, however, managed to retain a foothold in the royal pagoda and in the French concession. Upon being informed of Rivière's death on May 26, the Minister of the Navy and of the Colonies dispatched

General Bouët, Commander in Chief of the French forces in Cochin-China, to Tongking. In addition he instructed the governor to send to Tongking all the troops he could spare.[24]

The Cabinet of Jules Ferry, soon after it had taken office, gave a demonstration of what it meant by its promise of a pacific though not inactive foreign policy. On April 16 it asked Parliament for a supplementary appropriation of 5,500,-000 francs in order to consolidate the French protectorate of 1874 over Annam and particularly over Tongking by permanently occupying the rich and densely populated delta of the Red River with naval and land forces totaling about 6,000 men. In a message sent to Parliament, and in speeches made before the Senate and the Chamber of Deputies by the Minister of Foreign Affairs, the Cabinet contended that such occupation was necessary in the face of the hostility shown the French by the Annamite mandarins. Rivière, who had captured Hanoi, Hongay Bay, and Nam-Dinh in open insubordination against the instructions of September, 1881, was represented as having done so in self-defense against insults, threats, and attacks, and the people of Tongking as longing for justice and order under French occupation and protection. France, it was said, was under a duty, so to speak, not to betray such trust. Emperor Tu-Duc was pictured as the originator of certain unspecified disturbances. Hence there could be no question of restoring and maintaining public order and security in Tongking upon the request of the Emperor, "without charge," as was provided for in Article 2 of the Traité Politique of 1874. All the expenses incurred by the occupation were to be reimbursed by the Annamite customhouses functioning under French customs collectors. In his speech before the Chamber of Deputies of May 15, 1883, Challemel-Lacour particularly emphasized that France, in spite of the bombardment and capture of Hanoi, a skirmish at Hongay Bay and the "classic" battle of Nam-Dinh, was not at war with Annam, but simply on a "footing of hostility." In his speech before the Senate of May 24 he called what was planned an "expedition" against Annam.[25]

The Senate on May 24 granted the new credit by a vote of 209 to 4. The news of Rivière's death reached the Palais Bourbon most conveniently for the Cabinet in the early afternoon of May 26, at exactly the hour when the Chamber was considering the request for the new appropriation. The Chamber, impressed by the bad news, granted the request unanimously.[26]

The government appointed Harmand, French consul in Bangkok, to the office of High Commissioner in Tongking. The diplomatic relations between France and Annam had been broken off after Rheinart, the French chargé d'affaires, had left Hue upon being informed of the bombardment and capture of Nam-Dinh.[27]

In spite of the favorable vote in May, 1883, of both houses of Parliament, opposition made itself felt against the "expedition" in Tongking. The Second Empire, born in 1851–52 under Louis Napoleon's rallying cry of "*L'empire c'est la paix,*" and ending in disaster at Sedan, soon after the abortive expedition into Mexico, had left a heritage of anticolonial and antiwar sentiment. Public opinion in France was opposed in principle to all kinds of foreign enterprises. It had its mouthpieces in the progressive press, which favored an exclusive policy of internal reforms; and it so happened that public opinion was soon to be deeply impressed by new developments in European politics. About the middle of June, 1883, information reached French quarters regarding the Triple Alliance secretly concluded by Germany, Austria-Hungary, and Italy. Prince Bismarck was suspected of entertaining aggressive intentions against France. Many a Frenchman considered the situation to be grave, and counseled prudence. The opponents of the "expedition" in Tongking pointed to the dangers involved in the dispatch of a part of the land and naval forces into the Far East at a time when France, threatened on her very frontiers, might need all her means of defense to face an enemy in the Alps and in the Vosges.[28] There entered into consideration, furthermore, a question of constitutional law. The French Constitutional law Regarding the Relations among the Public Powers, of July 16, 1875, provided in Article 9: "The Presi-

dent of the Republic cannot declare war without the preliminary assent of both Houses." [29]

This constitutional provision had a strange fate. The history
of the Third Republic abounds with instances of battles
fought by the French land and naval forces in foreign lands.
Yet, from 1875 down to 1940, no French Cabinet ever went
before Parliament with a proposal for a declaration of war.

In 1883 there was proceeding, besides the "expedition" in
Tongking, an "expedition" against the Queen of Madagascar.
On June 1 the French bombarded and captured the important
harbor of Tamatave on the east coast of the island. Two years
before, the first Cabinet of Jules Ferry, by an "expedition"
against the helpless Bey of Tunis, then still a vassal of the crum-
bling Ottoman Empire, had launched France upon the imperialistic career which was to make it the second colonial power
of the world. That "expedition," which resulted in the snatch-
ing of Tunis and its establishment as a French protectorate
under the hungry and frenzied eyes of Italy, had cost heavy
sacrifices in French blood and money. It was the cause, moreover, of the long and bitter enmity between France and Italy
which soon caused the Roman Government to climb on Bismarck's bandwagon, and which was only temporarily abated
during the first World War. In the Chamber of Deputies,
Ferry had been repeatedy accused of carrying on a belligerent
enterprise without the consent of Parliament. Two years later,
in the face of the "expedition" in Tongking, the question again
arose quite naturally: Do not such "expeditions" constitute
war and hence require a declaration issued with the consent of
Parliament? [30] This question was answered most emphatically
in the affirmative by both the monarchist-clerical Right and
the extreme Left. It served the monarchist-clerical opposition
as a welcome lever of attack against the infant Republican
regime. The extreme Left, on the other hand, was animated
no doubt by a resolve to take up the cudgels for an essential
institution of representative democracy.

On July 10, Granet, a member of the extreme Left, questioned the government in the Chamber of Deputies regarding

its policy in Tongking and in the Far East. Challemel-Lacour answered the interpellation. In a surprising reversal of the stand taken by him in both Houses in May, he admitted that no illusion was longer possible. "This is war, indeed, and nobody, I think, hitherto has doubted it." The answer created a tumult among the members of the Right. There were shouts of "Respect the Constitution!" and of "Don't repeat the case of Tunis!" The Minister of Foreign Affairs, however, dodged a constitutional debate. A Rightist firebrand exclaimed: "We have war! France heard it—France will remember it—and soon we shall be able to repeat that word before our constituents." [31]

Ten days later, the Duke de Broglie, leader of the monarchist-clerical opposition in the Senate, asked Challemel-Lacour whether, in using the term "war" before the Chamber, he had intended to give it "the scope and the precision which it has in international law. Everybody knows that in international law war is rigorously defined." The Minister of Foreign Affairs, swinging back again to his stand taken before both Houses in May, now replied that there existed with Annam "no open war." The Duke de Broglie confessed that he found it difficult to understand the Foreign Minister's answer. [32]

On July 19, almost the day on which Challemel-Lacour spoke before the Senate on the absence of "open war" with Annam, Colonel Baden performed an effective sortie against the Annamite troops which at that time were blocking Nam-Dinh. He succeeded in driving the "enemy" from the outskirts of the city. The number of Annamite dead left on the field of battle was at first officially reported to be 200, which was later changed to 700, and a third official report gave the number as more than a thousand. [33]

On July 30 High Commissioner Harmand, General Bouët, and Rear Admiral Courbet, Commander in Chief of the newly created naval division off Tongking, met in Haiphong, and adopted a plan of campaign. In Hue Tu-Duc was no more. He had died the middle of July, and the succession to the throne still was hanging fire. The Queen Dowager, at one with the royal princes and the *Comat* (Council of Ministers), on that very July 30 issued a decree calling to the throne Hiep-Hoa, a younger half-brother of the late Emperor. This, however, was something the triumvirate in Haiphong could not yet know. They, therefore, decided to take advantage of the vacancy of the throne and to direct their first "war operation" against Hue, about 500 kilometers to the south of Tongking. Once in possession of Hue, they hoped to prevent further commands, ammunition, and subsidies from reaching the Annamite troops in Tongking. Brun, Minister of the Navy and of the Colonies, had subscribed in advance to such a sideshow in Annam, in spite of the Cabinet's promise to Parliament to confine the "expedition" to the delta.[34]

From August 18 to 20 a French squadron of seven men-of-war bombarded the fortifications of Thuan-An. These protected the mouth of Hue River, and formed the only serious defenses of the capital. At 5:45 A.M. on the 20th, landing forces disembarked to the strains of "La Marseillaise." Three hours later the French flag was hoisted over the fortifications. The French reported six of their own wounded and 600 of the enemy killed. In the small hours of the 21st Hiep-Hoa's Minister of Foreign Affairs arrived in Thuan-An and asked for an armistice. This was granted by Harmand for forty-eight hours under the condition of immediate evacuation of the twelve forts located between Thuan-An and Hue.[35]

In Tongking, French occupation had been far from progressing according to schedule. General Bouët did not take the field before the middle of August. After a series of stiff engagements in which the Annamites fought gallantly, he carried Haidzuong after some spasmodic resistance, but was unable to dislodge the enemy from Bac-Ninh and Son-Tay. The Annamites, with France and Annam officially still hanging somewhere in the balance of peace and war, lost almost 3,000 men either killed or wounded. On August 23 General Bouët wired the Minister of the Navy and of the Colonies, that the growing number of the enemy, their armament, their undeniable valor and their defended positions covering a front of several kilometers, made it necessary to mobilize a complete division on a war footing, with all its services and material and garrison artillery and tank guns as well. In other words, the expeditionary corps in Tongking was to be increased to about 10,000 men. During the summer recess of Parliament the Cabinet dispatched the requested reinforcements without hesitation, "confident of responding to the thoughts of the Chamber and to its actual intentions." They amounted to about 4,600 men and began to arrive in Tongking in the first days of November. The French naval forces in both Tongking and the South China Sea, on the other hand, then comprised a complement of 32 vessels manned with a crew of 4,500.[36]

After a summer recess of almost three months, Parliament met again on October 23. On the 30th Granet, in the Chamber of Deputies, again questioned and assailed the Cabinet on account of its policy in Tongking. He was supported by Clemenceau, at that time standard-bearer of the extreme Left and its fabulously impressive speaker. Clemenceau rejected any kind of colonial policy, and in particular the system of protectorates, as contrary to the interests of France. Ferry told the Chamber that the "expedition" now had no other purpose than to complete the possession of the delta by the occupation of the fortresses of Son-Tay and Bac-Ninh. After this, General Campenon, Minister of War, rushed into the fray with a flamboyant speech in which he declared:

Here is the principle: When the flag of France, the flag of the Republic floats somewhere, it must, under penalty of being completely done for, under penalty of no longer standing for anything in this world, be upheld, respected and honored by each and everyone, from the first to the last, under all circumstances, whatever may happen and in spite of all.[37]

The majority responded to this rousing appeal with lengthy rounds of applause and other marks of strongest approval. After eight hours of debate the Chamber passed by 325 votes against 155 an *ordre du jour* approving "the measures taken by the government in order to safeguard the interests, rights and honor of France in Tongking."[38]

In the late fall of 1883 Ferry asked for and obtained from Parliament fresh appropriations for the "expedition" in Tongking, 9,000,000 francs as a supplementary credit for the year 1883, and 20,000,000 for 1884.[39] The report of the Chamber Commission charged to examine the draft statute concerning the supplementary credit for 1883 contained important news with respect to China. It revealed that in August and September the enemy in Tongking had been effectively aided by contingents of Chinese regulars and irregulars. It was known furthermore that on November 17 Ferry had notified the Chinese Minister in Paris that the French expeditionary corps had orders to march on Bac-Ninh and Son-Tay, and that on the same day the Chinese Minister had informed the French Government that the Celestial Empire had sent troops into both fortresses in order to defend there what it called "its own interests and those of its vassal." [40]

The question, therefore, arose whether the French Cabinet, dodging a declaration of war and violating constitutional law, was now waging war not only against Annam, but against China as well. On December 10 Clemenceau asked Ferry for an answer in the Chamber of Deputies. Ferry, who several weeks before had taken over the portfolio of Foreign Affairs from Challemel-Lacour, denied the existence of a war with China by emphasizing that the projected occupation of Bac-Ninh and Son-Tay amounted to only "a limited, localized, geographically circumscribed action." Clemenceau rejoined by saying bluntly that Ferry was fooling only those that wanted to be fooled. A week later the Chamber was witness to a strange incident. Ferry, by a slip of the tongue, admonished the Chamber not to call upon the Government to reveal its plan of campaign "in the midst of war." He was interrupted by an outburst of heckling coming from the Right and the extreme Left, and immediately withdrew the word "war" by saying instead "in the midst of action." The uncertainty as to whether France was or was not at war with China resulted in noteworthy statements in both branches of Parliament. On December 8, Camille Pelletan, a member of the extreme Left, said in the Lower House in a speech full of dash and wit: "Today, you know, one no longer declares war—this was all right for the remote period in which the constitution was drafted, way back in 1875—today one goes in for 'military operations,' an altogether different thing." The Duke de Broglie, on December 20, made an equally trenchant comment in the Senate. He said: "Do you know anything as difficult to define as the present situation of our relations with China? Is it peace, is it war? Formerly nothing was more simple than the distinction between peace and war. . . . Today, however, the definition has become almost impossible. They bombard cities without being at war with their possessors. At this very moment there are perhaps regular Chinese soldiers behind the walls of Son-Tay which our soldiers are attacking, yet we are not at war with China. Since war has become a state which has its consequences in the constitutional law of this country, it has, at the same time, turned into some sort of metaphysical entity of which a definition is no longer possible." [41]

The Chamber, at the end of its debate on December 10, was faced with five motions for an ordre du jour. Among these was one presented by Messrs. Archard and Rivière, which ran as follows: "The Chamber, affirming the right to deal with questions of peace and war which the Constitution has bestowed exclusively upon Parliament, and resolved not to tolerate any interference with this right through ministerial machinations, proceeds to the calendar of the day." This motion was indirectly defeated, in that priority was given to an ordre du jour similar to that adopted October 31. The latter was carried by 308 votes to 201. [42]

On December 16, the French, after a desperate battle that had lasted forty-eight hours, wrested Son-Tay from the Black Flags. In January, 1884, a brigade with two batteries and a company of engineers sailed from France further to reinforce the expeditionary corps in Tongking, the command of which was taken over by General Millot. General Millot completed French possession of the delta by capturing Bac-Ninh from the Chinese in March, 1884, and by the occupation of various other strategic points soon thereafter. By the middle of April the Chinese troops had been thrown back toward Yunnan Province and Langson. The program drawn up by the Cabinet of Jules Ferry was thus realized.[43]

For China, suzerainty over Annam had become by now an almost lost asset. The Chinese Government was getting ready to write finis beneath this chapter of China's past and it began to hold out the olive branch. Li Hung Chang, Vice-King of Chihli, was authorized to set on foot negotiations with Rear Admiral Lespès, Commander in Chief of the French naval division in Chinese and Japanese waters.[44] Lespès, with the consent of Ferry, dispatched Ernest F. Fournier, commanding the scouting vessel *Le Volta*, to meet Li Hung Chang in Tientsin. Fournier departed without any instructions. The part assigned to him was, in his own words, that of a "diplomatic scout" in a "diplomatic vanguard." Actually, however, Fournier, upon meeting Li Hung Chang, acted as a self-appointed negotiator for a treaty between France and China. This was entirely in keeping with the free and easy way of other French naval officers of that period. The singular negotiations between Fournier and Li Hung Chang lasted for only a day or two. After their conclusion Fournier, by cable, asked and obtained from the Cabinet in Paris authorization to sign.[45]

On May 11 Fournier performed what he later characterized as *"un veritable coup de main diplomatique."* On that day he and Li Hung Chang, with the consent of the Empress, signed in Tientsin what in the preamble was called "a preliminary convention the provisions of which will serve as the basis for a definite treaty." In Article 5, the parties agreed that their plenipotentiaries were to meet within three months after signature to work out the definitive treaty on the bases agreed upon in the preceding articles. The most important article was Article 2. According to it China implicitly recognized the French protectorate over the whole Empire of Annam. As far as Tongking was concerned this meant French occupation not only of the delta of the Red River, as held out by Ferry to the Chamber of Deputies on October 31, 1883, but French posses-

sion of the whole of Tongking, including the three provinces
bordering on China which had not yet been occupied by
French troops. From the legal point of view, Article 2 was a
blunder in that China consented to withdraw her garrisons
from Tongking "immediately," but neglected to specify
what she meant by that term. Two parties in good faith, however, could hardly have disagreed on the meaning of the term
"immediately." Article 2 was preceded by a preamble which
clearly characterized the whole treaty of Tientsin as a treaty
to make a treaty. Article 2, on the other hand, was followed by
Article 5 which, in turn, without any exception, referred to
"the" preceding articles as forming the basis upon which a
definite treaty was to be made. It is difficult to see how, under
these circumstances, any lawyer could interpret "immediately" otherwise than as meaning "immediately upon the
coming in force of the definitive treaty." Yet Ferry decided
otherwise.[46] He refused to submit the treaty to Parliament
for ratification on the ground that it was nothing but a
preliminary treaty, but from China he demanded the withdrawal at once of the Chinese garrisons from Tongking,
on the ground that, after all, the treaty, at least as far as Article
2 was concerned, was not merely preliminary. On May 13 he
cabled Fournier: "Regarding the evacuation of Tongking by
the Chinese, inquire as to where the imperial garrisons are and
notify me of the orders given for their withdrawal. Notify the
commander of our troops in Annam to the same effect." [47]

On May 17 Fournier and Li Hung Chang met again in the
vice-royal palace in Tientsin. At the opening of the meeting
Fournier handed to the vice-king an unsigned note. Fournier
bluntly informed Li Hung Chang that the French were entitled to occupy Langson and all the districts adjacent to the
Chinese provinces of Kwantung and Kwangsi on June 6, and
Laokai and the districts bordering on Yunnan Province on
June 26. Fournier then made the following threat: "At the
end of the respites allowed we shall proceed summarily to expel the Chinese garrisons tarrying on the territory of Tongking." [48]

The presentation of this note was followed by a lengthy conversation between Fournier and Li Hung Chang. Several months later Fournier told the story of this conversation under cross-examination and in statements which were to some extent inconsistent or foggy or obviously fabricated out of thin air, to the Tongking commission of the Chamber of Deputies. According to Fournier, the vice-king first declined to accept the note by pointing to the "fulminating" opposition it would provoke in Peking. Later on, so Fournier reports, Li Hung Chang veered around. He had his interpreter tell Fournier that he personally agreed to the terms of the note, and that he would try his best to have them accepted in time in Peking.[49]

Fournier, no doubt, was far from telling the truth and nothing but the truth. It is improbable that Li Hung Chang consented, even if *ad referendum* only, to terms so clearly inconsistent with the Treaty of Tientsin, and so injurious to the dignity of China as to foreshadow "fulminating" opposition on the part of the government in Peking. The vice-king, in a report to the Tsungli Yamen, contended that, far from consenting to Fournier's terms ad referendum, he not only had rejected them but had warned Fournier against any premature advance on the part of the French troops into districts still held by the Chinese.[50]

On May 17 Fournier cabled to Paris and sent a wire to General Millot. In both messages he described in nonchalant, sprightly fashion the terms of his note regarding the evacuation of Tongking as being embodied in an agreement concluded between himself and Li Hung Chang.[51] On May 20 Ferry read to the Chamber of Deputies both the text of the Treaty of Tientsin and the text of the "agreement" concluded on May 17 between Fournier and Li Hung Chang.[52]

Fournier left Tientsin on May 19 in order to carry the Treaty of Tientsin in person to Paris.[53] Before departing he told Lespès the story which he had wired to Paris and to General Millot. He represented the terms of his note to Li Hung Chang of May 17 not as being merely accepted ad referendum, but as being the terms of an accomplished agreement. Under these circumstances, Lespès naturally enough saw no reason to concern himself further with the "agreement" of May 17.[54]

In order to seal "the friendly understanding" between France and China, Lespès visited Peking from May 24 to June 7. On June 3 the Chinese capital witnessed a social event without precedent. Lespès gave a dinner party to the members of the Tsungli Yamen in the French legation. The party was "animated and very cordial." When the dessert course was reached, Lespès drank to the health of His Majesty, the Emperor of China, and Prince Kong toasted President Jules Grévy of France. Two days later the members of the Tsungli Yamen dined and wined Lespès and his entourage in the Chinese Foreign Office. On June 25 Li Hung Chang, with an escort of twelve Chinese men-of-war, visited Lespès in Chefoo and was given a brilliant reception on the flagship *La Galisson-nière*. Full-fledged, sweet peace seemed again to have descended on the Far East.[55]

The friendly understanding which Lespès had tried to seal was in reality a short-lived one. When the reception in Chefoo took place, the shadows had fallen again over Tongking.

On a day in early June, General Millot, Commander in Chief of the French military forces in Tongking, acted upon the fantastic telegram from Fournier informing him of the "agreement" of May 17. He ordered Lieutenant Colonel Dugenne to proceed with a column from Phu-Lang-Thuong on the 20th and to garrison Langson on the 24th.[56] In accordance with what appeared to be a perfectly pacific mission, Dugenne had been given explicit orders to refrain from taking upon himself any decision, and to report to the Commander in Chief at once in case his column encountered any resistance on the part of the Chinese.[57] Near Bac-Le, a village on the China highway roughly halfway between Hanoi and Langson, Dugenne received a warning from the Commander in Chief of a Chinese army that he would oppose with force any further advance of the French column.[58] When Dugenne, in spite of this warning and in spite of the orders from General Millot, tried to proceed into Chinese-occupied territory, the Chinese used force and defeated the French. The French casualties amounted to one officer and thirteen men killed and two officers and twenty men wounded.[59]

The tidings of Bac-Le reached Paris on June 26. The reaction of the Quai d'Orsay was one of moral indignation. Ferry, on the very same day, without knowing any details, accused China of having violated both the Treaty of Tientsin and the "agreement" of May 17. To Li Hung Chang he cabled: "We made a bona fide treaty. The ink is hardly dry on it and already it has been violated." [60] No expression seemed to Ferry to be strong enough to stigmatize the incident of Bac-Le. To him, in spite of all the subsequent information to the contrary, it remained "a disloyal surprise," "an act of bad faith," "treason," "a trap," "abominable perfidy." [61]

For several days Ferry was not in a position to know whether the "agreement" of May 17 was fact or fiction. He had been fooled by Fournier's cable of that date. On July 7, however, Fournier arrived in Paris. He thereupon handed to Ferry not only the original of the Treaty of Tientsin, but also the milder version of his fable, the version according to which Li Hung Chang had accepted his famous note ad referendum.[62] To Ferry, in spite of such an admission on the part of his representative, the note of May 17 continued to embody *"un arrangement complémentaire."* [63]

As things were, China might well have claimed damages for the losses suffered at Bac-Le. Damages, instead, were claimed by the French Government. On July 12 the French chargé d'affaires handed to the Tsungli Yamen an ultimatum, to be answered within a week, in which the French Government not only demanded the immediate evacuation of Tongking, but also damages amounting to "at least" 250 million francs.[64]

The French claim had no legal justification and was outrageously large. The various appropriations voted by the French Parliament for the campaign in Tongking from 1881 to July, 1884, amounted altogether to 37 million francs. This,

it was observed in the Chamber of Deputies, was not the traditional French way of doing business in international affairs.[65]
In August Ferry himself called the claim "exaggerated." [66]

The week following the presentation of the ultimatum of
July 12 was about to expire when China conceded the immediate evacuation of Tongking. This led to further negotiations between France and China, negotiations during which
Ferry blew now hot now cold. He no longer demanded "at
least" 250 million francs. Instead he called upon China to recognize at once that France had a claim for damages, and to
agree by August 1, at the latest, as to the amount thereof. Yet
the Chinese Government could not possibly admit that it owed
an indemnity without perjuring itself. On July 30 they offered
to pay 3,500,000 francs, not as an indemnity but in the way of
a conciliatory settlement.[67] This Ferry declined. He declined,
as he later explained before the Senate, not so much because he
thought that 3,500,000 francs was not enough, but because
the Chinese Government refused to plead guilty. Ferry's refusal, according to Clemenceau, was the act of a criminal, if
not of a lunatic.[68]

On August 3, three days after the expiration of the second
ultimatum, Ferry issued a third ultimatum. He summoned
China to choose between the payment of 50 million francs
"and not one cent less," or "war." [69]

Two days later Admiral Lespès, commanding a battleship,
a cruiser, and a gunboat, tried to seize the fortified port and the
coal mines of Kelung on the island of Formosa as a pledge.
After bombardment, Lespès succeeded only in occupying the
port. A few days later Chinese troops counterattacked. Lespès
lost 100 men, according to Chinese reports, and was compelled
to abandon Kelung.[70]

On August 3 Ferry had declared that his patience was at the
breaking point and that France and China now either had to
get it over quickly or fight it out. Yet Ferry began to mark
time. The ultimatum of August 3 had no time limit. The parliamentary records offer a clue to Ferry's Fabian tactic. Ferry
was clever at finding his way around obstacles. At this partic-

ular juncture he again had to find a way around the barriers which the constitution had placed in the way of war. A new discussion in the Chamber and in the Senate about France's relations with China, and in particular about the embarrassing question as to whether the two countries were at war, was likely to occur soon, since the Cabinet, for the purposes of its campaign in the Far East, had asked Parliament for a new appropriation amounting to 38 million francs.[71] The constitutionality of the action at Kelung, performed as it was without a declaration of war, already was likely to be questioned by the opposition. It was advisable to put off further coercive measures against China until Parliament had debated the new appropriation and had gone on vacation. Ferry, no doubt, expected by fall to have Tongking and the millions which he had demanded, and that, in the face of such a gratifying *fait accompli*, Parliament, when it reconvened in October, would care little about whether it had been obtained in conformity with or against the Constitution. This, it will be seen, turned out to be a case where Ferry gambled none too wisely.

The fresh appropriation of 38 million francs was debated in the Chamber of Deputies on August 14 and 15, and in the Senate on August 16. These days were well chosen. On August 16 Parliament was to adjourn sine die. Attendance during the last days of the session was small. Many Deputies and Senators had already left Paris. August 15 had the further advantage of being the date of the Feast of the Blessed Virgin. This was calculated to keep away many of the Deputies belonging to the clerical-monarchist opposition. Ferry talked to the Chamber about *"le traité supplémentaire"* of May 17, the "trap," and the "treason" of Bac-Le, about Chinese "disloyalty" and "perfidy," and about his own good faith.[72] He also talked about Admiral Lespès' operation against Kelung. Kelung was depicted as a pawn still held by Admiral Lespès. This, no doubt, was a deliberate misrepresentation. Since August 9 or 10, Ferry had known full well that Lespès had been compelled to abandon Kelung.[73] The gentlemen of the Chamber of Deputies had no idea of how brazenly they were being deceived. Ferry asked the Chamber to grant him, through an ordre du jour, authorization to seize further territorial pawns. The Chamber was assured that the bombardment of Kelung did not constitute war, and that further seizures of territory would not constitute war either. Ferry refused to ask for a declaration of war. Some members of the opposition were of the opinion that Ferry had violated the constitution and was perhaps about to do so again. There was some desultory heckling on this account, and even more desultory answers from Ferry, who, customarily, showed little talent when it came to answering hecklers. The Chamber eventually granted the 38 million francs by 334 votes to 140. By 173 votes to 50, with 324 Deputies absent, it further adopted an ordre du jour which, if it had not been engineered behind the scene by Ferry himself, had at any rate the advance approval of the government. This order was rather indefinite, and therefore open to various interpretations. It simply expressed confidence in the government's firmness in enforcing the Treaty of Tientsin. The Senate followed suit next day by granting the fresh appropriation by a vote of 174 to 1; about 125 Senators were absent. No sooner had the Senate voted than Ferry gave the go-ahead signal.[74]

On August 19 Ferry communicated to the Tsungli Yamen his fourth "last word." He summoned China to consent within forty-eight hours to the payment of 80 million francs in ten annual installments. On August 21 two officials of the Tsungli Yamen called on Semallé, French chargé d'affaires in Peking, and asked him how his passport should be worded. At the same time Li-Fong-Pao left Paris with the staff of the Chinese legation. Diplomatic relations between the two countries were thus broken off.[75]

Admiral Courbet, with the main body of the French naval division off Tongking and in the China Seas, had taken since the middle of July a position down the river Min in front of the naval dockyard of Foochow. The French naval strength before Foochow comprised four cruisers, three gunboats, two destroyers, and five steam launches, armed with Hotchkiss cannon. Foochow was in those days the chief Chinese naval and supply base. The arsenal of Foochow, according to Ferry, held "all the military and naval wealth of China." The main body of the Chinese fleet was likewise at Foochow. This fleet, incidentally, was not merely a puny collection of anemic junks. It consisted of eleven warships, which, to be sure, were without armor plating, eleven large junks, seven steam launches, three or four rowboats, and a certain number of fire ships. The two fleets had been anchored opposite each other in watchful preparedness for more than five weeks, when on August 21 the diplomatic relations between France and China were broken off. During these weeks Courbet had actually blockaded Foochow against Chinese shipping. Moreover, he had orders to interpret any kind of defensive measure on the part of the Chinese, the laying of mines, for instance, as an "attack," and to reply by a counterattack. Yet not even the news of the bombardment of Kelung caused the Chinese to "attack." Between the French crews and the civilian population there continued to be "business as usual." On board the French ships Chinese merchants sold ice and laundrymen called for and delivered laundry. Ten days after the bombardment of Kelung, China celebrated the birthday of the Empress. On the preceding day a Chinese officer, in conformity with maritime custom, called on board the French flagship and requested that the French men-of-war be dressed in honor of the sovereign. Courbet complied with the request. On August 16 the Chinese flag fluttered from the main mast of the French ships. The next day a Chinese officer came to render thanks for this act of courtesy. Lieutenant Commander Loir, who served under Admiral Courbet and later on became the historian of the French Squadron of the Far East, seems to have been informed by some expert that all this amounted to an "intermediate state." He wrote later: "What a queer thing this intermediate state, made up of courtesies and bombardment!" [76]

Courbet originally had had orders to occupy Foochow as a territorial security in case the Tsungli Yamen persisted in its refusal to pay an indemnity. The taking of further territorial pledges, in addition to Kelung, was what Ferry had held out to the Chamber of Deputies on August 15. Instead, on August 22, as Loir relates, Courbet received orders to attack the Chinese fleet and to destroy the arsenal and the fortifications on the shores of the river Min. The occupation of Foochow probably appeared to be too hard a nut to crack. Courbet attacked on Saturday, August 23, shortly before 2:00 P.M. There developed a great naval battle in which 40 Chinese officers and 2,000 seamen and soldiers perished within an hour. The French reported only 6 killed and 27 wounded. On the following days the French either destroyed or badly damaged the arsenal and the fortifications around Foochow. The Chinese Government, in spite of the wreck and ruin of its fleet and of its chief naval and supply base, was far from contemplating surrender.[77]

In its answer to the ultimatum of July 12, the Chinese Government had offered to evacuate Tongking immediately. Ferry's policy prevented such evacuation. By fall the Chinese armies had in fact succeeded in advancing from their positions of July into the delta. The French expeditionary corps, numbering by this time about 18,000 men, now began to fight for territories which several months before they might have occupied without striking a blow. In October and November there occurred in Tongking a great many engagements between French and Chinese troops. On November 26 Ferry told the Chamber of Deputies: "For the expeditionary corps in Tongking, victory, daily victory, is the normal state of affairs." Most important among these engagements were two battles fought in the earlier part of October at Kep and Chu, strategically important villages situated 25 kilometers to the southwest and southeast, respectively, of Bac-Le, in the two defiles that lead from Langson into the delta. The Chinese, "fierce enemies," as General Brière de l'Isle, new Commander in Chief of the French expeditionary corps, called them, were defeated in both places. As Ferry told the Chamber of Deputies, they suffered 5,000 killed.[78]

In the meantime Admiral Courbet had sailed from the estuary of the river Min under instructions to seize the whole northern part of the island of Formosa as a territorial pledge. The coal mines in the neighborhood of Kelung were expected to be the chief asset of such a seizure. On October 1, under protection of the guns of the fleet, the French disembarked a landing force of about 2,000 men at Kelung. They succeeded in occupying the city and the near-by hills, but were then faced with resolute Chinese opposition and were unable to advance to the much-coveted mines. This failure was of great consequence for the further conduct of the French operations. The French Squadron of the Far East—since Foochow the two French naval divisions off Tongking and in the China Seas had been so designated—now became dependent for its coal supplies upon the British Crown Colony of Hongkong.[79]

In order to prevent reinforcements, ammunition, and victuals from reaching the Chinese forces in Formosa, the French Government now instructed Courbet to blockade the island. On October 23, 1884, there appeared on the first page of the *Journal Officiel de la République Française* a notification announcing that the ports and roadsteads of the north and the west coasts of the island of Formosa were to be placed in a state of effective blockade from that day, and that a delay of three days was to be given to friendly vessels to complete their cargoes and to quit the places under blockade.[80] This notification, which was communicated on the same day through diplomatic channels to the maritime powers, ended with the threat that blockade-running vessels would be proceeded against "in accordance with international law and the treaties in force." It did not say what the "international law" referred to was, or which the treaties in force were or what they provided. In spite of all this, it soon became clear how the French Government intended to proceed against blockade-running vessels of both China and third states. Such vessels were to be captured and condemned for breach of blockade.[81]

In Paris Ferry was bragging that the approaches to Formosa were "hermetically closed," and that no vessel had managed to outwit the blockading French.[82] The blockade was, in fact, far from "effective." It belonged to that kind of international Gilbert-and-Sullivan pressure which has come down in the history of international law under the name of "paper" blockade. To a large extent it existed only on the paper on which it had been proclaimed. Giers, Minister of Foreign Affairs of Alexander III of Russia, compared it to the bite of a wasp on the back of an elephant.[83] On a coast line about 800 kilometers in length, Courbet disposed of only one fourth the number of cruisers necessary to prevent blockade-running. The ineffectiveness of the blockade is best illustrated by the fact that 25,000 Chinese soldiers landed on Formosa during the period from September, 1884, to the end of January, 1885.[84]

Yet there was, besides the paper blockade of Formosa, the great naval battle of Foochow, won by Courbet, whom Ferry called "the brilliant victor of the river Min," [85] and there was —again in the words of Ferry—"the daily victory in Tongking," won against what General Brière de l'Isle had termed a "fierce enemy." In the spring of 1883 the French Minister to the Court of Peking had told Li Hung Chang that France would consider as a *casus belli* any assistance, open or disguised, given by China to the Emperor of Annam.[86] In his third ultimatum Ferry had summoned China to choose between the payment of 50 million francs "and not one cent less," and "war." Would the gentle reader now care to guess whether "the brilliant victor of the river Min" and General Brière de l'Isle with his "daily victory" over a "fierce enemy" in Tongking were winning their laurels in war or in peace?

The attitude taken by the Chinese Government was puzzling. After the battle of Foochow, the Tsungli Yamen made Luu-vinh-phuoc, chief of the Black Flags, a lieutenant general, and gave him orders to retake Tongking from the French. The Chinese naval commanders received orders to attack the French men-of-war and to capture French merchantmen wherever they were encountered.[87] Merchantmen flying the flag of third states, on the other hand, went their way unmolested. The Chinese naval commanders had no orders to stop, visit, and search them, for contraband of war.[88] Of a small number of third states the Chinese Government requested neutrality, but not a neutrality pure and simple. On August 28 the Tsungli Yamen handed to the representatives of Great Britain, Japan, and the United States a note requesting as a consequence of neutrality simply that no coal be supplied to French men-of-war in British, Japanese, and United States ports.[89] This request was made, in all probability, in view of the second of the famous "three rules of the Treaty of Washington," agreed upon by the Governments of Great Britain and the United States in 1871 for the purpose of having their differences in the *Alabama* claims settled by arbitrators, who were to convene in Geneva, Switzerland.[90] The special purpose of the Chinese note was to prevent coal from being furnished at Hongkong and Nagasaki. It had no practical implication, therefore, as far as the United States was concerned. John Russell Young, United States Minister to the Court of Peking, consequently made no reply beyond a simple acknowledgment. The American Minister did, however, participate in much discussion in the Peking diplomatic body as to whether or not there existed war between China and France. He was unable to discover any consensus of opinion among his colleagues. The strangest part of it was the impossibility of obtaining from Prince Kong, president of the Tsungli Yamen, with whom Young had several conversations, any declaration to the effect that China regarded itself at war with France. The Tsungli Yamen seemed to shrink from admitting explicitly what they had implicitly admitted by their request for neutrality. Young contended that without an explicit statement on the part of the Yamen it was impossible to know whether war existed. Both the British and, as it seems, the Japanese Minister shared this view, and, consequently, likewise took no steps to comply with the Chinese request of August 28.[91]

As far as France was concerned, according to Jules Ferry, the victims, both Frenchmen and "enemies," of the battles of Foochow, Kep, and Chu, and of all the other "daily victories" in Tongking, had died in peacetime. The foreign policy of peace which Ferry had advertised in his ministerial declaration of February 22, 1883, had, to be sure, become somewhat dynamic by this time, but it was still "not a bellicose policy." [92] Ferry called this sort of policy "a policy of taking securities" (*une politique des gages*) resulting in a "legal situation" which he termed a "state of reprisals." [93]

In November and December Ferry asked for and obtained from Parliament fresh appropriations for the expeditionary corps in Tongking, and for the French Squadron of the Far East. An appropriation of 14 million francs was made to take care of a deficit incurred during the second half year of 1884, and 43 million in anticipation of expenditures during the first half year of 1885.[94] The Chamber of Deputies debated these appropriations from November 24 to 28, together with two interpellations regarding Ferry's Far Eastern policy and a further interpellation on "the violation of the constitution through the war waged against China without the preliminary consent of Parliament." [95]

In the course of this debate, Granet asked the Cabinet the following precise question: "What, exactly, is our situation? Are we at peace? Are we at war?" [96] It was up to Ferry to show the Chamber of Deputies how he had derived the concept of that "legal situation" which he called a "state of reprisals," how the military operations undertaken by France against China fitted in with such a concept, and how it differed from war. Yet nothing of this sort happened. In his speech before the Chamber of Deputies on November 26, Ferry did not prove anything at all, and the "state of reprisals" remained a mystery. In the same speech the unaccounted-for "legal situation" which Ferry had originally termed a "state of reprisals" and which had allegedly resulted from a pacific, "nonbellicose policy" was also called "a state of hostility." A fortnight later Ferry spoke before the Senate of "demi-belligerency." [97] There was no particle of proof anywhere. Clearly this was the verbosity of a politician who tried to delude his listeners.

The declaration of the blockade of the island of Formosa of

October 20, 1884, failed to indicate the legal grounds on which France based her claim to prevent the ingress and egress of the vessels of all nations. In December Courbet temporarily lifted the blockade for the southwestern coast on account of bad weather and in order to give chase on the high seas to Chinese men-of-war. On January 3, 1885, he issued a new declaration of blockade for that area. On instructions from Paris, no doubt, it referred to "the state of reprisals existing between France and China." [98]

This reference to a "state of reprisals" in a declaration of blockade is unparalleled. There was one way, and only one way, for France to justify her claim to prevent vessels of all nations from ingress and egress. This was to invoke the Declaration of Paris, signed on April 16, 1856, by Austria, France, Great Britain, Prussia, Russia, Sardinia, and Turkey, and soon acceded to by forty-five other members of the family of nations.[99] It should be said that the fourth rule of the declaration, that regarding blockades, was recognized even by those states which, like the United States of America, were not a party to the Declaration.[100] But the fourth rule, like the three which precede it, is a statement of maritime law "in time of war." Its meaning is that blockades, in order to be binding for third states, may be established *only* "in time of war," and, in addition, must be effective, i.e., "be maintained by a force sufficient really to prevent access to the coast of the enemy." There is nothing in international law to bind third states by a blockade during a "state of reprisals."

It was perhaps with the Declaration of Paris in mind that Clemenceau asked Ferry in the Tongking commission of the Chamber of Deputies on October 24 how the blockade of Formosa could be reconciled with the absence of a declaration of war. Ferry's answer was to the effect that the blockade of Formosa amounted to only a "pacific blockade." [101] Ferry, as shown above, had made no attempt to prove the legal possibility of the existence of what he termed a "state of reprisals." In the meetings of the Chamber of Deputies on November 26 and

of the Senate on December 12,[102] he did, however, try to clear
the legal hurdles by attempting to prove that the blockade was
"pacific."

To make good Ferry had to prove two propositions: First,
that, generally speaking, a blockading power had, according
to international law, a right in time of peace to prevent ships
of third nations from ingress and egress and to capture and
condemn them for breach of blockade; and, second, that the
blockade of Formosa was such a pacific blockade.

On November 26 Ferry showered the Chamber of Deputies with no less than thirteen "precedents," calculated to
serve as evidence for the first proposition, "a very serious and
very correct proposition with respect to international law."
All or nearly all European Powers, according to Ferry, had in
the course of the nineteenth century had recourse in peacetime to blockades of the kind declared in the *Journal Officiel*
of October 23 for the island of Formosa.

What were the thirteen precedents offered by Ferry? Five
of the "precedents" must be ruled out because there was at the
date and place concerned no blockade whatsoever. This is especially true of "the most famous precedent," the blockade
allegedly established by France, Great Britain, and Russia in
1827 against the coasts of Greece. The three admirals in their
conference of October 18, 1827, it will be remembered, decided against establishing an expensive and perhaps useless
blockade.[103] Into the same category of make-believe blockades
belong those allegedly established by France and Great Britain
against the Netherlands in 1832, by Great Britain against the
ports of Naples in 1840, by Spain against the ports of Mexico
in 1860, and by Great Britain against the port of Rio de Janeiro
in 1862.[104]

Two of Ferry's "precedents" must be ruled out, if for no
other reason than because they were directed against vessels
of the blockaded state only. Such is the case with the blockade
established by France against Portugal in 1831, and by Great
Britain against Greece in 1850.[105]

Two of the "precedents" must be ruled out because the

blockade in question was established not in peace but in war. This is the case as to the blockade established by France against the states of the Dey of Algiers in 1827–30, [106] and as to the short-lived blockade established in January, 1861, by the government of King Victor Emmanuel II of Sardinia against the port of Gaeta, refuge of Francis II, last king of the Two Sicilies. The blockade of Gaeta was declared in accordance with the Declaration of Paris in view of the war then undoubtedly existing between Sardinia and the Two Sicilies.[107]

This accounts for nine "precedents" out of the total of thirteen offered by Ferry. What about the remaining four cases? Two further cases—the very brief blockade by Great Britain of the ports of New Granada in 1837, and the blockade by Great Britain and France of the ports of the Argentine Republic from 1845 to 1847 and from 1845 to 1848, respectively—cannot be compared with the blockade of Formosa, and therefore have to be eliminated if for no other reason than that, at the end of the blockade, the vessels of third states were restored to their owners.[108]

All that remains to be considered are two blockades established by France under King Louis Philippe. They are the blockade of the ports of Mexico in 1838, and the blockade mentioned above [109] of the Argentine ports in 1838–40.[110] These blockades, it is true, like the blockade of Formosa, were directed against both vessels of the blockaded states and the vessels of third states, and, like the blockade of Formosa, they were enforced through capture and condemnation of blockade-running vessels. One also will readily admit that they were both performed in time of peace. Still they did not, on that account, establish precedents. There certainly was no tacit consent of the members of the family of nations establishing the admissibility of this sort of blockade in time of peace. The Hanse towns, in a manifesto which they circulated among the diplomatic body of Hamburg, maintained the illegality of this newfangled fashion of blockading at the expense of third states in the absence of war. In a memorandum of September 10, 1838, which they sent to their diplomatic representative in

London, they advocated a world-wide protest. Palmerston agreed. There are no means of ascertaining what steps, if any, were actually taken. As far as the Hanse towns are concerned, the diplomatic correspondence of this period perished in the great fire of Hamburg of 1842. But be that as it may. There had existed since 1856, short-circuiting all possible talk about "precedents" established prior to 1856, the universally recognized fourth rule of the Declaration of Paris, according to which blockades, in order to be binding for third states, must be established *only* "in time of war."

This takes care of all Ferry's thirteen precedents designed to demonstrate that a blockade of the type declared on October 23 was admissible in time of peace according to international law. The blockade of Formosa, in particular, was preceded and accompanied by heavy fighting on land and at sea. Ferry, after parading the thirteen "precedents," altogether neglected to explain why, in spite of such fighting, the blockade of Formosa in particular still was to be considered as established in time of peace and, for that matter, as a "pacific blockade."

On the whole, then, it is important to note that Ferry, who had failed when it came to furnishing proof of the "legal situation" which he called a "state of reprisals," likewise failed to make good his proposition as to the "pacific blockade." There can be no doubt about the hollowness and the pretext of both the "state of reprisals" and the "pacific blockade." The thirteen precedents manifestly were a smoke screen to divert attention from what really mattered: the Declaration of Paris, invalidating the blockade of Formosa, if, indeed, as Ferry asserted, it had been established in time of peace.

Not all the deputies and senators saw the light as Ferry wanted them to see it. Yet Ferry's smoke screen of "precedents" had worn down and reduced even the doubting Thomases to a state where they could not see steadily or think straight. In this half-dazed condition nobody was ready to attempt the feat of debunking Ferry's argument by penetrating his legalistic subtleties. It was rather felt than clearly seen that

Ferry was bluffing. To Clemenceau, speaking before the Chamber of Deputies, "state of reprisals" and "pacific blockade" were but "baroque epithets." In the Senate, the Duke de Broglie referred to these "legal situations" ironically as "finesses of international law." [111]

What the French Parliament, or at least the opposition, had in mind was Article 9 of the French Constitutional Law of July 16, 1875, providing that the President of the Republic could not declare war without the preliminary assent of both Houses. The proceedings of the Chamber of Deputies of November 26 and 27, 1884, offer a striking example of how a nation can be taken along the road to war without a declaration of war and in spite of such a constitutional barrier. On August 15, eight days before the naval battle of Foochow, Ferry had told the Chamber of Deputies that the anticipated "policy of taking securities" was not to lead to war, and that, consequently, he was not going to ask Parliament for a declaration of war. The implication manifestly was that, in case he did anticipate war, he would ask Parliament to vote a declaration of war.

On November 26 the Chamber of Deputies listened to a sweeping reversal of this very way of thinking. Ferry, while still professing peace, asserted that the contest over the question as to whether there was war or peace amounted to mere shadow boxing. The Constitution, according to Ferry, did not provide for a special procedure regarding the commencement of war. The assent of Parliament to war was not necessarily to be obtained directly through a vote on a declaration of war. It could be obtained indirectly through a vote on appropriations for a given objective or through a vote on an ordre du jour. The Cabinet was conducting its "policy of taking securities," even if it were war, with the consent of Parliament, as was manifested from August 14 to 16 by the votes for appropriations in both Houses, and by the ordre du jour voted by the Chamber of Deputies. The dispute as to whether the Constitution was violated, under these circumstances, made no sense.

Eventually Ferry asked the Chamber of Deputies for authorization to resort in 1885 to all military operations necessary for the complete possession of Tongking. In addition he asked for blanket authority to undertake at sea all the operations which Admiral Courbet, "the brilliant victor"—victor in "peace," mind you—should declare necessary to break Chinese resistance against the payment of the "indemnity" for the "trap" of Bac-Le. On November 28, the Chamber of Deputies granted Ferry's request by adopting, by 295 votes to 176, an ordre du jour proposed by Messrs. Spuller and Sadi Carnot which ran as follows: "The Chamber, persisting in its determination to make sure that the Treaty of Tientsin be put into full force and effect, takes cognizance of the statements made by the Cabinet, relies upon its energy in enforcing the rights of France, and proceeds with the calendar of the day." [112]

There could be no doubt about the meaning of this ordre du jour. The Chamber of Deputies agreed that peace with China had not been interrupted. It, furthermore, approved of Ferry's manifestly dubious interpretation of Article 9 of the Constitutional Law of July 16, 1875, and in accordance with this interpretation eventually gave Ferry by indirection, in the way of an ordre du jour, a green light on the road to war. Ferry's cunning, and connivance on the part of the Republican majority in the Chamber, combined to thwart the constitutional requirement of a direct and explicit declaration of war.

Since the naval battle of Foochow, Admiral Courbet had had a very definite idea as to what would constitute a successful naval operation for breaking Chinese resistance. Courbet was well aware of the fact that merchant vessels of third nations, especially those of Great Britain and America, were carrying considerable cargoes of arms and ammunition into Chinese ports. Unlike Ferry, he was of the opinion that France and China were at war, and that, consequently, such cargoes constituted contraband of war. Courbet repeatedly urged for authorization to stop, visit, and search on the high seas what he called the "neutral" vessels. Ferry wanted to have none of it.

He informed Courbet that France was not entitled to visit and search in what amounted to only a "state of reprisals." [113]

After notification of the blockade of Formosa, Great Britain and her possible attitude began to loom very large. In the period under consideration it had long been an established practice for belligerents to notify third states of the outbreak of war so as to cause them to adopt an attitude of neutrality. In the case at hand, neither France nor China had made such notification. Both France and China also had abstained from asserting rights incident to the existence of war, those of visit and search of vessels of third nations on the high seas. The British Government, for all that, concluded that war existed, and hence decided to adopt an attitude of neutrality. Fighting on a large scale had already occurred on land and sea, and, in addition, there was the notification on the part of France of the blockade of Formosa of October 23, which notification, under the terms of the Declaration of Paris, was valid only under the assumption that France and China were at war.

The fact that both China and France refrained from exercising the rights of visit and search on the high seas was most advantageous to British commerce. The number of British vessels employed at this period in Chinese trade was 3,309, as against 294 American, 361 German, and 200 Japanese vessels.[114] The British Government naturally was bent upon preserving such a state of affairs. It was willing to offer France and China a *quid pro quo* to be laid down in an agreement regulating British neutrality.

On October 31 Earl Granville, Secretary of State for Foreign Affairs, informed Waddington, French Ambassador to the Court of St. James's, that the British Government in its observation of neutrality would confine itself to the enforcement of the provisions of the Foreign Enlistment Act and abstain from issuing the usual proclamation of neutrality provided the French Government had the intention of refraining altogether from exercising over neutral vessels on the high seas the belligerent rights of visit and search.[115] This offer, as can be gleaned from a speech delivered by Earl Granville in the House of Lords on February 23, 1885, was made with the knowledge and approval of the Chinese Government.[116]

Before an agreement was reached, the two governments briefly debated the term "pacific blockade," for the French Government in its reply of November 5 stated that the blockade of Formosa was merely a pacific blockade, and that, in line with the pacific character of the blockade, it had by no means the intention of asserting the right of belligerents to visit and search vessels of third nations on the high seas. The French Government took pains to point out, as it did later before the Chamber of Deputies, that the blockade was permissible in time of peace. In so doing, however, they prudently refrained from parading by verse and chapter the thirteen "precedents." Trying to fool the Chamber of Deputies in a speech was one thing; trying to fool the British Foreign Office in a diplomatic note was another. Instead they vaguely hinted at unspecified precedents allegedly provided by France and even by Great Britain, establishing for a blockading power the right to capture and condemn the vessels of third nations for forcing a blockade even if it was resorted to in time of peace.[117] It was left to the sagacity of the British Foreign Office to discover what was hinted at.

The British Government, in all probability with the Declaration of Paris in mind, would have none of this suggestion. In its notes to the French Government of November 11 and 26 [118] it rejected the French doctrine as being in conflict with well-established principles of international law, and it impressed on the French that it could not admit that British ships were liable to capture and condemnation for entering a blockaded port unless the blockade was established in time of war. It added that the "novel doctrine" of the French was opposed to the opinions of the most eminent statesmen and jurists of France and to decisions of the French prize courts; leaving it, in turn, to French sagacity to find out who the statesmen and jurists were and which the prize court decisions. As far as the blockade of Formosa was concerned, the British were prepared to recognize it as a valid war blockade on the ground that it had been preceded and was accompanied by large-scale military and naval operations quite inconsistent with a "state of peace."

There the Franco-British discussion on pacific blockades in general and on the character of the blockade of Formosa in particular came to rest. This discussion did not prevent the two parties from entering upon a *"modus vivendi"* in accordance with the objectives of the British offer of October 31. The French Government took cognizance of the declaration of the British Government that it would confine itself to the enforcement of the Foreign Enlistment Act and refrain from issuing the usual proclamation of neutrality, and declared on its own part that it did not propose to visit and search vessels of third nations on the high seas.[119]

This modus vivendi, according to Earl Granville, insured "a just and equal measure of neutrality toward both belligerents."[120] At the beginning, Great Britain, France, and China alike were gratified. British shipping went on unmolested by visit and search, and the Chinese could freely import arms and ammunition.

What were the advantages accruing to France from the modus vivendi? There was no great difference between the provisions of the Foreign Enlistment Act [121] and the wording of the usual British proclamation of neutrality. The proclamation of neutrality put forth by Great Britain in 1877, at the outbreak of the Russo-Turkish War,[122] recites the Foreign Enlistment Act, and, in addition, commands observance of the duties of neutrality resulting from international law. Among these duties was the prohibition of belligerent vessels to remain more than twenty-four hours in British ports unless detained by stress of weather.[123] Hence, in the absence of a proclamation of neutrality, French men-of-war were free to enter British ports and to remain there for an unlimited period of time. On the other hand the Foreign Enlistment Act of 1870 prohibits and penalizes the increase of the armament or *equipment* of a man-of-war of a belligerent in a British port (Sec. 10).

The term "equipping" is interpreted in Section 30 of the act. It includes the furnishing of a ship with any tackle, provisions, stores, or any other thing which is used in or about a ship for the purpose of fitting or adapting her for the sea or for naval service. It seems that this interpretation clause was for weeks overlooked by the French Government and disregarded by the British colonial authorities.

Under these circumstances, the advantages accruing to the French from the modus vivendi were enormous. The many French men-of-war and transports making for or returning from the Far East by the India route called at British ports such as Aden, Colombo, Singapore, and Hongkong, and freely repaired, revictualed, provisioned, and coaled. Hongkong was actually the supply base of the French naval operations against China.[124] The transportation of supplies by sea from Marseilles to Saigon would have taken much time and would have cost on the average 700,000 francs per vessel.[125] As to coaling, it will be remembered that the landing force of Admiral Courbet had been unable to wrest the coal mines near Kelung from the Chinese.

As early as November the Chinese Government made and twice repeated to the British Foreign Office a formal complaint of what it justly considered to be a violation of the modus vivendi. In consequence of these complaints, the British Government issued new instructions to the governors of its eastern colonies. Repairing and furnishing provisions and coal to belligerent ships in British ports were restricted to such as were necessary to enable the vessels to proceed to the nearest national port or nearer destination.[126] The French armored cruiser *La Triomphante* arrived in Hongkong on January 26, 1885. No sooner had she docked than an officer of the British ship *Victor Emmanuel* came on board and gave notice of the new instructions.[127]

Three days later Ferry performed the most spectacular about-face of his whole career as a statesman. Both the mysterious "state of reprisals" and the alleged "pacific blockade" of Formosa were suddenly tossed into the ash can. Ferry called

France a "belligerent," [128] and accordingly claimed the right to visit and search vessels of third nations on the high seas for contraband of war. The Declaration of Paris, quite recently a "forgotten" doctrine, was suddenly recalled to memory. The French Government declared that the right of capture was to be exercised strictly in conformity with the famous second and third rules of the Declaration of Paris. The neutral flag was to cover enemy's goods with the exception of contraband of war. Neutral goods, with the exception of contraband of war, were not to be liable to capture under the enemy's flag.[129]

Why this sudden change from the assertion of peace to an assertion of war? The answer is to be found in a most revealing sentence contained in a note handed by Waddington to Earl Granville on January 29, 1885. There no longer existed "any reason" for asserting peace, and for consequently refraining from visiting and searching vessels of third nations on the high seas because "the ships of our squadron no longer find in foreign ports the facilities which they have enjoyed until now." [130] This is clear enough. Until January, 1885, as far as third nations were concerned, Ferry asserted peace; he did this not because he had good reasons from a legal point of view but as a diplomatic stratagem calculated to induce third states, in particular Great Britain, to refrain from assuming the duties of neutrality, and thereby to preserve for French men-of-war peacetime facilities in foreign ports.

If anything were wanting to show the hollowness and the pretext of both the "pacific blockade" and the "state of reprisals," it is furnished by the anonymous "diplomat," author of the repeatedly quoted study, *L'Affaire du Tonkin.* The "diplomat," as is well known, was no less a person than Mr. Billot, director of the political and legal department of the French Foreign Office in 1884, and naturally a close collaborator of Jules Ferry.[131] Mr. Billot let the cat out of the bag by writing: "There was not and there was not supposed to be war between France and China." There was not *supposed* to be war! He adds that the French Government had not *legal* reasons, let there be no mistake about it, but "an evident *interest*" to assert peace "in order to avoid the application of the rules of neutrality, which rules would have operated to its detriment." [132]

The naval battle of Foochow has gone down in history. Because of the legalistic tricks resorted to by Ferry it has often been looked upon as a "battle in time of peace" and hence as a colorful and fantastic curiosity of nineteenth-century history. Let it be said again that this "battle in time of peace" is a diplomatic fabrication.

This case, so instructive for the student racking his brain about the much-talked-of border line between war and peace, might be closed here were it not for the fact that Ferry continued to assert peace for home consumption until the very overthrow of his Cabinet.[133] Said Granet to the Prime Minister and Foreign Secretary in the meeting of the Chamber of Deputies on March 28, 1885:

You are waging war against China; you say so everywhere save in the one place where you ought to admit it, that is to say, to the Parliament and the representatives of the country. On the one hand you have said to France and the representatives of the country: "We are not in a state of war with China." On the other hand, against Europe, you claim the rights of a belligerent! Whom are you deceiving? Is it the Chamber, is it Europe? [134]

It has been shown above that Ferry, speaking before the Chamber of Deputies on November 26, 1884, failed to establish the truth of his assertions of peace. He failed in his attempt to prove the "pacific" nature of the blockade of Formosa, and he did not even attempt to prove the legal possibility of the existence of a "state of reprisals." Ferry's assertions of peace for foreign consumption had had no foundation in international law. They were a diplomatic stratagem. The deputy Lockroy obviously was correct when, on November 24, 1884, he intimated that, similarly, Ferry's assertions of peace for home consumption could by no stretch of interpretation be reconciled with Article 9 of the French Constitutional Law of July 16, 1875, but were merely a political decoy calculated to keep Ferry in power.[135] After the adoption by the Chamber of the ordre du jour of November 28, which registered approval of Ferry's dubious interpretation of Article 9 of the above-mentioned constitutional law, Ferry, by admitting war, would no longer have exposed himself to overthrow on the ground that he was violating the constitution by not asking for a declaration of war; but to admit war would still have exposed him to accusation of violating the peace promises laid down in the ministerial declaration of February 22, 1883. The nation's collective mind was not properly conditioned for openly admitting at home the existence of war.

No peace—no coal from Hongkong, and impaired solidity and life expectancy of the Cabinet: this, in a nutshell, was the diplomatic and political background of Ferry's startling assertions of peace.

According to General Millot, who spoke before the Tongking commission on October 30, 1884, the Chinese Army was without courage and without fighting qualities. Admiral Peyron, Minister of the Navy, estimated their strength at but 20,000 poorly armed and underpaid hoodlums, scraped together from the byways and the hedges.[136] The French expeditionary corps, on the other hand, amounted to almost a whole army corps, composed of the best troops of France.[137] On November 26, 1884, Ferry told the Chamber of Deputies that the military situation in Tongking was "not only good, but excellent and reassuring." [138]

As far as Formosa was concerned, French hopes, however, were shattered. Various engagements occurred from November, 1884, to March, 1885, between Admiral Courbet's landing force and Chinese troops, but at all times the coal mines near Kelung and the port of Tamsui remained in possession of the Chinese.[139] Naval operations, apart from the blockade of Formosa, were an unimportant item, hardly worth bothering about. On February 15, two French torpedo boats attacked and put out of action a Chinese frigate and a corvette which had taken refuge in the harbor of Shipu.[140] Tongking, on the other hand, became the scene of important military events. On

February 13, General Négrier carried Langson. In early
March, he crashed the Gate of China and drove forward into
Chinese territory. The Chinese Army left in Tongking several thousand dead, and seemed to be approaching complete
collapse. On March 23 General Négrier, however, suffered a
defeat at the hands of the Chinese. He was hurled back
through the Gate of China and, with Langson recaptured by
the Chinese, was compelled to fall back toward the delta.[141]

It was this debacle which proved Ferry's nemesis. In the
afternoon of Sunday, March 29, news of the defeat burst upon
Paris like a bombshell. A hue and cry went up which brought
public opinion to the seething point. Waterloo, wrote
Waldeck-Rousseau, Minister of the Interior in Ferry's Cabinet, did not produce such a panic.[142] There was no staying the
wave of indignation that swept over France. This furious ex-
plosion of public opinion forecast Ferry's overthrow. Not for
a long time had France witnessed the great national pastime
of upsetting a cabinet. Responsibility for the defeat rested, to
be sure, not only with the Cabinet but with the Republican
majority that had voted the ordre du jour of November 28,
1884. Yet a great number of this majority was now seized by
wild panic and backed out in an attempt to disengage their
responsibility toward their constituents. General elections for
the Chamber of Deputies were only a few months away. The
strength of the opposition in the Chamber was thus greatly increased.

When, on the afternoon of March 30, Ferry went before
the deputies, an enormous mob was flooding the approaches
to the Palais Bourbon, shouting "Down with Ferry!", "Death
to Ferry!", "Into the water with Ferry!" The meeting of the
Chamber was one of the most baleful in French parliamentary
history. Pandemonium greeted Ferry's arrival.[143] His demand
for an extraordinary appropriation of 200 million francs for
the "war" with China met with a torrent of jeers from the
frenzied opposition. Clemenceau, the Cabinet killer of the
Third Republic, with all the fire and emphasis at his command,
was "blasting away" in what seemed to be a superb inspiration,

but was actually, as Waldeck-Rousseau's biographer reports, a speech carefully rehearsed for more than six months and held in store for just such an occasion.[144] Not one Republican came to the Cabinet's rescue. Ferry made no reply. He confined himself to asking that the Chamber vote the new appropriation first, and then vote an ordre du jour. This the Chamber refused by 306 votes to 149. Condemnation was imminent. Ferry saw the handwriting on the wall, and announced the Cabinet's resignation.

In spite of Chinese victory, peace was just around the corner. On February 20 France had declared that she would treat shipments of rice destined to any port north of Canton as contraband of war. Ferry had called such writers as Grotius, Vattel, Phillimore, and the practice of states to witness, in order to prove the lawfulness of this measure. The British Government, however, had taken exception, and protested against provisions being treated generally as contraband of war. It had declared that it would not consider itself bound by the decision of any prize court upholding a contrary doctrine.[145] As it was, fear of capture prevented the shipment of any cargoes of rice, and the occasion did not arise for any such prize court decision.[146] It is well known that rice constitutes the staple food of Northern China. In the period under consideration it was bought in South China, Indo-China, the Philippine Islands, and Japan and imported in the spring, following the thawing of the ice, by way of the ports of the Gulf of Chihli. By the end of February the rice depots in Northern China were nearly exhausted. The French measure thus spelled famine for Peking and Northern China. It also spelled prosecution for squeeze or graft, a venerable Chinese practice, against high Chinese officials commissioned with the administration of the rice depots in the north.[147]

In consequence of this, France and China accelerated fresh negotiations which had been going on behind the scene for several weeks.[148] On April 4, their representatives signed in Paris an armistice consisting of a protocol and an explanatory note.[149] China declared its readiness to ratify the Convention of Tientsin of May 11, 1884. France, on the other hand, declared it had no other claim beyond that (Art. 1). France thus implicitly abandoned her claim to an indemnity for the "trap" of Bac-Le. That claim, it will be remembered, originally had been made in the amount of 250 million francs "at least," then 50 million "and not one cent less," then 80 million. Instead of receiving an indemnity, France paid for Ferry's unjust and senseless war—unjust, because the claim to an indemnity was outrageously arbitrary; senseless, under any circumstance, because China was a notorious have-not—with at least 100 million francs and, as was said in the Senate, with the lives of 10,000 French soldiers.[150] China emerged from this war the victor. France and China agreed to stop military and naval operations as soon as orders to that end could be given by the two governments and received by their commanding officers. An officer, upon receiving the order, was to inform the enemy opposite him and to desist, thereupon, from further attack. Military commanders in the eastern and western parts of Tongking were to be informed by April 15 and 25, respectively, at the latest.[151] An important exception was agreed upon with regard to the cessation of naval operations. France, for the whole duration of the armistice and until the signature and ratification by China of a treaty of peace, retained the right to visit and search Chinese and neutral vessels on the high seas for contraband of war, including rice.[152]

On June 9, 1885, Patenôtre and Li Hung Chang signed in Tientsin a "Treaty of Peace, Amity, and Commerce." [153] In Article II China implicitly recognized the French protectorate over Annam. There was, in addition, an oral agreement made between Patenôtre and Li Hung Chang regarding the date and places for the exchange of prisoners of war.[154]

SECTION 3. THE MANCHURIAN CONFLICT, 1931–1933, AND THE SINO-JAPANESE "INCIDENT," 1937–1941

By the Treaty of Portsmouth of September 5, 1905, Russia transferred to Japan its lease of the Kwantung Territory and the Russian-controlled Manchurian Railway between Port Arthur and Changchun. In 1915, as a result of the "Twenty-one Demands," made by the Japanese, China extended the original twenty-five year lease of Kwantung Territory and the concession of the South Manchurian Railway to ninety-nine years. Along with the railway, Japan was to control and administer a narrow strip of territory running from the sea beyond the Kwantung Territory up into the heart of Manchuria. Within it were included several towns and sections of such populous cities as Mukden and Changchun. In this area Japan maintained a force of about 10,000 soldiers for the protection of the railway.[1]

It was under these unparalleled conditions that the Japanese campaign against China in 1931 started not at the border of, but within, Manchuria. The versions of the two parties as to the beginning of the campaign, as has happened time and again in military and naval history, were not only different but contradictory. According to the Japanese version, the campaign was set off the night of September 18 by the attack of a small group of Chinese soldiers on a Japanese force patrolling the tracks of the South Manchurian Railway to the north of Mukden. According to the Chinese version, the Japanese attacked the Chinese North Barracks at Mukden without provocation. The Japanese, no doubt, were the architects of the campaign. They threw into the action in the area of the South Manchurian Railway from Port Arthur to Changchun all their forces in Manchuria and some of those in Korea. Meeting with but little or no resistance, they captured Mukden, principal seat of the government, Changchun, and a series of small towns. These were the first steps in a campaign which resulted in the inauguration of the "Manchukuo Government," on March 9, 1932, the main political and administrative power of which rested in the hands of Japanese officials and advisers, and finally led to the military occupation of all Manchuria, an area as large as that of France and pre-Hitler Germany combined.[2]

The Japanese campaign of 1931 was notable for the ease with which the Japanese were able to occupy the greater part of Manchuria. At the end of 1931 Marshal Chang Hsüeh-liang, War Lord and chief of the administration in Manchuria, withdrew his troops south of the Great Wall, practically without having struck a blow. In 1932, however, the Japanese met with resistance from other Chinese regular troops and from volunteer armies engaging in guerrilla warfare. Much more important than all the engagements in Manchuria was the great battle fought between Japanese and Chinese troops during the period from January 28 to March 4, 1932, in consequence of a Japanese attack on Shanghai. The Chinese estimated their casualties in killed, wounded, and missing as 24,000 officers, privates, and civilians, and the total material loss at approximately 1,875,000,000 gold dollars.[3]

The Japanese operations against China which were touched off on July 7, 1937, by a night skirmish between Japanese and Chinese soldiers near the Marco Polo Bridge outside Peking developed into the biggest campaign in Japan's long history. When the Japanese attacked Pearl Harbor, they held most of China's major ports and had penetrated into some thirteen of the twenty-four provinces of China proper. The Chinese estimated their death toll at some three million soldiers and civilians and on July 7, 1942, announced that their troops had killed or wounded 2,500,000 Japanese in fourteen major battles and 10,375 smaller engagements.[4]

These two Japanese campaigns, though on a different scale, have many features in common.

There was no declaration of war in the Manchurian campaign. In the campaign against China proper, no declaration of war was made until December 9, 1941, on which day China declared war on Japan, Germany, and Italy.[5]

Diplomatic relations continued uninterrupted throughout the whole Manchurian affair. In the campaign against China proper the two parties withdrew their respective ambassadors the middle of January, 1938, but for some time continued to be represented by counselors.[6]

The Manchurian campaign involved no naval operations. Not only were there no engagements between Japanese and

Chinese men-of-war, but Japanese and Chinese private shipping continued entirely unmolested. During the operations
against China proper, naval activity seems to have been limited—up to December, 1941, at least—to the blockade
which Japan had instituted, August 25, 1937, against all Chinese shipping, official and private, along the Chinese coast
from the mouth of the Yangtze to near the southern tip of
China. On September 5 of the same year, this blockade was
extended to Chinwangtao, in the north, and to Pakhoi, near
Indo-China, in the south.[7]

Neither from 1931 to 1933, nor from 1937 to 1941 did
Japan or China request third powers to assume an attitude of
neutrality. In 1937, it is true, Japan informed France that if the
shipment of arms into China continued through Indo-China,
Japan would bomb the French railways running from Hanoi
north to Yunnan and east to Nanning.[8] In February, 1940,
Japan sought to obtain a formal French statement that France
would permit no traffic whatever over the French-controlled
railway between Indo-China and China that could be of assistance to China.[9] It was stated in high Japanese quarters that this
demand on France was not made as that of a belligerent to a
neutral but was purely opportunistic.[10]

In neither period was foreign trade interfered with on the
grounds of either contraband or blockade, with certain minor
exceptions.[11] Neither side issued contraband lists and the declaration of the above-mentioned blockade specifically exempted the vessels of third powers.

It is a matter of common knowledge that, according to statements made by Japan, China and third powers, neither the
Manchurian campaign nor the campaign against China proper
amounted to war. The military operations of 1931–33 accordingly have gone down in history as "the Manchurian conflict."
In official Japanese pronouncements the military and restricted naval operations of 1937–41 were usually referred to
as the China "incident" or the China "affair," as in the statement broadcast to the nation on October 18, 1941, by the new
Premier, Gen. Eiki Tojo: "The national policy calls for a

successful settlement of the China incident and the establishment of the Greater East Asia co-prosperity sphere as a contribution toward world peace." [12] It was only when speaking of Japan's far-reaching aims in China, such as "the Greater East Asia co-prosperity sphere," that Japanese officials occasionally referred to the campaign as "the holy war." In such a connection "holy incident" or "holy affair" apparently wouldn't do.[13]

In 1931 both China and Japan were members of the League of Nations. Under these circumstances the Manchurian campaign at once focused attention upon the system for the maintenance of peace laid down in the Covenant of the League. For this system the hour of fate had struck. It was the first time that a major issue had arisen between two Great Powers since the establishment of the League following the first World War. The main reliance for the assurance of peace embodied in the Covenant was Article 16, Paragraphs 1 and 2 of which ran as follows:

1. Should any Member of the League resort to war in disregard of its covenants under Articles 12, 13 or 15, it shall *ipso facto* be deemed to have committed an act of war against all other Members of the League, which hereby undertake immediately to subject it to the severance of all trade or financial relations, the prohibition of all intercourse between their nationals and the nationals of the covenant-breaking State, and the prevention of all financial, commercial or personal intercourse between the nationals of the covenant-breaking State and the nationals of any State, whether a Member of the League or not.

2. It shall be the duty of the Council in such case to recommend to the several Governments concerned what effective military, naval or air force the Members of the League shall severally contribute to the armed forces to be used to protect the covenants of the League.

It is not necessary to enter into the rather complicated details as to what constituted disregard of the covenants under Articles 12, 13, and 15. Suffice it to say that these articles provided for the settlement of international disputes either through the decision of a court or an arbitral award or through mediation by the Council or the Assembly of the League of Nations. Failure to have recourse to one of these procedures constituted the main instance of disregard of the above-mentioned covenants. There had been no resort to any procedure for the pacific settlement of the differences existing between Japan and China prior to September 18, 1931, when military operations were initiated.

On September 21 China appealed to the League of Nations by invoking not Article 16 but Article 11,[14] which provided in its first paragraph that in "any war or threat of war . . . the League shall take any action that may be deemed wise and effectual to safeguard the peace of nations." The second paragraph gave each member of the League the right to bring to the attention of the Assembly or the Council any circumstance whatever affecting the good understanding between nations. Hence, as far as its military aspect was concerned, the League dealt with the Manchurian conflict solely by virtue of Article 11. Article 16 was never openly referred to in either the Council or the Assembly. By not invoking Article 16 in conjunction with Article 11 the Chinese Government made it clear that it did not mean to assert the actual existence of "war." It was equally clear that China was not bringing to the attention of the League a circumstance that merely affected the good understanding between nations; it was asserting the existence of a "threat of war." Hence the Council considered it its duty to take the action that was deemed "wise and effectual to safeguard the peace of the nations." [15] Under the paralyzing unanimity rule of the Covenant, these actions had to be decided upon in agreement with Japan, and could hardly be expected to be "effectual."

What matters here is the question of whether or not the Manchurian campaign amounted to war. The proceedings of the Council and of the Assembly of the League of Nations throw little if any light on this question. No such lively exchange of views as that which characterized the proceedings of the French Parliament from 1883 to 1885 ever occurred in the international atmosphere at Geneva. The desire not to antagonize anyone and to preserve the proverbial diplomatic politeness was paramount.

The assertion that war existed was rarely heard. Sze, the Chinese delegate in the Council, repeatedly hinted at Article 16. The first time was on September 22, 1931, when he said, "it has become a serious question whether the application of other articles than Article 11 of the Covenant may not be required." [16] However, it was not until the battle of Shanghai had occurred that delegates bluntly spoke of war.

Said Mr. Beelaerts van Blokland (the Netherlands) in the second meeting of the General Commission of the Assembly on March 5, 1932: "Hostilities broke out in China which by whatever legal term they may be called have all the main features of *war*." [17]

Said Mr. te Water (South Africa) in the same Commission three days later: ". . . I am able to say bluntly that we have no other name for the state of affairs in China today than that of *war*." [18]

On March 4 even the Japanese delegate, Sato, speaking on the spur of the moment, admitted in the General Commission of the Assembly that there was "war" in Shanghai. In a previous speech Sato had just held out the possibility of a real and effective suspension of hostilities, the evacuation of Japanese troops from Chinese territory, and the restoration of order and peace in the Shanghai area. No sooner had Sato ended than the Chinese delegate Yen jumped to his feet, waving three telegrams in his right hand and asking the Commission to take their eyes away from the mirage which was being conjured up before them by the Japanese delegation. The Japanese Army at Shanghai was being reinforced, and was advancing farther and farther, fighting desperately to take the entire region between Shanghai and Nanking, Yen said. [19] In view of the great excitement into which the General Commission was thrown, Sato had to rebut quickly and offhand. As reported in the *Official Journal* of the League of Nations he began by saying:

"May I reply to Mr. Yen's statement concerning new Japanese reinforcements? Some days ago we announced that the extension of the *hostilities* compelled us to send certain rein-forcements. . . ." [20]

According to other members of the Commission and as re-liably reported by Swiss newspapers,[21] Mr. Sato said:

"May I reply to Mr. Yen's statement concerning new Jap-anese reinforcements? Some days ago we announced that the extension of the *war* compelled us to send certain reinforce-ments. . . ."

Clemenceau must have winked at Ferry as they watched the proceedings in Geneva from the Elysian Fields. In Decem-ber, 1883, a similar incident had occurred in the Palais Bour-bon.

The expression "war" in Sato's rejoinder was of course a slip of the tongue. Japan had denied throughout that it was conducting a war. The Japanese delegate, Yoshizawa, declared from the beginning, at the very first meeting of the Council devoted to the Manchurian conflict, that "it is far from our idea to make war on the Chinese Republic" and that Japan would continue, as it had done in the past, loyally to observe the terms of the Covenant.[22] The Japanese delegation adduced and frequently repeated two main arguments in support of its thesis that there was no resort to war. Time and again it as-serted that the Japanese forces in Manchuria were operating not against Chinese troops but against brigands.[23] In other words, the Japanese forces were engaged in mere police ac-tions.[24] There probably was a great deal of truth in the Japa-nese contention, though it was their practice to describe indis-criminately as "bandits" all the forces opposed to them after the withdrawal of Marshal Chang Hsüeh-liang's army south of the Great Wall. Banditry has always existed in Manchuria, as in China. Since September 18, 1931, there had been an un-paralleled growth of banditry and lawlessness in the country due partly to disbanded soldiery and partly to farmers who, having themselves been ruined by bandits, had to take to ban-ditry for a living.[25] The second reason, frequently advanced by the Japanese delegation, was the plea that their military operations were mere measures of self-defense and that the right thereto was implicit in the Covenant.[26] To put it in other terms: even if the Japanese military operations amounted to war—and they did not—Japan was not guilty of "resorting" to it; China was the aggressor.

From delegates of third states the assertion that war did not exist was as seldom heard as the assertion that it did exist. Particularly noted was a statement made by Briand in the meeting of the Council of December 10, 1931. According to Briand up to that date there had been "no resort to war" by Japan or China.[27] The Assembly, the body which had handled the Manchurian conflict since February 12, 1932, unfortunately evaded taking an unequivocal stand. In the *Lytton Report* the following ambiguous statement is made: "This is not a case in which one country has declared war on another country without previously exhausting the opportunities for conciliation provided in the Covenant of the League of Nations." [28] Of course this was not a case in which one country had declared war on another country. Everybody knew that. To say so was beside the point. The question that mattered was, had a member of the League of Nations, declaration or no declaration, resorted to war in disregard of its obligations under Articles 12, 13, or 15 of the Covenant? The final report on the Manchurian conflict, which the Assembly adopted on February 24, 1933, unanimously, save for Japan's dissenting voice, embodied verbatim the ambiguous statement of the *Lytton Report*.[29] The inactivity of the League spoke louder than its evasive words. The League never even considered application of the economic or military sanctions provided for in Article 16 of the Covenant. It was thus that the League clearly, though only by implication, denied the existence of war in Manchuria.

The view of the League was generally shared by theoreticians on international law. Professor Clyde Eagleton of New York University, writing in the early part of 1933, said: "It is admitted by all authorities that war in the legal sense did not exist and does not at the time of this writing." [30] It is difficult to see why this point of view was so generally held. The rea-

sons advanced by the theoreticians on international law were
as few and far between as they had been in the proceedings of
the Council or the Assembly of the League of Nations. Eagleton—like the *Lytton Report*—points out that neither side had
declared war and that no third state had issued a proclamation
of neutrality.[31] By "third" states are evidently meant states not
members of the League, since members of the League were
not expected to issue declarations of neutrality, in case of war,
but were to apply the sanctions according to Article 16. To
Eagleton's opinion might be added the view of a prominent
European writer. Professor Hans Wehberg, co-author with
the late Professor Walther Schücking of the German written
commentary on the Covenant, held that "war in the sense of
international law" did not exist, since operations occurred between particular detachments of the respective armies only,
with neither side intending to operate against the totality of
the armed forces of the other.[32] It will be noted that Eagleton
writes of "war in the legal sense," whereas Wehberg uses the
expression "war in the sense of international law."

Though legal experts seemed to vindicate the verdict of the
League, the opinion was frequently heard that in refraining
from sanctions it had been actuated not by legal but by purely
political considerations. Neither France nor the British Empire, it was said, for instance, was willing to antagonize a friend
in the Far East or to face—particularly in time of depression—
the loss of valuable trade connections.[33] Common sense refused to subscribe to the thesis that there was no war. The
greatest of modern Italian political thinkers, Guglielmo Ferrero, prophetically wrote:

"The League of Nations will perish if it lends itself to a
casuistry according to which there are wars which are not
war. The conscience of the world will never accept the demonstration by subtle jurists that invasion of a territory by an
army does not constitute a war. For common sense . . . this
is war." [34]

Strong support was given such a view by a debate in the
House of Commons on February 27, 1933, in the course of

which the Secretary of State for Foreign Affairs, Sir John Simon, declared: "There is one great difference between 1914 and now, and it is this: In *no circumstances* will this Government authorize this country to be a party to the struggle." [35] Such a statement was hardly reconcilable with other official declarations according to which the League of Nations was "the cornerstone of British Foreign Policy." Foreign Secretary Chamberlain, for instance, in a note to American Ambassador Houghton dated May 19, 1928, had affirmed that for "the Government of this country respect for the obligations arising out of the Covenant of the League of Nations . . . is fundamental." [36] The contention that it was the policy of the powers not to commit themselves to an expensive compliance with their duties under Article 16 and to avoid for that reason an admission that war existed derived further sustenance from an indiscreet disclosure made on September 21, 1934, by the Chinese delegate Liand in the first Committee of the fifteenth Ordinary Session of the Assembly. "Great pressure has been brought to bear on China not to bring up the question of application of Article XVI." [37]

So much for the problem of war and peace in the Manchurian conflict. Now to the same problem in the campaign which Japan, on July 7, 1937, started against China proper.

From the very beginning of the "incident," juristic attention was focused upon the so-called American Neutrality Act of May 1, 1937.[38] "Neutrality Act" was the unofficial abbreviation for the long-winded title of Public Resolution No. 27 adopted by the 75th Congress on April 30 and signed by the President on May 1, 1937. The "Neutrality Act" was properly so called. It intended to regulate the conduct of the United States during the existence of foreign wars on a basis of impartiality and abstention. This is of the very essence of rules on neutrality. The purpose of neutrality rules, international and municipal, is to protect third states against involvement in foreign wars by means of conduct characterized by impartiality and abstention. The purpose of the various neutrality acts adopted by the United States in the period from 1935 to 1939 [39] was to create an increased guaranty against the United States' getting involved in foreign wars by means of an abstention going far beyond that required by international law. The historic defense of freedom of the seas for American commerce, subject only to the belligerent rights of visit, search, and seizure in connection with contraband of war and breach of a blockade, was abandoned. It was replaced by the notion that the country should abstain from all contacts with belligerent powers which, in view of the differences with Germany and Great Britain in the period from 1914 to 1917 on the subject of belligerent rights, were deemed likely to draw it into a foreign war. The nation was to insulate itself, as the expression went.

In connection with the "incident," two provisions of the Neutrality Act were of major importance.

Section 1, which was mandatory, ordered the President, whenever he found "a state of war" existing between foreign states, to proclaim such fact. It was unlawful thereafter to export arms, ammunition, or implements of war to any such foreign state. This provision, it might be added, was directed against the "merchants of death," munition manufacturers, who, it had been asserted, had conspired with bankers eager to float war loans to force the United States into the European war in 1917. [40] That the antiplutocratic President Wilson had played the game of munition manufacturers and bankers was a shibboleth to which the American people were much exposed in the years following World War I.

Section 2 contained the discretionary "cash-and-carry" provisions. If the President found that restricting the shipment of still other articles or materials to belligerent states was necessary "to promote the security or preserve the peace of the United States or to protect the lives of citizens of the United States," he was likewise so to proclaim. It was unlawful thereafter for any American vessel to carry such articles or materials to any belligerent state. American ships were thus to be kept out of harm's way. Carrying was confined to foreign bottoms, at the risk of foreign shippers. After a proclamation issued in accordance with Section 2, it was also to be unlawful to export from the United States to any belligerent state any articles or materials whatsoever until all right, title, and interest had been transferred to some foreign government, agency, institution, association, partnership, or individual. Thus articles and materials to be sent to any belligerent state had to be paid for in cash before leaving the United States. There were to be no more American cargoes sent to a belligerent state.

After July 7, 1937, week followed week without the President's proclaiming a "state of war" to exist in the Far East. Individuals and peace organizations, though, claimed that a "state of war" existed and hence urged that the Neutrality Act be put into operation.[41] Asked on September 5 about the possibility of invocation of the Neutrality Act, the President replied that this was still a matter on a twenty-four-hour basis.[42] Soon, thereafter, it became apparent that the President in all probability would not choose to find that a "state of war" existed. In his speech delivered at Chicago on October 5 the President turned his back on the foreign policy prescribed in the Neutrality Act by pledging his administration to a "concerted effort" with "the ninety per cent of the world which wants peace" to "quarantine aggressor nations."[43]

On August 23, 1937, Senator Key Pittman of Nevada, chairman of the Senate Foreign Relations Committee, speaking over the radio, made a detailed explanation and defense of President Roosevelt's reluctance to declare that a "state of war" existed. Senator Pittman was the principal author and sponsor of the Neutrality Act which he had piloted through the Senate, and thus appeared to be best qualified to provide the nation with an explanation. While there was no indication whether the Senator's discussion of the subject was self-assumed or officially inspired, he was generally credited as being the Administration's principal Congressional spokesman on foreign affairs.[44] In a statement made on July 28 the Senator had issued a warning saying, "it is very difficult to determine that a state of war exists."[45] On August 23 he adduced the following points as legal reasons militating against the admission that a "state of war" existed:

1. Neither Japan nor China had declared war.
2. Both Japan and China denied that a "state of war" existed.
3. Japan and China continued diplomatic relations.
4. Neither Japan nor China had indicated an intention to conquer or to subdue its opponent.
5. Neither Japan nor China was interfering with the commerce of third states on the ground of either blockade or contraband of war.[46]

The second point calls for particular attention. It confirmed for the first time unofficial reports to the effect that not only Japan but also China denied that a "state of war" existed. Senator Pittman, it ought to be added, did not labor the above points. He did not explain *why* these were legal reasons for not applying the Neutrality Act. It is small wonder if, under these circumstances, John Q. Citizen was unable to follow what Senator Pittman proposed.

On November 17 a debate on President Roosevelt's refusal to proclaim a "state of war" broke out in the House. The fireworks were led by the Republican party's arch-isolationist, Representative Hamilton Fish, from New York. In the view of Representative Fish, the Administration had arbitrarily ignored the Neutrality Act. The President himself came in for his share of chiding. He was reminded of his Armistice Day speech of 1935 in which he had declared: "We are acting to simplify definitions and facts by calling war 'war' when armed invasion and resulting killing of human beings takes place." Secretary of State Cordell Hull was attacked without restraint. "If the President does not know that a state of war exists in China to-day, or if the Secretary of State does not know this, then the Administration had better get a new Secretary of State because there is no one in this country who does not know that a state of war exists in China at the present time." Representative Fish to some extent attempted to substantiate his thesis, though in his view its truth was self-evident. He recalled the war definition put forth in 1800 by Justice Washington in the case of *Bas* v. *Tingy* in order to convince the House that, in the determination of a "state of war," such things as the lack of a declaration of war and the continuance of diplomatic relations do not matter. "War is every contention by force between two nations in external matters under the authority of their respective governments." Justice Washington's definition, as has been pointed out above, was founded on sheer "belief." [47] Thus it can hardly be said that Representative Fish succeeded in making out his case.

Neither did Representative Sam D. McReynolds of Tennessee, chairman of the Foreign Affairs Committee and the Administration's foreign policy spokesman in the House. Representative McReynolds contended that the lack of a declaration of war, the lack of a declaration of neutrality on the part of any third state, and the continuance of diplomatic relations, did not harmonize with a "state of war," but, like Senator Pittman, failed to show why. The situation was most peculiar indeed. Congress had adopted the neutrality resolution of April 30, 1937, after long debates. Now there was nobody to make out a clear legal case either for or against the application of the law.[48]

As in the Manchurian conflict, the contention was often made that nonapplication of the law was due not to legal but to political considerations. The political arguments against the application of the Neutrality Act most frequently heard were these:

(1) Japan was virtually self-sufficient in arms, ammunition, and implements of war and hence would not be injured by an American embargo in accordance with Section 1 of the Neutrality Act. China, on the other hand, was dependent on outside supplies for such articles and an American embargo would handicap her.[49]

(2) In accordance with Section 2 of the Neutrality Act, the President might place the trade in other articles or ma-

terials on a "cash-and-carry" basis. Japan had large gold reserves and substantial dollar balances which could be used for "cash," and a large merchant fleet, which could be used to

"ARE YOU FELLOWS HAVING A WAR?"

Hutton © Philadelphia Inquirer

"carry." China, on the other hand, had a very small gold reserve and comparatively small dollar balances and no modern merchant fleet. The Neutrality Act would operate in favor of Japan and to the detriment of China.[50]

These political arguments, at the same time, seemed to explain why the Chinese Government denied the existence of a "state of war." Dr. Chengting T. Wang, Chinese Ambassador to the United States, declared on September 8, 1937, in an interview, that invocation of the Neutrality Act would hurt China more than Japan by cutting off supplies needed for the maintenance of China's economic life.[51] The other side of the picture, the reasons which prompted the Japanese Government to label the campaign against China as mere "incident," can only be guessed. Japan is a country where national psychology and national policy are often enigmatic and inscrutable. Japan had risen in recent years to be the third best customer of the United States. During the eighteen months prior to June, 1936, she had purchased 75 per cent of her oil and one half of her importations of iron ore and scrap iron from this country. For the first six months of 1937, American exports to Japan amounted to $165,519,000, as compared with $31,355,000 of exports to China. Measured in tonnage, about one fourth of the trade from the United States to Japan was carried in American vessels.[52] Japan, it would seem, had an interest in the preservation of the American share of that freight and hence in the nonapplication of the "cash-and-carry" plan of the Neutrality Act.

The contention that the President's failure to apply the Neutrality Act was due not to legal but to political reasons derived substance from the above-mentioned speech made in the House on November 17 by Representative Sam D. McReynolds. A resolution by Representative Francis H. Case of South Dakota, putting to President Roosevelt a series of questions regarding the Far East, referred to Representative McReynolds' speech as follows:

Is it a fact that the Department of State is using the Neutrality Act as an instrument of *policy* as indicated by the following statements of the Chairman of the Committee on Foreign Affairs on the floor of the House of Representatives on November 17, 1937, to wit:

"I think it will aid Japan and aid the Fascist countries of Europe more by putting this law into effect now than by not putting it into effect."

And again:

"I am not saying that we should help China but I want to stick a dagger in these countries that are trying to create dictatorship and trying to ruin the world."

To this Secretary of State Cordell Hull replied on December 4, 1937:

"The Department of State keeps constantly in mind the fact that the principal purpose of the Act is to keep the United States out of war." [53]

The answer manifestly was not directed to the point of the question. It could not be regarded as conclusive in one way or the other. The principal purpose of the Neutrality Act was indeed to keep the United States out of war, but such was also the purpose of the policy enunciated by the President in his speech made at Chicago on October 5. Both the Neutrality Act and the policy held out at Chicago were to serve the same purpose, but were intended to serve it by different means. The Neutrality Act prescribed indiscriminate, blindfolded isolation, i.e., isolation regardless of who was the aggressor. The Chicago speech, on the contrary, provided for discrimination and cooperation, for a "concerted effort" with other peace-loving nations to "quarantine aggressor nations."

According to Mr. Bernard M. Baruch, financier, philanthropist, and key figure on the American home front in two World Wars, testifying before the Senate Foreign Relations Committee on April 6, 1939, the existence of a "state of war" between Japan and China was a fact "as obvious as the sun in the sky." By invocation of the Neutrality Act, however, "we would be favoring Japan and prejudicing China. We have avoided that by refusing to recognize an existing condition of war." [54] We shall see whether the existence of a "state of war" between Japan and China was a fact "as obvious as the sun in the sky." However, the contention that the Neutrality Act was not applied lest Japan be favored, sounded plausible enough.

There remained, to be sure, for several years to come, a gap between such a contention and certainty. President Roosevelt himself closed it through publication on December 2, 1941, of the second installment of his *Public Papers and Addresses*, which covers his second term in the White House. The volumes make available, besides the text of speeches, messages to Congress, Executive Orders, etc., stenographic transcripts of presidential press conferences which, as is generally known, were never reported literally at the time. The transcript of the conference with the American Society of Newspaper Editors on April 21, 1938, makes particularly interesting reading. It discloses a statement by President Roosevelt upon the non-application of the Neutrality Act in the "China incident." The President frankly declared that his refusal to find a "state of war" had been "only an excuse" for not applying the Neutrality Act. He justified this by pointing out—not the policy of quarantining aggressor nations, but—the principle of impartiality which should govern rules on neutrality. The application of the Neutrality Act, the President explained, would have helped Japan against China,[55] for the reasons pointed out above.[56] In other words, as applied to China and Japan, the Neutrality Act would have had a decidedly unneutral effect.

After the frank admission of the President himself there could no longer be any doubt that, in the view of the Administration, the "China incident" amounted to a "state of war." The failure to find that a "state of war" existed and the non-application of the Neutrality Act were now admittedly the result not of legal but of political considerations. For the student of the problem of war and peace, however, the question arises: What has become now of the arguments with which Senator Key Pittman on August 23, 1937, attempted to prove to the nation that there was no "state of war" in East Asia?

PART II

THEORETICAL

CHAPTER V

Of Rules of Law on War

1. IN GENERAL

Lawmaking, international as well as municipal, has been concerned with war for centuries. There are modern rules of law on war and old ones, and many that are no longer in force. It is not always easy to know whether some rule of law on war is still in force or has become obsolete.

All rules of law on war are answers to one of two basic questions: (1) What conduct is to be observed in war? (2) Under what conditions may states resort to war? The answers to the first question form the so-called *jus in bello*, the answers to the second, the so-called *jus ad bellum*. Typical of jus in bello are the rules of the Annex to the Hague Convention (IV) of 1907 Respecting the Laws and Customs of War on Land.[1] Typical of internal jus ad bellum was Article 9 of the French Constitutional Law of July 16, 1875, which provided that the President of the Republic could not declare war without the preliminary assent of both Houses.[2] The outstanding example of international jus ad bellum until quite recently was furnished by the obligations in the Covenant of the League of Nations by which the members of the League had undertaken not to resort to war against each other except in certain specified circumstances.[3]

Rules of law may refer to war either directly or indirectly; directly, by using the terms "war," "state of war," "act of war," "threat of war"; indirectly, by employing some other term connoting the existence of "war," such as "breach of the peace," "aggression," "enemy," "belligerent," "neutral." The Act of Congress of March 2, 1799, for instance, declared that for ships and goods belonging to citizens of the United States, if retaken from "the enemy" after more than four days, the owners were to allow the recaptor one half of the whole value

for salvage.[4] The most important among recent indirect rules
of law on war, no doubt, is furnished by Article 39 of the
Charter of the United Nations. "The Security Council shall
determine the existence of any *threat to the peace, breach of
the peace, or act of aggression* and shall make recommenda-
tions, or decide what measures shall be taken in accordance
with the provisions of Articles 41 and 42,[5] to maintain or restore international peace and security."

2. INTERNATIONAL LAW

International rules of law on war can be easily ascertained
as such if they are written rules of law laid down in treaties.
Accurate copies of the authentic documents in which these
rules are embodied and knowledge of the language in which
the documents are drawn up are sufficient to ascertain the existence of such rules.

States have been concluding treaties on war for centuries,
and to a far greater extent than is generally realized. It was, for
instance, long the practice of states to conclude bipartite
treaties, or to insert in commercial treaties clauses regulating
their respective rights and duties in case one of them was a
belligerent and the other one neutral. The Treaty of Amity
and Commerce of February 6, 1778, concluded by France and
the Thirteen United States of North America is a treaty in
point.[6] Two hundred ninety-one bipartite treaties regulating
the treatment of the wounded and sick were concluded in Europe from 1581 to 1864.[7] A movement toward multipartite
treaties was inaugurated with the signing of the Declaration of
Paris on April 16, 1856. Among the multipartite treaties concluded since 1856 stand out the Hague Conventions and Declarations of 1899 and 1907. These two years are among the
most important for the history of international law. The principal Hague Conventions regulating war are (1) Conventions
(II) of 1899 and (IV) of 1907, Respecting the Laws and Customs of War on Land; (2) Convention (III) of 1907, Relative
to the Opening of Hostilities; (3) Convention (V) of 1907,

Respecting the Rights and Duties of Neutral Powers and Persons in Case of War on Land; (4) Convention (XIII) of 1907, Concerning the Rights and Duties of Neutral Powers in Naval War.[8]

The period between World War I and World War II was the golden age of neutrality pacts, alliances, guarantee pacts, friendship pacts, nonaggression pacts, and other political treaties. The jumble of these treaties became so bewildering that only a very few any longer understood who was going to be neutral, who was the ally or friend of whom, who had given a guaranty and who had promised nonaggression to whom.[9]

Suffice it to add a few words regarding neutrality pacts and alliances.

It goes without saying that the neutrality pacts without exception were supposed to become operative upon the existence of "war." The term "neutrality" points to the problem of the conduct of third states toward states engaged in war. In the neutrality pacts, war, as a rule, was referred to indirectly by the terms "attack" or "aggression." Neutrality was promised not to aggressors but solely to the victim of a war of aggression.[10]

Regarding alliances it may be recalled that under Article I of the Treaty of Alliance concluded on February 6, 1778, by France and the United States, the two countries were to be good and faithful allies in case "war" should break out between Great Britain and France.[11] Many more recent treaties of alliance could be quoted, the operation of which likewise hinged on the existence of "war," such, for instance, as the alliance concluded by Great Britain and France early in 1939.[12] Usually, however, assistance is promised in case of "unprovoked attack."[13] Assistance, like neutrality, as a rule is promised not to the aggressor but to the victim of an aggression, and of an unprovoked aggression at that. In addition to "war" and "unprovoked aggression," still other terms are used to specify the *casus foederis*. In Article III of the Rome-Berlin-Axis Pact of May 22, 1939, the contracting parties promised to support each other in case "either of them should become involved in

military entanglements with another power or powers." [14]
The student of history might well take a cynical attitude
toward treaties of alliance, and say that, from a practical point
of view, it matters little on what their operation depends,
whether on "war," on "unprovoked aggression," or what.
The path of history is strewn with broken alliances, and for
that matter with broken treaties of guaranty.

There exists for the period between World War I and
World War II a sharp contrast between the great number of
political treaties, the operation of which depended on the existence of war, and the small number of new treaties made for
the conduct of war. The most important of the latter are: (1)
the Geneva Protocol Prohibiting the Use in War of Asphyx-
iating, Poisonous, or Other Gases and of Bacteriological Methods of Warfare, of June 17, 1925; [15] (2) the Geneva Convention for the Amelioration of the Condition of the Wounded
and Sick in Armies in the Field, of June 27, 1929; [16] (3) the
Geneva Convention Concerning the Treatment of Prisoners
of War, of July 27, 1929; [17] (4) the Procès-Verbal Concerning Rules of Submarine Warfare, signed at London on November 6, 1936.[18]

There exists today an almost complete set of treaty provisions as far as warfare on land is concerned. Those respecting
naval warfare are far less complete, while hardly any treaty
provisions exist with regard to aerial warfare. As far as warfare at sea and in the air is concerned, no treaty corresponds
to the Hague Convention (IV) Respecting the Laws and Customs of War on Land. The incompleteness of the treaty provisions regarding naval warfare is chiefly due to the fact that
the elaborate Declaration of London concerning blockades,
contraband of war, unneutral services, and other important
items of prize law, signed on February 26, 1909, by delegates
of the United States and other powers has not been ratified.[19]

The provisions of treaties referring to war are supplemented
by rules of international customary law. The nature of international customary law is a matter of controversy among
doctrinal writers.[20] In accordance with the principle of the

independence of states, which rests "at the very basis of inter-national law," [21] to wit, the principle that members of the family of nations cannot be obligated against their will, inter-national customary law must be derived from the conduct followed by a state with the tacit understanding with one or several other states that they have a right to demand or a duty to tolerate such conduct. To put it in other terms, international customary law consists in *pacta tacita.* Internal customary law, of which the Anglo-American common law is the outstanding modern representative, is of a different nature.[22] An example concerning the formation of recent international customary law will serve to illustrate its nature. For aerial warfare there exists no treaty corresponding to the Hague Convention (V) Respecting Neutrality in Case of War on Land, or to the Hague Convention (XIII) Respecting Neutrality in Naval War. During the first World War, the Swiss Army had orders to fire at belligerent military aircraft passing over neutral Swiss territory and to compel them to land. Such aircraft were then interned, together with their crews. The Swiss Government, no doubt, considered this practice to correspond to a duty of neutrality in aerial warfare. This Swiss practice, coupled as it was with *animus obligandi* and acquiesced in by France, Ger-many, and other belligerents, may be said to have established between Switzerland, on the one hand, and such belligerents, on the other, a rule of international customary law which might be formulated as follows: Switzerland, as neutral state, must use the means at its disposal to compel belligerent aircraft which have entered the air space over its territory to alight, and must intern them and their crews.[23]

The task of establishing the existence of the unwritten rules of international customary law is a difficult one. Doctrinal writers, patriotically advocating the interests of their respec-tive nations, instead of objectively ascertaining international law, frequently assert the existence of a rule of international customary law where in fact there is none. Of interna-tional customary law in general, it has been said that many of the rules to be found in textbooks on international law are "mere fancies." [24] The uncertainty of the existence of rules of international customary law on war, in particular, was clearly shown by the difficulties which the first and the second Hague Peace Conferences in 1899 and 1907 encountered in their task of codifying the rules of war. More often than was generally realized, codification amounted to transformation into a treaty provision not of a rule of international customary law but of a mere rule *de lege ferenda*.[25] Even the London Naval Conference of 1908–9, one of the most important international conferences ever held, was reproached for rashly asserting the existence of international customary law. In a preliminary provision of the unratified Declaration of London concerning the Laws of Naval Warfare, of February 26, 1909, the signatory powers were agreed that the rules contained in the Declaration corresponded in substance "with the generally recognized principles of international law." In the General Report presented to the Naval Conference on behalf of its drafting committee, it was stated that the purpose of the conference, above all, had been to note, to define, and where needful to complete what might be considered "as customary law." [26] This statement was later on severely criticized by leading authorities on international law. Sir Thomas Erskine Holland, for instance, assailed the Declaration of London as "revolutionary" and as containing "a good many undesirable novelties." [27] Hjalmar Hammarskjöld, prominent Swedish jurist, likewise held that the London Naval Conference had attempted to do more than merely noting, defining, and completing "customary law." [28] On the whole, then, no clear-cut dividing line can be drawn between rules of customary law and mere customs.[29]

According to the positivist conception, international law is the outcome of contracts. It consists in the rules accepted by the members of the family of nations in the shape of either treaties or international customary law. However, in the past, states at variance did not confine their arguments to treaty provisions and international customary law. Often they had recourse to "natural" international law. "Natural" international law may have been meant when, in consequence of the French spoliations, the Cabinets of Washington and John Adams insisted upon the illegality of the conduct of France from the point of view of both the Treaty of Amity and Commerce of 1778 and "the generally recognized rules of civilized naval warfare." [30] "Natural" international law, in conjunction perhaps with international customary law and purely French precedents in prize court decisions, was meant when the notification of the blockade of Formosa of October 23, 1884, warned that blockade-running vessels would be proceeded against according to the treaties in force and "in accordance with international law." [31] "Natural" international law, pure and simple, was meant when Ferry, on February 20, 1885, called such writers as Grotius, Vattel, and Phillimore to witness in order to prove that shipments of rice could be lawfully treated as contraband of war.[32]

"Natural" international law is that branch of the old natural law which concerns rights and duties among states. The old natural law was the law as reasoned out by doctrinal writers, in contradistinction to the law made by states, by enactments or judicial and other decisions in the municipal field and by treaties and *pacta tacita* in the international field. Natural-law thinking proceeded on the assumption that the law, either in part or in whole, had been written into the hearts of men by the Bible, "nature," or "reason," as a body of unchanging rules, valid at all times and in all places, and that such a "naturally" existing law must be evident to all men of good will like the rules of logic or mathematics. Although speculation as to natural law is to be found in the theological philosophical writings of the Middle Ages, it becomes significant for the law at and after the Reformation. It had its hegemony in the seventeenth and eighteenth centuries.[33] There were the out-and-out naturalists, like Pufendorf (1632–94), who maintained that no positive law was possible; and there were Grotius and the Grotians and Vattel, who taught natural law and at the same time admitted the existence of positive law. The innumerable "systems" of the professors of natural law, by the way, were variously conceived and differed in their content; but whatever their conception and their content, they claimed eternal and universal validity.

The positivist school of thought refuses to recognize any such rules of a supposedly absolute or a priori validity. It does so for good reasons. Comparative legal studies have shown that every nation has its own laws. History teaches that the law of every nation has its own development. "The" law not only never existed, but the very concept of an a priori law conflicts with the appeal to reason as the foundation of the authority of rules of law. Rules of law, lest they become unreasonable and inequitable, must keep pace with the changing patterns of living conditions. Yesterday's answers are inadequate for today's problems. Under economic, social, and political conditions which change in the course of time and vary from nation to nation, there could be no appeal to reason and hence no authority in static and uniform rules of law. No body of legal rules is destined to be valid forever, or to be valid everywhere.

In municipal law, the old natural law is a thing of the past, at least as far as Continental and Anglo-American legal thought are concerned. In the international field, however, it is different. Although in the nineteenth century a great many law books entitled *Jus naturae et gentium* dropped from fashion, natural-law ideas continued to influence legal thought strongly. Even many a contemporary writer is a Mr. Facing-both-ways, arguing with positive law here and with natural law there. Natural law sometimes sails under the flag of "customary law" or of "general international law." [34] Thus the emancipation from natural law in the international field is not yet accomplished, and as a matter of fact is difficult of accomplishment in view of the incompleteness of the rules of positive international law. In the absence of positive international law, doctrinal writers and practicing lawyers not infrequently argue with "natural" international law instead of pointing to the rule which, under the existing conditions, would recommend itself *de lege ferenda* as reasonable and equitable.

After what has been said about international customary law

and "natural" international law, a word ought to be added regarding the expression "laws and customs of war." On August 21, 1798, the Attorney General of the United States advised the Secretary of State that there existed a maritime war between the United States and France and that consequently persons commissioned by France and aiding that nation in her naval operations would be treated as enemies and confined as prisoners of war. Captured crews of armed French vessels were in consequence treated as prisoners of war in accordance with "the laws and customs of war." [35] One hundred and sixteen years later, on April 21, 1914, Rear Admiral Fletcher, commanding a detached squadron of the United States Atlantic Fleet, conducted the landing operations against Vera Cruz, in accordance with "the laws and customs of war." [36] This expression has various meanings, depending upon the circumstances under which it is used. Generally speaking, "laws" refers to some system of "natural" international law and "customs" either to international customary law or to mere customs, customs which may have been purely national or shared in by other nations.[37] In connection with the American naval operations against France from 1798 to 1800, "the laws and customs of war" would seem to mean only precepts of some system of "natural" international law; at this period the young navy of the United States still had to develop both customs and customary law. In the case of the landing operations of American bluejackets and marines at Vera Cruz in 1914, the same expression, strangely enough, refers neither to precepts of some system of "natural" international law, nor to customary law or customs, but to the contractual obligations incumbent upon both the United States and Mexico as parties to the Hague Convention (IV) of 1907 Respecting the Laws and Customs of War on Land. Incidentally, the title of this Convention amounts to a contradiction in terms. It should read simply "Convention Concerning Warfare on Land." The very purpose of the Convention was to establish definite treaty provisions respecting warfare on land, and to replace thereby uncertain and varying "laws and customs."

3. MUNICIPAL LAW

In comparison with international law the rules of municipal law which refer to war are few in number, yet they appear in every field of the system. There are war clauses in constitutions, and in statutes such as civil, commercial, penal, and military penal codes. Other statutes and decrees are laws on war pure and simple; the application of all their provisions depends on the existence of war. Neutrality acts, and statutes and decrees regarding the organization, procedure, and the substantive law of prize courts, are examples in point. There are rules of internal customary law, the Anglo-American common law for instance, which likewise refer to war. The Anglo-American common law thus prohibited since the end of the eighteenth century and long before modern legislators made Trading-with-the-enemy acts, intercourse and especially trading with alien enemies, unless allowed by certain general exceptions or special license.[38] There are, finally, the war clauses written into all sorts of contracts, especially insurance policies.

To the more or less permanent rules on war in municipal law ought to be added the so-called "emergency legislation" of both belligerent and neutral countries—concerning finance, shipping, food supply, civilian defense, etc.—calculated to be valid "for the duration" only. Not every modern war entailed such special legislation. Italy, for instance, enacted no special legislation for her war with Ethiopia in 1935–36.

Those rules on war in municipal law are not all of equal interest to the student concerned with establishing the border line separating war from peace. The establishment of this line, to be sure, may become a matter of importance in any field of municipal law—constitutional law, statutory law, decrees, customary law, contracts and other legal transactions. The most interesting rules, however, are those of constitutional law, which purport to reserve the decision as to a declaration of war to the legislature. Article I, Section 8, Paragraph 11 of the Constitution of the United States has served as a pattern for other states. It has emigrated so to speak. Similar provisions have appeared since 1789 in many other constitutions, in those of the Central and South American republics, for instance, and in the new constitutions enacted in Europe after the first World War.[39] There these provisions stand as monuments to the wisdom and the vision of the revolutionary fathers, as eloquent testaments to the enduring nature of the philosophy of government which they proclaimed.

The provision has a particularly interesting history in French constitutional law. France has had fourteen constitutions since 1791. In seven of these constitutions the decision as to a declaration of war was a prerogative of the legislature. Such was the case with those of 1791, 1793, 1795, 1799, 1848, and with the Constitutional Law of July 16, 1875.[40] Such is again the case with the constitution adopted by referendum on October 13, 1946.[41] We have seen above how Jules Ferry found his way around the barriers which the Constitution of 1875 had placed in the way of war. It might be added that on April 3, 1814, the French Senate, "in a kind of heavy-hearted and gloomy silence," [42] declared and decreed that Napoleon Bonaparte had forfeited his throne. The decree was "like a verdict of destiny already given somewhere else, higher than the Senate and higher than the earth." [43] In one of the several considerations preceding the *Sénatus-Consulte* it was said that Napoleon Bonaparte had "undertaken a series of wars in violation of Article 50 of the Constitutional Act of the 22d of Frimaire, year VIII, which prescribed that a declaration of war be proposed, discussed, decided upon and promulgated like a statute." [44]

It matters little that the provision reserving to the legislature the decision as to a declaration of war has been written into the constitution of small, peace-loving nations without any imperialistic record whatever, or into the constitution of countries in which parliament has the power of a rubber stamp. It will be seen, however, that it does matter a great deal that the rule is to be found in the Constitution of the United States, in the French constitutional law of July 16, 1875, and in the Constitution of the German Empire of April 16, 1871.[45] The provision, on the other hand, does not exist in the constitutional law of Great Britain. In Great Britain the declaration of war is a prerogative of the crown. It has been exercised, though, at least during the last hundred years, with due consideration of the feelings and the wishes of the Commons in view of the control of that House over finances.[46]

CHAPTER VI

"The" Legal Definition of War

On July 20, 1883, the Duke de Broglie stated before the French Senate that "everybody knows that war is rigorously defined in international law." [1] The leader of the monarchist-clerical opposition evidently meant to say not "in international law," but "in the theory of international law." There are recent writers on international law who likewise contend that there exists a generally accepted definition of war. [2]

The preceding chapters show that such a contention is unwarranted. We have noted several statements which are set forth by their authors as "the" legal definition of war. "It may, I believe, be safely laid down that war is every contention by force between two nations in external matters under the authority of their respective governments," said Justice Washington in August, 1800, in the Supreme Court of the United States in the case of *Bas* v. *Tingy*. [3] One hundred and thirty-seven years later, on November 17, 1937, Representative Hamilton Fish, Republican from New York, quoted this definition in the House of Representatives in support of his contention that Japan and China were at war and that, consequently, President Roosevelt ought to apply the Neutrality Act. [4] Another definition was adopted by the Supreme Court in the prize cases in 1862, [5] by the Court of Claims in the French spoliation cases in 1886, [6] and by the Circuit Court for the District of Kansas in the case of *Hamilton* v. *McClaughry, Warden* in 1905. [7] The definition applied in these three cases is that made by Vattel in his famous *Le Droit des Gens ou Principes de la Loi Naturelle*, the first edition of which appeared in 1758. This much quoted definition reads as follows: "War is that state in which nations, under the authority of their respective governments, prosecute their rights by force." [8] Another textbook definition, but of a much later date, was used by Senator Hiram Bingham, Republican from Connecticut, in the United States Senate on April 21, 1928, to support his contention that the United States was not then at war with Nicaragua.[9] The book which served the Senator was Oppenheim's *International Law*, considered by many to be the best modern textbook on international law. As defined by Oppenheim, "War is the contention between two or more States through their armed forces, for the purpose of overpowering each other, and imposing such conditions of peace as the victor pleases."[10] It is probable that Senator Key Pittman of Nevada, chairman of the Senate Foreign Relations Committee, had Oppenheim's definition in mind when he spoke over the radio on August 23, 1937, in defense of President Roosevelt's reluctance to declare that a "state of war" existed between China and Japan. In his talk he stressed that neither Japan nor China had given any evidence of "an intention to conquer or to subdue its opponent."[11]

These three definitions which have just been quoted and which have appeared in the historical part of this study make it evident that war is not "rigorously" defined in the theory of international law.

The three definitions quoted above constitute, as a matter of fact, only a small percentage of the definitions of war that might be quoted from the many textbooks available in a first-class library on international law. Fauchille and Rolin, leading French and Belgian international lawyers respectively, hardly exaggerate when they assert that almost every writer on international law has his own definition of war.[12] It is indeed easy to draw up a list of ten, twenty, fifty, a hundred, and more definitions even if the cataloger confines himself to a small number of languages and to textbooks on international law published during the short period from the turn of the century to World War II.[13] The student confronted with such a list blinks in surprise. He brings to mind the student conversing with Mephistopheles in *Faust:*

> As if a mill wheel turned in my head,
> I feel confused by what you have said.

Legal thinking in connection with the basic notions of war and peace seems to be hopelessly confused, all the more so if we bear in mind the terminology which is to be found at the end of Chapter II.[14] However, it can be said that the difficulties are by no means as great as they appear to be.

The definition of war, according to some legal writers and courts, represents "war in *the* legal sense." According to others, it represents more specifically "war in the sense of international law." [15] The Reichsgericht used the expression "war in the sense of international law" in the case of *F.* v. *Reichsfiskus*,[16] the Supreme Court of the United States the expression "war in the legal sense" in the case of *Sutton* v. *Tiller*.[17]

Before examining these two expressions some observations ought to be made on defining words employed in rules of law. The aim of such defining is to get at the meaning of equivocal terms in the light of the intent and purpose which motivated the making of the rule of law. Thus, for the lawyer, to define means to interpret. There is no need of dealing here in detail with the difficult problem of legal interpretation. Suffice it to say that the interpretation of legal transactions, such as wills and contracts and, for that matter, treaties in international law, is one thing and the interpretation of constitutions, statutes, and decrees another. The interpreter of a legal transaction considers the *actual* intent and purpose of its maker or makers. The interpreter of a treaty, for instance, seeks to ascertain not what two or more reasonable and just parties ought to have stipulated, but what they actually did agree upon, whether it be reasonable and just or not.[18] The interpreter of constitutions, statutes, and decrees, on the contrary, according to legal philosophical thinking and the legal tradition in many lands, presumes the intent and purpose of the makers of the law to have been reasonable and just and tries to make ambiguously worded rules of law fit this hypothesis.[19] "The intention of the legislator is always supposed to be equity," says Hobbes in *Leviathan*.[20]

It is with this in mind that one must approach the idea of

"war in *the* legal sense." What will be said regarding it covers also the idea of "war in the sense of international law."

It is easy enough to see that there can be no such notion as "war in *the* legal sense," to wit, war in the sense of *all* the rules of law on war, both international and municipal. In order to establish the notion of "war in *the* legal sense" one would have first to compile and then to interpret every single rule of law on war *ever* made. All who know anything about legal history will readily admit that it would be wholly impossible to compile all these rules on war of international law, let alone the rules on war of municipal law. Yet even a knowledge of all the rules ever made would not be enough. In order to arrive at the allegedly *ever* valid notion of "war in *the* legal sense" one would in addition have to anticipate and be able to interpret all the rules of law on war that might be made in the *future*. Such a proposition is so absurd as to need no comment.

It would be a delusion to assume that at least all the rules of law on war *in force* could be gathered together. Such an undertaking also would obviously be beyond the powers of anyone, even if it were confined to international law. The linguistic difficulty of doing research in dozens of languages, it is true, might be overcome, but other hurdles cannot be taken. It has been pointed out that it is not always easy to know whether a rule is still in force or not.[21] It will be remembered, furthermore, that no clear-cut dividing line can be drawn between rules of international customary law and mere customs.[22] Finally, a compilation of rules in force, assuming such a compilation could be made for today, might, as a result of some new rule, become incomplete overnight.

A word or two about the idea of interpreting rules of law en masse. This idea is implicit in any definition of "war in *the* legal sense," no matter whether or not the writer is aware that such implication exists. Every lawyer knows that interpretation is sometimes child's play or entirely unnecessary. In all branches of the law there are, fortunately, many rules which are perfectly clear and do not need to be interpreted. In other instances, however, the task of interpreting would drive a lawyer to despair. Article 16 of the Covenant of the League of Nations is a striking illustration of the difficulties of interpretation. The exact intent and purpose of the members of the League of Nations with regard to Article 16 of the Covenant [23] has never been established. The Pact of Paris of August 27, 1928, otherwise called the Briand-Kellogg Pact, which was hailed as the dawn of a new era, presents another example of the difficulties of interpretation. It has never been possible to ascertain the exact intent and purpose of the states which in Article 1 of that treaty renounced "war" and in particular "war as an instrument of national policy." [24] In short, interpretation of a single rule of law can be difficult enough to discourage any thought of interpreting rules of law en masse.

For the above reasons, if for no other, one thing is clear. The definition of "war in *the* legal sense" is impossible of achievement. It never has been achieved. It never will be. The idea of "war in *the* legal sense," although handed down from year to year, from decade to decade, and even from century to century, is a futile one. No matter how teeming with wisdom textbooks on international law may be in other respects, we shall have to throw into the discard, permanently, and to forget the definitions of war which they contain.

It seems as if no useful purpose could be served in considering the book definitions of war any further after it has been established that they cannot possibly be the result of the interpretation of the rules of law on war. One of Josh Billings' epigrams comes to mind. "It is better to know nothing than to know what ain't so." However, one recognized way of explaining a thing is to tell what it is not. It will be seen that it is interesting and even useful to ask the question: what reality lies behind the book definitions of war?

The answer is not an easy one. In textbook after textbook on international law, with but a few exceptions, the definition is set forth without substantiation. The definition, as a rule, issues full grown from the brain of its author as Minerva sprang with her panoply of war from the brow of Jupiter. (Which is, of course, to put it mildly, no way of presenting a definition.) Hence as a rule it cannot be seen out of what material the definition has been hewn. Its origin, under these circumstances, becomes a matter of conjecture. Regarding most definitions the researcher feels inclined to shrug his shoulders and let it go at that. However, it is fairly safe to say that every book definition falls into one of four categories.

A first category is represented by Oppenheim's definition. "War is the contention between two or more States through their armed forces for the purpose of overpowering each other, and imposing such conditions of peace as the victor pleases." [25] Why should states alone be parties to war? Why is the essence of war "a contention through their armed forces"? Why this purpose and no other, or, for that matter, any definite purpose at all? Oppenheim's textbook leaves all these questions unanswered. The writer found the answers by chance in Oppenheim's article "The Science of International Law, Its Task and Method," published in 1908 in the *American Journal of International Law*. War, according to Oppenheim, is what his definition says that it is because "history" presents such a definition.[26] In other words, if historians speak about "war," they mean war in the sense of the above definition. Since historians speaking about war do not resort to any technical language but simply use the word in its everyday meaning, Oppenheim might just as well have said: war is what my definition says that it is because my definition corresponds to the common meaning of the word "war."

It does not matter whether or not Oppenheim's definition corresponds to such a meaning. The definition is not acceptable even if it does accurately bring out the everyday meaning of the word "war." It is an inadmissible procedure to promise a *legal* definition of the term "war" or of any other term employed in a rule of law, and then to consider and to define some extraneous issue. The legal meaning of a word frequently deviates from its everyday meaning. It will be seen in the next chapter that this is true also of the word "war" in the rules of law on war. This is why Oppenheim's definition must be rejected.

It can be taken for granted that many other definitions simply represent what their authors consider to be the everyday meaning of the word "war," or "war in the material sense," as it is sometimes called. The meaning of a word in common parlance, indeed, is a trap into which we fall easily. Confronted with a certain word, such as the word "war," we always think of its everyday meaning first. Foulke, an American author,[27] and de Louter, a distinguished Dutch writer,[28] while defining war, openly declared that they were concerned with war as a mere fact. This is another way of saying: war as the word is commonly understood. Such writers as the Englishman Westlake,[29] the Dane Matzen,[30] and the Austrian Strisower,[31] who follow more or less closely in the footsteps of Grotius, should also be mentioned here. Grotius, as will be seen presently, also made his definition in accordance with what he believed to be the common meaning of the word "war." The tendency of looking upon the meaning of the word "war" in common parlance and of defining it accordingly in textbooks on international law is strikingly revealed by a recent French writer. In 1928, ten years after the close of World War I, Moye flatly refused to define war in his textbook on international law on the assumption that every Tom, Dick, and Harry knows from experience what is meant by "war." "It would be a tragic irony to try to define war after the upheavals which have ravaged Europe for five years. Their painful repercussions have afflicted all mankind. Each of my readers knows only too well what war is. There is no need for laboring this point." [32]

It is of the utmost importance to mention now Hugo Grotius and his once celebrated work *De Jure Belli ac Pacis Libri Tres*, first published in Paris in 1625. Grotius, like Oppenheim, as has been said before, defined the word "war" in accordance with what he believed to be its common meaning.[33] While he was meditating on a definition of war from that angle, an obvious and indisputable fact imbedded itself in his mind. This fact was that nations are said to be at war not merely when their armed forces are fighting; nations are said to be at war as soon and as long as they are conducting operations against each other. Combat operations often proceed without actual fighting and sometimes they are lacking altogether. What we commonly call a "war" may temporarily consist in nothing but logistic operations.

Two examples will suffice to illustrate this common conception of war.

In the eighteenth century Europe had its stagnant wars in which no fighting occurred for months. That was especially the case during the winter. The armies hibernated in their quarters and the soldiers had virtually nothing to do but try to keep warm and polish their buttons. But despite the fact that no fighting occurred during the winter months, the princes, Frederick the Great and Maria Theresa, for instance, were said to be at war.

During World War I and World War II it repeatedly happened that major combat operations necessitated months of preparation or of waiting for favorable weather during which the eventual assailant refrained from fighting in a chosen sector in the hope that his opponent also would remain quiet. Thus a strange quiet brooded over the western front from September 3, 1939, when France declared war on Germany, till May 10, 1940, when Germany invaded the Netherlands, Belgium, and Luxemburg. Many Americans spoke of a "phony war." The French and German troops seemed to observe an armistice. Except for a few minor scouting episodes, there was not a single encounter between the French and German Armies worth mentioning. Operations were almost exclusively logistic. Still France and Germany were said to be at war.

Historical parallels to cases like these, it can clearly be seen, preoccupied Grotius.[34] Cicero had thought that the word "war" [*bellum*], as commonly understood, means a contention by force [*certatio per vim*]. War to Cicero was, broadly speaking, some sort of *action*. Grotius refused to concur with Cicero. He considered the fact that nations are said to be at war not merely when their armed forces are engaged and, strangely enough, concluded that it would be wrong to say that "war" means some sort of *action*. The word, he contended, means a "state," to wit, "the state of those contending by force." What he meant by "state" Grotius did not deign to say.

However, his failure to explain is of no importance whatever. Combat operations, certainly, are *actions*, no matter whether or not the armed forces of the opponents are engaged. Logistic operations, whether accompanied by combat operations or not, also are *actions*. To contend that the word "war," in its common usage, means, broadly speaking, anything else but action, to contend that it means a "state," was not to inform but to mystify. It is, it will be granted, an ungracious task to accuse Grotius of having obscured the problem as to what constitutes war. But affection for Grotius must not blind us to the fact that his definition of war is a mistake. It is a mistake, first, because it turns on the extraneous issue of the meaning of the word "war" in common parlance and, secondly, because even from that angle it does not make sense.

If the definition of Grotius had been only a mistake, it could be let alone. However, it proved to be a dangerous mistake. The impression produced by *De Jure Belli ac Pacis Libri Tres* was singularly great. Forty editions of this work appeared in less than a hundred years and it became the code of international law for Europe after its reconstruction by the treaties of Westphalia in 1648.[35] Grotius was the accepted oracle of jurisprudence in a time when authority continued to be mistaken for argument. The word "state," under these circumstances, soon managed to surround itself with an aura of legal erudition. From blindly acknowledging that there is such a thing as "war in *the* legal sense" and that such a thing is a "state," it was only a slight step for the followers of Grotius to say "state of war" instead of "war in *the* legal sense." "State of war," as a matter of fact, became the expression par excellence for saying "war in *the* legal sense" or "de jure war," or "war in the technical sense." As a result of Grotius' definition the French began to speak of "état de guerre," the Germans of "Kriegszustand," the Spanish of "estado de guerra," and so forth.

To Mr. Bernard M. Baruch, testifying before the Senate Foreign Relations Committee on April 6, 1939, the existence of a "state of war" between Japan and China was a fact "as obvious as the sun in the sky." [36] Senator Key Pittman, chairman of the Senate Foreign Relations Committee, on the contrary, issued a warning on July 28, 1937, in which he said "it is very difficult to determine that a state of war exists." [37] To these two expressions of opinion a third one might be added. On June 24, 1937, Congressman Shanley of New Haven, Connecticut, told the House of Representatives that "it would take a council of international jurists working overtime" to define the expression "state of war." [38] The truth of the matter is that it is absolutely impossible to define the expression "state of war." It is impossible to define the expression "state of war" because it is a substitute for the expression "war in *the* legal sense." We have seen already, and we shall see even more clearly in the next chapter, that there can be no such thing as "war in *the* legal sense." Hence there is a fundamental and, if not corrected, fatal weakness in rules of law the application of which has been made dependent upon the existence of a "state of war." Such rules cannot be applied if they are taken literally. Statutes like the American Neutrality Acts of 1936, 1937, and 1939 must be corrected in accordance with the maxim that the intent and purpose of the legislator are always reasonable and just. The correction consists in reading "war" where the legislator wrote "state of war."

Now to the second category of book definitions.

The second category is exemplified by the definition which Justice Washington made from the bench of the Supreme Court of the United States in August, 1800, in the case of *Bas* v. *Tingy*. That definition, it will be remembered, was merely the result of Justice Washington's belief. "It may, I believe, be safely laid down that war is every contention by force between two nations in external matters under the authority of their respective governments." [39] Definitions, as a matter of course, ought to be statements of which we know—not guess, but know—that they are true. It is safe, however, to say that the above definition is not an isolated sample of reliance on belief. Stockton, for instance, in 1914 in his textbook on international law gave what in his "belief" was "the best definition extant." [40] To contend that many an author of a definition of war relied on "belief" does not necessarily mean that he has felt his way in a hit-or-miss fashion toward that extraordinary conception of "war in *the* legal sense." It seems fair to say that such a writer may well interpret this or that rule of law on war and then only believe in the definition on the assumption that it applies to *all* the rules of law on war. Such an assumption, it will be seen, is an unwarranted generalization. But unwarranted generalizations are another trap into which we fall so often and so easily.

Now to the third category.

This is the category of what might be called *mixed definitions*. As far as the parties to and the essence of war are concerned, the definitions to be considered now belong in all probability either to the first or the second category or to both. These definitions, however divergent they may be in regard to the parties to and the essence of war, agree on one point. War, according to these definitions, has a purpose: either litigation or the enforcement of rights. War, in short, is an instrument of justice.

The classical example of a mixed definition is Vattel's definition of 1758, which was so frequently cited, particularly in the United States. "War is that state in which nations, under the authority of their respective governments, *prosecute their rights by force*." [41] Contemporary authors of mixed definitions, among many others, are the American Stowell,[42] the Italian Olivi,[43] and the Spaniard Orúe.[44] The presence of the term "state" in Vattel's definition is, of course, due to the fact that Vattel followed uncritically in the footsteps of Grotius in defining the essence of war. But why did Vattel and many others define war as an instrument of justice? Their agreement in this respect is no mere coincidence. The definitions are manifestly echoes of what always has been the supreme war tenet of the natural-law school of thought.[45] Its chief concern has always been not jus in bello but jus ad bellum. The answer given to the question "When may states go to war?" however formulated by the various writers has been in principle uniform through the ages. War is unjust, if it is—what it usually is [46]—an instrument of politics. War, on the contrary, is just, if it is what many a declaration of war has asserted, namely, an instrument of justice. "It is the iniquity of the opponent which confers upon a wise man the right to wage a just war," proclaimed Saint Augustine in the fifth century.[47] This tenet of Saint Augustine has been adopted by innumerable Catholic and Protestant writers of the natural-law school of thought.[48] The Bible, it might be added, is replete with proofs of care, of certain victories, of triumphs without losses, of guidance and sheltering for soldiers of a righteous cause.[49] Theological philosophical writers now seldom stress that the gospel of love and peace is not to be confounded with an unconditional pacifism and that certain iniquities occur where not only is it permitted, but it is criminal weakness and neglect of *duty* not to resist with force. On September 23, 1940, the official Vatican radio station said:

. . . it may be a *duty* to wage war for the vindication of a vital right that has been wantonly violated by an enemy nation. Any contrary principle would guarantee impunity to tyrants, robbers, or those for whom the might of arms makes right, and who condemn the law-abiding to an intolerable labor. . . . When that is the case, we all have the *duty* to go out and meet all the agonies of war.[50]

Because the truth of the principle that states may resort to war as an instrument of justice was self-evident, it appealed to the adherents of the natural-law school of thought and to positivists alike. In the absence of agencies for the pacific settlement of international disputes and for the enforcement of international law, war, though a primitive and fallible procedure like a duel, was the last means of self-help, the ultima ratio of governments.[51] Former Secretary of War Henry L. Stimson still heard Theodore Roosevelt say that he put peace above everything except righteousness, when the two came into conflict he supported righteousness.[52]

After the above digression on the purpose of war in mixed definitions we shall now take up a criticism of these definitions. Mixed definitions, as far as the parties to and the essence of war are concerned, are open to the same objections as are the definitions of the first two categories. The meaning of the word "war" in common parlance, or mere belief, are no basis for making a definition. Regarding the purpose of war—the description of war as an instrument of justice—one might well say that mixed definitions are based not on a rule of positive law, but on a tenet of the systems of natural law, and let it go at that. However to define war as an instrument of justice is a mistake even from the point of view of the natural-law systems. Mixed definitions manifestly fall short of considering *all* the rules of law on war of these systems. They fail to cover the many rules of the "natural" jus in bello, the rules as to the treatment of captives and of noncombatants such as minors, the aged, the feeble, women, and ecclesiastics, the rules regarding the immunity of sacred places, the rules against wanton destruction, and so forth, in short the whole fabric of rules by which the authors of systems of natural law strove to mitigate the horrors of war. Mixed definitions suggest that the party resorting to war as an instrument of justice was bound by the above rules, whereas, on the other hand, the party waging an unjust war, which, according to the definition, is no war at all, was entitled to employ any means whatever, even the most treacherous and cruel ones, against the enemy. In fact he who resorted to war as an instrument of justice and he who waged an unjust war, of course, were supposed to be equally bound by the rules for the conduct of war found in the systems of natural law. It is only too clear that mixed definitions do credit to the humanitarianism of their authors, not to their legal acumen. Their description of war as an instrument of justice is not inspired by a desire to define, but by a desire to suppress war as an instrument of policy. This has been openly admitted by Bluntschli, the founder of the Institut de Droit International and himself author of a mixed definition. "There exists a great humanitarian interest to conceive of and to describe war as an instrument of justice in order to restrict thereby recourse to it." [53]

Now to the fourth and last category.

It consists of a small number of definitions based upon etymological considerations. A recent author of an etymological definition is Marquis de Olivart, a Spanish writer and the original owner of the "Olivart International Law Library" of the Harvard Law School. Olivart writes:

The term "guerra" derives etymologically from the Germanic word *war*, i.e., *defense*, and means in all languages in one way or another a state of defense by force of one's right. We believe that the term war can be defined as the litigation between nations which are defending their rights and in which force is the judge and victory serves as the judgment. [54]

He who would explain the legal meaning of a word by resorting to its etymology is on the wrong track. It is one thing to explain the history of the meaning of a word, another to make out its meaning if it is employed in a rule of law.

In recapitulation the following can be said about the reality that lies behind the book definitions of war: They consist in the main of statements based upon what authors consider to be the meaning of the word "war" in common parlance and of statements based upon mere belief. Mixed definitions, furthermore, set forth the chief tenet as regards war taught by the writers on natural law, the tenet that war be an instrument of justice. A small number of definitions are based on etymological considerations.

Having dealt with textbook definitions of war, we now turn to monographs concerned with the problem of how war ought to be legally defined.

It is amazing how little detailed attention has been paid to this problem. The monographs, it appears, can be counted on the fingers of one hand and are all rather brief. All are attempts to define "war in *the* legal sense," and are inevitably doomed to failure.

Suffice it to consider briefly two monographs which happen to be written in English. The respective authors are McNair, an Englishman, and Eagleton, an American.

McNair's monograph, entitled "The Legal Meaning of War and the Relation of War to Reprisals," is a paper which its author read before the Grotius Society in London in 1925.[55] McNair's first proposition concerns the essence of war. After having examined eight book definitions which follow the Grotian pattern, he concludes that "any good definition" must bring out that war is a "state or condition." The involved exposition which follows is likewise not, as it should be, concerned with the meaning of the word "war" in the rules of law on war. It is offered, instead, "in the light of deductions from actual experience." [56] This puts McNair's definition squarely into the first category of definitions, the definitions which turn upon what their authors hold to be the common meaning of the word "war."

Eagleton's study is entitled *The Attempt to Define War*. It was published in 1933 by the Carnegie Endowment for International Peace, Division of Intercourse and Education, as No. 291 of the pamphlet series "International Conciliation." It is intended for lawyers and laymen alike. Yet lawyers will find it extremely difficult not to become confused in making their way through this monograph, while laymen will certainly not be able to meet the challenge of its involved presentation. The author, with commendable frankness, concedes that his discussion leaves one with "a great deal of uncertainty." [57] His main line of argument, like McNair's, follows book definitions. He concludes from a small number of such definitions that states only can be parties to war [58] and that fighting is "ordinarily" characteristic of its essence.[59] Confronted with conclusions like these, one can only repeat that all book definitions are fallacious.

The theory of "war in *the* legal sense"—or the state-of-war theory, as it may also be called—however we may regret the existence of such a theory, can do no harm as long as it is confined to textbooks and to the academic discussions of learned societies. However, legal thinking is done not for academic but for practical purposes. The same theory becomes anything but harmless if it is followed by students of law who in practical life are called upon to make, to apply, and to enforce the rules of law on war or, for that matter, the rules of law on peace. The application of the American Neutrality Acts of 1936, 1937, and 1939 should not have been made dependent upon a proclamation by the President of the United States that "a state of war" among foreign states exists. The expression "state of war," employed as it was in the pivotal rules of these acts, threw their whole mechanism out of gear. The chairman of the Senate Foreign Relations Committee should not have alluded to Oppenheim's definition in defense of President Roosevelt's refusal to apply the Neutrality Act of 1937 in the Japanese-Chinese "incident." [60] Congressman Hamilton Fish should not have quoted Justice Washington's definition when he criticized President Roosevelt's refusal to apply this act.[61] The writ of habeas corpus in the case of *Hamilton* v. *McClaughry, Warden,* should not have been denied the petitioner by a court attempting to prove with Vattel's definition that the Boxer Expedition was a war.[62] Neither should the Supreme Court in the "prize" cases [63] nor the Court of Claims in the French spoliation cases [64] have resorted to the definition of the illustrious Swiss. He who resorts to book definitions of war instead of fixing his attention on what the rules of law on war mean is a poor servant of the law. This is why the theory of "war in *the* legal sense" or state-of-war theory cannot be tolerated indefinitely.

CHAPTER VII

The Relativity of War and Peace

SECTION 1. GENERAL CONSIDERATIONS

The definition of "war in *the* legal sense" is impossible of achievement for still another and a more simple reason. The rules of law on war are not all made with one and the same intent and purpose. The particular rules are calculated to serve particular functions. The word "war" in each rule must be interpreted accordingly. Thus what has to be looked for is not one over-all legal definition of war, but a variety of legal definitions, each made in the light of and in relation to the particular intent and purpose of the rule which happens to be under consideration.

Each legal definition of war has its counterpart in a corresponding legal definition of peace. The narrower the definition of war in the sense of a particular rule, the broader the corresponding definition of peace. The wider the definition of war in the sense of a particular rule, the narrower the corresponding definition of peace.

It is to a consideration of such relativity of the legal meaning of the two terms "war" and "peace" that the present chapter will be devoted. The thesis that in law the word "war" requires not one, but a variety of definitions, is new only in theory. In practice those who must apply the rules of law on war have often balked at the consequences of the false and confusing theory about "war in *the* legal sense," and have yielded, though they hardly knew how or why, to the theory of the relativity of war and peace.

Every single characteristic of a legal definition of war depends upon the intent and purpose of the rule concerned. The two most often recurring themes in the definitions of "war in *the* legal sense" are to the effect that the parties to war are states, and that its essence is an armed contest. It will be seen that not even that much should be taken for granted. Much less do other general statements about what in law constitutes war hold good for all the rules of law on war, such as the assertion that legally war does not exist as long as operations occur between particular detachments of the respective armies only, with neither side intending to operate against the totality of the armed forces of the other.[1]

There exists a marked difference between the meaning of the term "war" as used in common parlance and various legal meanings of "war." Common sense sometimes does not recognize as war what must be considered as war in the sense of some rule of law on war. Common sense, on the other hand, sometimes does recognize as war what cannot be considered as war in the sense of some other rule. The language of the soldier under these circumstances sometimes quite naturally conflicts with the technical language of the lawyer. In July, 1883, the Cabinet of Jules Ferry, having in mind Article 9 of the French Constitutional Law of July 16, 1875, refused to consider France as being at war with Annam. About the same time Colonel Baden reported that he had succeeded in driving the "enemy" from the outskirts of Nam-Dinh, and the triumvirate Harmand, Bouet, and Courbet decided to direct what they called their first "war operation" against Hue.[2] Seemingly paradoxical statements may result if one and the same person speaks now in technical language, now in common parlance. Such statements were made by Ferry in the Chamber of Deputies on November 26, 1884. At that date Ferry, again with an eye on the French Constitution, still denied that France and China were at war. At the same time he boasted in common parlance about the "victory" won day after day in Tongking by the French expeditionary corps over Chinese troops.[3]

History shows that states employ their armed forces in a great variety of modes usually against another state or states. A limited number only of these modes has been pointed out in the historical part of this study.

In some operations the *number* of the armed forces engaged on either one side or both was conspicuously small. In 1915

Germany assisted Austria-Hungary at the outbreak of the war between Austria-Hungary and Italy with three divisions.[4] In the "battles" of San Ignazio and of Carrizal of June 15 and 21, 1916, two diminutive fractions of the American army, just two troops of cavalry in each case, clashed with equally diminutive numbers of Mexican soldiers.[5]

A number of other operations were *geographically limited*. The American naval operations against France in 1798–1800 were confined to American territorial waters and to the high seas; they were not to extend into French territorial waters.[6] On December 10, 1883, Ferry, in a speech before the Chamber of Deputies, denied the existence of a war between France and China by emphasizing that the projected occupation of Bac-Ninh and Son-Tay amounted to only "a limited, localized, geographically circumscribed action." [7] The military operations during the Boxer Expedition in 1900–1901 were practically limited to the province of Chihli. In regions south of the Tientsin-Paotingfu line, French and Chinese troops camped peacefully together.[8] The "shoot on sight" order, issued by President Roosevelt on September 11, 1941, restricted American naval and aerial operations against Germany and Italy to American "defense waters." [9]

The American naval operations against France in 1798–1800, and the American naval and aerial operations against Germany and Italy in 1941, were restricted not only geographically, but also as to their *objectives*. The former were directed against *armed* French vessels only, not against unarmed French merchantmen; the latter only against Axis submarines and Axis surface raiders.[10]

There have been naval operations, the American naval operations of 1798–1800, for instance, which were not supplemented by operations on land, and, on the other hand, military operations without corresponding naval operations. During the Boxer Expedition there occurred practically no naval operations. The Allied men-of-war, on the whole, did not attack the Chinese men-of-war and refrained from capturing Chinese merchantmen and vice versa. The commerce of third powers was not interfered with on the grounds either of contraband or of a blockade of any portion of the Chinese coast.[11] The Japanese campaign in Manchuria in 1931–33 likewise involved no naval operations. While parts of the Japanese and the Chinese Armies fought each other on land, Japanese and Chinese warships and merchantmen met in the Pacific and passed each other peacefully; foreign trade continued entirely unmolested. During the Japanese military operations against China proper in 1937–41, naval activity on the whole seems to have been limited to the blockade which Japan instituted against all *Chinese* shipping along the Chinese coast from Chingwangtao, in the north, to Pakhoi, in the south.[12]

In spite of the great variety of modes in the employment by states of their armed forces, historians in general do not find it difficult to give some name to each concrete mode. In general they accept without hesitation the appellation which one or the other party employs officially. The military operations of the powers in China in 1900–1901, for instance, went down in history not as a "war" but as an "expedition," because the Allied governments had styled them an "expedition." The restricted American naval operations against France in 1798–1800, and against Germany and Italy in 1941, the restricted German military operations against Italy in 1915–16, and other operations never were styled officially. Under these circumstances, the historian is left to choose his own appellation. It matters nothing whether in such cases he chooses the term "war," or some other appropriate designation, as, for instance, the word "hostilities." The historian's task is well done if he succeeds in describing the past accurately, in one way or another, and in interpreting it in the light of his own philosophy.

The task of the lawyer is of a different nature. Unlike the historian he is not concerned with adequate appellations, but with finding out whether a concrete mode of employing the armed forces of a state constitutes war in relation to and in the sense of some rule of law on war, and whether, in consequence, such rule applies or not. A comparison of Article 16 of the

Covenant of the League of Nations with Sections 1 and 2 of
the American Neutrality Act of May 1, 1937, will serve as a
first illustration for the contention that operations which constitute war in relation to one rule of law on war may not constitute war in the sense of another, and that hence the rules of
law on war call for a variety of war definitions.

The exact intent and purpose of the members of the League
of Nations with regard to Article 16 of the Covenant has never
been gauged.[13] Still, there was one definite limit to such uncertainty. In Article 10 of the Covenant the members of the
League undertook to respect and to preserve as against external
aggression "the territorial integrity and existing political independence" of all members of the League. The members therefore at any rate could not possibly refuse in good faith to consider as a "resort to war" in the meaning of Article 16 of the
Covenant, and as calling for sanctions, *any* employment by a
member of the League of its armed forces against another
member, provided that such employment was resorted to in
disregard of the obligations respecting the settlement of disputes among members, and provided further that such employment threatened or impaired "the territorial integrity and
political independence" of the other member. It mattered not
whether the territorial integrity or political independence of
the other member was impaired through an all-out effort.
War, in the meaning of Article 16 of the Covenant, might
have been resorted to with limited military forces, with geographically restricted military operations, without the support
of naval operations, in particular without interference with
foreign trade through contraband lists or blockade.

The same limited kind of employment of armed forces by
foreign states, the same somewhat pale hue of war, was sufficient to constitute war—a "state of war" as the makers of the
law unfortunately said—in the meaning of Section 1 of the
American Neutrality Act of May 1, 1937. Section 1 was directed against "the merchants of death" and prescribed an
embargo on the export of arms, ammunition, and implements
of war to foreign states which were in a "state of war." [14]

"Merchants of death," it goes without saying, will proceed to their sinister machinations not only in all-out military and naval efforts, but in almost any kind of operations, provided they last long enough.

The kind of war—the "state of war" in the language of the act—required for the application of the discretionary "cash-and-carry" provisions of Section 2, on the other hand, was of an entirely different nature. It cannot be said that any kind of operations was sufficient to constitute war in relation to Section 2. The intent and purpose of that section was to keep American ships and cargoes out of harm's way as created through the establishment of blockades and the proclamation of contraband lists. Hence, interference with foreign trade on the grounds of either blockade or contraband, or both, were the requisites of a war in the sense of Section 2. The military and restricted naval operations of Japan against China in 1937–41 were conducted without interference with foreign trade. Hence, they constituted war in relation to the intent and purpose of Section 1, but not in relation to the intent and purpose of Section 2. Nothing in the conduct of either Japan or China would have justified the President in renouncing the historic defense of the freedom of the seas for American commerce and in putting the "cash-and-carry" plan into operation. President Roosevelt's refusal to find that a "state of war" existed rested insofar on sound legal grounds and needed no excuse. In relation to the kind of war required for the application of Section 2, Japan and China were at peace from 1937 to 1941. It was, to be sure, a kind of technical peace which strangely contrasted with the common-sense meaning of the word "peace." Among the five points which Senator Key Pittman in his radio address of August 23, 1937, enumerated in defense of President Roosevelt's reluctance to declare that a "state of war" existed, point 5—noninterference with foreign trade by both China and Japan—happened to be well chosen as regards Section 2, but out of place as regards Section 1.[15] The five points of the address were unintelligible, because the senator failed to show what they had to do with war as required for the application of the provisions of the Neutrality Act.

There are writers on international law who proclaim the "indivisibility" of war and peace. Hautefeuille, for instance, wrote: "War and peace are indivisible; one cannot at the same time be at war and at peace with another people." [16] The dogma of the "indivisibility" in law of war and peace, in reality, is as false as the doctrine about war in "the" legal sense. Since operations which constitute war in relation to one rule of law on war do not necessarily constitute war in the sense of another, states may, as far as the law is concerned, well be at war and at peace simultaneously; at war, in relation to the intent and purpose of one rule, not at war, and consequently at peace, in relation to the intent and purpose of another rule. The question whether a state at a given time is legally at war or at peace is not one to be answered absolutely with "Yes" or "No," as the traditional theory would have it, but instead with "it depends upon which rule of law on war you have in mind."

The argument as to whether the limited naval operations of 1798–1800 between the United States and France constituted war is still going on, 150 years after the event. Historians should never have hesitated to call them "war" or, maybe, "hostilities," and let it go at that. "It was, of course, actual warfare," President Franklin D. Roosevelt once said.[17] As regards the law, the answer will never be found as long as the perspective is obscured by the doctrine of war in "the" legal sense. The answer that everybody expects is either a clear-cut "Yes" or a clear-cut "No." Yet, what in fact ought to be given is not one answer but several. A "Yes" with regard to certain rules of law on war, a "No" with regard to other rules.

The important statute of July 9, 1798, entitled "An Act Further to Protect the Commerce of the United States," authorized the commanders of ships of war and of commissioned private vessels, under instructions from the President, to subdue, capture, and bring into port for adjudication any *armed*

French vessel found within the *jurisdictional limits* of the United States or elsewhere on the *high seas*, and to recapture American vessels, goods, and effects captured by such French vessels.[18] The seventh section of the statute entitled "An Act for the Government of the Navy," passed March 2, 1799, declared that for ships and goods belonging to citizens of the United States, if retaken from the *"enemy"* more than four days after capture, the owners were to allow one half of the whole value for salvage.[19] In the case of *Bas* v. *Tingy*,[20] the argument before the Supreme Court turned chiefly upon the question whether France was an "enemy" of the United States. This appeared to be a difficult problem only because the justices of the Supreme Court in their opinions failed really to look into the intent and purpose of the seventh section of the Act of March 2, 1799. The intent and purpose of this provision were perfectly clear. Skill and courage of American recaptors were to receive an adequate reward. It could not possibly make any difference whether such skill and courage were shown during an all-out military and naval effort or during naval operations which were restricted both geographically and as to their objectives. Hence, from 1798 to 1800 France was an enemy in the light of and in relation to the seventh section of the Act of March 2, 1799. During this period France and the United States were *insofar* at war. The decision of the Supreme Court of the United States in the case of *Bas* v. *Tingy* is correct, though the opinions of the three justices are dimmed through legally unintelligible considerations about "imperfect," "limited," and "partial" war, and through Justice Washington's introduction of a definition of war in "the" legal sense, in which he "believed."

The naval operations between the United States and France constituted war in still another respect, despite the fact that they were limited both geographically and as to their objectives and despite the fact that they were not supplemented by military operations on land. The many engagements between American and French public and private armed vessels were conducted according to "the laws and customs of war." [21]

Captives held by each government were dealt with as prisoners of war. This constituted not merely "very strong, but still inconclusive" evidence of the existence of war, as the Court of Claims contended in *Gray, Administrator*, v. *United States* and in *Cushing, Administrator*, v. *United States*. Actually it constituted conclusive evidence that in law war *insofar* existed. The "laws and customs of war," in connection with the American naval operations of 1798–1800, can refer only to the precepts of some natural-law thinker, such as Vattel.[22] Such precepts were looked upon as immutable and universally valid expressions of reason and justice. They were to be applied accordingly. The application had to yield a reasonable and equitable result. It would have been most unreasonable and unjust to refuse to treat captives as prisoners of war on the grounds that no operations were undertaken on land, or in French territorial waters. In addition, it would have been extremely unwise to do so. Rules regarding the treatment of captives as prisoners of war have a sanction of their own. Nonapplication by one party usually "boomerangs," and leads to mutual ill treatment, or even slaughter of those captured.

Other rules of law on war could be pointed out in relation to which the United States and France were at war, but there is another side to the picture— rules of law on war in relation to which the two countries were technically at peace.

First of all there is Article I, Section 8, Paragraph 11 of the Constitution of the United States, the rule which prescribes that Congress shall have the power to declare war. Since the President alone, as head of state, and not Congress, represents the United States in its foreign relations, and since, consequently, the President alone can issue a declaration of war to a foreign power, the real meaning of the rule is that the President shall not declare war without the consent of Congress. Nor should the President undertake an undeclared war without such consent. It is not necessary to establish here in detail what "war" in this connection means. The plain intent and purpose of the rule is to safeguard the United States against autocratic impulses of the President. The American naval operations against France in 1798–1800—unlike the military operations against China during the Boxer Expedition, for instance—were undertaken not by the President of the United States in his capacity as Commander in Chief of the Army and Navy, but were, instead, authorized by Acts of Congress of May 28 and July 9, 1798.[23] Under these circumstances, for Congress to have "declared" war would have made no sense. Even all-out military and naval operations against France would not have constituted war in relation to the intent and purpose of Article I, Section 8, Paragraph 11 of the Constitution and, consequently, would not have required a declaration of war in the sense of that provision, provided only that they were authorized by Congress.

It has been shown above that there is one aspect to the American naval operations against France in which the right answer to the question as to whether they constituted war or not is still worth more than $3,000,000.[24] Do the French spoliation claims originate from what were originally valid claims of the Government of the United States against the Government of France? In the French spoliation cases the United States contended that from 1798–1800 war existed with France and as the United States could have no claims against France for indiscriminate captures, condemnations, and confiscations, followed by and committed during a war, of the private property of its citizens at sea, neither could the claimants have any resulting claims against them.[25] The Court of Claims, on the contrary, arrived in the above cases at the conclusion that there had been no war between France and the United States and that, hence, the spoliation claims were founded on valid obligations of France to the United States, that the United States had surrendered these claims to France for a valuable consideration benefiting the nation, and that this use of the claims raised an obligation on the part of the United States to compensate the individual claimants.[26] Why war and consequently no valid spoliation claims according to the United States? Why peace and consequently valid spoliation claims according to the Court of Claims? It is important to note that the United States failed to specify the rule or rules of law on war in relation to which it claimed the existence of war and in consequence the invalidity of the spoliation claims. It is equally important to note that the Court of Claims likewise failed to make clear and to concentrate its arguments upon some rule or some rules of law on war in relation to which it might have claimed the existence of peace and in consequence the validity of the spoliation claims. There can be no doubt though about the rules of law on war to which the United States should have referred for its contention that war existed, and the Court of Claims for its opposite contention. The validity of the spoliation claims, as far as positive law is concerned, depends upon the right answer to the question whether, in spite of the American naval operations against France in the period from 1798 to 1800, Articles XIV and XXIV–XXVII in the Treaty of Amity and Commerce of February 6, 1778, remained applicable.[27] These provisions dealt with capture, condemnation, and confiscation of ships and cargoes belonging to citizens of the contracting parties and were made by France and the United States to apply in case France should be engaged in a maritime war with a third power while remaining at *peace* with the United States, and vice versa. The point to be established, therefore, is whether the American naval operations of 1798–1800 overthrew the kind of peace that was required for the application by France of the above neutrality rules in the Treaty of Amity and Commerce of 1778. The answer does not depend upon considerations of reasonableness and equity. It is, as has been said before,[28] the *historical* intent and purpose of the contracting parties that matters in the interpretation of *contractual* obligations. There is plenty of evidence as to the intent and purpose of the contracting parties. The Cabinets of Washington and John Adams uniformly insisted upon the illegality of the French captures, condemnations, and confiscations of American ships and cargoes in the war between France and Great Britain, and never failed to demand full compensation for all losses and damages from the point of view of the Treaty of Amity and Commerce of 1778.

France, on the other hand, never denied her liability for captures, condemnations, and confiscations which were unjustifiable from the same point of view. She freely admitted the principle of the American contention.[29] In the historic "bargain" of 1801 the United States finally swapped the spoliation claims for a release from all obligations founded upon the treaties of 1778, especially the burdensome guarantee of the French possessions in America.[30] The American naval operations of 1798–1800 did not upset the peace in relation to the neutrality provisions in Articles XIV and XXIV–XXVII of the Treaty of Amity and Commerce of 1778; and the spoliation claims, in consequence, were founded on valid obligations of France to the United States, because the contracting parties wanted it so to be. This is the main reason why the United States long ago should have compensated the sufferers from the French spoliations and why Congress should make an appropriation to pay at long last the awards of the Court of Claims that are still before Congress and unpaid.[31]

The great report on the spoliation claims made by Charles Sumner to the Senate on April 4, 1864,[32] and the *rationales* of the decisions of the Court of Claims in *Gray, Administrator,* v. *United States* and in *Cushing, Administrator,* v. *United States* [33] were written by firm believers in the doctrine of war in "the" legal sense and, therefore, bristle with untenable arguments. Yet, the decisions as such, which recognized the validity of the spoliation claims on the ground that there had been no war with France, are correct, correct like the decision of the Supreme Court in *Bas* v. *Tingy,* which, in relation to a different legal intent and purpose, on the contrary, declared France to be an enemy of the United States. The above decisions of the Court of Claims, on the one hand, and the decision of the Supreme Court, on the other, it will be observed, look like contradictory and inconsistent decisions under the doctrine of war in "the" legal sense. In reality each and every one represents sound legal judgment.

In summary, then, the following can be said about the famous old dispute as to whether from 1798 to 1800 France and the United States were legally at war: the American naval operations against France constituted war in relation to the intent and purpose of the seventh section of the statute of March 2, 1799, entitled "An Act for the Government of the Navy" and, furthermore, for the purpose of a reasonable and equitable application of the precepts taught in the second part of the eighteenth century by natural-law thinkers with regard to the treatment of prisoners of war. The same naval operations, on the other hand, left the United States and France at peace in relation to the intent and purpose of Article I, Section 8, Paragraph 11 of the Constitution of the United States and in relation to the intent and purpose of Articles XIV and XXIV–XXVII of their Treaty of Amity and Commerce of February 6, 1778.

This, incidentally, clearly demonstrates one thing. The answer to the question as to whether the United States is legally at war is a matter not of one determination, but of relative determinations, of as many determinations as there are rules of law on war in American municipal law and in the international law in force between the United States and other members of the family of nations. It cannot possibly be the well-settled law of the United States that the political department of the government, Congress, can provide the answer in one determination, and that the courts must take judicial notice of such determination and are bound thereby.[34]

Much confusion could be avoided by bearing in mind the simple verity that it is not possible to assert that certain operations do or do not *legally* constitute war, without relating such assertion to some rule of law on war. Arguing with *facts* alone will not do. Mere *facts* prove nothing. In *Gray, Administrator, v. United States* and in *Cushing, Administrator, v. United States* the United States substantiated its contention that between 1798 and 1800 there existed a war with France by pointing to the *fact* that battles were fought and blood was shed on the high seas. The Court of Claims admitted this and other *facts*, but contended that they did not constitute conclusive evidence of the existence of war.[35] In June, 1900, the British

Prime Minister, the Marquess of Salisbury, acknowledged the *fact* that the Taku forts had fired on the international forces without orders from the Government in Peking and then told the Chinese Minister in London that if the attacks by Chinese troops on Seymour's expedition were likewise without authority, there was no reason to consider that a "state of war" existed between the powers and China.[36] The Russian Minister of Foreign Affairs referred to another *fact*, the fact that the Czar had made known that Russia would evacuate Chinese territory immediately upon the restoration of orderly conditions, and he declared this *fact* to be "the best proof" for his contention that there was no war between Russia and China.[37] This was all "humbug" in the eyes of Kaiser Wilhelm II. He took it for granted that the powers and China were at war by considering other *facts*, the *facts* that—according to information that had reached him—representatives of the powers in Peking had been murdered, that hundreds of soldiers and marines had been killed, that the admirals of the international fleet at Taku were in distress, and that Peking had been stormed, burned, and sacked.[38] It is important to note that the United States, the Court of Claims, the British Prime Minister, the Russian Minister of Foreign Affairs, and Kaiser Wilhelm II all argued with mere *facts*, that they all failed to relate their findings to some rule of law on war. Their assertions as to the nonexistence or existence of war, therefore, were, from the *legal* point of view, altogether pointless, altogether "humbug."

Reasonable questions as to whether certain operations constitute war—like reasonable assertions as to the existence of war—must needs relate to some rule of law on war, if the questioner expects a *legal* answer. Unrelated questions are unanswerable, because they leave the person to whom they are addressed in the dark about the rule of law in relation to which he might either assert or deny the existence of war. Unrelated questions might well be parried by the request "Tell me what in law you are driving at." They are often answered, instead, by unrelated assertions or denials. Question and answer thus degenerate into an exchange of mere words without any legal meaning. Typical of such an exchange of mere words is the incident which occurred on February 14, 1854, in the House of Lords, when the Secretary of State for Foreign Affairs, Lord Clarendon, in reply to inquiries as to whether Great Britain then was at war or at peace with Russia, stated that the two countries were in "the intermediate state." [39] Another example of an unrelated answer to an unrelated question is the categorical "No" ventured either late in 1900 or at the beginning of 1901 in the Commission on the Budget of the Reichstag by the representative of the German Foreign Office in response to a debate as to whether Germany, in consequence of her participation in the Boxer Expedition, was in a "state of war," that is, at war, with China.[40] Why "No"? The debate from the legal point of view, it seems, was conducted *in vacuo*. It did not relate to any rule of law on war—not, for instance, to Article XI, Paragraph 2 of the Constitution of the German Empire of April 16, 1871, according to which the consent of the Bundesrat was required for a declaration of war by the Emperor, unless an attack were made upon the federal territory or its coasts.[41] It is interesting to note the appropriate answer given to an unrelated question by Secretary of War Henry L. Stimson when, on July 2, 1940, during a meeting of the Committee of Military Affairs of the Senate, he was asked by Senator Vandenberg whether or not opening of the American ports to the British and French navies would constitute an "act of war." Mr. Stimson finally replied, "I cannot answer that." [42] A question capable of receiving a legal answer might have been: "Would not opening of our ports to the British and French Navies for all repairs and refueling and other naval services constitute an act of war in relation to Article I, Section 8, Paragraph 11 of the Constitution and hence require the consent of Congress?"

It is sometimes not quite easy to see how certain operations can be related to any rule of law on war at all. Take, for example, the Spanish Civil War of 1936–39. It is a matter of common knowledge that during the Spanish Civil War the insurgent government at Burgos, headed by General Franco, was recognized by Germany and Italy as the Government of Spain and that General Franco, in his military operations against the Loyalist government in Valencia, was assisted by considerable contingents of German and Italian troops, such as the German "Condor Legion," which fought under their own command. No relation of international law existed between Loyalist Spain on the one hand and Germany and Italy on the other. German and Italian military operations, insofar, could not possibly constitute war in relation to any international rule of law on war. They did constitute war, however, in relation to certain German and Italian rules of municipal law. Captives taken by the German and Italian contingents were dealt with, it seems, in accordance with German and Italian army regulations concerning the treatment of prisoners of war.[43] It can be taken for granted, moreover, that the pay of German and Italian officers and men was increased to the amount which, according to law, was paid in time of war.

The answer to the question as to whether certain operations constitute war in relation to some rule of law on war and as to whether, in consequence, such rule applies, depends upon its intent and purpose. It is the business of interpretation to furnish that answer. It cannot be gleaned from anywhere else. Not from the fact that for or after the termination of operations the parties thereto conclude a treaty and style it a "treaty of peace." Not from the fact that titles of statutes enacted in connection with operations either do or do not speak of "war." Not from the fact that in diplomatic documents operations either are called "war" or are given some other name. Nor can the answer be gleaned from the fact that governments or members of parliament explicitly qualify operations as either constituting or not constituting "war." It is intended to consider these propositions more closely in the following paragraphs.

It sometimes happens that states conclude a treaty and style it a *"treaty of peace,"* even though neither of the contracting parties had conducted any operations against the other. Haiti and the Dominican Republic concluded a "Treaty of Peace, Friendship, and Arbitration" out of the blue sky on February 20, 1929.[44] Finland, three months after the Diet had declared her to be an independent state, concluded with Germany "the Treaty of Peace" of March 7, 1918, the fact notwithstanding that no military or naval operations had occurred between the two countries.[45] Czechoslovakia and Poland, though they had not yet existed in the period of World War I, belonged to the Allied and Associated Powers which, on June 28, 1919, signed with Germany the Treaty of Peace of Versailles. Nobody, it seems, would be prepared to conclude from these captions that among the contracting parties a war in any conceivable legal sense was terminated.

It is different, however, with "treaties of peace" that are concluded for or after the termination of operations. Nothing seems to be more natural than to point to the fact that for or after the termination of operations two countries conclude a treaty which they style a "treaty of peace" and to conclude from such a fact that they have been "legally" at war. In *Cushing, Administrator*, v. *United States* the United States substantiated its contention that there existed, from 1798 to 1800, a war between the United States and France by advancing, among others, the point that the treaty signed on September 30, 1800, between the French Republic and the United States was a "treaty of peace." [46]

Palmerston once reasoned in the same way. From September 24, 1845, to July 15, 1847, a British and a French squadron blockaded the ports and coasts of the province of Buenos Aires for the purpose of preventing ingress and egress not only of Argentine vessels, but of vessels of all nations. This blockade, like the French blockade of Buenos Aires and of the whole Argentine coast in 1838–40,[47] was accompanied by insignificant operations on land, operations which could not possibly be considered as constituting war in relation to the rules of customary law and of treaties which recognized such blockades as a means of warfare and of warfare only.[48] In a note of

December 7, 1846, to Lord Normanby, British Ambassador in Paris, Palmerston, then British Secretary of State for Foreign Affairs, wrote:

The real truth is, though we had better to keep the fact to ourselves, that the French and English blockade of the Plata has been from the first to the last illegal. Peel and Aberdeen [Prime Minister and Foreign Secretary respectively in the preceding British Cabinet] have always declared that we have not been at war with Rosas [dictator of the Argentine Confederacy]; but blockade is a belligerent right and . . . unless you are at war with a state you have no right to prevent ships of other states from communicating with the ports of that state. . . . I think it important, therefore, in order to legalize retrospectively the operations of the blockade, to close the matter by a *convention of peace* between the powers and Rosas.[49]

This line of reasoning is resorted to quite frequently in both theory and practice. It is fallacious nevertheless. Operations which do not constitute war in relation to a certain rule of law on war cannot be "converted" into war, war cannot be conjured up of nothing by the simple device of styling a treaty a "treaty of peace." It is a matter of no consequence that neither of the originals of the treaty signed by France and the United States on September 30, 1800, is obtainable—that supposed to be in the custody of France nor that supposed to be in the Department of State—and that hence the caption cannot be safely ascertained. Suppose that the contention of the United States in *Cushing, Administrator, v. United States* was correct and that the treaty had been styled a "treaty of peace." Such title could not possibly alter the fact that the naval operations conducted by the United States against France in the period from 1798 to 1800 did not constitute war according to a reasonable and equitable interpretation of Article I, Section 8, Paragraph 11 of the Constitution of the United States. Nor could such title alter the fact that these operations, according to the historical will of the contracting parties, did not constitute war in the meaning of Articles XIV and XXIV–XXVII of the Treaty of Amity and Commerce concluded by France and the United States on February 6, 1778.

It seems natural, on the other hand, to point to the fact that for or after the termination of operations two countries make a treaty which they do *not* style a "treaty of peace" and to conclude from such fact that "legally" they have not been at war. In the French spoliation cases the Court of Claims argued that the treaty of September 30, 1800, was merely a "Convention between the French Republic and the United States," not a "treaty of peace," and that, consequently, from 1798 to 1800 no war existed between France and the United States.[50] However, this line of reasoning too is fallacious, because the juridical nature of operations does not depend upon captions of treaties. Suppose that the Court of Claims was correct and that the treaty of September 30, 1800, was, indeed, merely a "Convention between the French Republic and the United States of America." Such title could not possibly alter the fact that the American naval operations of 1798–1800 did constitute war for the purpose of a reasonable and equitable application of the precepts taught in the second part of the eighteenth century by natural-law thinkers with regard to the treatment of prisoners of war, nor could such title alter the fact that these operations were war in accordance with a reasonable and equitable interpretation of the seventh section of the statute entitled "An Act for the Government of the Navy," of March 2, 1799.

Captions of treaties concluded for or after the termination of operations are chosen now for this reason, now for that.

The treaties by which the Ottoman Empire up to the middle of the eighteenth century terminated its numerous campaigns against Christian states, it seems, were always called "armistices." To make a "treaty of peace" with infidels was considered contrary to the Koran.[51]

The outstanding modern example of an unusual caption was furnished when the United States and Germany signed at Berlin on August 25, 1921, the "Treaty restoring friendly relations," [52] instead of the nonratified Peace Treaty of Versailles of June 28, 1919. This caption, certainly, was not intended to deny that the United States and Germany had been legally at war in a great many respects. It manifestly was chosen in consideration of the fact that the Congress of the United States had already passed the Knox-Porter resolution, approved July 2, 1921—a strange resolution as we shall see.[53] It had declared that the "state of war" between Germany and the United States had come to an end.

An important *legal* consideration seems to have been the reason why the powers terminated the Boxer Expedition by signing with China not a "treaty of peace," but the "Final Protocol" of September 7, 1901.[54] The military operations of the powers, it will be remembered, had been undertaken solely for the purpose of protecting the lives and property of foreigners. The United States had participated in the Boxer Expedition on orders issued by President McKinley, France on orders issued by President Loubet, Germany on orders issued by Kaiser Wilhelm II. The Congress of the United States, the French Chambers, and the Bundesrat had not been asked to consent to a declaration of war. It is significant that in the important Budget Commission of the Reichstag doubts could be heard as to the propriety of concluding with China under these circumstances a "treaty of peace." [55] The caption "Final Protocol," it seems, was deliberately chosen in order to point at those provisions in American, French, and German constitutional law which reserved the decision as to a declaration of war to the legislature. It served the purpose of denying the legal existence of war thus far and no further. It in no way prejudiced the decision in *Hamilton* v. *McClaughry, Warden* in which the Circuit Court for the District of Kansas recognized the American military operations during the Boxer Expedition as constituting war in the meaning of the fifty-eighth article of war.[56]

Titles of statutes enacted in connection with operations, like titles of treaties concluded for or after their termination, must be taken for what they are. Such titles are chosen for various reasons. They are not necessarily intended to qualify the operations to which they refer as constituting or not constituting war in relation to this or that rule of law on war. On May 28, 1798, Congress passed the important statute entitled "An Act More Effectively to Protect the Commerce and the Coast of the United States." In the French spoliation cases the Court of Claims considered that there was "nothing warlike" in this title and that nothing was said about war in the text; and it concluded that, therefore, in the opinion of Congress, no war was intended against France.[57] Yet, what mattered was not the title of the statute but what it ordered to be done. The act authorized the commanders of the armed vessels belonging to the United States to seize and to bring into port for adjudication any armed vessel of France which had committed depredations off the coast, or which should be found hovering off the coast for the purpose of committing depredations, and also to retake any American merchantman which might have been captured by any such armed French vessel.[58] To seize armed French vessels and to retake captured American merchantmen was not possible without engagements between French and American armed vessels and such engagements did constitute war for the purpose of a reasonable and equitable application of "the laws and customs of war." The right thing to do was to consider as enemies and to treat as prisoners of war captured persons commissioned by France and aiding that nation in her naval operations against American sea-borne commerce. The Act of May 28, 1798, in spite of its harmless caption and in spite of the fact that nothing about war was said in its text, thus started the United States on the road to war with France in relation to and as far as "the laws and customs of war" were concerned.

Likewise untenable is the conclusion that Congress intended no war against France, which the Court of Claims drew from the fact that two subsequent acts did not speak of war either. The Act of July 7, 1798, abrogating the treaty with France, spoke of the conduct of France as being "a system of predatory violence," and the Act of July 16 authorized an augmentation of the army for and during the "existing differences" with France.[59] France's indiscriminate seizure, condemnation, and confiscation of American ships and cargoes in her war with Great Britain, in other words, "the system of predatory violence," was one thing and the resulting "differences" with France another; still another was the American naval operations initiated by the Act of May 28, 1798, and intensified by the further Act of July 9, 1798.[60] There was no inconsistency in speaking of "a system of predatory violence" and of "existing differences" on the one hand and in recognizing, on the other hand, the American naval operations as constituting war in the sense of, for instance, the "laws and customs of war."

The fact that in *diplomatic documents* operations either are called "war" or are given some other name likewise should be taken at its proper value. The same is true of the fact that governments or members of parliament sometimes explicitly qualify operations as either constituting or not constituting war.

In *Gray, Administrator*, v. *United States* the Court of Claims contended that from 1798 to 1800 the United States and France had been at peace, because the uninterrupted continuance of peace was asserted in the diplomatic documents of that period and in statements made before both the Congress of the United States and the legislative assembly of France. It can easily be seen, however, that the quotation of these assertions of peace is beside the point. It is beside the point because —with one single exception—none of these assertions relates to the kind of peace upon the uninterrupted continuance of which the validity of the spoliation claims depended: peace, in spite of the American naval operations, in relation to Articles XIV and XXIV–XXVII of the Treaty of Amity and Commerce of February 6, 1778. The instructions of October 16, 1799, to Ellsworth, Davie, and Murray apparently depicted the restricted American naval operations as peaceful measures [61] in relation to a well-known rule of many "natural" international law systems, the rule in accordance with which only an all-out effort required a declaration of war.[62] John Marshall and Mr. Everett from Massachusetts, it would seem, had the same rule in mind, the former when, in his instructions of September 20, 1800, to the United States Minister to Great Britain, he referred to war only as a "probable event"; [63] the latter when he described the naval operations as "peaceful remedies and measures of defense" in his report submitted to the House of Representatives on February 21, 1835.[64]

Of other assertions of peace quoted by the Court of Claims it may well be doubted whether they concerned the American naval operations at all, let alone their relationship to Articles XIV and XXIV–XXVII of the Treaty of Amity and Commerce of 1778. Joseph Bonaparte and the other negotiators for France declared on August 11, 1800, that the "state of misunderstanding" which had existed for some time between France and the United States had not been "a state of war." [65] One year later the same plenipotentiaries contented themselves with characterizing "the relations" between the two powers at this period as an "almost hostile state." [66] Finally, when the report on the treaty of September 30, 1800, was laid before the legislative assembly of France, one of the French plenipotentiaries charged with its vindication announced that it was to terminate—not a war, but—a "misunderstanding" between France and the United States.[67] It is impossible to say whether or not the terms "state of misunderstanding," "relations," and "misunderstanding" were at all aimed at the American naval operations.

At least one assertion of peace referred to by the Court of Claims clearly does not concern the American naval operations at all but is merely a statement of French policy instead. "France . . . never thought of making war against them [the United States]," wrote Talleyrand as Minister of Foreign Affairs on August 28, 1798, at a time when he still was unaware of the Act of July 9.[68] Likewise an assertion, not of peace but of war, which the Court of Claims—quite unnecessarily—tried to refute, had nothing to do with the American naval operations. The Act of April 27, 1798, went no further than to authorize the President to procure and fit out a number of armed vessels, not exceeding twelve. It was passed in the House amid great excitement nevertheless. Edward Living-

ston, who closed the debate on the part of the opposition, said
he considered the country now in a "state of war" and "let no
man flatter himself that the vote which has been given is not a
declaration of war." [69] In spite of the pseudotechnical language in which it was wrapped, this was clearly a somewhat
extravagant *political* statement made for the purpose of accus-
ing President John Adams' Administration and the Federalists of dragging the United States into a war with France. It
had absolutely nothing to do with the American naval operations, operations which were instituted weeks later by the
Acts of May 28 and July 9, 1798. The statement, therefore,
was of no concern to the Court of Claims, whose task it was
to answer the question whether or not the American naval
operations constituted war in relation to Articles XIV and
XXIV–XXVII of the Treaty of Amity and Commerce of
1778.

Of all the assertions of peace quoted by the Court of Claims
only one is to the point because it relates more or less clearly to
the above treaty provisions, to the kind of peace upon the
uninterrupted continuance of which the validity of the spoliation claims depended. The report made by Mr. Chambers to
the Senate on May 24, 1828, says in substance that the conduct
of the United States ordered by the several acts of Congress
"cannot be considered as placing the two countries in the attitude of war, which would destroy the obligations of previously existing treaties." [70]

The above way of reasoning with diplomatic documents
and with statements made by governments and in parliaments
has many parallels in the legal history both of the United States
and of other countries. Suffice it to recall the speech made over
the radio on August 23, 1937, by Senator Key Pittman of
Nevada. In that speech the chairman of the Senate Foreign
Relations Committee defended President Roosevelt's reluctance to declare that a "state of war" existed in China and
thereby to put into operation the provisions of the Neutrality
Act of May 1, 1937. Both China and Japan, Senator Pittman
said, denied that a "state of war" existed.[71] This was strange

reasoning. The expression "state of war" (war in "the" legal sense), as has been said before, does not make sense. Let us suppose, therefore, that the operation of the Neutrality Act depended upon the existence of "war," and that Japan and China denied such existence. It would have been probable then, but not by any means certain, that Japan and China had the Neutrality Act in mind when they denied that "war" existed. Supposing they did, it still remains true that their denials, as a matter of course, would have been prompted by their respective interests and not by an objective interpretation of the Neutrality Act. Nothing, therefore, would have justified Senator Pittman in jumping from the Chinese and Japanese denials to the conclusion that no war existed in relation to and in the meaning of the Neutrality Act.

In this connection the geographically restricted military operations and the rudimentary naval operations which have gone down in history as the "Boxer Expedition" are of particular interest. They are referred to in diplomatic documents by the greatest variety of expressions. These expressions seemingly run the whole gamut from "most cordial relations" to "war." [72] An attempt to answer the question of the applicability of rules of law on war through reference to the expressions used in the diplomatic correspondence will from the outset come to naught in cases like this one. The variety of expressions seems to be perplexing. Yet it is perplexing only to him who fails to realize that there are also a variety of standpoints from which the Boxer Expedition could be looked at. Except for "de facto state of war," an expression as senseless as "state of war," something is to be said for every one of the expressions employed, depending upon the point of view one chooses. The terms "war," "actual warfare," "warlike acts," "hostilities," "military measures," "military action," and "enemy" (with regard to the Chinese armed forces), are each appropriate from the point of view of common sense and common parlance. So also are the expressions "intervention," "armed intervention," "expedition" and "punitive expedition." The latter expressions, moreover, are plausible from a legal point of view, in the light, namely, of American, French, and German constitutional law. They served the purpose of emphasizing that in the opinion of the respective governments the operations of the Boxer Expedition did not constitute war in relation to those provisions in American, French,[73] and German constitutional law which reserved the war-making power to the legislature. The term "most cordial relations," which the Emperor of China employed in his letter to President Loubet of France, it goes without saying, was not aimed at the Allied operations at all. It was used, instead, for the political purpose of underscoring the conciliatory disposition of the Chinese Government and of projecting a rapprochement between China and France.

The answer to the question as to whether certain operations constitute war in relation to some rule of law on war ought not to be given by relying upon names employed in diplomatic documents or upon explicit qualifications made by governments, even if it can be established that such names and such qualifications do have a legal bearing, and a legal bearing, at that, upon exactly that rule of law on war the applicability of which we should like to ascertain. It would be a mistake to accept at their face value the language of diplomatic documents and of declarations made by governments. Governments, in order to escape from the legal or political consequences of their conduct, sometimes do not say what they mean or do not mean what they say. On April 23, 1793, at the start of the war between France, the ally of the United States, and Great Britain, Washington issued what was in substance a declaration of neutrality, but sidestepped the word "neutrality" in conformity with a compromise arrived at in the Cabinet.[74] The Traité Politique signed by France and Annam on March 15, 1874, established in fact a French protectorate over Annam but the word "protectorate" had been crossed out at the last moment. In the same treaty the Court of Hue was dubbed an "allied government" as though it were a partner in a love match, not in a shotgun marriage.[75] It is with such information in mind that one also should approach diplo-

matic documents and explicit qualifications made by governments. Names and explicit qualifications sometimes are used
as a smoke screen in special pleading. Ferry, no doubt, knew
that the operations against Annam in 1882–84 and against
China in 1883–85 constituted war in relation to the war-
making power of the chambers. He was resolved, however,
to humbug and "manage" a pacifically disposed Parliament
from behind a façade of misrepresentation. In order to short-
circuit the democratic process of a declaration of war Challemel-Lacour, Minister of Foreign Affairs, referred to the operations against Annam as a "footing of hostility," "expedition,"
and Ferry to the operations against China as "state of reprisals," "state of hostility," "demi-belligerency." [76] Both Challemel-Lacour and Ferry tried to get around the Constitution
by conspiring with each other to call a spade by another name.

Attention ought to be drawn here to one further untenable
way of arguing the question as to whether certain operations
constitute war in relation to a given rule of law on war. The
answer to that question sometimes is gleaned from the fact that
some *other* rule of law on war either does or does not apply.
Both the United States and the Court of Claims reasoned that
way in the French spoliation cases. [77]

It will hardly be necessary to insist upon the fallacy of this
way of reasoning. It overlooks the all-important fact that the
various rules of law on war have different intents and purposes. It proceeds from the illusion that the definition of war
required by the various rules of law on war is *semper idem*. It
rests, in other words, on the obsolete theory of war in "the"
legal sense. The fact that some rule of law on war applies does
not mean that all others should apply also. Vice versa, the fact
that some rule of law on war does not apply does not by any
means settle the question as to the existence of war "in all its
bearings." [78]

Incidentally, the doctrine of war being legally semper idem
would, if followed in practice, lead to tragic results. Fortunately states often meant less than what they said, if they contended that they were "legally" not at war. Often what they

meant to say in fact was that they were not at war in relation to this or that rule of law on war.

Thus Ferry's denial that France was legally at war with China in 1883–85 was by no means intended to include "the laws and customs" of war on land. Both the Minister of War and the Minister of the Navy assured Clemenceau in the meeting of the Tongking Commission of October 24, 1884, that captured Chinese soldiers were being treated as prisoners of war.[79] In 1885 the prisoners of war were exchanged in accordance with an oral agreement.[80]

In 1931–32 the Japanese Government denied that their military operations against China in Manchuria and around Shanghai amounted to war. Yet what the Japanese Government actually denied was that the Japanese military operations constituted war in the meaning of Article 16 of the Covenant of the League of Nations. Both Japan and China are parties to the Hague Convention (IV) of 1907 Respecting the Laws and Customs of War on Land. The Japanese third fleet operating with marines around Shanghai enlisted the service of Dr. Jumpi Shinobu, Japan's greatest authority on international law, in order to make sure that the operations were conducted in accordance with the provisions of this convention.[81] From 1937 to 1941 the Japanese Government again contended that it was not conducting a war against China. Whatever the meaning of the Japanese contention, it clearly was not intended to mean that the Japanese military operations did not constitute war in the meaning of the Hague Convention (IV). In September, 1937, the Japanese Government unofficially acknowledged that the "incident" insofar did constitute war.[82] After the capture of Nanking in December, 1937, the Japanese Army—certain units excepted—disregarded the above acknowledgment. It indulged in wholesale looting of the city, violation of women, and mass execution of Chinese captives. Civilians of both sexes and all ages were likewise shot by the Japanese. It is noteworthy, however, that high Japanese officers and diplomats, while admitting the excesses, tried to explain them by saying that a section of the

Japanese Army got out of hand and that the atrocities were being committed unknown to the Japanese High Command in Shanghai.[83]

The definitions of war required by the various rules of law on war vary greatly in their respective latitudes. Some rules, the "laws and customs" of war on land or at sea, for instance, spring into life at the slightest provocation. Others are less likely to become applicable. Such, for instance, is the case with certain rules respecting the conduct of neutral powers. Still other rules call for a very narrow definition of war. Such rules, therefore, remain dormant while most other rules apply. Article I, Section 8, Paragraph 11 of the Constitution of the United States is a rule in point. It has been pointed out above that there is no reason why Congress should enact a declaration of war as long as operations are instituted by Congress itself and not by the President in his capacity as Commander in Chief of the Army and Navy.[84]

It is interesting briefly to compare "the laws and customs" of war on land and at sea with rules respecting the conduct of neutral powers.

First, the "laws and customs" of war on land. In the Hague Convention (II) of 1899 and (IV) of 1907 the contracting powers agreed on such important provisions as the prohibition of the use of poison or poisoned weapons; the prohibition of killing or wounding an enemy who, having laid down his arms or having no longer means of defense, has surrendered at discretion; the prohibition of employing arms, projectiles, or material calculated to cause unnecessary suffering; the prohibition of pillaging a town or place; the treatment of the armed land forces of the enemy, in case of capture, as prisoners of war.[85] The intent and purpose of these provisions is to humanize operations on land. In the preamble of the two conventions the contracting parties stated that the drafting of the rules was "inspired by the desire to diminish the evils of war." Whether or not military operations are accompanied by naval operations, whether they are geographically limited or not, whether they are conducted by large units or merely by minute detachments, whether they extend over a period of years or last a few minutes only, all this cannot possibly make any difference for the application of the above rules of law on war. Mere border incidents, engagements which in common parlance nobody would call a "war," are thus elevated to the rank of war in relation to the above provisions. The "battle" of San Ignazio of June 15, 1916, was fought between a detachment of seventy-five officers and soldiers of the Constitutionalist Army of Mexico and two troops of United States cavalry. It lasted for about half an hour early in the morning and was over when President Wilson heard about it.[86] Still it was considered as constituting war between Mexico and the United States in the meaning of Article 3 of the Annex to the Hague Convention (IV) of 1907. The Court of Criminal Appeals of the State of Texas decided that the defendants in the case of *Arce et al.* v. *the State of Texas* were not "bandits" but Mexican soldiers, and it actually recognized them to be prisoners of war. They were treated with all the consideration due to their status and turned over to the Mexican consul at Laredo, Texas, to be taken back to Mexico.[87]

In the period from May 24, 1915, to August 27, 1916, Germany assisted Austria-Hungary in its military operations against Italy with three divisions. It has been established that both Germany and Italy considered the German military operations in this period as being war in the sense of the Red Cross Convention of 1906.[88] It can be taken for granted that both Germany and Italy likewise applied the Hague Convention (II) of 1899 Respecting the Laws and Customs of War on Land.[89] The two conventions are inspired by the same idea, the humanization of warfare.

Secondly, rules on neutrality. Two illustrations will suffice to demonstrate that rules on neutrality are slower in becoming operative than are "the laws and customs" of war on land or at sea.

There are operations which constitute war in relation to the "laws and customs" of war on land or at sea, but do not constitute war in the sense of any rule on neutrality. This can be the case if operations on land or at sea are of short duration. The battle fought off Oran, Algeria, between a British and a French battle squadron on July 3, 1940, is an example in point. It will be remembered that it was fought to determine the issue whether France should carry out a previous agreement to hand over its navy to Great Britain or abide by the terms of the Franco-German armistice, which stated that all warships should be taken to French ports and disarmed. The action lasted an hour and twenty-seven minutes and ended in the destruction or crippling of the French warships which lay at Oran.[90] It was over when the third powers heard about it. The question as to whether they should adopt an attitude of neutrality in conformity with the rules on neutrality did not present itself at all. The battle of Oran, on the other hand, no doubt, constituted a naval war in relation to and in the meaning of, for instance, the customary rule of international law which prescribes that as soon as an attacked or counterattacked vessel hauls down her flag, and thereby signals that she is ready to surrender, she must be given quarter and be seized without further firing.[91]

Other operations do not raise the problem of neutrality at all though they are conducted during a considerable length of time. The Boxer Expedition was conducted practically without naval operations.[92] Third powers, therefore, did not have to consider their rights and duties as neutrals in naval warfare. The military operations, on the other hand, were participated in by all the powers bordering on China, with the exception of Korea, and were confined to the province of Chihli.[93] Under these circumstances it is small wonder that third states were not expected to issue declarations of neutrality in warfare on land.

Following the preceding observations on the rules of law on war as they are, something remains to be said de lege ferenda. The interpretation of a legal term sometimes is not delegated to those who must apply the rule of law concerned. It is supplied, instead, by the makers of the rule. The makers of a rule of law on war themselves thus might interpret the word "war" in accordance with their intent and purpose. It is a delicate but not by any means an impossible task to decide whether such an interpretation ought to be furnished and, if so, how it ought to be formulated, provided only that the why and wherefore of the rule is clearly kept in mind.[94] In this connection an incident might be recalled which occurred on July 12, 1907—seven years after the Boxer Expedition—in the second subcommission of the second Hague Peace Conference. Colonel Ting, Chinese delegate, suggested that "war" be defined by agreement for the purpose of Article 1 of the Hague Convention (III) of 1907 Relative to the Opening of Hostilities in which "the contracting Powers recognize that hostilities between themselves must not commence without previous and explicit warning, in the form either of a reasoned declaration of war or of an ultimatum with conditional declaration of war." [95] Colonel Ting stated: "It might be well to define what is meant by the term 'war,' for it has often been made under the name of expedition as may be learned from numerous instances that can be found in the history of my own country." [96]

The suggestion by the delegate of China, however, was not even debated. The consequence is that Article 1 of the Hague Convention (III) of 1907—like Article 16 of the Covenant of the League of Nations—lacks precision. It is not clear just what operations constitute "war" and, consequently, ought to be declared in accordance with this important provision of international law.

The relative meaning in rules of law of the terms "war" and "peace" could be discussed ad infinitum. In the subsequent sections of this chapter the discussion will be confined to some outstanding aspects of such relativity. Before approaching these aspects attention must once more be given to the great variety of terms pointed out at the end of Chapter II.[97]

First, terms in connection with the ideas of war and peace as such.

It has been shown above why there can be no such thing as

a "state of war" or "de jure war" (war in "the" legal sense). There can, in consequence, be no such thing as a "state of peace" or peace in "the" legal sense.

Regarding the term "war" it has been pointed out that much confusion could be avoided by bearing in mind a simple verity. It is not possible to assert that certain operations constitute war *legally* or that they do not without relating such assertion to some rule of law on war.[98] The same, of course, is true of the expressions "act of war," "de facto war," and "belligerency." The assertion that certain operations are an "act of war" or "de facto war" or "belligerency," in order to make sense *legally*, must relate to some rule of law on war. There is no potency in these terms irrespective of the intent and purpose of a rule of law on war.

Secondly, terms in connection with the idea of war part way.

The expressions "imperfect state of war," "limited state of war," "partial state of war," "incomplete state of war," and "quasi state of war," it goes without saying, stand and fall with the expression "state of war." Their highly technical ring is likely to mystify the unsuspecting student. Says Mephistopheles:

> "Man usually believes, if only words he hears,
> That also with them goes material for thinking."

The expressions "imperfect war," "limited war," "partial war," "incomplete war," and "quasi war" likewise are useless as far as the law is concerned. Their uselessness is obvious. The mere expression "partial war," for instance, tells nothing. It immediately raises the question: "partial" in relation to and in the meaning of which rule of law on war? Yet what is the use of stating that certain operations do not have all, but only a part of the characteristics required for the application of some rule of law on war? It is tantamount to stating that such rule does not apply. Rules of law either apply or do not. *Tertium non datur*. There can be no "partial" application.

Thirdly, terms suggestive of a twilight zone of war: "intermediate state," "state of hostilities," "measures short of war."

"Intermediate state." The uselessness of this term again is evident. It represents some of the worst kind of legalistic verbiage that can be imagined. There could be no "intermediate state" even if there were such things as a "state of war" (war in "the" legal sense) and a "state of peace" (peace in "the" legal sense). To assert that certain operations constitute an "intermediate state" would be tantamount to asserting that they constitute neither war nor peace. The rules of law on war would be inapplicable because there is no war and applicable at the same time because there is no peace. This is a contradictory and, hence, an unintelligible assertion.

The motive which prompted Lord Clarendon to coin the expression "intermediate state" in the House of Lords on February 14, 1854, shortly before the outbreak of what in history is called the Crimean War, was not the inherent merits of the words, on any level, but a genius for putting the obvious in terms of the unintelligible which always has been a trade practice of diplomacy. The Secretary of State for Foreign Affairs merely wanted to say that Great Britain was drifting toward war. Instead of leaving it at that, he added, ". . . I consider that we are in the intermediate state." One of the lords laughed aloud. He did well to laugh.[99]

"State of hostilities." Makers of rules of law sometimes employ the term "hostilities." It is as good a term as "operations." In Article 1 of the Hague Convention (III) of 1907, for instance, the contracting parties might well have spoken of "operations," instead of agreeing that "hostilities" between themselves must not commence without previous explicit warning, in the form either of a reasoned declaration of war, or of an ultimatum with a conditional declaration of war.[100] The term "hostilities," if employed in a rule of law, must be understood in the light of the intent and purpose of such a rule. Its meaning is apt to vary from rule to rule. There can be no "state of hostilities" (hostilities in "the" legal sense) for the same reasons which stand in the way of a "state of war" (war in "the" legal sense).

Sir William Scott (later Lord Stowell) referred on December 7, 1798, in the case of the *Santa Cruz*, to the American naval operations against France as "the present state of hostilities (if so it may be called) between America and France" because he was "embarrassed" and unable to make out whether these operations were legally war or peace.[101] It is in the nature of man to appease any frustration of his inquisitiveness by giving a name to a phenomenon that he cannot understand and to accept that as an explanation.

It is easy to discern the reason which prompted the Japanese Government in 1940 to assert the existence of a "state of hostilities" in China.[102] France was under no obligation whatsoever to see to it that no ammunition and military supplies were reaching Generalissimo Chiang Kai-shek from Indo-China. The high-sounding but empty term "state of hostilities" was a veil thrown about the Japanese claim to hide its lack of justification.

"Measures short of war." In a much-noted article which appeared in the *Rivista di Diritto Internazionale* in 1915, Arrigo Cavaglieri, prominent Italian jurist, pointed to the complete dissension among writers on international law as to the enumeration and classification of "the measures short of war." He attributed such dissension to a lack of methodical thinking.[103] This is a thesis to which one can readily subscribe. Studying some dissertation on "measures short of war" as a rule leaves the student more puzzled and amazed than he was before the exposition began.[104] The core of the objections against the dissertations on "measures short of war," including Cavaglieri's above-mentioned article, lies in the fact that their authors invariably adhere, in one way or another, to the state-of-war theory or theory of war in "the" legal sense. The meaning of the word "war" in the rules of law on war, as will be abundantly clear by now, cannot be squeezed into a mold of a particular size and shape. The expression "measures short of war," as such, in consequence, is legally meaningless. It immediately raises the question "short of war in relation to and in the meaning of which rule of law on war?" Yet there is no practical need for stating that such and such measure is short of war in the sense of some rule of law on war, of Article I, Section 8, Paragraph 11 of the Constitution of the United States, for instance. Such a statement is the same thing as the statement that Article I, Section 8, Paragraph 11 of the Constitution does not apply. There is, of course, no objection to "measures short of war" as an expression in common parlance. It may be so used, like "war," "peace," or "act of war." President Roosevelt employed the term in that sense in 1939.[105] The lend-lease aid extended by the United States to various countries in the course of World War II thus can be appropriately termed a "measure short of war." As a technical, legal term, however, the expression "measures short of war" ought to be sponged off the slate.

It is said, by and large, that there are three kinds of "measures short of war": armed intervention, armed reprisals, and pacific blockade. The meaning of these terms will be considered separately in the three subsequent sections of this chapter.

SECTION 2. ARMED INTERVENTION

Complaints about the dissension prevailing in legal writings with regard to the term "measures short of war" reach a crescendo with some legal writers who have more particularly dealt with "intervention." Here exists "the most absolute disagreement" according to Cavaglieri.[1] "With regard to no other term probably have so many stupidities been said and so many errors been committed," stated Ellery C. Stowell, Professor of International Law at the American University of Washington, D.C., in a lecture on intervention at the Hague Academy of International Law in 1932.[2] To this one will readily subscribe after having ploughed through the vast legal literature regarding intervention.

What are the basic facts from the legal point of view? Consulting writers on international law conveys the impression that there exist a great many rules of international law prescribing the conditions under which intervention is allowed or prohibited. It would, however, be a mistake to take it for granted that such actually is the case. What are passed off as rules of international law on intervention are on the whole not rules consented to by two or more members of the family of nations in the shape either of a treaty provision or of international customary law. These rules, on the contrary, are a discordant medley of natural law,[3] of hastily construed rules of international customary law,[4] which in fact are "all mere book rules, fancies of their authors," [5] and of preachments for political purposes. Some writers manifestly expand and others contract the circle of conditions under which intervention is allowed or prohibited according to the policy of the country to which they belong and the national interests which they try to promote. The alleged rules of international law on intervention, in short, are on the whole not rules of positive law. Past interventions of states between other states or in the internal affairs of another state thus, as a rule, were not resorted to in accordance with or in disregard of particular rules of law on intervention. They were based instead solely on considerations of political expediency.

Rules of positive law on intervention are very rare, so rare that any international lawyer will find it difficult to enumerate a full dozen. The outstanding example of a rule of law on intervention in American legal history is furnished by Article III of the amendment which Congress appended to the Army Appropriation Bill of 1901 on a motion brought forward by Senator Orville H. Platt of Connecticut. The Platt amendment contained the conditions under which the United States would evacuate Cuba. Its provisions were made treaty provisions in the treaty concluded on May 22, 1903, by the United States and Cuba.[6] They were, furthermore, appended to the Constitution of Cuba of February 21, 1903.[7] As expressed in Article III of the treaty of May 22, 1903, the terms of the Platt amendment were:

The Government of Cuba consents that the United States may exercise the right to intervene for the preservation of Cuban independence, the maintenance of a government adequate for the protection of life, property and individual liberty, and for discharging the obligations with respect to Cuba imposed by the Treaty of Paris on the United States, now to be assumed and undertaken by the Government of Cuba.

On May 29, 1934, the two parties, in accordance with President Roosevelt's "Good Neighbor" policy, concluded a new treaty which abrogated the right of the United States to intervene in Cuba.[8]

Most important among all the rules of law on intervention ever made, no doubt, is Article 8 of the Convention on the Rights and Duties of States, signed at Montevideo, December 26, 1933, by the United States and other American republics. "No State has the right to intervene in internal or external affairs of another." [9] In Article 1 of the Additional Protocol, signed at Buenos Aires, December 23, 1936, "The High Contracting Parties declare inadmissible the intervention of any *one* of them, directly or indirectly, and for whatever reason, in the internal or external affairs of any other of the parties." [10]

Now to the problem of defining intervention legally. It is generally held that the student can look up "the" legal definition of intervention in the textbooks on international law. Yet "the" legal definition of intervention cannot be accomplished. It cannot be accomplished for the same reasons which stand in the way of "the" legal definition of war. It would be difficult, if not impossible, to gather together for interpretation all the past and present rules of law on intervention though they are few in comparison with the legion of past and present rules of law on war. It is, furthermore, impossible to interpret unknown rules of law on intervention, rules that might be made in the future. There is, above all, the possibility that the various rules of law on intervention, like the rules of law on war, are made with varying intents and purposes and that hence they require various legal definitions of intervention.

The term "intervention," like the term "war," might be made precise and unequivocal through an express agreement as to what it means. The delegation of the United States to the Seventh International Conference of American States at Montevideo in 1933 signed the Convention on the Rights and Duties of States with a reservation in which *inter alia* it is said:

I feel safe in undertaking to state that under our support of the general principle of *non-intervention*, as has been suggested, no government need fear any *intervention* on the part of the United States under the Roosevelt administration. I think it unfortunate that during the brief period of this conference there is apparently not time within which to prepare *interpretations* and *definitions* of these fundamental terms. . . . Such interpretations and definitions would enable every government to proceed in a uniform way without any difference of opinion of interpreting. I hope that at the earliest possible date such very important work will be done.[11]

It is not too much to say that there are almost as many textbook definitions of intervention as there are of war. Almost all of these definitions, like almost all of the textbook definitions of war, are unsubstantiated.[12] As regards the few writers who have gone to the trouble of arguing their definitions, it is easy to show that they have made one or another of the mistakes that have been made in arguing the question as to what legally constitutes war. To give an example, the fact that a certain way of conduct has been *called* intervention, no matter where and by whom, is no reason for considering it as legally constituting "intervention."[13] He who relies upon what has been *called* "intervention" might conclude his investigation with the statement that intervention by a state may be anything from standing aside and doing nothing to participation in a world war. The Cabinet of Dr. Ramon Grau San Martin, Provisional President of Cuba from September 10, 1933, to January 15, 1934, was not recognized by the United States. In October, 1933, Dr. Grau urged recognition by the United States among other reasons "because non-recognition in our case signals a new type of intervention—intervention by inertia—if nothing else, in our internal affairs."[14] It will be remembered, on the other hand, that in May, 1915, Italy decided upon "intervention" in World War I. Prominent among the "*interventisti*" were D'Annunzio and Mussolini.

The term "intervention," as applied to *operations*, it would seem, is not more than about 120 years old. The very word "intervention" conjures up the memory of the Holy Alliance and the policy which it pursued in the interest of legitimacy after the downfall of Napoleon. It brings to mind, among other things, the military operations to restore the absolute monarchy which Austria conducted against Naples and Piedmont in 1821 and France against Spain in 1823. These and similar military operations have gone down in history as "interventions." They were, however, not officially so styled. Neither the Protocol of the Congress of Troppau of 1820 nor the Declaration of the Congress of Laibach, in which the courts of Austria, Prussia, and Russia affirmed and reaffirmed their policy of upholding absolute monarchy wherever threatened, employs the term "intervention." [15] The official appellation, instead, was "interference" or "interposition." In his famous message to Congress of December 22, 1823, President Monroe referred to the French "interposition" in Spain and warned the powers of the Holy Alliance against any such "interposition" with the former Spanish colonies and new republics of Latin America.[16]

Other operations have been styled "intervention" *officially*. President Taft in his annual message to Congress of December 3, 1912, for instance, referred to the "intervention" of the United States in Nicaragua.[17]

In still other instances the official appellation varies. Operations are styled sometimes this way, sometimes that way. The Loyalist Government of Spain usually denounced as "intervention" the operations by which Italy and Germany from 1936 to 1939 aided the cause of the Nationalist (Insurgent) Government of Generalissimo Franco.[18] Now and then, however, it called these operations "war." [19] The Italian contingent of "volunteers," numbering 100,000 men at its maximum strength, and the German Condor Legion—some 15,000 strong and dispatched secretly to fight under the camouflage of Spanish uniforms—were long publicly denied by their own governments. The Condor Legion did not come into its own until its return home from the Civil War in Spain. The German Government then finally acknowledged the Condor Legion as part of its regular armed forces, organized by its army, navy, and air force staffs and sent to Spain at the command of the Führer and Chancellor of the Reich. On June 6, 1939, the Legion held its victory parade in Berlin before Adolf Hitler and was then welcomed home in a speech in which Hitler defiantly proclaimed: ". . . your *war* in Spain was a lesson to our enemies and therewith also a *war* for Germany." [20] Simultaneously Premier Mussolini, in an order of the day, greeted 20,000 Italian troops returning to Naples "after thirty months of victorious *war* against the democracies and bolshevism." [21] The Italo-German operations in Spain thus were officially now "intervention," now nameless, now "war."

Both lawyers and historians might well ponder the question why it is that in the nineteenth and the twentieth centuries so many operations have been *officially* styled "intervention." This question, however, cannot be answered with certainty. It is often impossible to say what the exact motives of representatives of states were in referring to operations of their armed forces as "intervention." There is no acid test for the intended meaning of such words. One has to hazard personal judgments in such matters.

What interests Americans most is the series of armed interventions in the Caribbean and in Central America which began under the first administration of President Theodore Roosevelt and ended with the evacuation of Haiti in 1934. In this series there are cases which have been officially styled as "intervention" and other cases which were only unofficially thus called. It is not easy to separate one category from the other. A perusal of the messages and papers of the presidents, of the published diplomatic correspondence of the United States, of the annual reports of the Secretaries of War and of the Navy, and of occasional statements released by the State, War, and Navy Departments to the press conveys the impression that there were but a few cases which have been officially called "intervention." President Taft, in his annual message to

Congress of December 3, 1912, as mentioned above, referred to the "intervention" of the United States in Nicaragua.[22] President Theodore Roosevelt and Secretary of State Elihu Root termed as "intervention" the occupation of Cuba by the Army of Cuban Pacification in 1906–9.[23] Rear Adm. H. S. Knapp, Military Governor in the Dominican Republic in 1917 and special emissary to Haiti in 1920, employed the term "intervention" for the operations of the Marine Corps in Haiti and in the Dominican Republic.[24] It must be left undecided whether President Wilson and his Secretaries of State and of the Navy did so too. There are signs that they did.[25] After 1920 it seems no American operations occurred which were officially styled as "intervention." Presidents Coolidge and Hoover and their Secretaries of State and of the Navy did not apply the term "intervention," for instance, to the extended operations of the Navy and of the Marine Corps in Nicaragua in 1926–33. These operations in fact remained nameless.

Various interpretations can be put upon the above ex officio uses of the term "intervention."

No speculative mind reading is needed to explain its use in connection with the operations of the Cuban Army of Pacification in 1906–9. The occupation of Cuba by sailors, marines, and an expeditionary force of the regular army in consequence of the Cuban Revolution of 1906 clearly was intervention under the authority of and in relation to the Platt amendment.[26]

It likewise seems to be clear why the Military Governor in the Dominican Republic and the special emissary of the State and Navy Departments to Haiti spoke of "intervention." The term "intervention," like the term "war," has its more or less precise meaning in common parlance. It conveys the idea of a state dealing with affairs, internal or external or both, of another state. It can be assumed that Rear Admiral Knapp, being an officer and not a lawyer or statesman, simply used everyday language. Dealing on the part of the United States, and on a vast scale at that, with affairs of other states, this, indeed, is what occurred in Haiti from 1915 to 1934 and in the Dominican Republic from 1916 to 1924. In the Dominican Republic, for instance, the Marine Corps not only established internal peace by wiping out banditry and by creating a national constabulary but, through all sorts of governmental activities, laid the foundation for a stable and self-supporting democratic government capable of maintaining order by itself and of observing its international obligations. The military government thus engaged in road building, sanitation, and development, in reforms of public instruction, of the internal revenues, and of the tariff, in a reorganization of the mail service and of the telegraph and telephone lines, and in the establishment of a topographical and cadastral survey and of a meteorological service.[27]

From a purely military point of view, it ought to be added, the operations in both Haiti and the Dominican Republic were minor affairs as far as American battle casualties are concerned. From 1915 to 1920, the period of the relatively most intensive operations, the marines suffered in Haiti a total of forty-one battle casualties.[28] These operations, furthermore, were not conducted against the Haitian or Dominican Armies. In Haiti they were directed against the "Cacos," bandits pure and simple and makers of one Haitian revolution after another,[29] and in the Dominican Republic against rebel soldiers, released convicts, and bands of outlaws.[30] The operations of the marines in both Haiti and the Dominican Republic thus were in the nature of police measures. One hesitates to call such operations "war." "Intervention" surely was a more appropriate term.

In contrast to this there seems to be a calculated *political* and *legal* design running through the term "intervention" as used by President Taft with regard to the operations of the Navy and of the Marine Corps in Nicaragua in 1912 and as supposedly used by the State Department and President Wilson with regard to the operations of the Marine Corps in Haiti and the Dominican Republic.

First a *political* design. "Intervention" was an appropriate term to indicate that the United States was not actuated by

any land hunger, that, on the contrary, it pursued the following objectives: (1) To give adequate protection to American
lives and property and to foreign interests as well.[31] (2) To
stiffen the independence and to strengthen the political and
economic stability of the republics in the strategic proximity
of the Panama Canal in order to prevent pretexts or justifica-
tions for intervention—after the fashion of Venezuela [32]—by
some non-American power that might threaten the new
Atlantic-Pacific life line of the United States.[33] The Government of the United States plainly assured the Haitian and Dominican peoples that it had no design upon their territorial
integrity and political independence.[34] It is significant that
President Theodore Roosevelt thought that "intervention"
was the right word to characterize operations undertaken in
pursuit of such a policy. In his annual message to Congress of
December 6, 1904, he said:

Chronic wrongdoing, or an impotence which results in a general
loosening of the ties of civilized society, may in America, as elsewhere, ultimately require *intervention* by some civilized nation,
and in the western hemisphere the adherence of the United States
to the Monroe Doctrine may force the United States, however
reluctantly, in flagrant cases of such wrongdoing or impotence,
to the exercise of international police power.[35]

Secondly, a *legal* design. "Intervention" was an appropriate
term to indicate that, in the opinion of the Taft and Wilson
Administrations, the operations in Nicaragua, Haiti, and the
Dominican Republic did not constitute an executive assumption of the war-making power which, according to Article I,
Section 8, Paragraph 11 of the Constitution of the United
States, belongs to Congress. To give such indication was important in a governmental system of "checks and balances"
with its accompanying jealousy of prerogatives and watchful
suspicion, aggravated by the fact that the chief executive in
the United States is the leader of a party. In 1920 Senator Warren G. Harding, as Republican nominee for president, made
an issue of both Haiti and the Dominican Republic in one of

his front-porch addresses at Marion, Ohio. The United States, he asserted, was at war then with the two little helpless republics "through the usurpation by the Executive of powers not only never bestowed upon him but scrupulously withheld by the Constitution." [36]

The question of how far the chief executive can go in using the armed forces of the United States without legislative permission commanded the particular attention of William H. Taft. In 1906, while Secretary of War, in agreement with the Judge Advocate General, he informed President Theodore Roosevelt that the United States under the Platt amendment could intervene in Cuba without such permission.[37] Ten years later ex-President Taft touched upon the subject again in a series of lectures delivered at Columbia University.[38]

Most important, however, is the fact that the Taft Administration took great pains to justify constitutionally the intervention of 1912 in Nicaragua. It did so through an elaborate memorandum of the solicitor for the Department of State of October 5, 1912, entitled *Right to Protect Citizens in Foreign Countries by Landing Forces.*[39] It appears from the memorandum that time and again American presidents have used the armed forces of the United States without legislative authority for the purpose of protecting American lives and property in foreign parts whenever it was necessary to do so and that Congress, by silent acquiescence, has approved of such practice. The exigencies of the situation, by the way, would often have rendered it impossible for the President to ask Congress, by its consent or leave, and an effort to do so would in many cases have resulted in a failure to give timely protection. This clearly means that a substantially uniform practice, approved of by Congress, has come to recognize such use of the land and naval forces of the United States as a right of the President and as not constituting war in relation to and in the meaning of Article I, Section 8, Paragraph 11 of the Constitution. It is a prerogative that grew up and developed from the power of the President as Commander in Chief of the Army and Navy and from his duty of conducting the foreign relations of the United

States. The operations in Nicaragua in 1912, in Haiti from 1915 to 1934, and in the Dominican Republic from 1916 to 1924 were all partly conducted for the purpose of giving protection to American lives and property. In consideration of Article I, Section 8, Paragraph 11 of the Constitution of the United States the term "intervention," therefore, was well chosen by the Taft and Wilson Administrations.

These operations, as has been pointed out previously, were also conducted in pursuance of the Panama policy of the United States, a policy which was most clearly expressed in the Platt amendment. In 1906 President Theodore Roosevelt, under the Platt amendment, had sent the Cuban Army of Pacification into Cuba without asking for legislative permission. The Congress had acquiesced in such use of the Army, Navy, and Marine Corps by the Chief Executive. It was only a small step from this to acquiescing in the use of the armed forces of the United States by the President in pursuance of the same policy toward other countries situated in the strategic proximity of the Panama Canal. Congress could be reasonably expected so to interpret its power under Article I, Section 8, Paragraph 11 of the Constitution, even though, when the interventions were started, there existed no treaty provisions after the fashion of the Platt amendment between the United States on the one hand and Nicaragua, Haiti, and the Dominican Republic on the other.[40] It did, in fact, so interpret it without serious questioning. Neither was such interpretation seriously questioned by public opinion.[41] With a view to constitutional law it can be said once more that in the above instances the term "intervention" was well chosen.

The official employment of the term "intervention" in the United States in the present century, be it said again, seems to be motivated by a consideration of mere facts and by political and legal designs.

It is the legal design which requires some additional elaboration. It cannot be strongly enough emphasized that the term "intervention" employed with this design meant peace in relation to Article I, Section 8, Paragraph 11 of the Constitution of the United States. The implied denial of the existence of war went that far and no further.

The intervention in Nicaragua in 1912 was in the words of ex-President Taft "quite a campaign." [42] The Secretary of the Navy, in his annual report for the fiscal year 1913, refers to this campaign as "an illustration of the courage and conduct of the officers and men of the navy under fire and during the most trying conditions." [43] The operations performed in Haiti, particularly in the period from July 9, 1915, to December 6, 1915, again were a real man's work, requiring of the personnel of the Navy and the Marine Corps all the qualifications of good soldiers. To commemorate their services the Haiti campaign badge was issued to all officers and enlisted men who participated in those operations during the above-mentioned period.[44]

It goes without saying that the pay of the officers and men who participated in the intervention in Nicaragua in 1912 and in the intervention in Haiti during the above period would have been increased to the amount provided for in time of war if the Navy Appropriation Act of June 30, 1909, which at this time regulated the pay of the navy personnel,[45] had differentiated between peace and war. Such, however, was not the case. The Act for the Better Organization of the Line of the Army of the United States of April 26, 1898, which regulated the pay of the army,[46] provided for a differential pay; the Act of June 30, 1909, did not. It is interesting, however, to note that certain officers and men of the Marine Corps who participated in the operations in Haiti in 1915 are now entitled to a war pension. In August, 1917, the Navy Department announced the award of medals of honor to certain officers and men of the Marines Corps "for conspicuous gallantry in the presence of the enemy in Haiti in 1915." [47] An Act of April 27, 1916,[48] concerns persons at the age of sixty-five who have served in the military or naval service of the United States "in any war" and who have been awarded a medal of honor for having in action with an enemy distinguished themselves conspicuously by gallantry or intrepidity, at the risk of their lives, above and beyond the call of duty. Such persons, if honorably discharged from service, shall by the Secretary of War or of the Navy be listed on "the Army and Navy Medal of Honor Roll" and be entitled to a special pension of $10 per month for life. Judging from the practice of the Navy Department [49] there could never be any doubt that the above-mentioned recipients of the medal of honor are entitled to such pensions. In relation to and in the meaning of the Act of April 27, 1916, the Cacos were an "enemy" and the intervention in Haiti a war.

The Articles for the Government of the Navy list certain offenses of persons in the naval service of the United States, such as desertion, sleeping on watch, and leaving station, [50] which are differently punished depending on whether they are committed "in time of war" or "in time of peace." Such offenses, if committed "in time of war," may be punished by death. None of these offenses were committed either in the course of the "intervention" in Nicaragua in 1912 or during the above-mentioned period of the "intervention" in Haiti. But let us assume, for the sake of the argument, that they did occur. There can be no doubt that the court-martial would have considered them as having been committed "in time of war." The manifest intent and purpose of the above rules is to give the navy, while engaged in combat operations, increased protection against the dereliction of important duties. The navy needs such increased protection no matter against whom its operations are conducted. The opposing forces may be a regular army or navy. They may be a revolutionary army as was the case during the "intervention" in Nicaragua in 1912. They even may consist of brigands as was the case with the Cacos during the "intervention" in Haiti in 1915–33.

Lastly, the Government of the United States, in accordance with a general principle of law, considers as an international delinquency and makes reparations for injurious acts committed by its armed forces to another state in time of peace. It thus has paid the Swiss Government $16,000,000 for damages done inadvertently in World War II when American fliers

dropped bombs on the peaceful and friendly city of Schaffhausen and other places in Switzerland.[51] The United States
Government did not assume such responsibility for the losses
sustained by Nicaragua, Haiti, and the Dominican Republic
in consequence of the American "intervention." In other
words, it considered these "interventions" as *insofar* constituting war.

In brief, then, it amounts to this: Operations which, for one
reason or another, are called "intervention," may well constitute war in relation to and in the meaning of many a rule of
law on war.

SECTION 3. ARMED REPRISALS

Regarding the term "reprisals" there is one basic legal fact
which ought to be clearly kept in mind. Of positive rules of
law on intervention it has been said above that they are very
rare. Of positive rules of law on reprisals it must now be stated
that they are extremely rare in municipal law and completely
absent in modern international law. Article I, Section 8, Paragraph 11 of the Constitution of the United States contains a
rule of law on reprisals and a perfectly obsolete one at that.
Article I, Section 8, Paragraph 11 gives to Congress not only
the power to declare war, but also the power to "grant letters
of marque and reprisals."

From what has been said above about "the" legal definition
of war and "the" legal definition of intervention it is clear that
any attempt to lay down "the" legal definition of reprisals
must likewise come to naught. The same cogent reasons which
prevent the achievement of "the" legal definition of war or of
intervention likewise prevent the achievement of "the" legal
definition of reprisals. The expression "state of reprisals" (reprisals in "the" legal sense) is a mocking term like the expression "state of war" (war in "the" legal sense). A legal definition of the term "reprisals" thus must relate to some specific
rule of law on reprisals in the same way as a legal definition of
war must relate to some specific rule of law on war and a legal

definition of intervention to some specific rule of law on intervention. Hence the possibility of a variety of legal definitions also for the term "reprisals." Textbook definitions of the term "reprisals"—they are as a rule unsubstantiated assertions—are as useless as the textbook definitions of war, of intervention, and many other allegedly legal definitions.[1]

It can easily be seen that the term "reprisals" in rules of law on reprisals has various meanings.

In Article XIV of the Treaty of Peace of Rijswijk of September 20, 1697, concluded between France and England, William III, King of England, promised to issue in the future "letters of marque and reprisals" against the subjects of France only to those of his subjects to whom justice had been manifestly denied in France. King Louis XIV of France, vice versa, promised to issue in the future "letters of marque and reprisals" against the subjects of the English crown only to those of his subjects to whom justice had been manifestly denied in England.[2] What were meant here were *special* "letters of marque and reprisals," to wit, a document granted by a sovereign to an individual who had been injured abroad and was unable to get redress there. Such documents authorized the bearer to capture at sea an equivalent for his losses from any of the subjects of the state that refused to grant redress. The word "marque" (German, *die Marken*) indicated the permission to pass the jurisdictional limits of one's sovereign and the word "reprisals" the permission for a taking in return. This crude mode of redress through self-help flourished chiefly from the thirteenth through the sixteenth century. It began to disappear when state navies began to assume the control of the seas. It had sunk into entire disuse by the end of the eighteenth century, the time when the Constitution of the United States was made.[3]

The words "letters of marque and reprisals" in Article I, Section 8, Paragraph 11 of the Constitution of the United States, therefore, must mean something else. It is not possible to say with what intention the founding fathers wrote them into the Constitution since there was no comment or debate as to their

meaning in the Constitutional Convention. Practice, however
—as evidenced, for example, by the Act of June 24, 1812, declaring war between the United Kingdom of Great Britain
and Ireland and the United States [4] and by a further Act of
June 26, 1812 [5]—has taken these words as meaning two things,
both known as *general* letters of marque and reprisals. First, a
commission issued by Congress to a privately owned, fitted-
out, armed, and manned ship which, like her commission, was
called a "letter of marque and reprisals." Secondly, a commission issued by Congress to a privately owned, fitted-out,
armed, and manned ship which usually was called a "letter of
marque" or a "privateer." A ship called a "letter of marque
and reprisals" was an armed *trading* vessel that was authorized
to capture ships and cargoes belonging to citizens of a third
state. A "letter of marque" or "privateer" did no trading at all,
but was commissioned to serve solely as a cruiser.[6] The United
States never employed "letters of marque and reprisals." It is
interesting, however, to note that in 1834 President Jackson
recommended their employment against French merchantmen and cargoes when the Chamber of Deputies temporarily
refused to appropriate $25,000,000 which the government of
King Louis Philippe had acknowledged as being due by France
to the United States.[7] Regarding "letters of marque" or "privateers" it has been pointed out above [8] that probably over a
thousand were commissioned in the course of the American
naval operations against France in 1798–1800. Commissions
were again issued for the war of 1812.[9] It might be added that
in 1861–65 the Navy of the Confederate States of America
consisted solely of "letters of marque" or "privateers."

The parties to the famous Declaration of Paris of April 16,
1856, evidently intended to suppress the employment of both
types of ships, "letters of marque and reprisals" and "letters of
marque" or "privateers" when in its first article they declared:
"Privateering is and remains abolished." [10]

Something different, therefore, is meant if Great Britain in
modern Orders in Council uses the term "general reprisals."
The term in this connection means the operations of the Brit-

ish fleet for the purpose of seizing all enemy ships and goods.[11]

Indeed it can easily be seen that the meaning of the term "reprisals" in the rules of law on reprisals varies.

Although the rule of law on reprisals in Article I, Section 8, Paragraph 11 of the Constitution of the United States is obsolete, it is interesting to consider briefly the relationship of reprisals in the sense of this rule to war in the sense of some rules of law on war. The United States never employed ships called "letters of marque and reprisals," but came close to it, as has been said above, under President Jackson. Suppose that Congress had followed Jackson's recommendation and authorized "letters of marque and reprisals" to capture French merchantmen and cargoes on the high sea and to bring them into port for adjudication. Such reprisals under Article I, Section 8, Paragraph 11 of the Constitution, because authorized by Congress itself, certainly would not have constituted war in relation to and in the meaning of the rule, likewise contained in Article I, Section 8, Paragraph 11, which confers upon Congress the power to declare war.[12] The task of making captures, of bringing them into port for adjudication, and of condemning them as lawful prizes, however, would have presented a different picture. There existed, with one single exception,[13] in this respect no rules of law on reprisals. Under these circumstances, if any, the rules of law regarding the making, bringing in, and condemnation of captures in *war* would have had to be applied.[14] The operations of American "letters of marque and reprisals" against French merchantmen and cargoes thus would have been reprisals in the sense of Article I, Section 8, Paragraph 11 of the Constitution of the United States and would at the same time have constituted war for the purposes of naval prize law. There are in other words operations which legally are both reprisals and war just as there are operations which in law are both intervention and war.

Operations officially styled as "reprisals" are not uncommon. Such ex officio employment of the term "reprisals," as a rule, however, cannot be traced and related to some rule of law on reprisals. Such rules, as has been said before, are extremely rare in municipal law and completely absent in modern international law. Operations in other words have been styled as "reprisals" not because they constituted reprisals in the sense of this or that rule of law on reprisals, but for some other reasons. What are these reasons? This question again cannot be answered with certainty. The motives which actuated officials in resorting to the term "reprisals" are often secrets locked in their breasts. One has again to hazard personal judgments. One thing only is certain beyond peradventure. Whatever the term "reprisals" is intended to mean, certainly it cannot mean that the operations concerned are "measures short of war."

In the eighteenth century the word "reprisal" in its wider ordinary sense simply meant some *limited* operation for the purpose of retaliation, such as the besieging of a town or the sinking of a fleet.[15] This meaning still lingers in the term as it is used today. It seems likely that the German Government employed the term with this meaning in mind, when on June 1, 1937, it declared that the day before German warships had bombarded the Mediterranean seaport of Almeria "in reprisal" for the Loyalist air attack on the pocket battleship *Deutschland*. Such interpretation is supported by the fact that Joachim von Ribbentrop, the German Ambassador to London, at once assured the British Government that Germany would not undertake any further retaliatory measures against the Valencia Government.[16] To emphasize the limited character of the German naval operation was important in view of the tense international situation created by the Almeria bombardment. The French Government in all probability had the same meaning in mind when it announced on September 25, 1940, that the day before French aviation had taken "reprisals" for the Free French and British sea attack on the French West African port of Dakar by a prolonged bombardment of Gibraltar.[17] The term "reprisals" characterized the bombardment of Gibraltar as an isolated operation. It indicated that

France had no intention of starting against Great Britain all-out operations with whatever armed forces were left to her after the armistices with Germany and Italy.

There is no use in raising the question what the bombardment of Almeria was in the light of this or that rule of law on war, at least not as far as international law is concerned. There were, as has been pointed out, no relations of international law between Germany and Loyalist Spain after Germany had recognized the Nationalist (Insurgent) Government of Generalissimo Franco as the government of Spain. From the point of view of international law the bombardment of Almeria was like shooting into no man's land. The question of how the "reprisals" against Gibraltar relate to the rules of law on war, on the contrary, might well be raised. At least four of the French bombers were shot down by a heavy antiaircraft barrage from shore guns and warships, chiefly on September 25 when waves of French bombing planes sweeping across the Straits from Morocco hammered Gibraltar in a second day of "reprisal" attacks.[18] Some of the attacking airmen parachuted on the "Rock" and were captured there. Such captives, it goes without saying, were not hired assassins and incendiaries, but prisoners of war in accordance with the Geneva Convention Concerning the Treatment of Prisoners of War, of July 27, 1929. They were prisoners of war, the fact notwithstanding that they had been ordered by the Vichy Government on a mission of "reprisals." A communiqué issued on September 25 by the military authorities of Gibraltar accurately spoke of "enemy" planes.[19]

There is still another meaning to the term "reprisals" in its ordinary sense, a meaning that dates back to the days when sovereigns used to issue *special* "letters of marque and reprisals." Such letters, as has been said above, were issued to individuals who had been injured abroad and there had suffered a *denial of justice*. From ages past this idea of a denial of justice still echoes in the term "reprisals." Operations thus may be styled as "reprisals" in order to proclaim that they are serving a just cause. "Right makes might." The sheer belief in right too makes might. The name "reprisals," no doubt, has often been advanced not as a bona fide assertion but as a red herring drawn across the trail of the main issue.[20] Suffice it to recall that in 1884 Jules Ferry applied the term "state of reprisals" to the French operations against China, senseless and unjust operations calculated to enforce the payment of an outrageous "indemnity" for the "trap" of Bac-Le.[21] This—besides being a legalistic trick with which we shall deal hereafter—in all probability was also an attempt to dress Ferry in a shining armor of innocence. While it had no relation to the truth, it certainly did have some propaganda value.

The term "reprisals," finally, is used for the purpose of camouflaging illegitimate operations—operations undertaken in contravention of this or that rule of law on war—as legitimate reprisal operations. Here then, lest we lose our bearing, we must not for one moment lose sight of the one hard fact that there are in modern international law no rules on reprisals. The total absence of rules on reprisals in modern international law, was acknowledged by Politis in 1934 at the Paris session of the Institut de Droit International.[22] Under modern international law, there can be, therefore, no reprisal operations, either legitimate or illegitimate. That Ferry spoke of a "state of reprisals" in order to advertise the righteousness of his cause is highly probable. That he used this term as a means of legalistic camouflage is certain. Ferry, it will be remembered, called that "state of reprisals" a "*legal* situation." What Ferry was accused of in the Chamber of Deputies in November, 1884, was a violation, through a war waged against China without preliminary consent of Parliament, of Article 9 of the French Constitutional Law of July 16, 1875. Instead of answering that accusation Ferry talked beside the point. The words "situation," "reprisals," and "state" were all part and parcel of a maneuver calculated to obscure the issue. The issue, in point of fact, was not a nebulous "situation," but something quite concrete, namely, the French military and naval operations against China. The issue, in point of law, was a provision of the French Constitution. Instead of dealing with the French Constitution

Ferry alluded to fictitious rules on reprisals in international law. Clemenceau was amply justified in ridiculing Ferry's "state of reprisals" as a "baroque epithet," and the Duke de Broglie in satirizing it as a "finesse of international law." [23] It is significant that Ferry never attempted to substantiate his assertion. Any attempt to do so would at once have laid bare the hollowness and pretext of this sort of verbiage.

From the legal point of view the French military and naval operations were war in many respects, notwithstanding the fact that they had been officially styled as a "state of reprisals." They were war, for example, in relation to and in the meaning of (1) Article 9 of the French Constitutional Law of July 16, 1875, (2) the "laws and customs" of war regarding the treatment of captives, (3) the rules of law on war which authorize the French fleet to capture vessels of third states for the carriage of contraband of war and for breaking a blockade.

Thirty-nine years later, on September 18, 1923, the Council of the League of Nations listened to an argument which reminds one of Ferry's "state of reprisals."

On August 27 General Tellini, chief of the Italian delegation in the international commission charged with establishing the frontier between Albania and Greece, had been murdered with his suite by unknown perpetrators on the street between Jannina and Santi Quaranta, that is, on Greek soil. The Italian Government held the responsibility of Greece to be involved. It seemed anxious to show that Fascist Italy could take up a determined position in foreign politics. In an ultimatum of August 13 it demanded reparation through the performance by the Greek Government of not less than four expiatory acts, including a solemn funeral service in the Catholic cathedral at Athens to be attended by the Greek Cabinet *in corpore* and the payment of fifty million lire. The Greek Government rejected several points of the ultimatum, in particular the demand for a pecuniary reparation. On August 31 an Italian squadron therefore bombarded and occupied the city of Corfu as a pledge to secure the reparation which Italy had demanded. Sixteen persons, almost all Greek refugees from Asia Minor and Armenian orphans, were killed; thirty-two persons were wounded.[24]

On September 1, the Greek Government brought its dispute with Italy to the attention of the League of Nations. The Greek appeal mentioned Articles 12 and 15 of the Covenant, but not Article 16, the article which provided for sanctions against any member of the League resorting to war in disregard of its obligations under Articles 12, 13, and 15 as to the settlement of a dispute.[25] Branting, the Swedish delegate to the Council meeting, nevertheless intimated that the Italian naval operation constituted an act of war under Article 16 and that it might set a dangerous precedent.[26] In the Council meeting of September 18 the Italian delegate Salandra attempted to refute such accusation by explaining the Italian naval operation "very clearly" and placing it "in its proper *legal* perspective." [27] Salandra, like Ferry, alluded to fictitious rules of international law on reprisals. These rules, he contended, had not been abrogated by the Covenant. They gave Italy a "right" to bombard Corfu and to occupy it temporarily to insure reparations. The Italian naval operation against Corfu, therefore, was "legitimate." Italy had committed no act of war. It is significant that Salandra made no attempt to prove when and how Italy had ever contracted such a rule of law on reprisals with Greece, let alone all the other states members of the League of Nations. Any attempt to do so would at once have come to naught. To allude, as Salandra did, to unspecified treatises on international law was beside the point. International law is a law made in the shape of contractual obligations by the states members of the family of nations, not a law "laid down" by writers on international law.[28] The truth of the matter is that before the advent of the League of Nations other states, France and Great Britain for instance, had now and then temporarily occupied foreign territories for the purpose of securing compliance with certain demands, such as a demand for reparation, and that such operations, either officially or unofficially, had been called "reprisals" as a matter not of right but of fact. Great Britain, as late as 1895, for a period of

about ten days had occupied the customhouse and other government buildings at Corinto, Nicaragua, and had seized all
vessels carrying the Nicaraguan flag in order to secure reparations from Nicaragua for the imprisonment and expulsion of
British subjects without due process of law.[29] France, as late
as 1901, had occupied the customhouse on the Turkish island
of Mytilene for the purpose of compelling the Porte to give
in to certain French demands.[30]

It is a moot question whether the bombardment and the
temporary occupation of Corfu was an act of war under Article 16 of the Covenant. This question might have been answered by the advisory opinion of the Committee of Jurists
which the Council of the League of Nations appointed after
the Corfu incident for the purpose of interpreting certain
provisions of the Covenant. This advisory opinion referred to
"coercive measures which are not intended to constitute acts
of war," but gave no explanation as to what these words
meant.[31] The definition of war in relation to and in the meaning of Article 16 of the Covenant hence remained uncertain.

Still it is certain that the Italian naval operation legally
would have constituted war in at least one respect provided
that both Greece and Italy had ratified the Hague Convention
(IX) Concerning Bombardment by Naval Forces in Time of
War.[32] Such, however, was not the case.[33] The commander
of the attacking Italian naval force, nevertheless, issued a warning before commencing the bombardment. He furthermore
directed the fire against the citadel, a military establishment,
not knowing, as Salandra later on assured, that it sheltered
refugees and orphans. He thus spared buildings not used for
military or naval purposes, such as sacred edifices and hospitals. Though he had been sent on a mission of "reprisals"
only, the Italian commander actually complied with Articles
2, 5, and 6 of the above-mentioned Convention regarding
naval warfare, as though both Greece and Italy had been
parties to it.[34]

To sum up: operations which for one reason or another are
called "reprisals"—like operations which for one reason or

another are called "intervention"—far from being "measures short of war"—may well constitute war in relation to and in the meaning of this or that rule of law on war.

In the final analysis it all comes down to this: names do not change the legal nature of operations. In the light of the rules of law on war they remain what they are regardless of their name and regardless of whether they are named at all. The operations of the United States marines in Nicaragua in 1926–33, characterized as "intervention" by historians, to give an example, were in relation to the rules of law on war what they were despite the fact that they remained officially nameless operations. Actions, as the Romans said, must be judged *non ex nomine sed ex re.*

Section 4. Pacific Blockades

The term "pacific blockade" is now just about a hundred years old. It was coined by Laurent Basile Hautefeuille, a prominent French lawyer and legal writer in the days of King Louis Philippe and Napoleon III. The expression made its first appearance in 1849 in Hautefeuille's "*Des Droits et des Devoirs des Nations Neutres en Temps de Guerre Maritime.*" [1] In the course of the second half of the nineteenth century "pacific blockade" turned up as a subject either advocated or opposed by practically every textbook on international law. The "pacific blockade," furthermore, has been dealt with in monographs on blockades [2] and in several special monographs.[3] Among the monographers Mr. Falcke stands head and shoulders above his fellow writers. His monograph published in 1909 and 1920 and translated into French by Dr. Contat, of Bern, is the result of many years of painstaking research and study. In addition to the private writings on "pacific blockade" there appeared in 1927 "A Memorandum on Pacific Blockade up to the Time of the Foundation of the League," issued by the legal section of the Secretariat of the League of Nations.[4]

With the exception of Mr. Falcke's monograph the writings

on "pacific blockade" are on the whole open to serious objections in points of fact. From the first to the last and including even Mr. Falcke's monograph, they are furthermore open to serious objections from the point of view of the law.

First, objections in points of fact. The writings on "pacific blockade" are filled with historical inaccuracies. Quite a few of these turn up in the thirteen "precedents" with which Ferry showered the French Chamber of Deputies on November 26, 1884.[5] Mr. Falcke has well taken care of these and many other factual errors. It is not necessary, therefore, to enter here upon a detailed historical criticism. Suffice it to give two striking examples of what is meant by historical inaccuracy.

It all started with Laurent Basile Hautefeuille. Hautefeuille, without quoting any source, wrote that in 1827 France, Great Britain, and Russia blockaded those regions of Greece which were then occupied by Turkish armies.[6] This, as we have seen above,[7] is not true.[8] Subsequent writers on international law, however, accepted Hautefeuille's statement without questioning. The assertions of peace made to the Sublime Port by the ambassadors of France, Great Britain, and Russia after the battle off Navarino [9] were later on erroneously taken as relating to the fictive blockade of 1827, and so arose what has been called the "mother" of the pacific blockades, "the pacific blockade of the coasts of Turkey of 1827." This "mother" has shown a remarkable vitality. She wandered from textbook to textbook and finally settled down at Geneva, Switzerland, exactly 100 years after the battle off Navarino. In the above-mentioned memorandum on pacific blockades issued in 1927 by the legal section of the Secretariat of the League of Nations we read, "The first blockade of this kind was established in 1827 when England, France, and Russia blockaded the coasts of Turkey. Since then there have been about twenty pacific blockades." [10]

Among the twenty blockades listed by the Secretariat of the League of Nations as "pacific" figures the blockade which the Sardinian admiral Persano from January 20 to February 13, 1861, directed against Gaeta, refuge of Francis II, last King of the Two Sicilies. This blockade has been called "pacific" for a strange reason. The diplomatic representative of King Victor Emmanuel II of Sardinia to the Court of Naples, it is said, was in Gaeta and assured Francis II daily of the friendship of his sovereign.[11] It has been pointed out above that these assertions of friendship never occurred. They belong to the realm of historical myth.[12]

The "mother" of "pacific blockades" and the "daughter" thus are both concoctions of fact and fiction. The mother is concocted of an imaginary blockade and actual assertions of peace. With the daughter it was the other way around. Her component parts are imaginary assertions of friendship and an actual blockade.

Secondly, objections in point of law. Students of international law complain that they do not understand the "theory" of pacific blockade, that they are unable to see what *legal* reasons make a blockade "pacific." No wonder. Who does understand the "theory" or rather "theories" on "pacific blockade"? The writings on "pacific blockade" are on the whole not only historically inaccurate but filled with unsolved legal perplexities and pitfalls.

Some supposedly legal dissertations on "pacific blockade" [13] are legal dissertations in appearance only. In point of law they are actually written *in vacuo*. Their authors argue constantly with the mere words "war" and "peace." The words "war" and "peace" as such and all by themselves are believed to be sufficient to make sense legally. This, as we have seen above,[14] is an illusion. It amounts to a mere play with words. The words "war" and "peace," in order to have a legal meaning, must relate to some rule of law on war, or maybe some rule of law on peace. Dissertations disregarding this simple verity necessarily defy understanding.

Other writers—the German Perels [15] and the Swede Söderquist,[16] for instance—measure blockades with the yardstick of what they consider to be "the" legal definition of war. "Pacific," according to them, are those blockades which do not measure up to such definition. War, Söderquist asserts, consists of operations and counteroperations. A blockade, therefore, is "pacific" if it is not reciprocated by operations on the part of the blockaded state. This line of argument needs hardly any comment. Enough has been said already against "the" legal definition of war.

It is easy to guess why the above-mentioned memorandum of the League of Nations lists the French blockade of the island of Formosa of 1884–85.[17] This blockade is considered as having been pacific on account of the assertions of peace made by Ferry before the French Parliament and to the British Government. But assertions of peace ought not to be run home on a legal single-track mind without any consideration for anything else. Such assertions do not necessarily have a legal meaning but might have instead—like the assertions of peace made in Constantinople in 1827—a political or some other meaning. Assertions of peace made with a legal intention, that is to say, assertions of peace aiming at this or that rule of law on war, might be feints, feints like Ferry's peace assertions of 1884–85. They should not therefore without questioning be accepted as correct. Ferry's assertions of peace were not by any means aimed at the blockade of Formosa and at the right of France to establish it. What Ferry actually had in mind was Article 9 of the French Constitutional Law of July 16, 1875, and the prohibitions under international law and under the British Foreign Enlistment Act of 1870 to use Hongkong as a supply base in case France and China were at war.[18]

If it comes to the problem of segregating the "pacific blockades" *legally* from the war blockades, one will find a flaw even in Mr. Falcke's otherwise level-headed and accurate treatise. In the first part of his treatise Mr. Falcke describes twenty blockades which by writers on international law have been *called* "pacific." [19] In the second part the writer eliminates at first two cases because the blockades said to have existed in fact never occurred. So far, so good. A flaw in the argument, however, appears when Mr. Falcke eliminates six cases more because there existed according to him "undoubtedly" a war between the blockading and the blockaded state. One is left to wonder why in six cases a war undoubtedly existed. Mr. Falcke, it seems, takes it for granted that a blockade remains legally "pacific" by virtue of mere *facts*, especially by virtue of the fact that it does not lead to any fighting between the forces of the blockading and the blockaded state. Blockades with only a small amount of fighting still are "pacific." Beyond a certain measure of fighting war begins. Mr. Falcke admits that there might be doubtful cases but recommends considering them as being "pacific."

This separation also is untenable. Above all, it is not a *legal* separation. It does not rest on any *legal* consideration. It is drawn solely in consideration of a fact, namely, the greater or lesser amount of fighting. Mr. Falcke himself does not show an absolute trust in his own method of segregation. The elimination of eight cases leaves him with twelve "pacific blockades." He leaves it to the discretion of the reader either to accept his list or further to eliminate one case or another.[20]

The question arises whether or not in the end the theories on "pacific blockade" represent an idle play with words, filled with pitfalls into which so many have fallen so often. After years of discussion the writers on "pacific blockade" still do not seem to know whether this term points to any practical problem at all. On December 17, 1902, Prime Minister Balfour stated before the House of Commons that "there can be no such thing as pacific blockade." [21] Has the glamour of the expression "pacific blockade" faded out? Ought it to be relegated to the limbo of things to be forgotten?

We submit that the expression "pacific blockade" after all does have a practical significance.

It does not make sense to expect *legal* results by measuring blockades with the yardstick of some book definition of war, the yardstick of official assertions of peace, or the yardstick of such facts as the greater or lesser amount of fighting between the blockading and the blockaded state. It does make sense, however, to measure blockades, like other naval operations, with the yardsticks of the various rules of law on war. A blockade is "pacific" if it does not measure up to what is meant by "war" in some rule of law on war. A blockade, while not measuring up to what is meant by "war" in one rule of law on war, might, however, still measure up to "war" in the meaning of a second rule. One and the same blockade can thus be both "pacific" and a war blockade, pacific in relation to and in the meaning of a first rule and a war blockade in relation to and in the meaning of a second rule. These rather abstract assertions will at once become clear by a concrete practical demonstration.

On August 25, 1937, Japan clamped down a blockade against all *Chinese* shipping, official and private, on the Chinese coast from the mouth of the Yangtze to near the southern tip of China. Twenty days later this blockade was extended to the whole length of China's 2,150-mile coastline, from the Manchukuo border to the border of Indo-China.[22] Was this a pacific blockade? The answer depends upon the kind of rule of law on war to which it relates. If one relates this blockade to Sections 1 and 2 of the American Neutrality Act of May 1, 1937,[23] the answers are both "Yes" and "No," "No" in relation to Section 1 and "Yes" in relation to Section 2. The war envisaged in Section 1, as has been shown above, is a different thing from the war that was required for the application of Section 2.[24] The blockade was a war operation, a war blockade in relation to and in the meaning of Section 1, because it was accompanied by fighting on a large scale on land, affording thus the American "merchants of death," against whom Section 1 was directed, an opportunity to proceed to their sinister machinations. From a purely legal point of view the blockade would amply have justified the laying of an embargo on the export of arms, ammunition, and implements of war to both China and Japan. The political considerations which explain the failure to find that war (a "state of war") existed and, in consequence, the nonapplication of the Neutrality Act have been pointed out above.[25] The same blockade, on the contrary, was a pacific blockade in relation to and in the meaning of Section 2. It was a pacific blockade because it was not operated against the shipping of third powers. It was directed against Chinese shipping only. There was no reason to proclaim that war (a "state of war") in the meaning of Section 2 existed and consequently to apply the "cash-and-carry" clauses, because it was the intent and purpose of Section 2, it was the *ratio legis*, to keep American ships and cargoes out of harm's way created through the establishment of blockades or the issuing of contraband lists. As it was, the Japanese Navy interfered with foreign trade on neither ground. Thus one and the same blockade can legally be both a pacific blockade and a war blockade.

The term "pacific blockade" in law, in other words, has a relative not an absolute meaning. It has a relative meaning like the terms "war," "peace," "intervention," "reprisals." Textbook definitions made with the intention of defining the term "pacific blockade" once and forever [26] are of no use. The term "pacific blockade" does not indicate what many think it does,[27] namely, a definite and stable legal "institution."

It is interesting to note that from the *legal* point of view a blockade can be pacific in spite of the fact that a great amount of fighting occurs between the blockading and the blockaded power and that, vice versa, a blockade can be a war blockade in spite of the fact that no fighting at all occurs. The above-mentioned Japanese blockade of the Chinese coast was pacific in consideration of Section 2 of the American Neutrality Act of May 1, 1937, in spite of the battles fought on Chinese soil between Japanese and Chinese troops. It would have been a different story with a blockade instituted in contravention of the Convention Defining Aggression signed at London on July 3, 1933.[28] In this Convention—which had been fathered by Litvinov—Afghanistan, Esthonia, Latvia, Iran, Poland, Romania, Turkey, and the Union of Soviet Socialist Republics defined "in the interest of general security" the kind of war which they previously had "renounced" through becoming parties to the Briand-Kellogg Pact of August 27, 1928. In Article II the contracting parties agreed to consider as an aggressor the state which first shall have committed one of a series of acts. The act enumerated in the fourth and last place of this series is a "naval blockade of the coasts or the ports of another State." *Any* blockade, even a blockade during which not one shot is fired, is thus declared to constitute a war blockade in relation to and in the meaning of the term "war" in Article I of the Pact of Paris.

The student of blockades has one task which in practical importance stands out above all others. This is the task of measuring blockades with the yardstick of those international rules of law on war which give a blockading power the right to enforce the blockade against the flag of third states. This right, it is important to note, is a purely belligerent right. It is a belligerent right like the right to interfere with the sea-borne commerce of third states on the ground of contraband. The rules of law conceding such right to a blockading power, in other words, always have been rules of law on *war*. They represent a compromise between prospective neutrals, interested in the complete freedom of the seas, and future belligerents, interested in cutting off all sea-borne commerce to and from an *enemy*. No blockade, therefore, ought to be enforced against the flag of third states as long as the blockading and the blockaded power are at peace. A pacific blockade enforced against the flag of third states, in other words, is an illegal blockade. The yardstick of *these* rules of law on war was meant by Prime Minister Balfour when on December 17, 1902, he stated before the House of Commons that "there can be no such thing as pacific blockade." [29] Most important among these rules is the universally recognized fourth rule of the famous Declaration of Paris of April 16, 1856, in which the contracting powers agreed that blockades in order to be binding must not be paper blockades but must be effective, "i.e., be maintained by a force sufficient really to prevent access to the coast of the *enemy*." The whole Declaration of Paris is a statement of maritime law "in time of *war*." [30] The United States, though with a small number of other states not a party to the Declaration of Paris, adheres to the above rule in practice. The United States, furthermore, has expressly accepted the principle of this rule in various treaties. Article XIII of the now terminated Treaty of Commerce and Navigation, signed between the United States and Italy at Florence on February 26, 1871, might be quoted. It ran as follows:

Article XIII. The high contracting parties having agreed that a *state of war* between one of them and a third Power shall not, except in the case of blockade and contraband of war, affect the neutral commerce of the other, and being desirous of removing every uncertainty which may hitherto have arisen respecting that which, upon principles of fairness and justice, ought to constitute a legal blockade, they hereby expressly declare that such places only shall be considered blockaded as shall be actually invested by naval forces capable of preventing the entry of neutrals, and so stationed as to create an evident danger on their part to attempt it.[31]

Here then these questions arise: Which operations constitute war in relation to and in the meaning of these rules of law on war? Which operations do not come up to war in this sense and therefore constitute a pacific blockade only, i.e., an illegal blockade?

The history of the nineteenth and the twentieth centuries knows of a small number of blockades which in one way or the other were enforced against the flag of third states in spite of the fact that no or almost no fighting occurred between the blockading and the blockaded power. Three British and two French blockades of this kind occurred in South America around 1840.[32] French operations supplementing the French blockade of 1838–40 against Buenos Aires and the whole Argentine coast consisted up to September, 1839—almost a year and a half after the beginning of the blockade—in nothing but the storming and capture of the pin point island of Martín García.[33] It is clear that this whole group of British and French blockades must be wiped off the slate. They cannot, because they occurred around 1840, throw any light upon what matters most now, namely, the question of how the term "war" in relation to the fourth rule of the Declaration of Paris has been understood in practice.

For the period from 1856 up to World War II one can count on the fingers of one hand the blockades which the blockading states declared to be binding for the flag of third states although no or almost no fighting occurred between the blockading and the blockaded powers. These blockades are:

First, the blockade instituted in 1897–98 by the Concert of Europe—Austria-Hungary, France, Germany, Great Britain, Italy, and Russia—against the island of Crete, which, though Turkish still, had been occupied by Greek troops. The blockading powers intended to and actually did prevent at that time the annexation of the island by Greece.[34]

Secondly, the joint blockade by Germany, Great Britain, and Italy in 1902–3 against Venezuelan ports for the purpose of compelling Venezuela to recognize a series of pending claims raised separately against it by the blockading powers on behalf of some of their subjects.[35]

Thirdly, the short blockade established by the Concert of Europe from April 10 to May 14, 1913—that is, in the course of the first war of the Balkans—against the coasts of Montenegro and northern Albania. The blockading powers intended to and actually did prevent the annexation by Montenegro of the Albanian city of Scutari, saving it thereby for the future state of Albania, then in *statu nascendi*.[36]

Lastly, the blockade of Greece by France in the period from December 8, 1916, to June 14, 1917. This blockade aimed in the last analysis at the abdication of the Germanophile King Constantine I, brother-in-law of Emperor William II, and the formation of a Greek Cabinet under Venizelos, then head of a provisional Greek government in Salonika. King Constantine abdicated on June 12. Two days later the blockade was raised.[37]

It is manifestly impossible to state whether "the family of nations"—minus the blockading powers—considered these blockades as pacific and consequently as illegal in relation to and in the meaning of the fourth rule of the Declaration of Paris. It is possible, however, to try to find out how they were looked upon by one or another of the members of the family of nations, the United States for instance.

The United States protested against the blockade of Crete

upon being notified thereof by the ambassadors of the six powers which formed the Concert of Europe. On March 26, 1897, the Government of the United States declared that it was "not conceding the right to make such a blockade as that referred to in your communication and is reserving the consideration of all international rights and of any question which may in any way affect the commerce or interest of the United States." [38] No further protest, however, was made when a few weeks after the notification there broke out what in history is known as the Greco-Turkish War of 1897. In this war the European Powers blockading Crete were de facto allies of the Porte. In the eyes of the Government of the United States, it seems, a blockade is not pacific but legal in relation to the fourth rule of the Declaration of Paris, though no or almost no fighting occurs between the blockading and the blockaded powers, if the blockading powers are de facto or de jure allied to a third power engaged in operations on a large scale against the blockaded power. It might be added by way of parenthesis that during World War II the British fleet operated a strict blockade against the coasts of Finland. This blockade apparently was hardly supplemented by other British operations. The British Empire and Commonwealth at any rate did not conduct any military operations against Finland. Great Britain operated this blockade in her capacity as an ally of the Union of Soviet Socialist Republics.

The Government of the United States, on the other hand, did not protest against the blockade of Venezuelan ports in 1902–3. Neither did it protest against the blockade of the coasts of Montenegro and northern Albania in 1913 or against the blockade of Greece in 1916–17.

Can this attitude be considered as constituting tacit agreements between the United States on the one hand and the surviving members of what once was the Concert of Europe on the other—agreements to the effect that these powers are entitled to enforce a blockade against the flag of the United States even though the blockade itself be their only effort made to overcome the resistance of the blockaded state? Not if one looks behind the circumstances. Under such an agreement war could be nonexistent and still be war in relation to and in the meaning of the term "war" in the fourth rule of the Declaration of Paris. It would allow the establishment of a blockade at too low a cost for American sea-borne commerce. The blockading powers would exercise the right of blockade without actually fulfilling their corresponding duty of waging a war.

What were the circumstances which accompanied the three blockades mentioned above?

It is easy to see why the United States made no protest against the blockade in 1913 of Montenegro and the coast of northern Albania. The United States seemed to have had no interest in this blockade in the Adriatic which lasted for only thirty-four days.[39] It was, furthermore, impossible to foresee from the notification of the blockade what the ulterior military intentions of the Concert of Europe were. It seemed quite probable at the time that the Austro-Hungarian Armies would march into Montenegro or that the blockading powers would disembark marines. Around April 20, 1913, King Nikita of Montenegro declared that he would consider landing parties as enemies.[40]

The reason why the United States made no protest against the French blockade of Greece in 1916–17 is a manifestly political one. This blockade served the Allied cause which the United States was about to join by its declaration of war against Germany of April 6, 1917. There ought to be no doubt that the consent of the United States to this blockade was meant as a consent *ad hoc* and not as a consent in principle.

Now to what is by far the most interesting case of all, the joint blockade in 1902–3 of Venezuelan ports by Germany, Great Britain, and Italy. This is the case of cases. It must be given special attention. The purpose of the blockade, as has been said before, was to compel the Venezuelan Government to recognize a series of claims raised against it by the Governments of Germany, Great Britain, and Italy on behalf of some of their subjects. Venezuela at that time was ruled by President Castro, one of the most unpleasant in a series of military dictators.

In July, 1902, the British and the German Governments began to confer with each other with a view to a joint action. By November 11 the German Government had acceded to a British suggestion that the first step should be the seizure of the Venezuelan Navy.[41] The German Government suggested that a second step should consist in a blockade enforced against the flags of all nations of the ports of Venezuela. This blockade the German Government intended to call a "pacific blockade." Why a "pacific blockade"? The German Foreign Office realized that a blockade by the German Navy would come under Article XI, Paragraph 2 of the Constitution of the German Empire of April 16, 1871, the provision which prescribed the consent of the Bundesrat for a declaration of war by the Emperor, unless an attack was made upon the federal territory or its coasts.[42] This provision of constitutional law the German Foreign Office intended to by-pass by resorting to the simple stratagem which twenty-seven years earlier had been applied by Ferry. It intended to make the proposed blockade look pacific by *calling* it a "pacific blockade." The German Constitution, of course, was a matter of no concern to the British Government. What mattered for Great Britain was the Declaration of Paris. The British Government therefore declined to accept the German proposal for a "pacific blockade." Prime Minister Balfour, as has been stated above, was soon to declare before the House of Commons that "there can be no such thing as a pacific blockade." The British Government likewise declined to accept a further German proposal to call the suggested blockade neither "pacific" nor "war blockade," but simply "blockade." The second step against Venezuela, in the British view, had to be a "war blockade," if it was intended to establish a blockade that was to be enforced against the flag of all nations. The German Government thereupon acceded to the wishes of Great Britain and decided to unite with Great

Britain in the establishment of a "war blockade." It was prepared now to ask the consent of the Bundesrat for a blockade
against Venezuela.[43]

Venezuela gave no satisfactory response to a joint British
and German ultimatum which was delivered on December 7,
1902. On the following day the British and German diplomatic representatives left Caracas and the British and German
Navies proceeded to the first step.[44] They seized within about
a week without opposition eleven out of the thirteen vessels
which composed the Venezuelan fleet. The torpedo boat *Mar-
garita* was not captured, but her engines and guns were removed, as she was inside the camber at La Guayra hauled up
for repairs and totally unseaworthy.[45] The Germans after
seizure sank the armed yacht *Crespo* and the armed launch
Tortuno of 137 tons each. The reason given was that the two
small boats were not sufficiently seaworthy to be permitted to
undertake the voyage to Trinidad, where the British Navy
had established a prize court.[46] Meanwhile the mob at Puerto
Cabello seized and looted a British steamer and imprisoned her
officers and crew. On December 13 the British cruiser *Charybdis* and the German cruiser *Vineta* shelled the two forts at
Puerto Cabello after the local authorities had failed to comply
with a demand for an apology made by the Commodore of the
Charybdis.[47]

Now the Government of the United States began to show
concern about the blockade which appeared to be imminent.
The German Government, through a *Promemoria* of the
German embassy in Washington, had informed the Government of the United States as early as December 20, 1901, that
it was considering the establishment of a "peace blockade"
against Venezuelan harbors. "Such a blockade would touch
likewise the ships of neutral [*sic*] powers, inasmuch as such
ships, although a confiscation of them would not have to be
considered, would have to be turned away and prohibited
until the blockade should be raised." [48] On December 12,
1902, Secretary of State Hay directed the American Ambassador in Berlin to say to the German Government that the

United States continued to adhere to the position taken by it with regard to the Cretan blockade in 1897.[49] The gist of that position was: no belligerents—no neutrals and no neutral commerce.[50] The German Government replied that Germany, though at first inclined to a pacific blockade, now intended to unite with Great Britain in a joint declaration of a "warlike blockade" in a few days. It added that Germany at present had no intention whatever to proceed beyond the establishment of a "warlike blockade." Secretary of State Hay now directed the American Ambassador in Berlin to ascertain discreetly what was intended by a "warlike blockade without war, especially as regards neutrals." [51] The reply of the German Minister for Foreign Affairs of December 18 consisted in a contention to the effect that there actually existed "a state of war" between Germany and Venezuela.[52]

By this time it had become clear that the Venezuelan Government was to remain adamant in spite of the seizure of their fleet. Germany and Great Britain therefore proceeded to the second step, the blockade of Venezuelan ports. In that second step they were joined by Italy. Italy dispatched two cruisers. On December 20 Germany, Great Britain, and Italy notified third powers of the blockade. Every vessel sailing under their flag and found by one of the blockading ships in the immediate neighborhood of a blockaded port was to receive a special notification to the effect that any attempt to communicate with the blockaded port was to be followed by seizure and detention of the vessel for trial in a prize court with probable ultimate confiscation of ship and cargo. Merchant vessels sailing under the Venezuelan flag were to be seized and treated as prizes of war.[53] Germany and Italy together blockaded one portion of the Venezuelan harbors, Great Britain another.[54] The blockade was raised on February 15, 1903, after the differences between the blockading powers and Venezuela had been settled through mediation by the United States.[55] The three European Powers thereafter restored to Venezuela both the fleet and merchant vessels which had been seized.[56]

Let us now turn to this question: Where, in the period from

December 20, 1902, to February 15, 1903, was the war which, under the fourth rule of the Declaration of Paris and under Article XIII of the above-mentioned treaty between the United States and Italy, entitled the blockading powers to enforce their blockade against American shipping? On January 17, 1903, the German gunboat *Panther*—the same *Panther* which in 1911 was on every tongue after her "leap to Agadir" —according to German reports, was fired at from Fort San Carlos. On January 21 the *Panther* and two other German war vessels retaliated by shelling and destroying that fort.[57] With the exception of this bombardment by the German Navy, an operation which was not planned but accidental, the blockading powers undertook no operations against Venezuela in addition to the blockade and the seizure of merchant vessels sailing under the Venezuelan flag. Thus, setting aside the seizure of Venezuelan merchant vessels, the war required by the fourth rule of the Declaration of Paris and by Article XIII of the Treaty of Commerce and Navigation between the United States and Italy but once, and for a short time only, rose above zero, and then dropped down again to the vanishing point, to stay there until the blockade was raised. On December 17, 1902, Mr. T. M. Healy asked the Prime Minister in the House of Commons whether the United States had assented to this sort of blockade. Prime Minister Balfour answered: "The question of the honourable and learned gentleman, the member for Lowth, does not arise when you are in a *state of war* with a third party." Confronted with the further question "a state of war! Has war been declared?" the Prime Minister asked: "Does the honourable and learned gentleman suppose that without a state of war you can take ships of another power and blockade its ports?"[58] The Marquess of Lansdowne, Secretary of State for Foreign Affairs, thought that "the establishment of a blockade created *ipso facto* a state of war between Great Britain and Venezuela. . . ."[59] In a debate on German foreign policy which took place in the Reichstag on January 23, 1903, Freiherr von Richthofen, Secretary of State of the Foreign Office, voiced the same opinion.

"The state of war between us and Venezuela was created with the establishment of the blockade." [60]

These statements evidently were evasive to the point of inanity. Nobody can understand just what is supposed to exist if it is contended that a "state of war" (war in "the" legal sense) exists. Assuming that the Prime Minister and the British and German Foreign Secretaries had said "war" instead of "state of war," their statements still would have twisted logic. They would have been attempts to represent the blockade itself as constituting war in relation to and in the meaning of the fourth rule of the Declaration of Paris, attempts, in other words, to justify the blockade by the blockade itself.

At the first superficial glance the strange part in the picture was the fact that the United States after December 20, 1902, made no protest against the molestation of American shipping even though the war supposed to accompany the blockade remained practically invisible and inaudible. By the simple device of labeling as a war blockade what actually was a pacific and therefore an illegal blockade, Germany and Great Britain, it seemed, after all had succeeded in calling upon the United States to submit to the position of a neutral and to tolerate a derangement of American trade. To Mr. Basdevant, a prominent French legal writer, the situation looked "slightly ridiculous." [61]

The situation in fact was far from being ridiculous. There was emphatically, another part in the picture.

It is utterly clear—though there is no evidence that this argument was made at that time in any quarter—that in the Venezuelan episode the principle of the freedom of the seas came in conflict with the Monroe Doctrine. The traditional American defense of the freedom of the seas was counterbalanced and precluded by the determination on the part of the Cabinet at Washington to defend the Monroe Doctrine first. The action of the three European Powers as such, to be sure, was not inconsistent with the Monroe Doctrine. Much of President Theodore Roosevelt's political credo is laid out in his first annual message to Congress of December 3, 1901. In this message the new chief executive had stated: "We do not guarantee any State against punishment if it misconducts itself, provided that punishment does not take the form of *acquisition of territory* by any non-American Power." [62] On November 13, 1902, Secretary of State Hay gave to Sir Michael Herbert, the British Ambassador at Washington, a specific assurance regarding the contemplated action against Venezuela. Mr. Hay stated "that the United States Government, although they regretted that European Powers should use force against Central and South American countries, could not object to their taking steps to obtain redress for injuries suffered by their subjects, provided that no acquisition of territory was contemplated." [63] The best way to forestall an acquisition of Venezuelan territory manifestly was to relax the traditional American defense of the freedom of the seas and to recognize the blockade as a valid one even though it was in fact a pacific blockade. A refusal on the part of the United States to do so might have forced the blockading powers to supplement the blockade by landing marines for a march on Caracas. This was something the Cabinet at Washington wished to avoid at any price. There existed in the United States in the latter part of 1902 and in the first months of 1903 a strong resentment against Germany. The German Emperor was suspected of having acquisitive designs in the Caribbean. That suspicion was shared by the administration, the press, and the public alike.[64] Senator Cullen, chairman of the Foreign Affairs Committee of the Senate, stated that the collection of Venezuela's debts might call for prompt action if the Allies were to march to Caracas, for it would have to be regarded as a first step toward permanent occupation or acquisition of territory, whether the Allies considered it so or not and by whatever name they described their operation.[65] President Roosevelt himself had no absolute faith in German assurances to the effect that Germany would respect the Monroe Doctrine. Freiherr Speck von Sternburg, German Envoy in Extraordinary Mission and "Specky" to T. R., [66] got this impression while riding horseback with his friend, the President of the United

States, shortly after the termination of the blockade.[67] It matters little that the documents in the Wilhelmstrasse which bear upon the Venezuelan blockade have been searched in the meantime by such distinguished scholars as Dexter Perkins and that not the slightest evidence of any acquisitive designs on the part of Germany has ever been discovered.[68] It is an undeniable fact that the United States was suspicious at the time of the blockade. That fact explains why the United States acquiesced in the Venezuelan blockade in the way in which it was performed. There ought again to be no doubt that the consent of the United States to this blockade was meant as a consent pro hoc and not as a consent in principle. The consent of the United States in other words must not be regarded as setting a precedent.

In the foregoing an attempt has been made to establish the attitude of United States toward blockades operated by the six great European Powers under the fourth rule of the Declaration of Paris and under Article XIII of the Treaty of Commerce and Navigation, signed by the United States and Italy in 1871. The latter treaty may be disregarded, since it has expired. The Declaration of Paris, however, is still in force. In conclusion it must be stated that no precise answer can be given to the question as to what operations in the eyes of the United States constitute war under the fourth rule of the Declaration of Paris. The United States in principle certainly does not tolerate any interference with American shipping through a blockade which is not or which is hardly supplemented by any other operations. It is impossible, however, definitely to state just what supplementary operations elevate a blockade to the rank of a war blockade.

In reviewing all our considerations on the subject of "pacific blockade" the most important fact is no doubt that the term "pacific blockade" as such has no legal meaning. The term "pacific blockade," in order to make sense legally, must relate to some rule of law on war or some rule of law on peace. It must relate, for instance, to the rule of constitutional law which reserves the decision to resort to war to parliament. Of the greatest practical importance in international law is the universally recognized fourth rule of the Declaration of Paris of 1856 in relation to which a blockade, in order to be enforced against the flag of third states, must be a war blockade; a pacific blockade is illegal.

It is not being overlooked that since World War I a great change has been occurring in naval warfare. Navies are no longer the offensive weapon that they once were. Mines and submarines and, above all, planes have made inadvisable certain kinds of naval activity, particularly some kinds of action close to shore such as the type of blockade regulated by the fourth rule of the Declaration of Paris. Navies, unless well protected by planes of their own, are helpless when they come within range of first-class shore-based air power. Close blockades with a cordon of ships in the immediate offing of the blockaded ports were still declared and maintained in no less than nine instances during World War I. Among these instances was the above-mentioned blockade of the coasts of Greece by France in 1916–17.[69] Twenty years later, during the Spanish Civil War, announcements of the intended establishment of close blockades were issued on six different occasions, twice by the Loyalist Government and four times by the insurgents.[70] The most important close blockade of World War II, no doubt, is the blockade which Japan instituted against the Chinese coast in 1937. Other important blockades established since World War I, however, no longer were close blockades, but so-called long-distance blockades operated through the establishment on the high seas of areas proscribed to and actually made dangerous for commercial navigation by the laying of mines.[71] The fourth rule of the Declaration of Paris entitles belligerents to enforce close blockades against the flag of third states. The operation of long-distance blockades is a question not of right but of might. No third state probably has ever recognized that belligerents have a right to appropriate for their naval operations certain areas of the high seas.

Section 5. On the Parties to War

According to many book definitions states only are parties to war. An examination of various rules of law on war, however, shows that there is no warrant for such a view. The parties to war are often, but not always, states. It all depends upon the intent and purpose of the rule of law on war which happens to be under consideration.

First, rules of law on war which are intended to apply only to operations conducted by a state against another state. Such rules abound. Of the greatest human interest and, therefore, most often thought of among these rules are the Hague Conventions (II) of 1899 and (IV) of 1907.[1] These are the Hague Conventions which carry the unfortunate title "Convention Respecting the Laws and Customs of War on Land," and which, as has been said before, might better have been called "Convention Concerning Warfare on Land." [2] The parties to war in relation to and in the meaning of these Conventions are states only, because it was expressly agreed that the provisions contained therein shall not apply except between contracting powers.[3] Articles 1 and 2 of the Annex to the Conventions regulate the all-important question as to what persons represent a state at war on land. A state is, of course, first of all represented by its army. The rights and duties under the Conventions, above all the paramount right of captives to be treated as prisoners of war, in addition apply to militia and volunteer corps fulfilling the following conditions:

1. To be commanded by a person responsible for his subordinates.
2. To have a fixed distinctive emblem recognizable at a distance.
3. To carry arms openly.
4. To conduct their operations in accordance with the laws and customs of war.

The rights and duties under the Conventions apply, furthermore, to the *levée en masse*. The inhabitants of a territory which has *not been occupied*, who, on the approach of the enemy, spontaneously take up arms to resist the invading troops without having had time to organize themselves into a militia or volunteer corps, are to be regarded as belligerents if they carry arms openly and if they respect the laws and customs of war.[4]

The rights and duties of persons carrying arms openly and respecting the laws and customs of war in a levée en masse in enemy-*occupied* territory are not clearly established.[5] At the first Hague Peace Conference of 1899 the British and the Swiss delegations attempted in vain to secure for such persons recognition as belligerents.[6] The preamble of the two Conventions, however, must not be overlooked. In the preamble of the Convention of 1907 the contracting parties state that it had not been possible "at present" to agree on provisions covering "all the circumstances which may arise in practice." It is further declared that the contracting parties clearly did not intend that "unforeseen cases" should, in the absence of a written undertaking, be left to the arbitrary judgment of military commanders. In such cases the belligerents and the *inhabitants* of an invaded country remain under the protection of "the principles of the law of nations, as they result from the usages established among civilized peoples, from the laws of humanity and the dictates of public conscience." The contracting parties declared that it is in this sense especially that Articles 1 and 2 of the Annex to the Convention must be understood. Similar declarations had been made in the preamble to the Convention of 1899. The formula "principles of the law of nations, as they result from the usages established among civilized peoples, from the laws of humanity and the dictates of public conscience" is a jumble of words into which it is impossible to read any concrete meaning. Yet, whatever the formula means, certainly it does not mean that the persons participating in a levée en masse in enemy-occupied territory are left without any legal protection and therefore may be considered as outlaws and be shot if captured.

"Unforeseen cases" of warfare on land occurred during

World War I. Other "unforeseen cases" occurred in the course of World War II. Outstanding among the latter cases are the operations which were conducted by the Chetniks and by the partisans of Marshal Josip (Tito) Broz against the German Army of Occupation in Yugoslavia and, more recently, the operations conducted by the F.F.I., the French Forces of the Interior, against the German Army of Occupation in France. The Chetniks, Tito's partisans, and the F.F.I. were under the command of officers who were responsible for their subordinates, they were provided with a distinctive emblem and carried arms openly. Gen. Dusan Simovic, Premier of the Yugoslav Government in exile, stated in a radio broadcast made from London on November 15, 1941, that the Chetniks—formed by regrouping and reorganizing remnants of the beaten Yugoslav Army under the command of General Mihailovic [7]—were willing to observe the laws and customs of war.[8] The same willingness could be reasonably assumed to have existed in the case of Tito's partisans. Respecting the F.F.I., Gen. Dwight D. Eisenhower asserted in a communiqué issued on July 15, 1944, that they were instructed to conduct their operations in accordance with the laws and customs of war.[9] The Chetniks, Tito's partisans, and the F.F.I. thus had the qualifications enumerated above which the Hague Convention (II) of 1899 and (IV) of 1907 require of belligerents.

This, however, was not the way in which Germany looked upon these forces. Respecting the F.F.I. Germany held that they were made up of citizens of France and were under the orders of the government of Marshal Pétain, a government with which Germany had concluded an armistice.[10] Respecting the Chetniks and the partisans of Marshal Tito, the German point of view probably was that these forces owed allegiance either to the Serbian puppet government of Gen. Milan Neditch, another government with which Germany had concluded an armistice, or to the government of the "kingdom" of Croatia, a country with which Germany had not been at war. Germany, in consequence, refused to consider the Chetniks, Tito's partisans, or the F.F.I. as belligerents. They were not even given the benefits of the above-mentioned formula regarding "unforeseen cases." On the contrary. Suffice it to quote but one German report out of many that come easily to mind. According to an eye-witness story written by a well-known German war correspondent and published in the Belgrade *Donau Zeitung* and *Novo Vreme* the Germans in the course of their western Serbian campaign in the fall of 1941 "shot out of hand" Chetniks, suspected Chetniks, and townspeople suspected of aiding the Chetniks. "In some villages the population met us with white flags; in some cases we respected them. In other cases we found unflattering slogans chalked on the walls, posters insulting the Führer. In those cases we sometimes shot one man out of ten in the entire village and sometimes burned the village to the ground." [11]

The German argument, altogether apart from what it was worth from the legal point of view, was a hazardous one to stress. It carried the threat of backfire and it did backfire in the case of the Chetniks and of Tito's partisans where it led to a mutual no-quarter fight. By the middle of July, 1944, Germany ultimately had admitted the claim of these forces for recognition as belligerents.[12] It seems that Germany finally was compelled to grant this recognition also to the F.F.I.[13] In 1940 the Germans had stated that they would treat as *franc-tireurs* the crews of French ships and planes belonging to the French Legion formed in Britain by General de Gaulle. They reconsidered this statement in 1942 after the Free French forces had captured large numbers of German prisoners.[14] Gen. Dwight D. Eisenhower, in his above-mentioned communiqué of July 15, 1944, warned the enemy to cease treating the F.F.I. as franc-tireurs, and declared that any German treating them thus would have to face the consequences.

Secondly, we now turn to rules of law on war in relation to and in the meaning of which the parties to war are not necessarily two states. Examples again abound. There might be quoted certain rules of municipal law which provide for neutrality both in wars between states and in civil wars. The parties to war under the United States Foreign Enlistment Act of 1818, for instance, were "a foreign Prince, State, Colony, district, or people, in war, by land or by sea, against any Prince, State, Colony, district, or people with whom the United States are at peace." [15] Article 102, Paragraph 9 of the Swiss Constitution of 1874 [16] confers upon the Federal Council the duty of protecting the permanent neutrality of Switzerland. This rule in practice is understood to mean neutrality both in wars between states and in civil wars.[17] The Federal Council thus issued several decrees for the protection of Swiss neutrality during the Spanish Civil War of 1936–39.[18] In relation to and in the meaning of certain rules of law on war the parties to war might even be a state on the one hand and bands of brigands or pirates on the other. We have met with such rules before. The words "in any war" employed in the Act to Establish in the War Department and in the Navy Department a Roll Designated as "the Army and Navy Medal of Honor Roll," of April 27, 1916, and the words "in time of war," employed in the Articles for the Government of the Navy, as has been pointed out above, cover the operations which the Marine Corps conducted against the Cacos in Haiti in 1915.[19]

The assertion so persistently made in one book definition after another, that the parties to war are states only, is both untenable and dangerous. It is a dangerous assertion, because it can and actually has been used to circumvent certain rules of law on war.

The prejudice that war in law can exist only between states thus was shrewdly exploited by the first Cabinet of Jules Ferry when it prepared the "expedition" which in 1881 resulted in the establishment of the French protectorate over Tunisia. This "expedition" was actually directed against the state of Tunisia, but was dressed up as "operations against the Kroumirs," [20] nomadic tribes living in the desert lands to the east of the frontier between Algeria and Tunisia. These operations, according to the "authorities," did not amount to war. They could be undertaken without a declaration of war and without the assent of Parliament required by the French Constitution,[21] an assent which at the time was clearly unobtainable. As against this maneuver a member of the opposition in either the Senate or the Chamber of Deputies might well have pointed to the intent and purpose of Article 9 of the French Constitutional Law of July 16, 1875. The manifest intent and purpose of this rule of law on war was to protect French treasure and blood and the conduct of French foreign policy against *le pouvoir personnel*. Operations against border tribes also involve the risk of a waste of treasure and blood. Operations against border tribes can, and in the case of Tunisia actually did, lead to operations against the border state. Such operations, in turn, can, and in the case of Tunisia actually did, result in an important change in French foreign relations. These were reasons enough to consider the "expedition" against Tunisia, even under the cloak of "operations against the Kroumirs," as a war in relation to and in the meaning of the above provision of the French Constitutional Law.

In the "Manchurian conflict" in 1931–33, Japan denied throughout that it was conducting a war against China. In support of this thesis the Japanese delegation to the League of Nations adduced and frequently repeated the argument that the Japanese forces in Manchuria were operating not against Chinese troops, but against brigands.[22] Here again an effective rejoinder could have been made by pointing to the intent and purpose of the rule of law on war upon which juristic attention was focused. This rule of law on war was Article 16, Paragraph 1 of the Covenant of the League of Nations.[23] The exact intent and purpose of this rule, as has been stated repeatedly, has never been gauged. Still there was one definite limit to such uncertainty. The members of the League could not possibly refuse in good faith to consider as a "resort to war" in the meaning of Article 16, Paragraph 1 of the Covenant and as calling for sanctions *any* operations conducted in disregard of the obligations respecting the pacific settlement of disputes among members of the League which threatened or impaired "the territorial integrity and political independence" of another member.[24] Japan was violating Article 16, Paragraph 1 of the Covenant even in fighting against bands of brigands, if the operations against bands of brigands, as actually was the case, were only preliminary steps in the virtual annexation of Manchuria. Article 16, Paragraph 1 of the Covenant, in other words, belonged to those rules of law on war in relation to and in the meaning of which the parties to war are not necessarily two states.

SECTION 6. AUTHORIZED AND UNAUTHORIZED OPERATIONS

In the historical part of this study we have met with several cases in which officers conducted operations without authority from their respective governments. In 1827 the commanders of the British, French, and Russian squadrons in the Mediterranean destroyed the Turko-Egyptian fleet off Navarino not only without instructions but contrary to their instructions.[1] In the course of the military operations which resulted in the conquest of Tongking by France, French officers acted repeatedly in contravention of instructions given by the Cabinet in Paris.[2] To these examples others might be added. In testifying before the War Crimes Tribunal in Tokyo on June 28, 1946, Reijiro Wakatsuki, the Japanese Premier who was in power when the "Manchurian Conflict" broke out, declared that this "conflict" was really started, as the world had always assumed, by the Japanese military clique and that the Japanese Army plunged ahead over the protests of the Imperial Government.[3]

Can unauthorized operations constitute war? In the case of *Bas* v. *Tingy* Justice Washington stated his belief that "war is every contention by force between two nations in external matters under the authority of their respective governments." [4] We must not, however, forget that any definition of war in "the" legal sense is impossible. We have just seen that the parties to war are not necessarily two states or nations. The above question—can unauthorized operations constitute war?—thus can only be asked in consideration of those rules of law on war which are intended to apply only to operations conducted by a state. In consideration of these rules it cannot be safely laid down that operations, in order to constitute war, must always be authorized by the respective government. We shall again have to distinguish.

War in relation to and in the meaning of certain rules of law on war consists only of authorized operations. Take the rule in accordance with which the thanks of the British Parliament are voted to officers for triumphs achieved in war through their zeal, skill, and gallantry.[5] The British Parliament clearly does not vote its thanks to officers for triumphs achieved contrary to either explicit or implicit instructions. It naturally enough did not consider the battle off Navarino as constituting war in the sense of the above rule and, hence, refused to vote its thanks to Vice-Adm. Sir Edward Codrington.[6]

However, war in relation to and in the meaning of other rules of law on war does not necessarily consist of authorized operations.

Take the rules which entitle captives to treatment as prisoners of war. So far as this writer knows it has never been argued that captives ought to be refused treatment as prisoners of war because they participated unwittingly in unauthorized operations. Such an argument would be utterly unfair toward the officers and men who, after all, fight and kill in compliance with orders they receive from their superiors. It furthermore would carry the threat of tit for tat.

In the battle off Navarino both sides made and later exchanged prisoners of war [7] in accordance with what at that time were "the laws and customs of war." [8] Both sides rightly considered the battle off Navarino as *insofar* constituting war.

It is in this sense that the United States understands and expects others to understand the Hague Convention (II) of 1899 and (IV) of 1907 Respecting the Laws and Customs of War on Land. The defendants in *Arce et al.* v. *the State of Texas* [9] belonged to a force of the Constitutionalist Army of Mexico which, on June 16, 1916, invaded Texas in all probability without instructions from the Carranza government. The Court of Criminal Appeals of the state of Texas, nevertheless, recognized these defendants as prisoners of war after considering the fact that at the time of the "battle" of San Ignazio they were commanded by their officers.[10]

In the "battle" of Carrizal of June 21 the situation was the reverse of what it had been at San Ignazio. At Carrizal the officer commanding the two troops of the United States cavalry attacked. He did so apparently without authorization.[11] Forty-six Mexicans were said to have been killed. Twenty-four Americans were captured. They were released upon the prompt demand of President Wilson, probably before General Carranza had made up his mind what to do with them. The fact that they had been confined in a penitentiary instead of in a camp for military prisoners had boded no good.[12] Treatment of the captives by Mexico as outlaws, no doubt, would have had the most serious consequences.[13]

Section 7. War and Diplomatic Relations

Many book definitions assert that war presupposes a severance of the diplomatic relations. War, in other words, cannot legally exist as long as the diplomatic relations continue.[1]

In practice this assertion is seldom made. It was made, however, by the United States in the French spoliation cases. France and the United States were at war from 1798 to 1800, the United States contended, because, among other reasons, diplomatic and consular intercourse was interrupted.[2] In 1937 Senator Pittman, on the contrary, pointed to the continuance of diplomatic relations between China and Japan to support his thesis that the "incident" did not amount to war (a "state of war") and that hence the Neutrality Act could be ignored.[3]

The assertion that legally there can be no war as long as diplomatic relations continue is untenable. It is untenable because it is made not in consideration of the rules of law on war but made instead in consideration of the operations which commonly are called a "war." It is in short—like the definition of war taught by Oppenheim [4]—the product of historical not of legal thinking.

The above assertion, though, is not even from the historical point of view entirely correct. What as a rule actually happens at the outbreak of what commonly is called a "war" is that the respective diplomatic representatives are either recalled or given their passports. The diplomatic relations in more recent times, however, continue either directly or indirectly. On October 6, 1941, the British and German Governments thus spoke to each other directly back and forth through their radio stations on details of an exchange of wounded prisoners of war.[5] Indirect diplomatic relations continue through the intermediary of a friendly neutral power, a protecting power to which belligerents turn over their embassy and legation buildings and to which they entrust the care of their interests. In the course of World War II the charge of belligerent interests was in the great majority of cases taken over by Switzerland. On December 17, 1941, the Department of State announced that Switzerland had been entrusted with the care of American interests in all countries with which the United States was at war. As during World War I there was added to the Swiss Foreign Office a special Division of Foreign Interests.[6]

As a rule diplomatic representatives are either recalled or given their passports. Exceptions, however, occur.

In certain wars the diplomatic representatives of belligerents were conspicuously slow in leaving the enemy country. The often-quoted case of Metternich's staying on in Paris as Austrian Ambassador in April and May, 1809, and enjoying there the pleasures of society as though France and Austria had not been at war, is not quite to the point. Metternich actually was not allowed to leave Paris until he could be exchanged for the personnel of the French embassy to the Court of Vienna.[7] More recent wars offer much better examples of slow departures of diplomatic representatives. In the Italo-Ethiopian War operations started on October 3, 1935. The Italian Minister, however, departed from Addis Ababa on October 26 and the Ethiopian chargé d'affaires from Rome on October 28.[8]

In other cases the diplomatic representatives did not leave the seat of the enemy government at all. During the eighty-hour war between the Soviet Union and Iran in August, 1941, the Iranian Ambassador to Moscow and the Soviet representative to Teheran remained at their posts.[9]

But these are all historical, not legal statements. What we must consider in order to reach legal conclusions is not war as history presents it to us, but the meaning of the term "war" in the various rules of law on war. Such a consideration seems to leave no substance whatsoever in the assertion that there can be no diplomatic relations between belligerent states. In the light of one rule of law on war after the other, states can be belligerents no matter whether they entertain diplomatic relations or not. In practice rules of law on war have been applied accordingly over and over again regardless of untenable theoretical assertions. The following instances are only a few out of the many that come to mind quickly.

According to the old "laws and customs of war"[10] and according to Article 3 of the Annex to the Hague Convention (II) of 1899 and (IV) of 1907 persons belonging to the armed forces of belligerent parties have, in the case of capture by the enemy, a right to be treated as prisoners of war. These rules, naturally enough, have never been understood as permitting a merciless no-quarter fight as long as the respective diplomatic representatives remain at the capital of the opponent. It would be very sad, indeed, if it were so. These rules were understood as applying from the start in the Italo-Ethiopian War in 1935 [11] and in the "incident" between Japan and China in 1937,[12] two cases in which the respective diplomatic representatives departed late.[13] The same rules were understood as applying to the "battle" of San Ignazio in 1916 [14] and to the "Manchurian conflict" in 1931–32,[15] two cases in which no departure at all of the respective diplomatic representatives occurred.[16]

The manifest intent and purpose of the rule of law on war in the fifty-eighth Article of War [17] is to tighten the discipline of the army when engaged in combat operations. It goes without saying that the need for tightened discipline exists regardless of where the respective diplomatic representatives happen to be. On February 4, 1901, the general court-martial convened and sitting at Peking found Private Hamilton guilty of murder in violation of the fifty-eighth Article of War [18] regardless of the fact that during the Boxer Expedition the American Minister to China and the Chinese Minister to the United States remained at their stations.[19]

Was it possible to wage war in relation to and in the meaning of Article 16 of the Covenant [20] as long as the diplomatic representatives of the aggressor and of the victim of aggression remained at their respective stations? The answer, of course, is "Yes." On October 10, 1935, the Assembly of the League of Nations rightly declared that Italy had violated Article 16 of the Covenant.[21] The departure of the respective diplomatic representatives from Rome and Addis Ababa, as pointed out above, occurred from two to three weeks later.

Section 1, Paragraph 1 of the American Neutrality Act of August 31, 1935,[22] on the whole corresponded to Section 1, Paragraph 1 of the American Neutrality Act of May 1, 1937.[23] It was directed against "merchants of death." A war in relation to Section 1 of the Act of 1935, like a war in the meaning of Section 1 of the Act of 1937, consisted of operations between two or more foreign states which were extensive enough to give "merchants of death" an opportunity to embark upon their sinister machinations, no matter, of course, whether the respective diplomatic representatives remained at their stations or not. On October 5, 1935, only two days after the start of the Italian operations against Ethiopia and long before the departure of the Italian and Ethiopian diplomatic representatives from Addis Ababa and Rome respectively, President Roosevelt thus rightly proclaimed that war unhappily existed between Ethiopia and Italy and that the exportation of arms, ammunition, and implements of war from the United States to either belligerent had become unlawful.[24] In 1937 the Neutrality Act was ignored, ignored as we have seen for *political* reasons.[25] Senator Pittman's argument that Japan and China continued diplomatic relations and that the "incident," therefore, did not amount to war (a "state of war") [26] defies legal understanding.

SECTION 8. WAR WITH AND WITHOUT CLASH OF ARMS

In 1912 and 1913 Bulgaria, Greece, Montenegro, Romania, and Serbia fought and won against the Ottoman Empire the first and second Balkan wars.[1] What followed was a quarrel among the victors about the distribution of the spoils. At the end of June, 1913, fighting started between the Greek and Serbian Armies on the one hand and the Bulgarian Army on the other. Two weeks later Romania invaded Bulgaria. The Bulgarian Army, heavily engaged as it already was against the Greeks to the south and against the Serbs to the west, was unable to take on a new enemy to the north. The Romanian Army thus entered Bulgaria without firing a shot. The Bulgarians retired and were disarmed "like sheep."[2]

In 1938 and 1939 the German Army scored one bloodless conquest after another. Adolf Hitler's "dynamic peace policy" gathered in first Austria, then Czechoslovakia, then Memel —all without fighting and bloodshed, if you discount a few incidental assassinations. In April, 1940, the German Army occupied Denmark practically without fighting. According to German sources only twelve persons were killed in the course of the German operations.[3]

History knows of many other victories which were won either without or almost without fighting. Such victories were particularly numerous in the eighteenth century. From the death of Louis XIV up to the French Revolution conscription existed in Europe only in a rudimentary and sporadic form. Soldiers were hard to find and the professional armies hence were small. The high military quality which compensated for the small numbers in eighteenth-century armies was achieved only by years of meticulous training. These armies were a costly instrument, difficult to replace, and hence to be used with caution. It was necessary to let as few be killed as possible. Having to economize their men, generals tried to avoid fighting battles. The object of warfare was the execution of skilful maneuvers, of threats and feints, and not the annihilation of the enemy. A victory without battle and without spilling one white corpuscle was considered the ideal of military leadership. In short, generals were superior chess players.[4]

A radical change in warfare occurred after the French Revolution had introduced the principle of universal compulsory service. Fighting against and annihilation of the enemy became the characteristic features of Napoleonic warfare and of Clausewitz' classical war theory which drew its chief inspiration from Napoleon.[5] War for Napoleon was a policy which engendered *battles* instead of chessboard moves. The spirit of Clausewitz' war theory culminated in the one sentence: "The soldier is enlisted, clothed, armed, drilled, he sleeps, drinks, eats and marches solely for the purpose of *fighting* at the right place and at the right time."[6] "War means fighting," said Gen. Stonewall Jackson, because he had made his own the method of war of Napoleon.[7]

Can operations without fighting, such as the invasion of Bulgaria by the Romanian Army in 1913, constitute war from the point of view of the law? This question has often been raised. Some say "Yes."[8] Many more say "No."[9] These answers, however, are never found to be supported by any legal evidence. The truth of the matter is that both sides are mistaken. The answer to the above question is easy enough, if we consult the only thing that ought to be consulted, namely, the rules of law on war. It is neither a categorical "Yes" nor a categorical "No." We must distinguish again between the various rules of law on war. If we do so, we find that the answer is now "Yes," now "No."

In considering the problem of the pacific blockade we already encountered one rule of law on war in relation to and in the meaning of which a war may be waged without fighting. The rule involved is Article II of the Litvinov Treaty of 1933. It will be remembered that war in the sense of this rule can be waged simply by establishing a "naval blockade of the coasts or the ports of another State."[10]

Let us consider, furthermore, the Hague Convention (IV) of 1907 Respecting the Laws and Customs of War on Land

and Article 16, Paragraph 1 of the Covenant of the League of Nations.

First, the Hague Convention (IV) of 1907.[11] There are, to be sure, in the Annex to this convention some rules which do not apply in military operations conducted without fighting because they regulate fighting itself. It is, for example, prohibited to fight with arms such as dumdum bullets, which are calculated to cause unnecessary suffering (Art. 23, Paragraph e). In relation to most of the rules of the Hague Convention (IV), however, military operations are war no matter whether they are conducted with or without fighting. It stands to reason that the absence of fighting does not make any difference in the applicability of the rules regarding prisoners of war (Arts. 4–20), the inviolability of the bearer of a flag of truce (Art. 32), the military authority over the territory of the enemy state (Arts. 42–56), and so forth and so on. Suppose that in 1913 Bulgaria had not only signed but, like Romania, ratified the Hague Convention (IV) of 1907.[12] The invasion of Bulgaria by Romania then would have constituted war in the meaning of the above rules of law on war.

Secondly, the rule of law on war in Article 16, Paragraph 1 of the Covenant of the League of Nations.[13] On October 4, 1921, the Assembly of the League adopted a set of resolutions and proposals for amendments to Article 16. The Assembly declared these resolutions and proposals, as long as they were not put into force, to constitute rules for guidance "which the Assembly recommends in connection with the application of Article 16." [14] The third resolution implied that a state member of the League could "resort to war" under Article 16 even in the face of continued nonresistance by the state attacked. The other members of the League, hence, were even in such a case considered as being bound at the outset to apply sanctions, economic sanctions first and military sanctions, maybe, later on.

The wisdom of this resolution might well be doubted. It promised the state attacked help no matter how passively and supinely it behaved, instead of proclaiming the principle of "help yourself, and the League will help you." Subsequent events have shown how difficult it is in practice to keep such a promise. Observers of the "Manchurian conflict" of 1931–33 will readily admit that Chinese resistance against Japan was far below what could be reasonably expected. The often denounced "betrayal" of China by the League assumes a different aspect if it is kept in mind that a great country was impotent for its own defense and that the risk and the cost of defending it would have fallen much too heavily on other shoulders. Operations without fighting, it appears, should not have been considered as constituting war under Article 16, Paragraph 1 of the Covenant. There is much to be said for a statement made on December 5, 1935, by Sir Austen Chamberlain in the House of Commons. "In a system of collective security each Member of the League ought to bring its proportionate quota of strength to the defence of its own land and to the common defence of the world." [15] Determined resistance by well-trained and skilled soldiers despite marked numerical inferiority and great odds can be decisive within the framework of a coalition. Evidence offered at the Nuremberg war-crimes trial shows that the heroic resistance of the Yugoslavs and of the Greeks in the spring of 1941 delayed the German invasion of Russia for almost a month.[16] Such resistance, in all probability, prevented the German Army from reaching its objective, the banks of the Volga,[17] before the unusually early advent of an extremely cold winter.

Let us then stop here for a moment and look back on the road which we have traveled. In the 1941 edition of Webster's Dictionary we find reproduced the formula which Justice Washington in August, 1800, presented to the Supreme Court of the United States as being "the" legal definition of war.[18] Justice Washington said: "It may, I believe, be safely laid down that war is every contention by force between two nations in external matters under the authority of their respective governments." [19] As against this definition we have seen up to now, first, that the parties to war are not necessarily two nations or states; secondly, that armed forces, provided they belong to a state, must not necessarily operate under the authority of their own government; thirdly, that even operations without fighting can constitute war.

The above definition thus goes to pieces. So would any other of the innumerable book definitions of war if tested by the various rules of law on war. It all goes to show how unsafe it is to lay down anything as necessarily belonging to the definition of war in relation to and in the meaning of no-matter-what rule of law on war. Not one element is knowable in advance, a priori so to speak, and without regard to the process of interpreting the rule of law on war whose meaning we should like to ascertain.

Section 9. On Declarations of War

In 1931–33 neither Japan nor China declared war. It seems to have been widely assumed abroad that hence there had been no "resort to war" in Manchuria, and that, consequently, no call had arisen for the application of Article 16 of the Covenant.[1] The Lytton Report mentioned the absence of a declaration of war as though to explain the inactivity of the League.[2]

The same argument could be heard five years later on this side of the Atlantic. Among the five points made by the chairman of the Senate Foreign Relations Committee on August 23, 1937, with regard to the Japanese-Chinese "incident," the absence of a declaration of war occupies first place. The Japanese-Chinese "incident," according to Senator Pittman, did not constitute war (a "state of war") and hence did not call for the application of the Neutrality Act of 1937 because, first of all, neither side had declared war.[3]

On January 18, 1938, President Roosevelt at his press conference touched upon the fact that still no declaration of war had been made. The President left the impression that nothing short of a declaration of war would move him to put the

Neutrality Act into effect. The implication was that from the point of view of the rules of law on war a declaration of war undoubtedly constitutes war.[4]

The above paragraphs bring to the fore the two paramount questions which present themselves in any discussion about declarations of war. First, can war legally exist only after a declaration of war? Secondly, can the existence of war in relation to and in the meaning of the rules of law on war no longer be doubted after a declaration of war has been issued?

First, can war legally exist only after a declaration of war? In a note handed by Litvinov, People's Commissar of Foreign Affairs, on August 31, 1928, to the French Ambassador in Moscow we read that war "in the legal sense" presupposes a declaration of war.[5] But there is, as we have seen, no such thing as war in "the" legal sense. From the point of view of the law there can be war only in relation to and in the meaning of the various rules of law on war. If we examine these we find that rules which are intended to become operative only after a declaration of war are extremely rare. In many years this author has come across but one rule of this nature. Article 126 of the Italian rules of land warfare of November 22, 1882, ran as follows: "The state of war [*sic*] begins with a declaration of war. A State invaded without a declaration of war, therefore, is entitled to treat the enemy soldiers as individuals who commit an aggression by force of arms." [6] This rule seems to go back to Roman law. " 'Enemies' are those who declare on us or on whom we publicly declare war. All others are 'brigands' and 'robbers.' " [7] In the nineteenth century this rule strangely enough still was advocated by such writers as Hautefeuille [8] and Fauchille.[9] Whatever it may have amounted to in Roman law, to propose it for modern warfare was both unrealistic and unfair toward the officers and men who have to obey their marching orders no matter whether their government has declared war or not. Anzilotti, the illustrious Italian lawyer, disapproved of Article 126 of the Italian rules of 1882.[10] So did Gemma, another greatly respected Italian.[11] The unfortunate rule, it is interesting to note, was ignored in practice. In the first Italo-Ethiopian War of 1895–96 Italy conducted her operations strictly in accordance with the laws and customs of war although neither side had issued a declaration of war.[12]

The history of warfare in modern times, indeed, would be very sad to behold if the rules of law on war became operative only after a declaration of war. Historians, to be sure, report a great many declarations of war made during the last 300 years. We are informed, for example, that on June 18, 1812, "the United States declared war on Great Britain," [13] and we forthwith assume that on that day the American Secretary of State handed to the British diplomatic representative in Washington a diplomatic note containing the declaration of war. Such, however, was not the case. Declarations of war presented by one state to another were in vogue during the Middle Ages but fell into disuse in the seventeenth century.[14] In 1657 Sweden still declared war against Denmark in the good old decent fashion, to wit, by a herald-at-arms sent to Copenhagen. From that year on, however, it would be difficult to find an instance of war being expressly declared at the court against which it was directed until in 1870 the French chargé d'affaires in Berlin handed to Count von Bismarck the French declaration of war.[15] During the interval what may have been presented to the other courts were notes declaring a rupture of negotiations, notes which were so worded as to be substantially declarations of war. What historians report as declarations of war for this period are documents which were issued *at home*, documents bearing the name of declaration of war or that of manifesto. A declaration of war made by the United States, like that of June 18, 1812, was an act of Congress in conformity with Article I, Section 8, Paragraph 11 of the Constitution.[16] War for more than two hundred years thus would have been an utterly lawless business if the applicability of the rules of law on war had depended on the presentation of a declaration of war properly so called.

Even after the adoption by the second Hague Peace Conference of 1907 of the Hague Convention (III) Relative to the Opening of Hostilities it still remains true that the rules of law on war become operative regardless of a declaration of war. In Article 1 of the Hague Convention (III) of 1907 the contracting parties agreed "that hostilities between themselves must not commence without previous and explicit *warning*, in the form either of a reasoned declaration of war or of an ultimatum with conditional declaration of war." [17] The meaning of this rule is clear although there was at the second Hague Peace Conference no debate about the consequences of a failure to observe it. Article 1 of the Hague Convention (III) of 1907, emphatically does not mean what it was said to mean in a paper read at a recent meeting of the American Society of International Law. It does not mean that other rules of law on war, such as the Hague Convention (IV) of 1907 Respecting the Laws and Customs of War on Land or the Hague Convention (V) Respecting Neutrality in War on Land, do not become operative until a declaration of war has been made.[18] The above rule means precisely what it says. It is simply intended to establish the duty of giving a "warning" before war is commenced. The United States experienced at Pearl Harbor what it means if an aggressor sneaks up in the dark and strikes without warning.

Let us consider for a moment a state, party to the Hague Convention (III), which begins "without previous and explicit warning, in the form either of a reasoned declaration of war or of an ultimatum with conditional declaration of war" operations that constitute war under the Hague Convention (III). Such a state, to be sure, commences war illegally, but its operations nevertheless are war in relation to and in the meaning of all the rules of law on war which alike would be applicable upon a declaration of war. The Hague Conventions are all written in French. Article 1 of the Hague Convention (III) of 1907 begins with the words: "*Les Puissances contractantes reconnaissent que les hostilitiés entre elles ne doivent pas commencer sans un avertissement préalable.* . . ." [19] These words read as follows in the English translation furnished by the Carnegie Endowment for International Peace, Division of International Law: "The contracting powers recognize that hostilities between themselves must not commence without previous and explicit warning. . . ." [20] It has been justly observed that a more correct rendering is that hostilities "*should* not" or "*ought* not to" commence without, etc.[21]

This interpretation is borne out in more than one way. It is borne out by the historical background of the Hague Convention (III) of 1907, by certain rules of law on war, and, furthermore, by the practice of states.

The making of the Hague Convention (III) of 1907 was inspired by a careful study undertaken by a committee of the Institut de Droit International. This study finally led to the adoption by the Institut, at its Ghent meeting in 1906, of a resolution the meaning of which is correctly rendered by the following translation made by Sir Thomas E. Holland: "It is in conformity with the requirements of international law, to the loyalty which the nations owe to one another in their mutual relations, as well as to the general interests of all States that hostilities *ought not* to commence without previous and unequivocal warning." [22] In the course of the Ghent meeting of the Institut it had been repeatedly stated that the rules of law on war are applicable regardless of a declaration of war. These statements were gainsaid by none.[23]

Some scattered rules of law on war have been expressly declared to apply even in the absence of a declaration of war. Among these rules is Article 1 of the Briand-Kellogg Pact of August 27, 1928, in which the contracting parties renounced war as an instrument of national policy. In Article II of the Convention Defining Aggression, in relation to the Briand-Kellogg Pact, signed at London on July 3, 1933,[24] the contracting parties declared to consider as an aggressor the state which shall first have committed an "invasion with his armed forces, even without a declaration of war, of the territory of another State."

In the practice of states, as it has developed since 1907, the function of a declaration of war time and again has been considered to be what it was held to be at the Ghent meeting of the Institut in 1906. Thus time and again operations have been conducted in accordance with the rules of law respecting the conduct of war, even in the absence of a declaration of war. In 1915 and 1916 both Germany and Italy considered the German military operations against Italy as being war in the sense of the Red Cross Convention of 1906 even though no declaration of war was made until August 27, 1916.[25] In 1931–33 the Japanese Government recognized the Hague Convention (IV) of 1907 Respecting the Laws and Customs of War on Land as applying to the "Manchurian conflict" even though a declaration of war was never made.[26] In 1937 the Japanese Government acknowledged that the "incident" constituted war under the same Hague Convention even though again neither side had declared war.[27] In the face of the practice of states it looks almost like a measure of overprecaution that the fifteenth International Conference of the Red Cross, at its Tokyo meeting in 1934, should have adopted a resolution in which it expressed the wish that the Red Cross Convention and the Geneva Convention Concerning the Treatment of Prisoners of War of July 27, 1929,[28] be applicable also in armed conflicts between states not accompanied by a declaration of war.[29] Dr. Armin Daeniker, at that time Swiss chargé d'affaires in Tokyo and delegate to the fifteenth International Conference of the Red Cross, has told the author that this resolution was strongly resented by the Japanese Government which, it will be remembered, in 1932 had sent its greatest authority on international law to Shanghai in order to make sure that the Japanese operations would be conducted in accordance with "the laws and customs of war." [30]

What is true of the rules of law respecting the conduct of war is true, as far as one can see, of the rules of law on war in general. They all apply irrespective of a declaration of war. To suggest, as the Lytton Report did, that Article 16 of the Covenant of the League of Nations was inapplicable because in 1931–33 neither Japan nor China had declared war was beside the point. To say, as Senator Pittman did, that for the same reason the Neutrality Act of 1937 could be ignored likewise was beside the point. The intent and purpose of Section 1 of the Neutrality Act of 1937, was to hamstring the "merchants of death." [31] The intent and purpose of Article 16 of the Covenant of the League of Nations, at any rate, was to protect the territorial integrity and political independence of the states members of the League.[32] Do "merchants of death" get busy only after a declaration of war? Can the territorial integrity and political independence of a state be impaired or destroyed only through operations accompanied by a declaration of war? To ask such questions is to deny them. Neither Italy nor Ethiopia declared war in 1935–36. Both the President of the United States and the League of Nations, nevertheless, promptly recognized the Italian military operations against Ethiopia as constituting war, the President of the United States in relation to Section 1 of the Neutrality Act of 1935,[33] the League of Nations in relation to Article 16 of the Covenant.[34]

There remains to be mentioned another interesting question which caused some embarrassment at the second Hague Peace Conference. On July 12, 1907, Colonel Ting, Chinese delegate, stated in the meeting of the second subcommission of the second commission that "it would be very important to settle the point as to whether a declaration of war can be considered by the State towards which it is directed as a unilateral act and whether the latter could regard it as null and void." [35] No one replied to this question though to answer it would have been easy enough. The answer, as a matter of course, must be given in accordance with the intent and purpose of Article 1 of the Hague Convention (III) of 1907.[36] It is beside the point to ask whether a declaration of war "can" be considered as a unilateral act. A declaration of war as required by Article 1 of the Hague Convention (III), no doubt, *is* a unilateral act and *must* so be considered. Such a declaration of war, in other words, is not an offer or a challenge that requires consent and acceptance in order to be effective. To "accept" or to "reject" a declaration of war does not make sense from the legal point of view. Such moves might make sense, however, as *political* demonstrations. So far as this author knows no case of an "acceptance" has occurred since 1907.[37] There have been, however, cases of a "rejection." To some of these cases we now turn.

On December 13, 1941, the Governments of Bulgaria, Hungary, and Romania declared war on the United States.[38] These declarations of war, however, were "ignored" by the Government of the United States for about half a year. They were "ignored" until, on June 2, 1942, President Roosevelt, in a gesture of friendship and support for Soviet Russia,[39] asked Congress to recognize that the United States was at war with the three Balkan countries. The temporary refusal to recognize their declarations of war, it seems, served the political purpose of demonstrating that no quarrel existed between the people of the United States and the peoples of Bulgaria, Hungary, and Romania. Support is lent to such interpretation by President Roosevelt's message to Congress of June 2, 1942, in which he said: "The Governments of Bulgaria, Hungary and Romania have declared war against the United States. I realize that the three Governments took this action not upon their own initiative or in response to the wishes of their own peoples but as the instruments of Hitler." [40]

A unique case of a rejection occurred in 1943 when Italy changed sides after the overthrow of Mussolini. On October 13, the German Overseas Radio announced that a representative of the "traitor" Badoglio had tried to hand the German Ambassador in Madrid a declaration of war but was shown— with his declaration—the door.[41]

Now to the second paramount question in a discussion about declarations of war.

Does a declaration of war issued by one country against another constitute evidence that they are at war in accordance with the rules of law on war? The answer unanimously given to this question by writers on international law is "Yes." "This much seems sure, amid many uncertainties," wrote a recent student of declarations of war.[42] President Roosevelt thus had the backing of legal theory when, in 1938, he intimated that he would have had no choice but to apply the Neutrality Act in case either China or Japan should declare war.[43]

The above thesis, though it is adhered to generally, is untenable. It is untenable because those who adhere to it take the declarations of war at their face value instead of taking them for what they really are.

The historic French declaration of war against Prussia of July 19, 1870, ended with the following words: "The Government of His Imperial Majesty . . . considers itself from now on to be in a *state of war* with Prussia." [44] This declaration of war has served as a pattern for others. At least fifty declarations of war were issued in the period from 1914 to 1918. About half of this number were declarations of war properly so called, i.e., declarations presented to the states against which they were directed. The rest consisted of either legislative acts or executive announcements issued at home. The great majority of these declarations of war in a wider sense followed more or less closely the French pattern of 1870. A, from such and such date, "considers itself to be in a *state of war*" with B. The government of A "declares that a *state of war* exists" between A and B from such and such date. These were the expressions most often used.[45] On May 23, 1915, to give an example, the Italian Ambassador in Vienna handed to the Austro-Hungarian Minister of Foreign Affairs the Italian declaration of war against Austria-Hungary which ended with the following sentence: "His Majesty the King declares that from tomorrow he will consider himself in a *state of war* with Austria-Hungary." [46] On August 14, 1917, to give another example, the Chinese Government handed to the Minister of the Netherlands in Peking a declaration of war for transmission to the German Government in which it was said: "The Chinese Government . . . now declares that a *state of war* exists between China and Germany from ten o'clock A.M. of the fourteenth day of the eighth month of the sixth year of the Republic of China." [47] It is the wording of such declarations of war which forms the pith of the contention that a declaration of war constitutes conclusive evidence that two countries are at war legally. The states issuing such declarations announce themselves that they are legally at war. Why doubt it?

There are two reasons which stand in the way of a literal interpretation of such declarations. In the first place it will be observed that these declarations assert the existence of a "state of war." The term "state of war," like the term "war in *the* legal sense," as we have seen, does not hold water in consideration of the varying intents and purposes of the rules of law on war. This term signifies a merely imaginary concept, somethings which cannot possibly come into "existence." What we can realistically assert is the existence of war in relation to and in the meaning of specific rules of law on war, not "war in *the* legal sense." It is strange that governments at the threshold of war should address each other or their own nation in such an unrealistic, almost mystical kind of language. Yet it is a fact that many a government, though not every government, that has declared war has expressed itself this way.[48]

Attention must be drawn in the second place to the words "considers itself to be" and "exists." There are, to be sure, on the record of recent history a few declarations of war which deviate from the French pattern of 1870 insofar as they do not speak of a "state of war," but of "war," declarations in which it is said that a government "considers itself to be at *war*" or that "*war* exists." [49] Even such declarations ought still to be viewed with circumspection. The words "considers itself to be" or "exists" do not necessarily mean that war in any conceivable legal sense has actually materialized. Such wording may well have been chosen for a paramount political purpose. A government runs the risk of being considered as an aggressor if it openly "declares war upon" another state. A government simply stating that it "considers itself to be at war" or that "war exists," on the contrary, dresses itself in an armor of innocence.

To sum up: the usual wording of the declaration of war ought not to be considered as evidence of any legal existence of war.

The question whether a declaration of war constitutes war

in the sense of the various rules of law on war cannot, in fact, be answered *in abstracto*. It can be answered only in relation to specific declarations of war. A government may declare that "war exists." It may declare that it considers another government as an "enemy." It may declare that it has been obliged "to break the peace." It may choose some other kind of declaration. No matter what wording is chosen, we are always confronted with the task of figuring out what a specific declaration amounts to in terms of action before we are able to say whether it constitutes war in the sense of this or of that rule of law on war.

The truth about declarations of war is that they have the most varied meanings. In terms of action a declaration of war can mean anything from nothing—absolutely nothing—to all-out operations. Declarations of war which mean nothing in terms of action are those which ought to be given special attention. They are arresting phenomena. At least ten declarations of this kind were issued during World War I. Future historians will report an even greater number for World War II. During the week following the tragic day of Pearl Harbor, December 7, 1941, to give an example, Costa Rica, Cuba, the Dominican Republic, El Salvador, Guatemala, Haiti, Honduras, Nicaragua, and Panama issued declarations of war against Germany, Italy, and Japan.[50] Haiti and Nicaragua soon issued, in addition, declarations of war against Bulgaria, Hungary, and Romania.[51] With the information available it is at this writing on the whole still too early to pass judgment on these and similar declarations of war made in the course of World War II. It is safer, under those circumstances, to go back to World War I and to recall that in 1917 and 1918 the above states—with the exception of the Dominican Republic and El Salvador—issued declarations of war against Germany.[52] Cuba, Nicaragua, and Panama, in addition, made declarations of war against Austria-Hungary.[53] The outcome of these declarations is well known. None of the states above mentioned contributed as much as a single soldier or a single ship to the Allied war effort. The wars which they had announced existed on paper only. In analogy to "paper block-ade" the term "paper war" would seem to be proper for cases like these.

One moment of thought given to paper wars at once discloses the hollowness of the dogma that a declaration of war constitutes evidence of the existence of war in law, that is to say, of war in the sense of the rules of law on war. In Article III of the Convention Defining Aggression, of July 3, 1933,[54] the contracting parties agreed to consider as resorting to war in contravention of the Briand-Kellogg Pact any party which first commits any one in a series of acts. The act named in the first place is a "declaration of war upon another State." War in contravention of the Briand-Kellogg Pact thus could be waged by a mere declaration. Questions may be raised concerning the wisdom of such a rule. It represents at any rate a rare exception. A mere declaration almost invariably does not possess the magic of producing war under any of the rules of law on war. It is action—operations—not words, that counts.

This is obvious in consideration of most of the rules of law on war. It is evident, to start with, that a paper war is no war at all under the provisions of the Hague Convention (IV) of 1907 Respecting the Laws and Customs of War on Land. The Hague Convention (IV) is from beginning to end a treaty regulating military operations. It deals with the composition of the armed forces on land, prisoners of war, the conduct of military operations, spies, flags of truce, capitulations, the military authority in enemy-occupied territory, the internment of armed forces, and the care of the wounded in neutral countries. According to Article 29 of the Annex "a person thus can only be considered a spy when, acting clandestinely or on false pretense, he obtains or endeavors to obtain information in the *zone of operations* of a belligerent, with the intention of communicating it to the hostile party." [55] A paper war, to give another example, does not transmute a state into a belligerent entitled to interfere with the freedom of the seas on the ground of contraband of war as provided in the second rule of the Declaration of Paris of 1856.[56] According to Jane's *Fighting*

Ships Haiti had in 1918 a small fleet consisting of two old gun-boats, two old avisos, and an old cruiser. Should Haiti in 1918 have been entitled to visit, search, and, eventually, to capture, say, Dutch or Scandinavian merchantmen simply because on July 12 the President of Haiti had proclaimed that "a state of war exists" between Haiti and Germany? The answer certainly is "No."

It would be easy to go on for a long time enumerating rules of law on war in relation to and in the meaning of which a paper war is no war at all. It will be more advisable, however, to draw attention, instead, to the fact that a state after waging a paper war, may conclude with its opponent a "treaty of peace." Cuba, Guatemala, Haiti, Honduras, Nicaragua, and Panama are parties to the "treaty of peace between the Allied and Associated Powers and Germany," signed at Versailles June 28, 1919.[57] Cuba, Nicaragua, and Panama, in addition, are parties to the "treaty of peace between the Allied and Associated Powers and Austria," signed at Saint-Germain-en-Laye September 10, 1919.[58] The fact that two states are parties to a "treaty of peace," as has been pointed out above,[59] is no proof that they have been at war in any legal sense whatever.

Some objections of a rather delicate nature will be raised against the contention that a mere declaration almost invariably does not produce war. Is it not a fact that states have treated subjects of the state against which their declaration was directed as *enemy* aliens and their property as private *enemy* property? Is it not a fact too that merchant ships sailing under the flag of the opponent and found in ports of such states have been requisitioned as *enemy* merchant ships? All this, no doubt, is true. The declarations of war in 1917 and 1918 by Costa Rica, Cuba, Guatemala, Haiti, Honduras, and Panama thus were followed by measures against *enemy* aliens or private *enemy* property or both.[60] Haiti, for instance, passed a law on July 22, 1918, investing the executive with the power to expel or control the movements of enemy aliens and to sequester their properties. Presidential decrees thereafter restricted the movements of all Germans residing in the republic and placed the leading German commercial houses under sequestration.[61] Cuba placed five German merchant ships under armed guard and later on transferred them as a gift to the United States.[62] The Governments of China and Siam, upon issuing against Germany declarations of war which alike meant nothing in terms of operations, also seized all German merchant vessels lying in their ports.[63]

The answer to such objections is that the above measures cannot be justified through a mere declaration of war.

The status of aliens is usually regulated either by rules of international customary law—*pacta tacita*—or by treaties of commerce, navigation, friendship, and the like. Such rules usually grant aliens equality with citizens as far as their freedom of movement and respect of property are concerned. Such freedom and respect are sometimes granted even in case the contracting parties should become engaged in war. Nicaraguans residing in Germany and Germans residing in Nicaragua, to give an example, were given such liberal status by Articles XI and XII of the Commercial Treaty between Germany and Nicaragua, signed February 4, 1896.[64] Under such treaty provisions property of aliens cannot lawfully be transmuted into private enemy property in consequence of a war consisting of operations. Much less can property of aliens be subjected to such transmutation in consequence of a war consisting in nothing but a declaration.

Suppose, however, that both freedom of movement and respect of property are granted for so long only as the contracting parties remain at peace. The question which then presents itself is this: can a mere declaration of war put an end to the condition of peace upon which freedom of movement and respect of property rest and are states waging a paper war, in consequence, free to treat aliens as *enemy* aliens and their property as private *enemy* property? The answer to this question must be "No," because such abrogation of peace is wholly inconsistent with the reasons which, according to modern conceptions, justify a state in enacting rules regarding enemy aliens and private enemy property. Such abrogation can, therefore, not possibly correspond to the mutual bona fide will of the contracting parties. To prevent males from returning home and enlisting; to prevent acts of sabotage against means of national defense; to prevent espionage; to protect aliens from mob violence when passions wax hot in consequence of reverses, of operations in contravention of international law, and the like; to prevent the withdrawal of private property which may be made use of in a manner prejudicial to the national defense—such are the reasons which may justify a state in supervising and even interning or expelling aliens as *enemy* aliens and in sequestering their property as private *enemy* property. There is no justification for such measures upon the issuance of declarations of war which are destined to remain meaningless in terms of operations.

This becomes all the more clear if it is recalled that in the nineteenth and the twentieth centuries great campaigns have been conducted without discriminating at all against subjects of belligerents who had taken up domicile in the enemy country. During the Franco-Prussian War of 1870–71 Frenchmen remained entirely unmolested in Prussia and in the territories of those German states which were allies of Prussia. The subjects of the latter states in turn were permitted to remain practically without molestation in France. In consequence of the German invasion and of the siege of Paris the French Government ordered all Germans to leave the department of the Seine. That was the only restriction placed on their freedom of movement. The war of 1898 between the United States and Spain, the Sino-Japanese War of 1894, and the Russo-Japanese War of 1904–5 likewise were conducted without special measures against subjects of the enemy and their property.[65]

Little needs to be said about the question whether in a paper war a merchant ship of the opponent lying in a port of the state issuing the declaration of war is transmuted into an *enemy* merchant ship and whether, in consequence, such a ship may be requisitioned. The answer clearly is "No," at least if the states concerned are parties to the Hague Convention (VI) of 1907 Relating to the Status of Enemy Merchant Ships at the

Outbreak of Hostilities.[66] Under Article 2 of this Convention a merchant ship of one country lying in a port of another is transmuted into an *enemy* merchant ship only through the commencement of "hostilities." [67]

Concerning empty declarations of war one might well ask the question why they are made at all. They are not warnings of impending operations given to an opponent in conformity with Article 1 of the Hague Convention (III) of 1907.[68] Neither do they make sense as legislative acts calculated to safeguard the war-making power of the legislature. They must have other functions instead. It is as a rule not possible to state with certainty what these functions are. They can only be guessed since there is no acid test to the exact motives of governments issuing declarations of a paper war. One and the same declaration may well have various functions.

Quite a number of past declarations of a paper war, it seems, had first of all a political function, the function of constituting the strongest possible expression of political solidarity with states actually conducting or prepared to conduct operations against the opponent. The declarations of war made in 1917 by Cuba against Germany and Austria-Hungary belong to this category.[69] There can be little doubt that they were intended primarily as expressions of political solidarity with the United States.[70]

Costa Rica's declaration of war against Germany of May 23, 1918, was of a different nature. Costa Rica, in many respects the most progressive of the Central American states, was from 1917 to 1918 under the tyrannical and arbitrary rule of the Tinoco brothers, Federico being President and Joaquim Vice-President and Minister of War. The Tinoco administration was refused recognition by the United States, in line with President Wilson's policy of not recognizing a government which had come into power in consequence of a revolution. The example of the United States was followed by the Entente and by the larger South American republics. The prevalent motive of the declaration of a paper war against Germany, it seems, was a desire on the part of the Tinoco brothers to curry favor with the United States and the other Great Powers and to secure recognition. This diplomatic stratagem, however, failed to placate the United States and the Allies. World War I came to an end with the Tinoco regime still unrecognized by any of the Great Powers—save Germany! [71]

The declaration of a paper war against Germany with which Guatemala jumped on the Allied bandwagon on April 20, 1918, provides a strange reflection on the old saying that politics makes strange bedfellows.[72] The National Legislative Assembly which decreed the declaration was at that time actually a mere rubber-stamp parliament. It was an instrument in the hands of the all-powerful Dictator-President Manuel Estrada Cabrera, who had been ruling Guatemala since 1899 with the ruthlessness and the despotism of an oriental satrap. In the considerations to the above decree it was said that "the continental solidarity, the geographical position of the country, and the ties, historical and of an international order, existing between the United States and Guatemala indicate to the latter its line of conduct in the present case." The sincerity of this official explanation may well be doubted if one considers the national economy of Guatemala in the days of World War I and a series of acts which immediately followed the declaration of war. The most important of the coffee plantations, chief source of the nation's wealth, were either controlled or owned by Germans. German capital had branched out into other fields as well. It has been conservatively estimated that 60 per cent of the country's wealth was in German hands. Following the declaration of war a considerable number of concessions which had been granted to German companies were at once rescinded. The holdings, especially coffee plantations, of Germans and German companies were sequestered. According to a communication made by Admiral Caperton to a subcommittee of the Senate Committee on Foreign Relations, the declaration of war was even seized upon as an opportunity to *confiscate* large German estates although there had grown up through the whole of the nineteenth century a usage and practice that belligerents—*actual* belligerents, not paper belligerents!—should not confiscate private enemy property on their territory.[73] Such methods were in many ways exceedingly profitable to Dictator-President Cabrera in person. One of the motives, if not the prime motive, of the above declaration of a paper war, it is not too much to say, was to furnish a semblance of justification and a cloak of legality for measures against private "enemy" property.[74]

Regarding World War II it might be added that at the Crimean Conference in February, 1945, the Big Three, at the insistence of the U.S.S.R., decided that a declaration of war against an Axis power up to March 1, be made a condition of participation in the San Francisco World Security Conference, which was to frame the Charter of the United Nations.[75] In order to stake a claim for representation at the Conference Argentina, Chile, Ecuador, Lebanon, Paraguay, Saudi Arabia, Syria, Turkey, Uruguay, and Venezuela issued what, according to the available information, were mere declarations of a paper war.[76] The inviting powers recognized these declarations, like many previous declarations of a paper war, as valid declarations of war. The price of admission to the San Francisco Conference, indeed, was low for those members of the family of nations—democracies, pseudodemocracies, and dictatorships—which happened to be in the good graces of one or the other or of all of the Big Three. But as against this it might be said that World War II was fought by the United Nations as the champions of liberty and democracy. Participation in the San Francisco Conference, therefore, should not have been made dependent upon a farcical declaration of war. In the name of liberty and democracy it should at any rate have been open to all peace-loving and really democratic nations. It should have included states like Eire, Iceland, Sweden, and Switzerland. Iceland was actually urged to stake a claim for representation, but refused to declare war against Germany even when much pressure was exerted by the big powers following the Crimean Conference. The position of the Reykjavik Government was that this would have been ridiculous and slightly indecent for a country without armed forces.[77]

Beside the declarations of a mere paper war one ought not to overlook declarations of war which are made in the midst of operations but mean nothing in terms of *additional* operations. Operations between Italian and German troops had been going on in the Austrian Alps for fifteen months when on August 27, 1916, Italy, through the Swiss Federal Council, declared war against Germany.[78] Operations between Paraguayan and Bolivian troops had been going on for eleven months when on May 10, 1933, President Ayala of Paraguay signed a decree declaring war against Bolivia.[79] The Japanese-Chinese "incident" had been going on for almost four and a half years when, on December 9, 1941, the Chinese Government declared war against Japan.[80] In each instance operations remained what they had been before the declaration of war.

Here again one might well ask the question why such declarations are made at all. They are not warnings of impending operations given to an opponent in accordance with Article 1 of the Hague Convention (III) of 1907.[81] Neither do they make sense as legislative acts safeguarding the war-making power of the legislature. They must have other functions instead. As with declarations of a paper war it is usually not possible to state with certainty what these functions are. They can, as a rule, only be guessed. Suffice it to consider briefly the Paraguayan declaration of war of May 10, 1933. Its motive was exceptionally clear. The decree of May 10, 1933, furnishes a plausible explanation. This declaration of war constituted a bid for declarations of neutrality by third states, especially the neighboring republics of Argentina, Brazil, Chile, and Peru. The Paraguayan Government, it is important to note, emphasized that it would have been entitled to make such a bid at earlier stages of the Chaco conflict. It, however, had temporarily waived its rights under the rules of neutrality in war on land in order to give efforts at reconciliation a chance.[82]

This conveniently brings into relief a general proposition.

Operations which do not constitute war in relation to and in the meaning of a certain rule of law on war cannot be transmuted into war by the device of topping them with a declaration of war which means nothing in terms of additional operations. The blockade by Germany, Great Britain, and Italy of Venezuelan ports in 1902–3 was a pacific and, hence, an illegal blockade in relation to and in the meaning of the fourth rule of the Declaration of Paris of 1856.[83] Some think that some day in December, 1902, the blockading powers declared war and that such declaration "turned" the pacific blockade into a war blockade, a blockade to which the United States could no longer object. Such, as we have seen, was not the case. The blockading powers never issued a declaration of war. A mere declaration of war, had it actually been made, still would have left the United States free to consider the blockade as pacific and as an illegal encroachment upon her sea-borne commerce. The United States, in fact, tolerated the blockade for a paramount political reason.[84]

This brings us back to where we started. There existed at the outbreak of the Japanese-Chinese "incident" healthy legal reasons for considering the Japanese operations against China as not constituting war in relation to the cash-and-carry clause of Section 2 of the Neutrality Act of 1937.[85] Suppose that Japan had declared war against China in, say, 1938, would such a declaration have constituted war under the above rule? The answer is "No" if, like other declarations of war, it had meant nothing in terms of additional operations. It is "Yes" if it had meant additional operations calculated to interfere with the sea-borne trade of third states on the grounds of either contraband of war or blockade or both.

Section 10. On the Duration of War

When does war legally begin?

This question ought not to be confounded with a question confronting historians, the question, namely, of how historians should date the beginning of what in history is called a "war."

Lawyers are confronted with a different problem. There are scattered rules of law on the "beginning," on the "duration," or on a "time" of war. The meaning of the words "beginning," "duration," and "time" in such rules of law depends on the intent and purpose of the rules concerned.

Apart from this there is a more general problem, the problem of determining the exact point of time at which rules of law on war become applicable.[1] This likewise depends upon the intent and purpose of the rule of law on war that happens to be under consideration. Operations may constitute war in relation to certain rules of law on war while not, or not yet, constituting war in the sense of others. Operations, as they progress, in other words, begin to be war legally at diverse points of time. The question "When does war legally begin?" thus requires not one but several answers.

A mere border skirmishing such as the "battle" of San Ignazio fought for half an hour early in the morning of June 15, 1916, between two handfuls of Mexican and American troops [2] is sufficient to constitute war under Article 3 of the Annex to the Hague Convention (IV) of 1907,[3] the rule of law on war which entitles captives to the treatment of prisoners of war.[4] Other rules of law on war, however, remain dormant during such a border incident. A border incident must develop into fighting on a much larger scale in order to constitute war in the meaning of, say, the Hague Convention (V) Respecting the Rights and Duties of Neutral Powers and Persons in Case of War on Land,[5] or the Hague Convention (XIII) of 1907 Concerning the Rights and Duties of Neutral Powers in Naval War.[6] Operations sufficient to constitute war under these two conventions still do not entitle the states conducting the operations to their immediate application. Article 2 of the Hague Convention (III) of 1907 Relative to the Opening of Hostilities provides that the existence of such a war—the existence of a "state of war," as the framers of the Convention unfortunately put it—does not obligate third powers to assume a neutral conduct until after the receipt of a notification or until they have otherwise become aware of it.[7] The government of a neutral power, after receipt of a notification, or after having otherwise become aware of the existence of war, no doubt is under an obligation to declare its neutrality at once and to see to it that such declaration reaches as quickly as possible all parts of its territory, its diplomatic representatives abroad, and its warships wherever they may be. It is clear, however, that such a declaration does not take effect in regard to distant addresses until it has become known to them.[8] Operations thus may begin to be legally war at diverse points of time even in consideration of one and the same set of rules of law on war.

The question might be raised whether or not the above argument is vitiated by the wording of the many declarations of war which follow more or less closely the pattern of the historic declaration of war that France issued against Prussia on July 19, 1870. "A, from such and such date, considers itself to be in a *state of war* with B." "The government of A declares that a *state of war* exists between A and B from such and such date." [9] The beginning of the "state of war" is sometimes fixed to the minute. The British Government, to give an example, declared to the German Government in 1914 "that a state of war exists between Great Britain and Germany as from eleven P.M. on 4 August." [10] It is on the strength of such declarations of war that many international lawyers [11] hold that war begins legally to exist at one and the same point of time and that, provided a declaration of war is made, such beginning is marked by the time named in the declaration.

This, however, is an untenable argument. War, to be sure, may exist simultaneously in the diverse senses of a great many rules of law on war. There is, however, no such a thing as "war in *the* legal sense" or a "state of war." A statement to the effect that at such and such point of time a "state of war" begins is in fact a statement which passes legal comprehension. The declaration of war which the Italian Foreign Minister, Count Galeazzo Ciano, handed to the American chargé d'affaires at Rome in the afternoon of December 11, 1941, like certain other declarations, did not speak of a "state of war." It simply stated that "as from December 11, 1941, Italy considers herself *at war* with the United States." [12] Even such declarations do not make sense if they are taken as establishing *the* legal beginning of war. Declarations of war to the effect that a state considers itself at war as from a certain point of time, while not making sense as announcements establishing *the* legal beginning of war, do make sense, however, if they are taken as establishing a *terminus a quo* operations might be commenced. Whether operations are started at all and, if so, when, what sort of operations they are, and in relation to and in the meaning of which rules of law on war they constitute war, all these points remain subjects for legitimate debate.

Attention ought to be drawn in this connection to a peculiar and most perplexing kind of declaration of war. Certain declarations of war, if taken literally, convey the impression that they *antedate* "the" legal beginning of war. On June 22, 1941, at 11 A.M., Mr. Ivan Gorelkin, the Russian Ambassador to Italy, was summoned to the Palazzo Chigi, where Foreign Minister Count Ciano read him the Italian declaration of war against the U.S.S.R. It informed the Russian Ambassador "that Italy considers herself in a state of war with the U.S.S.R. from five-thirty A.M. June 22, 1941." Mr. Gorelkin had been unaware of that "state of war" for five and one-half hours.[13] On January 13, 1942, the Royal Yugoslav Government in exile decided that "the Kingdom of Yugoslavia breaks all her relations with Japan and proclaims that she is in a state of war with that power *from December 7, 1941,* when Japan attacked the United States of America and Great Britain." [14] Five months later, on June 1, 1942, the President of Mexico declared "that *since the 22d of May, 1942,* a state of war has existed between Mexico and Germany, Italy and Japan." [15]

Such declarations are open to the same objections as are the declarations which postdate the beginning of a "state of war." Since the terms "state of war" or "war in *the* legal sense" are fallacious "war in *the* legal sense" never begins. There is no commencement therefore which could be either postdated or antedated. A postdated or antedated "war in the legal sense" is past comprehension. Suppose, however, that the above declarations had not been worded according to shopworn teachings, suppose that they antedated not the beginning of a "state of war," but the beginning of "war." Even if worded this way the declarations would still be beyond legal comprehension because there is no such thing as "the" legal beginning of war. There are the many legal beginnings in the diverse senses of the various rules of law on war. Declarations of war which antedate the beginning of war have a chance of making sense only if they are taken not as legal statements, but as factual, historical statements respecting a past point of time at which operations began. If viewed in this light they still leave us confronted with several questions. Were operations started at all? If so, were they started at the past point of time given in the declaration of war? In relation to which rules of law on war did war begin? In relation to which rules did it start at subsequent points of time? Italy certainly did not start operations against the U.S.S.R. at 5:30 A.M. of June 22, 1941. "Our first contingents will leave in three days. The Duce is very much excited at the idea of this participation of ours in the conflict, and telephones me that tomorrow he will review the troops," wrote Count Ciano in his diaries on June 24, 1941.[16] On the other hand, the Yugoslav and the Mexican declarations of war of January 13 and June 1, 1942, respectively, are openly at variance with the historical truth. Each declaration antedated the beginning of a mere paper war. One is left to wonder whether even their authors could plausibly explain why they resorted to dating at all. The Mexican declaration of war of June 1, 1942, antedating the beginning of "war" to May 22—the day on which the Mexican Cabinet took cognizance of the German refusal to receive Mexico's protest against the sinking of a Mexican merchant ship off Florida—was apparently calculated to constitute the strongest possible expression of continental solidarity.[17] It would seem that for such function a simple declaration of war, a declaration neither postdating nor antedating the beginning of war, would have been more adequate.

In 1898 the United States antedated the beginning of the war against Spain. This is a most instructive case.

On April 19, 1898, after more than three years of revolution in Cuba against the dominion of Spain, the Senate and the House of Representatives passed the historic joint resolution which sounded the death knell of the last remnants of the Spanish colonial empire. It proclaimed the independence of Cuba. It demanded that Spain at once relinquish its authority and withdraw its land and naval forces from Cuba and Cuban waters. It directed the President to use the entire land and naval forces of the United States and to call into actual service the militia of the several states to such extent as might be necessary to enforce the above demands. President McKinley signed the joint resolution next day, April 20, and directed General Woodford, the Minister of the United States in Madrid, to communicate it immediately to the Government of Spain and to say that the President would proceed without further notice to use the power conferred upon him if by the hour of noon, April 23, the Government of Spain had not communicated to that of the United States a full and satisfactory response to the American demands.[18] This was in substance, though not in name, an ultimatum with a conditional declaration of war. The Spanish Government knew about President McKinley's approval of the joint resolution of April 19 and was aware of the impending ultimatum. It managed to reject it without receiving it. Early in the morning of Thursday, April 21, at 7:30 A.M., before the ultimatum could be transmitted to Spain, the Spanish Minister of Foreign Affairs notified General Woodford that the diplomatic relations between Spain and the United States were broken off. General Woodford's cable announcing the rupture reached Secretary of State Sherman within less than two hours, at 9:02 A.M.[19]

Four days later, on Monday, April 25, 1898, the Senate and the House of Representatives passed and President McKinley signed a bill which ran as follows:

Be it enacted by the Senate and the House of Representatives of the United States of America in Congress assembled, First. That war be, and is hereby declared to exist, and that war has existed since the twenty-first day of April, A.D. 1898, *including said day*, between the United States of America and the Kingdom of Spain.

Second. That the President of the United States be, and hereby is, directed and empowered to use the entire land and naval forces of the United States, and to call into actual service of the United States the militia of the several States, to such extent as may be necessary to carry this act into effect.[20]

Why this act of Congress? The second paragraph evidently was a superfluous and sterile piece of legislation. It merely re-enacted the powers already bestowed upon the President by the Act of Congress of April 20, a power which the President had not hesitated to use since April 21. Why the first paragraph, which antedated the beginning of war to midnight of Wednesday, April 20, nine hours ahead of the time when the Government of the United States learned that Spain had rejected the ultimatum? The proceedings in both branches of Congress throw no light on this question. The House of Representatives passed the bill without debate. The Senate considered it behind closed doors.[21] Likewise, the message to Congress by which President McKinley recommended the enactment of the bill does not explain why the beginning of war was antedated or, for that matter, dated at all.[22] A comparison of the text of the message with the text of the bill, nevertheless, shows what Congress intended. There can be no doubt that Congress intended to date "the" legal beginning of war as midnight, April 20.

A few observations regarding the sequence of the American operations will show the unworkability and futility of any dating, be it postdating, be it antedating, of "the" legal beginning of war. The war which the United States conducted against Spain in 1898 began progressively, step by step, to be war from the point of view of the various rules of law on war. The first paragraph of the Act of Congress of April 25, 1898, was worse than merely sterile legislation. It became a source of confusion, perplexing legal writers long after it had been passed.[23]

Certain rules of law on war became applicable almost at once. On April 21 the North Atlantic Squadron of the United States Navy lay at Key West or in that vicinity. At 4 P.M. it received over the wires from Washington the news that the United States was to conduct a war against Spain.[24] For the Navy there thus began, in the course of the afternoon of April 21, the "time of war" during which certain offenses, such as desertion, sleeping on watch, and leaving station, may be punished by death in accordance with the Articles for the Government of the Navy.[25] The North Atlantic Squadron almost simultaneously received orders to institute a blockade of certain ports of the north coast of Cuba, lying between Cardenas and Bahia Honda. This blockade was established in the course of Saturday, April 23.[26] Then, and not until then, did the United States become a belligerent under the fourth rule of the Declaration of Paris of 1856, according to which a blockade must be effective in order to be binding. On May 1 the Asiatic Squadron of the United States, under Commodore Dewey, destroyed a Spanish squadron in Manila Bay. On May 2 and 3 Commodore Dewey occupied the naval station at Cavite and Corregidor Island.[27] Then, and not until then, did the United States become a belligerent under the laws and customs of war on land.

Section 7 of the act entitled "An Act for the Better Organization of the Line of the Army of the United States," approved April 26, 1898, provided that *"in time of war*, every officer serving with troops against an enemy, who shall exercise under assignments in orders issued by competent authority, a command above that pertaining to his grade, shall be entitled to receive the pay and allowances appropriate to the command so exercised." [28] When did "the time of war" in relation to and in the meaning of this rule begin? The Paymaster General of the Army held that it did not begin until operations were conducted in the immediate presence or at least in the near neighborhood of the enemy. The Attorney General, on the contrary, thought that it would be very difficult to make up the pay rolls, if it were held that one rate of compensation is due to officers when the enemy confronts them in the field, and a lesser rate from the very moment that the enemy has disappeared from their front. He, therefore, arrived at the conclusion that the above rule applied to all operations where the troops of the United States were assembled into separate bodies, such as regiments, brigades, divisions, or corps, for the purpose of subduing the forces of Spain. Army troops assembled for this purpose at camps in the United States, consequently, were considered as "in time of war operating against an enemy" even when their service was confined to the ordinary routine of camp life.[29] This "time of war," it is interesting to note, could reasonably have been considered as having begun precisely at midnight of April 20, if on that day the above-mentioned act of Congress already had been in force.

A lawmaker cannot possibly attempt to determine "the" legal beginning of war without riding roughshod over the diverse intents and purposes of the various rules of law on war. He may, however, usefully determine the beginning of war in relation to and in the meaning of some specific rule of law on war. Section 2 of the Trading with the Enemy Act, of October 6, 1917, to give an example, provides that "the words 'the beginning of the war,' *as herein used*, shall be deemed to mean midnight ending the day on which Congress has declared or shall declare war. . . ."[30]

One final observation remains to be made about the beginning of war from the point of view of the law. War in relation to and in the meaning of certain rules of law on war is in practice sometimes considered as having started surprisingly early. Thus it would be easy to quote prize court decisions characteristic of the partisanship that is apt to dominate the deliberations of national prize courts, decisions in which war was considered as having begun surprisingly early—both in relation to the right to capture private enemy property on the high seas and in relation to the right to capture merchant vessels of third states for the carriage of contraband of war—because such early beginning suited the national economic and political self-interest of the state concerned.

When does war legally end?

This question again ought not to be confounded with a question confronting historians, the question, namely, of how historians should date the termination of what in history is called a "war."

The problem of determining the end of war from the point of view of the law is of an entirely different nature. Certain rules of law refer to the "end" or the "close" of war. Article 5 of the Hague Convention (VIII) of 1907 Relative to the Laying of Automatic Submarine Contact Mines is an example in point. "*At the close of the war*, the contracting Powers undertake to do their utmost to remove the mines which they have laid, each Power removing its own mines." [31] It clearly is the business of interpretation to find out what is meant by "end," or "close."

Apart from this there is the more general problem of establishing the exact point of time at which the various rules of law on war cease to be applicable. The answer to this question again is a matter of interpretation. It depends upon the intent and purpose of the rule of law on war that happens to be under consideration. The "end" or "close," and the applicability in relation to certain rules of law on war is a different thing from what it is in relation to others. There is, in other words, no such a thing as "the" legal end of war, even though such a uniform legal end has time and again been asserted by those who proceed on the fictitious theory of "war in *the* legal sense" or the "state of war."

These rather abstract assertions will at once become convincing by illustration through some practical examples.

It is a matter of common knowledge that there are in the main three different ways in which may be terminated what, from the historical point of view, we call a "war." A small number of wars have ended through simple cessation of operations. In 1867 the war—by many called "intervention"—of France against Mexico ended that way. Diplomatic relations between the two countries remained suspended until they were restored in 1883.[32] More numerous are the instances in which war ended through *debellatio* or subjugation. Thus Italy came into existence in 1859–60 through the subjugation by Sardinia of the Kingdom of the Two Sicilies, the Grand Duchy of Tuscany, and the Duchies of Parma and Modena. In 1870 there followed the subjugation of the Papal States by Italy. The most frequent mode of terminating a war, however, is a treaty of peace, negotiated either while operations continue or after the conclusion of a general armistice. That war ends from the legal point of view at different times can best be seen if we consider this last and, so to speak, normal mode of terminating what in history is called a "war."

According to Article 2 of the Hague Convention (V) of 1907 Respecting the Rights and Duties of Neutral Powers and Persons in Case of War on Land, belligerents are forbidden to move troops or convoys of either munitions or supplies across the territory of a neutral power.[33] Article 24 of the Hague Convention (XIII) of 1907 provides that, if, notwithstanding the notification of a neutral power, a belligerent ship of war does not leave a port where it is not entitled to stay, the neutral power is entitled to take such measures as it considers necessary to render the ship incapable of taking the sea *during the war*. On November 11, 1918, the Allied and Associated Powers concluded with Germany a general armistice about the nature of which there could be no doubts.[34] It was concluded because Germany could no longer continue the struggle and desired peace. The Netherlands and Sweden rightly held that with the armistice of November 11, 1918, the war between Germany and the Allied and Associated Powers had come to an end in relation to and in the meaning of the two rules of law on war mentioned above. The Netherlands, therefore, allowed disarmed bodies of German troops to retreat through the Netherlands.[35] Sweden, immediately after the armistice of November 11, 1918, dismissed the German submarines which she had interned in her ports.[36]

For other rules of law on war the date of the signature or ratification of a treaty of peace is a natural point of time at which their applicability comes to an end. Thus desertion in the United States Navy committed after December 10, 1898, the date on which the treaty of peace with Spain was signed, was considered as no longer being committed "in time of war" under Article 4 of the Articles for the Government of the Navy.[37]

War in relation to and in the meaning of still other rules of law on war outlasts the date on which a treaty of peace comes into force. It is particularly interesting in this respect to unearth older peace treaties, peace treaties concluded in days when no telephone and cable lines and no radios were available to inform the armed forces of the conclusion of peace. Take, for instance, Article II of the Treaty of Peace and Amity, signed by Great Britain and the United States at Ghent on December 24, 1814, and ratified on December 31, 1814, and February 17, 1815, respectively.[38] It named various regions of the globe and stipulated for each of them a period of time, subsequent to the ratification by both sides of the treaty of peace, after which operations by sea and by land had to cease. The period was twelve days for the British and Irish channels, the Gulf of Mexico, the West Indies, the eastern coast of the United States and as far eastward in the Atlantic as 36° west longitude from the meridian of Greenwich. It was forty, sixty, ninety, and one hundred and twenty days, respectively, for more distant regions. Thus merchant ships sailing under the United States and the British flags remained in the regions and for the periods of time concerned subject to the treatment according to the rules of law on war regarding the capture, the bringing into port, and the adjudication of enemy merchant vessels. As against this there might be quoted, by way of contrast, the Peace Treaty signed in Moscow on March 12, 1940, by the U.S.S.R. and Finland. It was negotiated without a preceding armistice and came into force immediately upon being signed. In the protocol attached thereto the contracting powers agreed that both sides were to cease operations at noon March 13, 1940, Leningrad time.[39]

From among modern rules of law on war the applicability of which is likely to outlast the conclusion of a treaty of peace might be quoted a great many of the provisions of the elaborate Geneva Convention Concerning the Treatment of Prisoners of War, of July 27, 1929.[40] According to Article 75 of the Convention the repatriation of prisoners of war shall in any case be effected as soon as possible after the conclusion of peace. Captives, it goes without saying, remain prisoners of war and are entitled to the human treatment and protection in accordance with their status until they are brought to the frontier and handed back to their government. The victor owes such treatment to the vanquished beyond the conclusion of a treaty of peace and vice versa.

War in relation to and in the meaning of certain rules of law on war is in practice sometimes considered as having ended surprisingly early. In the sense of other rules of law on war it is, on the contrary, considered as having ended surprisingly late. There are all sorts of reasons for these surprisingly early or late endings.

In this connection "the laws and customs of war on land," now embodied in Hague Conventions (II) of 1899 and (IV) of 1907,[41] are again of the greatest interest. At what time is it permissible for one contracting party to consider another as being subjugated and no longer existing? At what date, therefore, may "the laws and customs of war on land" be considered as being no longer applicable? History, especially the history of Western imperialism, presents many cases of premature annexations, of annexations proclaimed for the double purpose of making a show of political strength at home and of getting rid of the restrictions imposed on warfare by "the laws and customs of war on land." Troops of "backward peoples" who for some time were treated as parties to war under "the laws and customs" were suddenly declared to be bands of "brigands" and hunted down accordingly. Regular warfare gave way to "pacification." Captives were no longer treated as prisoners of war but were eliminated, instead, through mass executions. Villages and towns were no longer respected as private enemy properties but were put to the torch.[42]

One of the latest cases of a premature annexation concerns

Ethiopia. It was at 4 P.M. on May 5, 1936, that Marshal Pietro Badoglio led a cavalcade of Italian soldiers on their final dash into Addis Ababa, the capital of Ethiopia. A few hours later Premier Mussolini, speaking to a multitude from a balcony in the Piazza Venezia in Rome, declared: "I announce to the Italian people and to the world that the war is over. I announce to the Italian people and to the world that peace has been re-established. . . . Ethiopia is Italian." On May 14 and 16, respectively, the Italian Chamber of Deputies and the Senate unanimously approved a bill presented by Premier Mussolini, annexing Ethiopia and proclaiming King Victor Emmanuel Emperor.[43]

There can be no doubt that Ethiopia was not subjugated when its annexation was announced. Whether subjugation was ever accomplished and, if so, when, is extremely hard to determine. There were conflicting reports which could not be verified on account of Italy's refusal to permit accredited journalists to enter Ethiopia.[44] According to a report published in *The Times* of London, Ethiopia—with the exception of the bigger towns, where means of communication were such that military aid could be secured quickly in cases of emergency—was in the autumn of 1937 still governed by Ethiopian chieftains who carried on guerrilla warfare against the Italians, harassing them at every opportunity.[45] In a memorable debate which took place at the Council table of the League of Nations on May 12, 1938 [46]—memorable above all to the student of a policy of appeasement toward aggressor states—Lord Halifax declared: "The situation, according to our information, is that the Italian Government has obtained control of virtually all the former territory of Ethiopia, and while resistance is still continuing in certain parts of the country, there is no organized native authority and no central native administration with the slightest prospect of reconquering the country." [47] As against this Emperor Haile Selassie, in a courageous replication, pictured Italy as still holding only a fraction of Ethiopia and said his chiefs were more loyal than ever to him. "The fact is that the war continues." [48]

However that may have been, certain it is that the annexation, in the Fascist way of thinking, at once reduced whatever fighting occurred thereafter to the status of suppressing "brigandage." After May 5, 1936, a great number of Ethiopians caught with arms were executed, according to press reports. Credibility was lent to such reports by the savage repressive measures which were taken after the abortive attempt to kill Marshal Rudolfo Graziani, the Viceroy, on February 19, 1936. Two thousand Ethiopians were seized in Addis Ababa and all those who possessed arms on their persons or in their homes were shot by firing squads.[49] Three days later Premier Mussolini expressly declared "death for every native chieftain or officer who opposes Italian troops even in territory yet unoccupied."[50] Emperor Haile Sclassie, in a letter addressed to the Secretary General of the League of Nations, soon thereafter denounced the killing of Ethiopian captives as a violation of the Hague Convention (IV) of 1907 Concerning the Laws and Customs of War on Land.[51] Both Italy and Ethiopia were parties to that Convention.[52, 53]

Now as to rules of law on war in relation to and in the meaning of which war has sometimes been considered as ending conspicuously late. As examples might be quoted the rules of the Declaration of Paris of 1856 which entitle belligerents to interfere with the sea-borne commerce of third states on the grounds of contraband or blockade.[54] In the armistice agreement signed at Paris on April 4, 1885, France and China agreed that France was to retain the right to visit and search neutral vessels on the high seas for contraband of war during the whole period of the armistice and until the signature and ratification by China of a treaty of peace.[55] This looks like a rather strange agreement indeed. After combat operations have been terminated because a definite decision has been reached, cargoes can no longer reasonably be considered as constituting contraband of war. Third states, one might think, should have protested in accordance with the principle that a treaty made between others cannot create duties for them. *Pacta tertiis nec nocent nec prosunt.* The above agreement between France and China, however, reflected but a general practice. Belligerents, with few exceptions,[56] have time and again insisted on exercising the right of interfering with the freedom of the seas on the grounds of contraband of war or blockade during the whole period of a general armistice and until the conclusion of a treaty of peace.[57] Such practice was defended by invoking the artificial "principle" that war does not end until the ratification of a treaty of peace by the respective sovereigns.[58] It was given support by Article 92 of the Draft Code of Maritime Warfare, adopted by the Institute of International Law at its meetings at Oxford in 1913.[59] The truth of the matter is that such a rule is too rigid. There are basically two kinds of general armistices, first, general armistices after which operations might be continued and, secondly, general armistices asked for and granted because a continuance of operations by the losing side is out of the question. The general armistices granted by the Allied and Associated Powers to the Central Powers in 1918 belong to the second category. So does the general armistice granted on September 19, 1944, to Finland by the U.S.S.R. and other members of the United Nations. A renewal of operations by Finland was so much out of the question that some peace terms were forthwith incorporated into the armistice agreement.[60] To interfere with the sea-borne commerce of third states any longer on the grounds of contraband of war or of blockade after the conclusion of a general armistice of the latter category may serve the economic and political self-interest of the victor. It cannot be justified, however, by invoking such rules of law on war as the Declaration of Paris.[61]

Similarly, attention ought to be drawn again to the case of *Hamilton* v. *McClaughry, Warden.*[62] The operations of United States troops in China in 1900–1, for reasons which have been indicated above,[63] were called an "expedition." Both the general court-martial convened and sitting at Peking and the Circuit Court for the District of Kansas, nevertheless, held that these operations constituted war under the fifty-eighth article of war, according to the Revised Statutes of the

United States of 1873–74. There is nothing surprising in such
a view. It is surprising, however, that the defendant was convicted of murder committed "in time of war," even though
he served at the time of the homicide, December 23, 1900,
with a troop of cavalry whose sole function for several months
had been to maintain order in certain sections of Peking. A
legislative lacuna, it seems, was the basic reason for such a finding. There existed no rule of law to convict the defendant of
murder committed *abroad* "in time of peace." The general
court-martial, in other words, was faced with the alternative
either of convicting the defendant of murder committed "in
time of war" or of rendering a judgment of acquittal. *Nullum
crimen sine lege.* Faced with such an alternative the court
stretched the "time of war" in the fifty-eighth article of war
in such a way as to include the period of time during which
the United States troops were charged with nothing but police
duties.[64]

It has been pointed out above what reasons stand in the way
of decreeing "the" legal beginning of war. The same reasons
stand in the way of decreeing "the" legal end of war. War in
relation to and in the meaning of certain rules of law on war
comes to an end sooner than it does in relation to and in the
meaning of others. War, from the legal point of view, in other
words comes into and goes out of existence gradually. Peace
from the legal point of view, vice versa, goes out from and
comes back into existence step by step.

Quite a few instances, no doubt, could be quoted where
states have proclaimed either "the" legal end of war or "the"
legal restoration of peace. The student of World War I will
remember the dramatic announcement with which Leon
Trotzky, at a certain break in the Brest-Litovsk peace negotiations, threw up his cards altogether. On February 10, 1918,
Trotzky, the President of the Russian delegation at the Brest-
Litovsk peace conference, denounced the treaty of peace
proffered by Germany and its allies during negotiations under
an armistice and announced that Russia, while desisting from
signing the treaty of peace, declared "the *state of war* with

Germany, Austria-Hungary, Turkey, and Bulgaria as ended."
The Russian Government simultaneously gave orders for
complete demobilization of the Russian forces on all fronts.[65]
China, to give another example, after having refused to sign
the Treaty of Peace of Versailles, decreed on September 3,
1919, that a "state of peace" between Germany and China had
been restored.[66] Such announcements are legally as unintelligible as are the expressions "state of war," or "war in *the* legal
sense," and "state of peace," or "peace in *the* legal sense."

Official statements simply announcing the end of war (not
the end of a "state of war") or the restoration of peace (not
the restoration of a "state of peace") do make sense from various points of view.

Such statements often are meant as simple common-sense
statements and are made with no legal intention whatever.
Thus on November 11, 1918, at one o'clock in the afternoon,
President Wilson in person announced to Congress the terms
of the armistice agreement concluded on that day between the
Allied and Associated Powers and Germany. After having
made known the terms, the President added: "The war thus
comes to an end; for having accepted these terms of armistice,
it will be impossible for the German command to renew it." [67]
It is quite clear that President Wilson simply intended to announce through Congress to the entire country that the combat operations of the Great War had come to an end.

Other official statements to the effect that war has come to
an end or that peace has been restored are *political* statements.
Such, for instance, is the case with a stock phrase that can be
found in one peace treaty after another, that "from the day of
the exchange of the ratifications of the present treaty there
shall be peace and friendship" or "peace and friendship in per-
petuity" between the contracting powers.[68] Such stipulations
are more or less serious mutual announcements of a future policy of peace and not by any means agreements that war in
every conceivable legal sense has come to an end. The faithful
observance of certain international rules of law on war, such
as most of the rules of the Geneva Convention Concerning the

Treatment of Prisoners of War, of 1929, may demand that they be applied beyond the conclusion of a treaty of peace. Equity and justice may demand that war in relation to certain municipal rules of law on war also be considered as continuing beyond the conclusion of a treaty of peace. Suppose that a belligerent has enacted "for the duration" of a war special rules of law in order to meet a housing shortage that may have been caused through devastating aerial bombardments. Equity and justice demand that war in the meaning of such emergency legislation be considered as continuing as long as the shortage lasts and regardless of a stipulation in a treaty of peace to the effect that "from the exchange of ratifications of the present treaty there shall be peace and friendship between the contracting parties."

Official statements that war has come to an end, finally, do make sense as legal statements if they concern specific rules of law on war and not the rules of law on war *in toto*. Lest the application of specific rules of law on war be continued by some courts or administrative authorities while being discontinued by others, the legislature will do well to determine the end of their applicability. Section 2 of the Trading with the Enemy Act of 1917 thus provides: "The words 'end of war,' *as used herein*, shall be deemed to mean the date of proclamation of exchange of ratifications of the treaty of peace, unless the President shall, by proclamation, declare a prior date, in which case the date so proclaimed shall be deemed to be the 'end of war' within the meaning of this Act." [69]

Free communication, as it were, and the resumption of trade relations with Germany were authorized on July 14, 1919, by a general enemy license issued by the War Trade Board Section of the Department of State.[70] A joint resolution of Congress, approved March 3, 1921, declared that—with certain exceptions—rules of law in acts of Congress, joint resolutions, and proclamations of the President relating to the duration or date of termination of the war between Germany and Austria-Hungary on the one hand and the United States on the other were to be interpreted as if such a war had come to an end on the date when the resolution became effective.[71] So far so good. With the applicability of much of America's wartime legislation gone, what remained to be done in the near future was to pass a second joint resolution declaring that war in relation to all other American municipal rules of law on war had come to an end. Instead of doing so, Congress passed the Knox-Porter resolution, approved July 2, 1921, which declared that the *state of war* between Germany and Austria-Hungary on the one hand and the United States of America on the other had come to an end.[72] The debates in the House on June 30 and in the Senate on June 30 and July 1 which preceded the passage of the Knox-Porter resolution were marked by confusion.[73] The representatives and senators could not possibly understand just what was supposed to have come to an end. Some members thought that Congress was merely registering a fact, the fact that combat operations had come to an end long ago. President Wilson had stated this fact in his address to Congress, November 11, 1918.[74] Others, on the contrary, were under the impression that something "technical," that some legal issue was involved.[75] The general uneasiness that prevailed in both branches of the Congress plainly came to the fore in a frank admission by Senator Jones of New Mexico:

Mr. President, in the proceedings of this body I have always endeavored to obtain some clear notion of my own as to what the Senate was trying to do. I think I have generally succeeded in satisfying my own mind, but I must confess that the action which the Senate is called upon to take is not clear. I confess great confusion of thought as to what the joint resolution is.[76]

The truth of the matter is that Congress had proceeded on a theory that defies understanding, when by the Acts of April 6, 1917, and December 7, 1917, respectively, it declared that a "state of war"—war in *the* legal sense—had been thrust upon the United States by Germany and Austria-Hungary.[77] It proceeded on that fictitious theory again while passing the Knox-Porter resolution in 1921. The Acts of Congress of

April 6 and December 7, 1917, to put it bluntly, recognized the existence of a phantom; the Knox-Porter resolution, on the contrary, declared that it had vanished.

Is it permissible to conclude considerations of a serious problem in a lighter vein? There remains something to be said about wars that apparently never end. Every once in a while press dispatches allege that certain states have been "technically" at war for an unusual length of time.

A Paris wireless to the *New York Times* of March 31, 1938,[78] reported a change of sovereigns in Liechtenstein, the tiny principality of approximately 12,000 persons on the upper Rhine between Austria and Switzerland. The dispatch repeated the often-heard story that Liechtenstein and Prussia have been "technically" at war since 1866. What is the background of this extraordinary assertion?

Liechtenstein is a remnant of the 360 or so states which in the eighteenth and up to the beginning of the nineteenth century formed the Holy Roman Empire, the German Empire which had been founded by Charlemagne and was dissolved in 1806. In 1815 Liechtenstein joined with all the other German states in the German Confederation, which had been framed at the Congress of Vienna and was presided over by Austria. In the meeting of the federal diet of June 14, 1866, the delegate of Liechtenstein voted for and helped to carry the motion for the enactment of the decree mobilizing the federal army. This decree was in substance, though not in so many words, a declaration of war against Prussia. It ended the long diplomatic duel for ascendancy between Austria and Prussia and led at once to the Seven Weeks' War between Austria and the German states siding with her on the one hand and Prussia and the German states siding with her on the other. The war culminated in the crushing Austrian defeat of Königgrätz on July 3. Liechtenstein's contingent to the federal army, consisting of a company of ninety-odd sharpshooters commanded by a first lieutenant, took no part in the military operations against Prussia. Without firing one shot it assisted, however, the Austrian Army of the South in protecting the southern frontier of Austria during the short war which Austria concurrently and successfully fought against Italy, the Ally of Prussia. The Seven Weeks' War was followed by the dissolution of the German Confederation and the creation under the hegemony of Prussia of the North German Federation, the predecessor of the Second Empire proclaimed in Versailles in 1871. These developments isolated Liechtenstein politically. The contingent of ninety-odd sharpshooters lost its raison d'être. In 1868 Liechtenstein, hence, completely disarmed. Its armed force ever since has consisted of a number of policemen that can be counted with the fingers of one hand.[79]

Why then should Liechtenstein in 1938 still have been "technically" at war with Prussia? Liechtenstein, as has been said before, participated in the declaration of war against Prussia of June 14, 1866. According to a delusion mentioned above [80] a declaration of war leads, as inevitably as day follows night, to the creation of that technical phantom called "state of war," war in *the* legal sense. According to another delusion this phantom continues in existence until something has been done to remove it. The conclusion of a treaty styled "treaty of peace" or a legislative pronouncement in the nature of the Knox-Porter resolution will exorcise it. Prussia signed the peace treaty of Prague with Austria on August 23, 1866.[81] It signed special peace treaties with other German states that had conducted military operations as Allies of Austria, to wit, the Kingdoms of Württemberg, Bavaria, and Saxony, the Grand Duchies of Baden and Hesse, the Duchy of Saxe-Meiningen, and the principality of Reuss elder line.[82] It annexed the Kingdom of Hannover, the Electorate of Hesse-Cassel, the Duchy of Nassau, and the Free City of Frankfurt-on-the-Main.[83] It did not, however, negotiate a treaty of peace with the Principality of Liechtenstein.[84] Hence the "state of war" which in 1938 was still hovering over little Liechtenstein and promised to become a permanent phenomenon in the European political picture.

There are other communities living under some permanent "state of war." Berwick-on-Tweed is said to have been in the last century neither English nor Scottish. So treaties made by the United Kingdom had to include Berwick as a special party. In the treaty of peace signed after the Crimean War at Paris, March 30, 1856, Berwick was overlooked. So Berwick is "technically" still at war with Imperial Russia.[85]

The Republic of San Marino is said to have declared war on Turkey in 1915. It is not, however, a party to the treaty of peace of Lausanne of 1923. A "state of war," therefore, still exists between San Marino and Turkey.[86]

The Tuscarora Indian tribe of New York state, part of the Iroquois group, is reported as having declared war on Germany in 1917 as an "independent people." The Tuscarora tribe, however, never offered to smoke the peace pipe with a German representative during peace negotiations and therefore a "state of war" with Germany still exists.[87]

It is all nonsense, although certainly most attractive nonsense.

Section 11. Observations Regarding War and Peace under the Charter of the United Nations

At this writing it is still difficult to comment legally upon war and peace under the Charter of the United Nations, the successor to the Covenant of the League of Nations. In the fall of 1944, representatives of the United States, the United Kingdom, the Soviet Union, and China met at Dumbarton Oaks and agreed upon proposals for a general international organization to maintain international peace and security.[1] The important Dumbarton Oaks conversations were secret. The Charter is the result of discussions at San Francisco from April 25 to June 26, 1945, between representatives of fifty states, discussions based upon the proposals of Dumbarton Oaks. The plenary sessions and the commissions of the Conference of San Francisco were held in public. The committees and subcommittees in which the real work of the Conference was done, however, were not public. Their minutes still await publication. Without a knowledge of the *travaux préparatoires* it is often not possible to be sure of the intents and purposes which motivated the wording of the Charter.

The United Nations surely is, first of all, an antiwar agency. A perusal of the Charter as a treaty establishing an antiwar agency reveals a striking fact: the apparent absence of rules of law on war. The Charter refers to war as such [2] but once. It does so not in any of its 111 articles but in the preamble only. "We the peoples of the United Nations determined to save succeeding generations from the scourge of *war*,[3] which twice in our lifetime has brought untold sorrow to mankind, . . . have resolved to combine our efforts to accomplish these aims." The accent in the Charter is on peace, not on war. It refers to "peace and security" not less than thirty-two times. The United Nations, in other words, is an antiwar agency by means of rules of law on peace. There is, on the whole, nothing surprising in this. An antiwar agency manifestly can be established either through rules of law for the maintenance of peace or through rules of law against war. The framers of the Covenant of the League of Nations had chosen the second alternative. The framers of the Charter have preferred the first one. What is surprising, however, is the fact that the word "war" appears in the Charter not even in places where one would expect it on the basis of common sense and common parlance. Take, for instance, Article 1, which states the purposes of the United Nations. Peace and security, one should think, can be maintained or restored by the prevention and removal of threats to the peace (or threats of *war*) and by the suppression of *war*. The wording of Article 1, however, is not as simple as that. Article 1 proclaims the first and overriding purpose of the United Nations is "to maintain international peace and security, and to that end: to take effective measures for the prevention and removal of *threats to the peace* and for the suppression of *acts of aggression* or *other breaches of the peace*. . . ."[4] Here and elsewhere in the Charter the word "war," the word which has caused so much trouble and controversy in the past, no doubt has been studiously avoided. The *travaux préparatoires*, it is to be hoped, will reveal why the framers of the Charter endeavored to steer clear of it. Such endeavor perhaps can be traced to the conclusion of the widely noted treatise criticized above [5] on "The Attempt to Define War," published by the Carnegie Endowment for International Peace, Division of Intercourse and Education, in 1933. The author, after an attempt to find "the" legal definition of war, an attempt which, as we have seen, was doomed to failure, concludes that "it is desirable to eliminate the word [war] with all its unpleasant psychology from the vocabulary of international affairs" and to restate the rules of law on war in other terms.[6]

However that may be, one thing is certain: a treaty establishing an antiwar agency may rest on rules of law on peace and thereby avoid the controversial word "war," but it cannot avoid the notion of war. Every single rule of law on peace in the Charter is an indirect rule of law on war. The easiest way to prove that peace exists is by proving that war does not exist. The easiest way of proving that peace does not exist is by proving that war does exist. Under Chapter VI of the Charter the Security Council can deal with a dispute among members of the United Nations only if its continuance "is likely to endanger international peace and security." In the meeting of the Security Council of January 30, 1946, Mr. Vishinsky, Soviet Vice Foreign Commissar, demanded that the dispute between Iran and the U.S.S.R. be removed from the agenda of the Security Council. It is no accident that Mr. Vishinsky should have done so by contending: "We have no intention of waging *war* on Iran and Iran has, I believe, no intention of waging *war* upon us." [7] Under Article 39 the Security Council, in order "to maintain or restore international peace and security," shall in the first place "determine the existence of any *threat to the peace, breach of the peace*, or *act of aggression*." [8] It is clear that a *threat of war* exists if international peace and security need to be maintained. It is likewise clear that *war* exists if international peace and security need to be restored. The words "breach of the peace, or act of aggression," therefore, simply paraphrase the expression "recourse to war" just as the expression "threat to the peace" paraphrases the expression "threat of war." By way of parenthesis it might be added that the Charter could only have gained in clarity if the words "act of aggression" had been omitted. These words are superfluous in the first place. The idea of "recourse to war" is sufficiently covered by the expression "breach of the peace." It is, furthermore, logically incorrect to say "breach of the peace, *or* act of aggression." "Aggression" is, but "breach of the peace" is not, a term of opprobrium. It will be observed also that the expression "act of aggression" is not used consistently. Article 1 speaks of "the suppression of acts of aggression or *other* breaches of the peace." [9] Under Article 39, however, the Security Council is charged with the duty of determining the existence of any "breach of the peace, *or* acts of aggression." [10] The inconsistency is so obvious as to need no comment. One is left to wonder why it was not corrected by the Coordinating Committee of the San Francisco Conference.

What, then, constitutes war, paraphrased by the expressions "breach of the peace" and "act of aggression," in relation to Article 39 of the Charter of United Nations? What is the essence of and which are the parties to such a war? Is it characterized by any specific purpose? At San Francisco the Bolivian delegation moved that the Charter should contain a definition of the term "aggression" as it stands now in Article 39 of the Charter, the provision in which are concentrated the most important powers of the Security Council. The Bolivian motion, however, was defeated chiefly because Committee 3 (Enforcement Arrangements) of Commission III (Security Council) thought it impossible that a definition could be made so tight as to leave no loophole. [11]

The answer to the question as to what constitutes war under the Charter must under these circumstances be found through interpretation. According to Article 24 (1) the members of the United Nations "confer on the Security Council primary responsibility for the maintenance of international peace and security." Under Article 24 (2) the Security Council shall in discharging these duties "act in accordance with the Purposes and Principles of the United Nations." [12] It would seem, however, that besides the purposes and principles there must also be considered the preamble of the Charter. The question whether or not the preamble of a legal instrument contains rules of law is differently answered in different systems of law. The Report to the President on the Results of the San Francisco Conference made by former Secretary of State Edward R. Stettinius, Jr., states, however, that "the Conference did not doubt that the statements expressed in the Preamble constitute valid evidence on the basis of which the Charter may hereafter be interpreted." [13]

If one considers both the preamble on the one hand and the purposes and principles on the other, one will find that no clear-cut answer can be given to the question as to what is the *essence* of war. In the preamble the United Nations declare their determination "to ensure, by the acceptance of principles and the institution of methods, that *armed* force shall not be used, save in the common interest." [14] Under Article 2 (4), however, "all members shall refrain in their international relations from the *threat or use of force* against the territorial integrity or political independence of any state, or in any other manner inconsistent with the Purposes of the United Nations." [15] The inconsistency again is so obvious as to need no comment. It is interesting to note, however, that the text of Article 2 (4) corresponds to the Atlantic Charter of August 14, 1941, and to the Declaration by the United Nations of January 1, 1942, in which the signatory powers declared that "they believe that all the nations of the world, for realistic as well as spiritual reasons, must come to the abandonment of the *use of force*." [16] The Government of the United States has made known that it considers not only *armed* force but every threat or use of force in any manner inconsistent with the purposes of the United Nations as being prohibited by the Charter. On February 28, 1946, Secretary of State James F.

Byrnes declared before the Overseas Press Club of America: "The Charter forbids aggression and we cannot allow aggression to be accomplished by coercion or pressure or by subterfuges such as political infiltration." [17] Such interpretation would entitle the United Nations to cope with that modern form of making war which starts with the activities of the fifth column and would present an entirely new legal concept of war. Whereas war in relation to and in the meaning of the rules of law on war with which we have met before consists almost invariably of operations,[18] war under the Charter would consist not only of operations but of every use of force in any manner inconsistent with the purposes of the United Nations.

The *parties* to war in relation to and in the meaning of Article 39 of the Charter are *states* and states only. It is not the task of the Security Council to maintain or restore internal peace if an insurrection or civil war threatens or breaks out. Under Article 1 (1) the United Nations are to maintain *"international* peace and security" and under Article 2 (7) "nothing contained in the present charter shall authorize the United Nations to intervene in matters which are essentially within the domestic jurisdiction of any state." On the other hand, both members of the United Nations and states which are not members can be parties to war. The Charter, to be sure, does not and cannot obligate states which are not members of the United Nations. Under Article 2 (4), however, the members "shall refrain from the threat or use of force against the territorial integrity or political independence of *any* state" [19] and under Article 2 (6) the United Nations shall insure that states which are not members of the United Nations act in accordance with the principles of the Charter "so far as may be necessary for the maintenance of international peace and security."

In the light of Article 2 (4) war in the sense of Article 39 of the Charter consists in the use of force "in any manner inconsistent with the purposes of the United Nations." Consistent with the Charter is the use of force only in two cases. (1) Under Articles 107 and 53 (1) the use of force against the defeated enemy states under special treaties [20] or under regional arrangements directed against renewal of aggressive policy on the part of any such state has been exempted from the scope of the Security Council. The United Nations may, however, at some future date on request of the governments concerned, be charged with the responsibility for preventing further aggression by such states. This puts for an unspecified length of time the enforcement of peace terms, for example,[21] and the application of the mutual-assistance treaties the U.S.S.R. has made with Poland, Yugoslavia, Czechoslovakia, and other states since 1942 beyond the scope of the United Nations Charter. (2) Under Article 51 individual or collective self-defense is permitted "if an armed attack occurs against a member of the United Nations until the Security Council has taken measures necessary to maintain [*sic*] international peace and security."

There is no purpose in theorizing still further about an anti-war rule of law which, we know, has not been enforced in the past and will not be enforced in the foreseeable future. It is all too clear by now that the United Nations cannot be relied upon for preventing and suppressing war. During the few years of its existence the Charter has been violated with impunity many times through the illegal use of *armed* force and (under the United States' interpretation) through other more subtle uses of force which have their origin in the effort to extend the power of Soviet communism throughout the world. The Charter is shadowed already by the Atlantic Pact, a new alliance for peace against the danger of Soviet aggression.

In spite of this, brief attention must now be invited to a final aspect of the problem as to what constitutes war under the Charter of the United Nations. The relevant provisions are Articles 42 and 43 (1). Under Article 42 the Security Council "may take such action by air, sea, or land as may be necessary to maintain or restore international peace and security." Under Article 43 (1) the members of the United Nations undertake to make armed forces available to the

Security Council, "on its call and in accordance with a special agreement or agreements."

Today an "international police force" is no nearer realization than it was when the United Nations started. Not one agreement under Article 43 has been concluded. It is extremely unlikely that given the present Great Power differences this force can be formed at all. For the sake of argument let us suppose, however, that Article 43 will not remain a dead letter indefinitely. Would operations conducted by contingents as provided for under Article 43 (1) constitute war legally? Such operations, if they should ever come to pass, will look like but in all probability will not be called "war." They will be called "preventive action" or "enforcement action," as in Article 2 (5) of the Charter, or will be given some other more pleasant name than "war." We have seen, however, that the name of operations (or lack of a name) should not be depended upon in answering the question as to whether they constitute war legally.

In the report submitted to the Senate on November 8, 1945, by Tom Connally on S. 1580 (concerning the participation of the United States in the United Nations),[22] we read: "Preventive or enforcement action by these forces upon the orders of the Security Council would not be an act of war but would be international action for the preservation of the peace and for the purpose of preventing war."[23] This statement sounds reasonable enough. However, it is not what it was intended to be, namely, a *legal* statement. It is not a legal statement because it was made *in vacuo* as far as the rules of law on war are concerned.[24]

If one considers operations of contingents as envisaged in Article 43 (1) of the Charter in the light of the various rules of law on war, one will find that in relation to certain rules they do constitute war whereas in the sense of others they do not. Will the contingents of states which in the preamble of the Charter have reaffirmed their faith "in the dignity and worth of the human person" observe such rules for the conduct of war as laid down in the Hague Conventions (II) of

1899 and (IV) of 1907 [25] and in the Geneva Convention Concerning the Treatment of Prisoners of War, of July 27, 1929? [26] Will the states whose laws provide for special pay for officers and men "in time of war" contend that their contingents are on a mission of peace? To ask such questions is to answer them.

On the other hand, to give only one example, operations under Article 42 of the Charter ought not to be considered as constituting war in relation to those rules of constitutional law of the states represented in the Security Council which reserve the decision as to a declaration of war to the legislature. Such operations, if they are to be effective, may have to be undertaken at short notice, without long-drawn parliamentary debates and hearings. The governments of the states represented in the Security Council, therefore, ought to be free to instruct their delegates to order their contingents into action through a decision of the Security Council and without asking for the consent of the legislature. Section 6 of the United States Participation Act, approved December 20, 1945,[27] recognizes that the president of the United States does have such freedom. Operations to maintain or restore international peace and security by armed forces of the United States on order of the Security Council do not constitute war in relation to Article I, Section 8, Paragraph 11 of the Constitution of the United States if the armed forces are not in excess of what will be stipulated in a special agreement between the United States and the Security Council. Such operations, on the contrary, do constitute war in relation to the warmaking power of the Congress and will require its authorization if the United States is to furnish armed forces in excess of what will be stipulated.

Indeed, what is true of other operations is true also of the "preventive action" or "enforcement action" of the United Nations. The answer to the question as to whether they constitute war cannot be given with either Yes or No. These operations furnish a final illustration of the thesis in the defense of which this study has been made, the thesis of the relativity in the realm of the law of the legal concepts of war and peace.

BIBLIOGRAPHY

This bibliography contains on the whole only publications which have been cited more than once and in an abbreviated form.

Allen, Gardner W. *Our Naval War with France*. Boston and New York, 1900.

Anzilotti, Dionisio. *Corso di Diritto Internazionale*, volume terzo, parte prima. Roma, 1915.

—— *Lehrbuch des Völkerrechtes*, Band 1. Einführung— Allgemeine Lehren. Berlin und Leipzig, 1929.

Baker, Joseph Richardson, and McKernan, Louis W. *Selected Topics Connected with the Laws of Warfare as of August 1, 1914*. Washington, 1919.

Baker, Ray Stannard. *Woodrow Wilson; Life and Letters . . .* Garden City, N.Y., 1927–39. 8 vols.

Basdevant, Jules, "L'Action Coercitive Anglo-Germano-Italienne Contre le Vénézuela (1902–3)," *Revue Générale de Droit International Public*, XI (1904), 362–458.

Baty, Thomas, "Professor Westlake on War," *The Law Magazine and Review*, 5th ser., XXXIII (1907–8), 451–457.

Bemis, Samuel Flagg. *A Diplomatic History of the United States*. Revised ed., New York, 1942.

—— *The Latin American Policy of the United States*. New York, 1943.

Borchard, Edwin, "When Did the War Begin?" *Columbia Law Rev.*, XLVII (1947), 742–748.

—— and Lage, William Potter. *Neutrality for the United States*. 2d ed. New Haven, 1940.

Bordwell, Percy. *The Law of War*. Chicago, 1908.

Bouinais, A., et Paulus, A. *L'Indo-Chine Française Contemporaine*, tome second. Paris, 1885.

Bourchier, Lady Jane (Codrington). *Memoirs of the Life of Sir Edward Codrington . . .* London, 1873. 2 vols.

Burckhardt, Walther. *Methode und System des Rechts*. Zürich, 1936.

Burlamaqui, Jean Jacques. *The Principles of Natural and Politic Law*. London, 1774. 2 vols.

Brandt, Max August Scipio. *Dreiunddreissig Jahre in Ostasien. Erinnerungen eines deutschen Diplomaten*. Leipzig, 1901. 3 vols.

Cady, John F. *Foreign Intervention in the Rio de la Plata 1838–1850.* Philadelphia, London, 1929.

Calvo, Carlos. *Le Droit International Théorique et Pratique,* . . . 5me éd. Paris, 1896. 6 vols.

Carnegie Endowment for International Peace. *The Proceedings of the Hague Peace Conferences. Translation of the Official Texts Prepared in the Division of International Law of the Carnegie Endowment for International Peace under the Supervision of James Brown Scott, Director. The Conference of 1907,* Vol. III: *Meetings of the Second, Third and Fourth Commissions.* New York, 1921.

Carnegie Endowment for International Peace, Division of International Law. *Prize Cases Decided in the United States Supreme Court, 1789–1918.* Oxford, 1923. 3 vols.

Cavaglieri, Arrigo. *L'Intervento nella sua Definizione Giuridica. Saggio di Diritto Internazionale.* Bologna, 1913.

——— "Note Critiche su la Teoria dei Mezzi Coercitivi al difuori della Guerra," *Rivista di Diritto Internazionale,* IX (1915), 23 ff.

Chassigneux, Edmond, "L'Indochine," *Histoire des Colonies Françaises et de l'Expansion de la France dans le Monde,* par Gabriel Hanotaux et Alfred Martineau, V (Paris, 1932), 313–575.

Ciano, Conte Galeazzo. *The Ciano Diaries 1939–1943,* ed. by Hugh Gibson. Garden City, N.Y., 1946.

Clausewitz, General von. *Vom Kriege,* herausgegeben von Oberstleutnant a. D. P. Creuzinger, 13. vermehrte Auflage, Berlin und Leipzig, 1918.

Clemens, Paul H. *The Boxer Rebellion, a Political and Diplomatic Review,* "Studies in History, Economics and Public Law," ed. by the Faculty of Political Science of Columbia University, LXVI, No. 3. New York, 1915.

Clercq, Alexander Jehan Henry. *Recueil des Traités de la France; publié sous les Auspices* . . . *[du] Ministère des Affaires Étrangères, 1713–*[1906]. Paris, 1880–1917. 23 vols.

Clowes, William Laird. *The Royal Navy, a History from the Earliest Times to the Present.* Boston and London, 1897–1903. 7 vols.

Dareste [de la Chavanne], François Rodolphe, et Dareste [de la Chavanne], Pierre. *Les Constitutions Modernes. Recueil des*

Constitutions Actuellement en Vigueur dans les Divers États d'Europe, d'Amérique et du Monde Civilisé. 4me éd. entièrement refondue par Joseph Delpech et Julien Laferrière. Paris, 1928–34. 6 vols.

Deák, Francis, and Jessup, Philip C. *A Collection of Neutrality Laws, Regulations and Treaties of Various Countries.* Washington, 1939. 2 vols. Publications of the Carnegie Endowment for International Peace, Division of International Law.

Diguet, E. *Annam et Indo-Chine Française.* Paris, 1908.

Un Diplomate. *L'Affaire du Tonkin, Histoire Diplomatique de l'Établissement de Notre Protectorat sur l'Annam et le Notre Conflit avec la Chine, 1882–1885.* Paris, n.d.

Dodd, Walter Fairleigh. *Modern Constitutions; . . .* Chicago, London, 1909. 2 vols.

Dupuis, Jean. *Le Tonkin de 1872 à 1886, Histoire et Politique.* Paris, 1910.

Eagleton, Clyde, "The Attempt to Define War," *International Conciliation, 291* (June, 1933), 235–287.

———— "The Form and Function of the Declaration of War," *American Journal of International Law,* XXXII (1938), 19–35.

Editorial, "La Nostra Dichiarazione di Guerra alla Germania," *Rivista di Diritto Internazionale,* X (1916), 403–423.

Falcke, Horst P., "Die Friedensblockade," *Zeitschrift für internationales Privat- und öffentliches Recht,* XIX (1909), 67–175; *Niemeyers Zeitschrift für internationales Recht,* XXVIII (1920), 36–182.

———— *Le Blocus Pacifique . . .* traduit de l'allemand . . . par Ant. Contat . . . Leipzig, 1919.

Fauchille, Paul. *Du Blocus Maritime . . .* Paris, 1882.

Fedozzi, P. *Saggio sul Intervento.* Modena, 1898.

Fisher, A. H. L. *A History of Europe.* London, 1936.

Flournoy, Francis. *Parliament and War.* London, 1927.

Gaillardin, Casimir. *Histoire du Règne de Louis XIV; . . .* Paris, 1871–76. 6 vols.

Garner, James Wilford. *International Law and the World War.* London, Bombay, Calcutta, and Madras, 1920. 2 vols.

Gautier, Hippolyte. *Les Français au Tonkin, 1787–1883.* Paris, 1884.

Geffcken, Friedrich Heinrich, "La France en Chine et le Droit

International," *Revue de Droit International et de Législation Comparée*, XVII (1885), 145–151.

———— *Das Recht der Intervention*, Separatabdruck des im Erscheinen begriffenen Handbuch des Völkerrechtes, herausgegeben von Prof. Dr. von Holtzendorff. Hamburg, 1887.

Gemma, Scipione, "Rassegna Criticha di Dottrina, Legislazione e Giurisprudenza. Nuovi Appunti e Discussioni di Diritto Bellico (A Proposito di Qualche Recente Publicazione)," *Rivista di Diritto Internazionale*, I (1906), 319–340.

Grotii, Hugonis. *De Jure Belli ac Pacis Libri Tres, in Quibus Jus Naturae & Gentium, item Juris Publici Praecipua explicantur* . . . Amsterdami, MDCXLVI.

Gretschanino, Georg von. *Politische Verträge, Eine Sammlung von Urkunden*, herausgegeben von Viktor Bruns. Berlin, 1936, Vol. I.

Grob, Fritz. *Seventy War Definitions Presented by International Lawyers in the Period from 1900 to 1940*, MS, Widener Library of Harvard University, Cambridge, Mass.; Library of Congress, Washington, D.C.; Swiss National Library, Bern.

Guizot. *Histoire Parlementaire de la France*. Paris, 1863–64. 5 vols.

Halleck, Henry Wager. *International Law or Rules Regulating the Intercourse of States in Peace and War*. 4th ed. London, 1908. 2 vols.

Hammarskjöld, H. J. "La Neutralité en Général," *Bibliotheca Visseriana*, III (1924), 53–141.

Hansard's *Parliamentary Debates*. 1st to 4th ser. London, 1820–1909.

Hardy, Georges. *Histoire de la Colonization Française*. 3me éd. Paris, 1938.

Hautefeuille, Laurent Basile. *Des Droits et des Devoirs des Nations Neutres en Temps de Guerre Maritime*. Paris, 1848–49. 4 vols.

Hearnshaw, F. J. C., "The European Revolution and After, 1848–1854," *The Cambridge History of British Foreign Policy, 1783–1919*, II (New York, 1923), 287–359.

Hertslet, Sir Edward. *The Map of Europe by Treaty;* . . . London, 1875–91. 4 vols.

Hettlage, Karl, "Die Intervention in der Geschichte der Völkerrechtswissenschaft und im System der modernen Völkerrechtslehre," *Niemeyers Zeitschrift für internationales Recht,* XXXVII (1927), 11–88.

Hodges, Henry G. *The Doctrine of Intervention.* Princeton, 1915.

Holland, T. E., "War *sub modo,*" *The Law Quarterly Review,* XIX (London, 1903), 133–135.

——— *Letters to "The Times" upon War and Neutrality.* 3d ed. London, 1921.

Holtzendorff, Franz von. *Handbuch des Völkerrechtes.* Berlin, 1885–89. 4 vols.

Huber, Max, "Die Fortbildung des Völkerrechtes auf dem Gebiete des Prozess- und Landkriegsrechtes durch die zweite internationale Friedenskonferenz im Haag 1907," *Jahrbuch des öffentlichen Rechtes der Gegenwart,* II (1908), 470–649.

Hudson, Manley O., "The Present Status of the Hague Conventions," *American Journal of International Law,* XXV (1931), 114–117.

——— *International Legislation; a Collection of the Texts of Multipartite International Instruments of General Interest Beginning with the Covenant of the League of Nations.* Washington, 1931–41, Vols. I–VII.

Hyde, Charles Chency. *International Law Chiefly as Interpreted and Applied by the United States.* Boston, 1922. 2 vols.

Jefferson, Thomas. *The Works of Thomas Jefferson,* ed. by Paul Leicester Ford. New York and London, 1904–5. 12 vols.

Jessup, Philip Caryl, and Deák, Francis. *The Origins* [of Neutrality]. New York, 1935.

Lane-Poole, Stanley. *The Life of the Right Honorable Stratford Canning, Viscount Stratford de Redcliffe, from His Memoirs and Private and Official Papers.* London, 1888. 2 vols.

Lanessan, Jean Louis de. *L'Indo-Chine Française, Étude Politique, Économique et Administrative sur la Cochinchine, le Cambodge, l'Annam et le Tonkin.* Paris, 1889.

Latané, John Holladay, and Wainhouse, David W. *A History of American Foreign Policy 1776–1940.* New York, 1941.

Latourette, Kenneth Scott. *The Chinese, Their History and Culture.* New York, 1934. 2 vols.

Lawrence, Thomas Joseph. *Documents Illustrative of International Law.* Boston, New York, Chicago, 1914.

Leyret, Henry. *Waldeck-Rousseau et la Troisième République (1869–1889)*. Paris, 1908.

Lingelbach, W. E., "The Doctrine and Practice of Intervention in Europe," *Annals of the American Academy of Political and Social Science*, XVI (1900), 1–32.

Loir, Maurice. *L'Escadre de l'Amiral Courbet*. Paris, 1892.

MacNair, Harley Farnsworth. *Modern Chinese History Selected Readings*. Shanghai, 1923.

McNair, Arnold D., "The Legal Meaning of War and the Relation of War to Reprisals," *Transactions of the Grotius Society*, XI (1926), 29–51.

Malkin, H. W., "The Inner History of the Declaration of Paris," *The British Yearbook of International Law*, 1927, pp. 1–44.

Malloy, William M. *Treaties, Conventions, International Acts, Protocols and Agreements between the United States of America and Other Powers, 1776–1909*. Washington, 1910. 2 vols.

Martens, F. de. *La Paix et la Guerre*. Paris, 1901.

Martin, Percy Alvin. *Latin America and the War*. Baltimore, 1925.

Maurel, M. *De la Déclaration de Guerre*. Paris, 1907.

Meurer, Christian. *Die Haager Friedenskonferenz*. München, 1905–7. 2 vols.

Miller, David Hunter. *Treaties and Other International Acts of the United States of America* . . . Washington, 1931–[1942]. Vols. 2–[7].

Moore, John Bassett. *A Digest of International Law* . . . Washington, 1906. 8 vols.

———— *International Adjudications, Ancient and Modern; History and Documents, Together with Mediatorial Reports, Advisory Opinions, and the Decisions of Domestic Commissions, on International Claims* . . . Modern ser. New York, 1929–33. 6 vols.

Nicolson, Harold. *Diplomacy*. London, 1939.

Un Officier de la Flotte, "Affaires de Buenos-Ayres. Expéditions de la France contre la République Argentine," *Revue des Deux Mondes*, XXV (Paris, 1841), 301–370.

Oppenheim, L., "The Science of International Law; Its Task and Method," *The American Journal of International Law*, II (1908), 313–357.

———— *International Law, a Treatise*, 5th ed. by H. Lauterpacht. London, etc., 1935, 1937. 2 vols.

Padelford, Norman J. *International Law and Diplomacy in the Spanish Civil Strife.* New York, 1939.

Perkins, Dexter. *Hands Off. A History of the Monroe Doctrine.* Boston, 1941.

Philippson, Coleman. *Termination of War and Treaties of Peace.* New York, 1916.

Pillet, A. *La Guerre et le Droit.* Louvain, 1923.

Pistoye, Alphonse de, et Duverdy, Charles. *Traité des Prises Maritimes . . .* Paris, 1859. 2 vols.

Portiez, Louis. *Code Diplomatique.* Paris, 1802. 2 vols.

Potter, Pitman B., "L'Intervention en Droit International Moderne," *Académie de Droit International, Recueil des Cours,* II (1930), 607–690.

Ragot, Ernest. *Le Blocus de l'Île de Formose.* Paris, 1903.

Rambaud, Alfred. *Jules Ferry.* Paris, 1903.

Rapisardi-Mirabelli, Andrea. *Il Significato della Guerra nella Scienza del Diritto Internazionale.* Roma, 1910.

Romanet du Caillaud, F. *Histoire de l'Intervention Française au Tong-King de 1872 à 1874.* Paris, 1880.

Roosevelt, Franklin Delano. *The Public Papers and Addresses of Franklin D. Roosevelt. With a Special Introduction and Explanatory Notes by President Roosevelt.* New York, 1941. 4 vols.

Rousseau, Ch., "Le Conflit Italo-Éthiopien," *Revue Générale de Droit International Public,* XLIV (1937), 681–728, XLV (1938), 53–123.

Rousset, Camille. *Guerre de la Crimée.* 3me éd. Paris, 1894. 2 vols.

Rutherford, Thomas. *Institutes of Natural Law; Being the Substance of a Course of Lectures on Grotius'* De Jure Belli ac Pacis . . . Cambridge, 1754, 1756. 2 vols.

Schuman, Frederik L. *War and Diplomacy in the French Republic; an Inquiry into Political Motivations and the Control of Foreign Policy.* New York and London, 1931.

Scott, James Brown. *The Hague Conventions and Declarations of 1899 and 1907, Accompanied by Tables of Signatures, Ratifications and Adhesions of the Various Powers and Texts of Reservations.* 3d ed. New York, 1918. Publications of the Carnegie Endowment for International Peace, Division of International Law, Washington, D.C.

Shinobu, J. *International Law in the Shanghai Conflict*. Tokyo, 1933.

Söderquist, Nils. *Le Blocus Maritime* . . . Stockholm, 1908.

Spaight, J. M. *War Right on Land*. London, 1911.

Staudacher, Hermann, "Die Friedensblockade, ein Beitrag zur Theorie und Praxis der nichtkriegerischen Selbsthilfe," *Staats- und völkerrechtliche Abhandlungen*, VII, 3. Leipzig, 1909.

Stowell, Ellery C., "La Théorie et la Pratique de l'Intervention," *Académie de Droit International, Recueil des Cours*, II (1932), 83–150.

Strisower, Leo. *Der Krieg und die Völkerrechtsordnung*. Wien, 1919.

―――― "Intervention," *Wörterbuch des Völkerrechtes und der Diplomatie*, begonnen von Prof. Dr. Julius Hatschek, fortgesetzt und herausgegeben von Dr. Karl Strupp. I, 581–591.

Strupp, Karl. *Wörterbuch des Völkerrechtes und der Diplomatie*, herausgegeben von Dr. Karl Strupp. Berlin-Leipzig, 1924–29. 3 vols.

Taft, William Howard. *Our Chief Magistrate and His Powers*. New York, 1916.

Thomsen, H. C. *China and the Powers*. New York and Bombay, 1902.

Turlington, Edgar. *The World War Period* [and Neutrality]. New York, 1936.

Valery, Jules, "De la Condition des Allemands en Italie postérieurement à la Declaration de Guerre à l'Autriche," *Journal du Droit International*, XLIII (Paris, 1916), 405 ff.

Vast, H. *Les Grands Traités du Règne de Louis XIV*. Paris, 1893–99. 3 vols.

Vattel, Emer de. *Le Droit des Gens ou Principes de la Loi Naturelle*. Londres, 1758.

Waldersee, Alfred Graf von. *Denkwürdigkeiten des General-Feldmarschalls Alfred Grafen von Waldersee* . . . , bearbeitet und herausgegeben von Heinrich Otto Meisner. Stuttgart und Berlin, 1923. 3 vols.

Waldkirch, Eduard von und Vanselow, Ernst, "Neutralitätsrecht," *Handbuch des Völkerrechtes*, Sechster Band, Fünfte Abteilung, Stuttgart, 1936.

Ward, Sir A. W., and Gooch, G. P. *Cambridge History of British Foreign Policy, 1783–1919*. Cambridge, 1922–23. 3 vols.

Warren, Charles. *The Supreme Court in the United States History*. Boston, 1924. 3 vols.

Wehberg, Hans. "Das Seekriegsrecht," *Handbuch des Völkerrechtes*, herausgegeben und mitbearbeitet von Prof. Dr. Fritz Stier-Somlo, Vol. VI, Stuttgart, 1915.

Westlake, John, "Le Blocus Pacifique," *Revue de Droit International et de Législation Comparée*, XIV (1909), 203 ff.

────── *International Law*. 2d ed. Cambridge, 1910–13. 2 vols.

Wharton, Francis. *The Revolutionary Diplomatic Correspondence of the United States* . . . Washington, 1889. 6 vols.

Wheeler-Bennett, John Wheeler. *Documents on International Affairs*. London, 1928, and later years.

Winfield, P. H., "The History of Intervention in International Law," *The British Yearbook of International Law*, III (1922–23), 130–149.

Official Publications

Austria

Bundesministerium für Heereswesen und Kriegsarchiv. *Österreich-Ungarns letzter Krieg, 1914–1918*, herausgegeben unter der Leitung von Edmund Glaise-Horstenau. Wien, 1930–36. 4 vols.

France

Chambre des Députés. *Annales de la Chambre des Députés, Nouvelle Série, Débats Parlementaires*, Session Ordinaire de 1881, Tomes I–III, Session Ordinaire de 1883, Tomes I–II, Session Extraordinaire de 1883, Tome III, Session Ordinaire de 1884, Tome II, Session Extraordinaire de 1884, Tome III, Session Ordinaire de 1885, Tome I.

Chambre des Députés. *Annales de la Chambre des Députés, Nouvelle Série, Documents Parlementaires*, Session Ordinaire de 1883, Tome I, Session Extraordinaire de 1884, Tome IV.

Sénat. *Annales du Sénat, Débats Parlementaires*, Session Ordinaire de 1881, Tome II, Session Ordinaire de 1883, Tomes I–II, Session Extraordinaire de 1883, Tome III, Session Ordinaire de

1884, Tome II, Session Extraordinaire de 1884, Tome III, Session Ordinaire de 1885, Tome II.

Sénat et Chambre des Députés. *Annales du Sénat et de la Chambre des Députés, Nouvelle Série, Documents Parlementaires*, Session Ordinaire de 1881, Tome I, Session Extraordinaire de 1883, Tome X, Session Ordinaire de 1884, Tome III.

Ministère des Affaires Étrangères. *Documents Diplomatiques, Affaires du Tonkin, Première Partie, 1874–Décembre 1882*. Paris, 1883.

Ministère des Affaires Étrangères. *Documents Diplomatiques, Affaires du Tonkin, Deuxième Partie, Décembre 1882–1883*. Paris, 1883.

Ministère des Affaires Étrangères. *Affaires du Tonkin, Exposé de la Situation, Octobre 1883*. Paris, 1883.

Ministère des Affaires Étrangères. *Documents Diplomatiques, Affaires du Tonkin, Convention de Tien-Tsin du 11 Mai 1884, Incident de Langson*. Paris, 1884.

Ministère des Affaires Étrangères. *Documents Diplomatiques, Affaires de Chine et du Tonkin, 1884–1885*. Paris, 1885.

Ministère des Affaires Étrangères. *Documents Diplomatiques, Affaires de Chine*, Paris, 1885.

Ministère des Affaires Étrangères. *Documents Diplomatiques, Chine, 1899–1900*. Paris, 1900.

GERMANY

Auswärtiges Amt. *Die grosse Politik der europäischen Kabinette, 1871–1914, Sammlung der diplomatischen Akten des auswärtigen Amtes*, im Auftrage des auswärtigen Amtes herausgegeben von Johannes Lepsius, Albrecht Mendelssohn-Bartholdy, Friedrich Thimme. Berlin, 1922–27. 40 vols.

Reichstag. *Sammlung sämmtlicher Drucksachen des Reichstages*, 10. Legislaturperiode, II. Session 1900/1901, Vol. I, No. 8, "Entwurf eines Gesetzes betreffend die Feststellung eines dritten Nachtrages zum Reichshaushalts-Etat für das Rechnungsjahr 1900, Denkschrift betreffend die Expedition nach Ostasien."

Reichstag. *Sammlung sämmtlicher Drucksachen des Reichstages*, 10. Legislaturperiode, II. Session 1900/1901, Vol. II, No. 132,

"Bericht der Kommission für den Reichshaushalts-Etat für das Rechnungsjahr 1900."

Great Britain

Foreign Office. *British and Foreign State Papers* [1812 and later years]. London, 1841–[1939]. 137 vols.

Foreign Office. *China*, 3 (1900). "Correspondence Respecting the Insurrectionary Movement in China," Presented to Both Houses of Parliament by Command of Her Majesty, July, 1900.

Foreign Office. *China*, 1 (1901). "Correspondence Respecting the Disturbances in China," Presented to Both Houses of Parliament by Command of His Majesty, February, 1901.

Foreign Office. *China*, 5 (1901). "Further Correspondence Respecting the Disturbances in China," Presented to Both Houses of Parliament by Command of His Majesty, May, 1901.

Foreign Office. *China*, 6 (1901). "Further Correspondence Respecting the Disturbances in China," Presented to Both Houses of Parliament by Command of His Majesty, August, 1901.

Foreign Office. *China*, 7 (1901). "Correspondence Respecting the Imperial Railway of North China," Presented to Both Houses of Parliament by Command of His Majesty, August, 1901.

Foreign Office. *Venezuela*, 1 (1903). "Correspondence Respecting the Affairs of Venezuela," Presented to Both Houses of Parliament by Command of His Majesty, February, 1903.

Foreign Office. *Spain*, 1 (1938). The Text of a Proposed Resolution Reaffirming and Extending the Non-Intervention Agreement and Providing for the Withdrawal of Foreign Volunteers from Spain, for the Grant in Certain Circumstances of Belligerent Rights to the Two Parties in Spain and for the Observation of the Spanish Frontier by Land and Sea. Adopted by the International Committee for the Application of the Agreement regarding Non-Intervention in Spain at a Plenary Session held on Tuesday, July 5, 1938, for Transmission to the Two Spanish Parties for Their Approval. Presented by the Secretary of State for Foreign Affairs to Parliament by Command of His Majesty. London, 1938.

Foreign Office. *A Commentary on the Charter of the United Nations Signed at San Francisco on the 26th June 1945*. Presented

by the Secretary of State for Foreign Affairs to Parliament by
Command of His Majesty. Cmd. 6666. Miscellaneous No. 9
(1945).

Parliament. *Hansard's Parliamentary Debates* (Official Report).
London, 1909—to date.

GREECE

Ministère des Affaires Étrangères. *Documents Diplomatiques,
Différend Italo-Grec, Août-Septembre* 1923 (Affaire Kaka-
via). Athènes, 1923.

LEAGUE OF NATIONS

Doc. A. 14. 1927. V. *Reports and Resolutions on the Subject of
Article 16 of the Covenant.* Geneva, 1927.

Doc. C. 663. M. 320. 1932. VII. Geneva, October 1, 1932. *Appeal
by the Chinese Government, Report of the Commission of Inquiry [Lytton Report].*

UNITED NATIONS

United Nations Conference, San Francisco, 1945. *Documents of
the United Nations Conference on International Organization,
San Francisco, 1945.* Published in Cooperation with the Library
of Congress. London, New York, United Nations Information
Organizations, 1945. 15 vols.

Security Council. *Journal of the Security Council,* Nos. 1–16.

UNITED STATES

House of Representatives, House Executive Documents, 25th
Congress, 3d Sess. Vol. 5, Doc. No. 211, *Blockades—Mexico
and Rio de la Plata. Message from the President of the United
States Transmitting a Report on the Subject of the Blockades of
the Mexican Coast and the Rio de la Plata.*

House of Representatives, 48th Cong., 1st Sess., 1883–84. Vol. V,
Report No. 1441, *French Spoliation Claims.*

Senate, 70th Cong., 1st Sess., Doc. No. 39. *Executive Assumption
of the War-Making Power.* Article from the *National University Law Review,* May, 1927, entitled "Executive Assumption

of the War-Making Power," by Albert H. Putney, Professor of Constitutional Law, National University Law School, Washington, 1928.

Senate, 79th Cong., 1st Sess., Report No. 717, *Providing for the Appointment of Representatives of the United States in the Organs and Agencies of the United Nations, and To Make Other Provisions with Respect to the Participation of the United States in Such Organization.*

Congress. *American State Papers, Documents, Legislative and Executive of the Congress of the United States* . . . Washington, 1832–61. 38 vols.

Congress. *The Debates and Proceedings in the Congress of the United States* . . . [1st Cong., 1st Sess.—18th Cong., 1st Sess.; half-title: *Annals of the Congress of the United States*]. Washington, 1834–56.

Congress. *The Congressional Globe* . . . [23d Cong. to the 42d Cong., Dec. 2, 1833, to March 3, 1873]. Washington, 1834–73. 46 vols.

Congress. *Congressional Record.* Washington, 1874, and later years.

Congress. *A Compilation of the Messages and Papers of the Presidents,* Prepared under the Direction of the Joint Committee on Printing of the House and Senate . . . of the United States. New York, 1897–1917. 20 vols.

Dept. of State. *Papers Relating to the Foreign Relations of the United States.* Washington, 1870, and later years.

Dept. of State. *Treaties and Conventions Concluded between the United States and Other Powers, since July 4, 1776.* Washington, 1871.

Dept. of State. *Declarations of War, Severance of Diplomatic Relations, 1914–1918.* Washington, 1919.

Dept. of State. *Treaty for the Renunciation of War, Text of the Treaty, Notes Exchanged, Instruments of Ratification and of Adherence, and Other Papers.* Washington, 1935.

Dept. of State. *Right to Protect Citizens in Foreign Countries by Landing Forces,* Memorandum of the Solicitor for the Department of State, October 5, 1912. 3d revised ed. with Supplemental Appendix up to 1933, Washington, 1934.

Dept. of State. *Charter of the United Nations, Report to the President on the Results of the San Francisco Conference by the*

Chairman of the United States Delegation, the Secretary of State, June 26, 1945, Dept. of State Publication 2349, Conference Ser. 71.

War Department. *Annual Reports of the War Department for the Fiscal Year Ended June 30, 1900, Report of the Secretary of War, Miscellaneous Reports.* Washington, 1900.

War Department. *Annual Reports of the War Department for the Fiscal Year Ended June 30, 1901, Report of the Lieutenant-General Commanding the Army*, Part 4. Washington, 1901.

War Department. Adjutant General's Office, No. XXXIII, *Reports on Military Operations in South Africa and China, July 1901.* Washington, 1901.

Navy Department. *Naval Digest Containing Digests of Selected Decisions of the Secretary of the Navy and Opinions of the Judge Advocate General of the Navy, 1916*, prepared by Captain Edwin N. McClellan. Washington, 1916.

Navy Department. Office of Naval Records and Library, *Naval Documents, Quasi War with France, Operations*, February, 1797–December, 1801. Washington, 1935–38. 7 vols.

Cases Quoted

The Santa Cruz, 1 C. Rob. 49 (1798).

Bas v. *Tingy*, 4 Dall. 35 (1800).

United States v. *One Hundred and Twenty-nine Packages*, 27 Fed. Cas. 284 (1862).

The Prize Cases, 2 Black 635 (1862).

Sutton v. *Tiller*, 98 Am. Dec. 471 (1869).

Gray, Administrator, v. *the United States*, 21 Ct. Cl. 340 (1886).

Hooper, Administrator, v. *the United States*, 22 Ct. Cl. 408 (1886).

The Ship Concord v. *the United States*, 35 Ct. Cl. 432 (1900).

Hamilton v. *McClaughry, Warden*, 136 Fed. Cas. 445 (1905).

The Schooner Endeavour, 44 Ct. Cl. 242 (1909).

Arce et al. v. *the State of Texas*, 83 Tex. Cr. 292 (1918).

Janson v. *Driefontein Consolidated Mines, Limited* (1902) A. C. 484.

F. v. *Reichsfiskus*, 58 Entscheidungen des Reichsgerichtes in Zivilsachen 328 (1904).

Vashti LaRue v. *Kansas Mutual Life Insurance Company*, 68 Kansas 539 (1904).

Kawasaki Kisen Kabushiki Kaisha of Kobe v. *Bantham Steamship Company, Ltd.* [1939] 2 K. B. 544.

New York Life Insurance Company v. *Bennion*, 158 F. (2d) 260 (1946).

Notes

Part I. Historical

CHAPTER I

Terms in Connection with the Ideas of War and Peace as Such

1. Deák and Jessup, *Neutrality Laws*, II, 1100–1116; 54 *Stat.* 4 (1939).
2. United States, Dept. of State, *Declarations of War 1914–1918*, pp. 11–73; United States, Dept. of State, *Bulletin*, Dec. 20, 1941, pp. 551–561.
3. *Ibid.*, Dec. 13, 1941, pp. 480–482.
4. *Ibid.*, p. 482.
5. *Am. Jour. Int. Law*, XXXV (1941), 36 f.
6. *N. Y. Times*, June 11, 1941, p. 11.
7. United States, Dept. of State, *Declarations of War 1914–1918*, p. 68. Italics supplied.
8. United States, Dept. of State, *Bulletin*, Dec. 13, 1941, p. 481.
9. Roosevelt, *Public Papers and Addresses* (1940), p. 391.
10. *Cong. Rec.*, LXXXVI (1941), 11354, 11364; *N. Y. Times*, Sept. 4, 1940, p. 16.
11. Roosevelt, *op. cit.*, p. 669. Italics supplied.
12. *N. Y. Times*, June 19, 1940, p. 17.
13. *Hearings before the Committee on Military Affairs, United States Senate, on Nomination of Henry L. Stimson to be Secretary of War*, 76th Cong., 3d Sess. (1940), pp. 19–21. Italics supplied.
14. *Cong. Rec.*, LXXXVI (1941), 7370. Italics supplied.
15. United States, *Messages and Papers of the Presidents*, X, 4292 f.
16. *Ibid.*, XIV, 6258–6261.
17. 325 *H. C. Deb.* (5th ser., 1937), 1171.
18. *N. Y. Times*, Dec. 8, 1939, p. 6.
19. *Ibid.*, Feb. 1, 1940, p. 1; *ibid.*, Feb. 9, 1940, p. 1; *ibid.*, Nov. 2, 1940, p. 3.
20. *Ibid.*, Dec. 20, 1941; *ibid.*, Oct. 4, 1943, p. 4.
21. United States, Dept. of State, *Bulletin*, Aug. 24, 1940, pp. 127 ff.
22. *N. Y. Times*, Dec. 10, 1941, p. 13.
23. *Ibid.*, Jan. 16, 1942, p. 5.
24. *Ibid.*, Dec. 17, 1939, pp. 1, 38.
25. *Am. Jour. Int. Law*, XXXV (1941), 32–34.
26. Ciano, *Diaries*, pp. 84, 582.
27. *Ibid.*, pp. 124, 127–129, 135, 137 f., 140.
28. *Ibid.*, pp. 157, 205, 219, 222, 239.
29. *Ibid.*, pp. 127 f., 142, 157, 160, 166, 167, 187, 194, 196, 211.
30. *Ibid.*, p. 132.
31. *Ibid.*, pp. 157, 178.
32. United States, Dept. of State, *Bulletin*, Nov. 11, 1939, pp. 544–546.
33. *N. Y. Times*, June 20, 1941, p. 3.
34. Deák and Jessup, *Neutrality Laws* (loose-leaf ed.), II, 947.
35. "Extracts from the Memoirs of Sir Samuel Hoare, now Viscount Templewood, Wartime British Ambassador to Spain," *N. Y. Times*, April 20, 1946, p. 4.
36. *Ibid.*
37. *N. Y. Times*, April 25, 1946, p. 2.
38. *Ibid.*, Aug. 23, 1943, p. 4.

39. "Digest of Documents on Franco Spain's Relations with Axis as Made Public in Washington," Docs. Nos. 9, 10, *N. Y. Times*, March 5, 1946, p. 12.

40. *Ibid.*, Doc. No. 2.

41. *Ibid.*, Doc. No. 1.

42. *Ibid.*

43. Martens, *Nouveau Recueil Général de Traités*, 3d ser., XXXIII (Leipzig, 1937), 331–333.

44. *N. Y. Times*, May 3, 1944, p. 8.

45. *Ibid.*, Feb. 13, 1946, p. 1.

46. See Robert R. Wilson, " 'Non-Belligerency' in Relation to the Terminology of Neutrality," *Am. Jour. Int. Law*, XXXV (1941), 121–123.

Chapter II

Terms in Connection with the Ideas of Operations Short of War and of War Part Way

1. Grotius, *De Jure Belli ac Pacis*, lib. III, cap. XXI, sec. 1.

2. (1902) A. C. at p. 497.

3. Rousset, *Guerre de la Crimée*, I, 1–71; Hearnshaw, "The European Revolution and After," pp. 340–358.

4. 130 *Parl. Deb.* (3d ser., 1854), 568.

5. *Ibid.*, p. 628.

6. *The Santa Cruz*, 1 C. Rob. 49, 64 (1798).

7. *N. Y. Times*, Feb. 15, 1940, p. 7.

8. Roosevelt, *Public Papers and Addresses* (1939), p. 3.

9. *N. Y. Times*, Jan. 5, 1939, p. 12.

10. Cf. *Bas* v. *Tingy*, 4 Dall. 35 (1800).

11. Warren, *Supreme Court*, I, 156.

12. *Ibid.*, pp. 33, 156.

13. United States, Navy Dept., Office of Naval Records and Library, *Naval Documents, Quasi War with France, Operations, Feb. 1797–Dec. 1801* (Washington, 1935–38). 7 vols.

14. *Brit. and For. State Papers* (1837–38), XXVI, 920–945.

15. Martens, *Nouveau Recueil Général de Traités* (1830–38), XV, 502–504; *Brit. and For. State Papers* (1837–38), XXVI, 972 f.

16. Un Officier de la Flotte, "Affaires de Buenos Ayres," p. 315; *N. Y. Times*, Sept. 8, 1940, p. 1.

17. *Ibid.*, p. 34.

18. 47 *Parl. Deb.* (3d ser., 1839), 1397.

19. Cf. Falcke, *Blocus Pacifique*, pp. 64–71; Cady, *Foreign Intervention*, pp. 22–92.

20. Hautefeuille, *Nations Neutres en Temps de Guerre Maritime*, III, 10–13, 183 f.

21. Guizot, *Histoire Parlementaire*, III, 415.

22. *H. R. Exec. Doc.*, No. 211, 25th Cong., 3d Sess. (1839), pp. 1, 50.

23. *Cong. Globe*, 26th Cong., 1st Sess. (1840), p. 513.

24. *Brit. and For. State Papers* (1837–38), XXVI, 186; Falcke, *op. cit.*, pp. 46–50.

25. 47 *Parl. Deb.* (3d ser., 1839), 1397; 49 *Parl. Deb.* (3d ser., 1839), 385, 397; 51 *Parl. Deb.* (3d ser., 1840), 573–575.

26. *Le Moniteur Universel*, 9 février 1841, p. 316.

27. Falcke, *op. cit.*, pp. 55–57.
28. United States, *Foreign Relations*, 1916, pp. 469 f.
29. United States, *Messages and Papers of the Presidents*, XVIII, 8103.
30. United States, *Foreign Relations*, 1916, pp. 581–583.
31. *Ibid.*, pp. 481 f.; *Current History*, VII (1916), 2 f.
32. United States, *Foreign Relations*, 1916, pp. 482, 586, 588; *Current History*, VII (1916), 2.
33. United States, *Foreign Relations*, 1916, pp. 484, 489, 491, 499, 518.
34. *Ibid.*, pp. 486 f., 491, 493, 497.
35. *Ibid.*, pp. 500, 521.
36. *Ibid.*, pp. 540–545, 572 f., 585.
37. *Ibid.*, pp. 514, 517, 556 f., 563, 585.
38. *Current History*, VIII (1916), 591.
39. *Ibid.*, pp. 834–837; *ibid.*, X (1917), 1016; United States, *Foreign Relations*, 1916, pp. 592, 597.
40. *N. Y. Times*, June 16, 1916, p. 5.
41. Vattel, *Le Droit des Gens*, Liv. III, Secs. 1–4.
42. *Arce et al.* v. *the State of Texas*, 83 Tex. Cr. 292 (1918).
43. Holland, "War *sub modo*," pp. 133–135.

CHAPTER III

War or Peace?

Section 1. American Naval Operations against France, 1798–1800 and against Germany and Italy, 1941

1. Cf. Moore, *International Adjudications*, V, 170–210.
2. Gray, *Administrator*, v. *United States*, 21 Ct. Cl. 340, 346 f. (1886).
3. Wharton, *Revolutionary Diplomatic Correspondence*, II, 526.
4. Gray, *Administrator*, v. *United States*, 21 Ct. Cl. 340, 348 f. (1886).
5. Miller, *Treaties*, II, 3 ff., 35 ff.
6. Arts. 25, 26.
7. A privateer was an armed vessel belonging to one or more private individuals, commissioned either by their own or by a foreign government to capture and to bring into a prize court either enemy vessels with their cargoes or neutral vessels for unneutral conduct, such as carrying of contraband or running of a blockade.
8. Arts. 14, 24, 27.
9. Art. 25.
10. Art. 14.
11. Arts. 19, 24.
12. Fisher, *History of Europe*, pp. 810 f.
13. Gray, *Administrator*, v. *the United States*, 21 Ct. Cl. 340, 377 (1886).
14. *Ibid.*, p. 360.
15. *Ibid.*, p. 377; Hooper, *Administrator*, v. *the United States*, 22 Ct. Cl. 408, 421 (1887).
16. Jefferson, *Works*, VII, 407 ff.; United States, *Messages and Papers of the Presidents*, I, 148 f.
17. *Am. State Papers, For. Rel.*, I, 377. Copy of the Decree of the National Convention, of May 9, 1793, second year of the Republic of France.
18. Miller, *op. cit.*, II, 245 ff.

19. Latané and Wainhouse, *American Foreign Policy*, pp. 89–96.

20. *Am. State Papers, For. Rel.*, VI, 28.

21. *Ibid.*, II, 30. Decree of the Executive Directory of March 2, 1797, Art. III, Pars. 3, 4.

22. United States, *Treaties and Conventions Concluded between the United States of America and Other Powers Since July 4, 1776* (Revised ed., Washington, 1873), p. 995. Notes by J. C. Bancroft Davis.

23. *Am. State Papers, For. Rel.*, II, 28 ff.

24. *Cushing, Administrator, v. the United States*, 22 Ct. Cl. 1, 44 (1886).

25. *Am. State Papers, For. Rel.*, II, 232.

26. *H. R. Rep.*, No. 1441, 48th Cong., 1st Sess. (1883–84), p. 32.

27. Great Britain, which had pursued a similar course in disregard of neutral rights, made ample amends under the action of a joint claims commission under the Jay Treaty of 1794, and Spain, which had countenanced the French spoliations and lent her ports in aid of it, did the same. *Gray, Administrator, v. the United States*, 21 Ct. Cl. 340, 360 (1886); *Cushing, Administrator, v. the United States*, 22 Ct. Cl. 1, 30 (1886). Cf. Moore, *op. cit.*, IV, V, 3–149.

28. *Am. State Papers, For. Rel.*, I, 732 f. The Minister of Foreign Affairs to the Minister Plenipotentiary of the United States of America, Paris, March 11, 1796. A summary exposition of the French Government against the Government of the United States.

29. *Ibid.*, pp. 745–747.

30. Latané and Wainhouse, *op. cit.*, p. 96.

31. *Ibid.*, p. 97; United States, *Treaties and Conventions*, pp. 996–998.

32. 1 *Stat.* 552 (1798).

33. *Annals of Cong.*, VII (1798), 1475 f., 1519.

34. 1 *Stat.* 553 (1798).

35. 1 *Stat.* 561 (1798).

36. 1 *Stat.* 578 (1798).

37. *Annals of Cong.*, VII (1798), 622.

38. 1 *Stat.* 604 (1798).

39. *Annals of Cong.*, VII (1798), 623.

40. 1 *Stat.* 578 (1798). Italics supplied.

41. 1 *Stat.* 565 (1798).

42. United States, *Messages and Papers of the Presidents*, I, 260.

43. United States, *Opinions of the Attorneys General* (1791–1838), p. 49.

44. 1 *Stat.* 724 (1799).

45. 1 *Stat.* 749 (1799), Sec. 1. Italics supplied.

46. 2 *Stat.* 7 (1800). Italics supplied.

47. *N. Y. Times*, August 26, 1940, p. 10; *ibid.*, August 24, 1941, p. 30; *ibid.*, March 10, 1942, p. 1.

48. United States, *Naval Documents* (Feb., 1797, to Oct., 1798), v f.

49. *Ibid.* (Nov., 1798, to March, 1799), pp. 326 ff.; *ibid.* (Jan., 1800 to May, 1800), pp. 160 ff.

50. Allen, *Naval War with France*, p. 222.

51. United States, *Naval Documents* (Nov., 1798, to March, 1799), pp. 327 f., 332.

52. *Ibid.*, pp. 332 ff.; John Adams, *The Works of John Adams, Second President of the United States* (Boston, 1853), VIII, 599, 661; Allen, *Naval War with France*, pp. 82, 89, 104 *et passim*.

53. United States, *Treaties and Conventions*, p. 999.

54. *Am. State Papers, For. Rel.*, II, 301. Italics supplied.

55. *Ibid.*, p. 306.

56. *Ibid.*, p. 318.
57. *Ibid.*, p. 325.
58. *Ibid.*, p. 334.
59. Miller, *op. cit.*, II, 458 f.
60. *Ibid.*, pp. 480 f.
61. *Am. State Papers, For. Rel.*, II, 615.
62. *Cong. Globe*, Appendix (1845–46), p. 864.
63. *H. R. Rep.*, No. 1441, 48th Cong., 1st Sess. (1883–84), p. 32; *Gray, Administrator, v. the United States*, 21 Ct. Cl. 340, 390 (1886).
64. 23 *Stat.* 283 (1885).
65. Secs. 3, 6.
66. Sec. 4.
67. *Cong. Rec.*, LXXXI (1937), 5047; *ibid.*, LXXXVI (1940), 8913–8915; *Sen. Rep.*, No. 618, 75th Cong., 1st Sess. (1937); *Cong. Rec.*, Appendix (1940), pp. 6851–6861.
68. *Gray, Administrator, v. the United States*, 21 Ct. Cl. 340, 367 (1886); *Cushing, Administrator, v. the United States*, 22 Ct. Cl. 1, 11, 17, 22 (1886); *The Ship Concord v. the United States*, 35 Ct. Cl. 432, 443 f. (1900).
69. *Gray, Administrator, v. the United States*, 21 Ct. Cl. 340, 367 (1886).
70. *Loc. cit., supra.*
71. *Loc. cit., supra.*
72. *Cushing, Administrator, v. the United States*, 22 Ct. Cl. 1, 12 (1886).
73. *Ibid.*, at 32 f.
74. *Gray, Administrator, v. the United States*, 21 Ct. Cl. 340, 369 f. (1886); *Cushing, Administrator, v. the United States*, 22 Ct. Cl. 1, 20 f. (1886). It will be remembered that the Supreme Court, in the case of *Bas v. Tingy*, did *not* succeed in establishing the existence in law of an imperfect, limited, or partial war.
75. *Gray, Administrator, v. the United States*, 21 Ct. Cl. 340, 367 (1886); *Cushing, Administrator, v. the United States*, 22 Ct. Cl. 1, 40 (1886).
76. *Gray, Administrator, v. the United States*, 21 Ct. Cl. 340, 372 ff. (1886); *Cushing, Administrator, v. the United States*, 22 Ct. Cl. 1, 32 (1886); *H. R. Rep.*, No. 1441, 48th Cong., 1st Sess. (1883–84), pp. 23 f.
77. *Gray, Administrator, v. the United States*, 21 Ct. Cl. 340, 371, 372 (1886); *H. R. Rep.*, No. 1441, 48th Cong., 1st Sess. (1883–84), p. 24. Italics supplied.
78. P. 47, above.
79. *Am. State Papers, For. Rel.*, VI, 1124. Italics supplied.
80. *Cong. Deb.*, XII (1835), 1456, Appendix 287.
81. Portiez, *Code Diplomatique*, I, 39.
82. *Gray, Administrator, v. the United States*, 21 Ct. Cl. 340, 368, 369 (1886); *H. R. Rep.*, No. 1441, 48th Cong., 1st Sess. (1883–84), pp. 24 f.
83. *Gray, Administrator, v. the United States*, 21 Ct. Cl. 340, 374 (1886); *H. R. Rep.*, No. 1441, 48th Cong., 1st Sess. (1883–84), pp. 24 f.
84. Clercq, *Recueil des Traités*, I, 400.
85. United States, *Treaties and Conventions*, p. 266.
86. 8 *Stat.* 178 (1846).
87. *Am. State Papers, For. Rel.*, II, 295.
88. *Gray, Administrator, v. the United States*, 21 Ct. Cl. 340, 368, 375 (1886); *Cushing, Administrator, v. the United States*, 22 Ct. Cl. 1, 32–34 (1886); *H. R. Rep.*, No. 1441, 48th Cong., 1st Sess. (1883–84), p. 25.
89. Vattel, *Droit des Gens*, Liv. III, Chap. V, Sec. 70.
90. *Gray, Administrator, v. the United States*, 21 Ct. Cl. 340, 374 (1886); *Cushing, Administrator, v. the United States*, 22 Ct. Cl. 1, 39, 40 (1886); *H. R. Rep.*, No. 1441, 48th Cong., 1st Sess. (1883–84), p. 23.

91. *The Schooner Endeavour*, 44 Ct. Cl. 242, 273 (1909).
92. *Cushing, Administrator*, v. *the United States*, 22 Ct. Cl. 1, 31 (1886).
93. Roosevelt, *Public Papers and Addresses* (1939), pp. 154–157.
94. *Boston Evening Transcript*, Jan. 27, 1941, p. 8.
95. United States, Dept. of State, *Bulletin*, Sept. 13, 1941, pp. 193–197.
96. *N. Y. Times*, Oct. 30, 1941, p. 1; *ibid.*, Nov. 1, 1941, p. 1; *ibid.*, Dec. 22, 1941, p. 1.
97. *Cong. Rec.*, LXXXVII (1941), 8611 f.
98. *N. Y. Times*, Sept. 14, 1941, Sec. 4, p. 3.
99. *Cong. Rec.*, LXXXVII (1941), 8151 f.
100. *Ibid.*, p. 8494.
101. *N. Y. Times*, Nov. 20, 1941, p. 20.

Section 2. The Boxer Expedition, 1900–1901

1. For the introductory considerations see Clemens, *Boxer Rebellion*, p. 101; MacNair, *Modern Chinese History*, pp. 560–568, 582–587; Latourette, *The Chinese*, I, 414 ff.
2. United States, *Military Operations in South Africa and China*, p. 525.
3. United States, *Foreign Relations*, 1900, pp. 132 ff., 190.
4. United States, *Military Operations in South Africa and China*, pp. 525–532.
5. *Ibid.*, pp. 533–540.
6. *Ibid.*, pp. 540–556.
7. *Ibid.*, pp. 557–579.
8. Waldersee, *Denkwürdigkeiten*, III, 36 ff., 47 f.
9. United States, *Foreign Relations*, 1900, pp. 161–167.
10. Great Britain, *China*, 1 (1901), No. 53.
11. Germany, *Die grosse Politik*, XVI, No. 4602.
12. Waldersee, *op. cit.*, III, 1 ff.
13. *Ibid.*, p. 17.
14. *Ibid.*, pp. 28, 32, 35, 39, 60, 68, 106, 114, 117, 124, 129.
15. *Ibid.*, pp. 143 f.
16. United States, *Foreign Relations*, 1901, pp. 306 ff.
17. United States, *Report of the Secretary of War* (1900), pp. 12 ff., 21 f.
18. United States, *Report of the Lieutenant-General Commanding the Army* (1901), pp. 441 f., 498, 509.
19. United States, *Foreign Relations*, 1900, p. 169.
20. Great Britain, *China*, 1 (1901), No. 33.
21. Waldersee, *op. cit.*, III, 74.
22. *Ibid.*, p. 82.
23. Thomson, *China and the Powers*, p. 132.
24. Waldersee, *op. cit.*, III, 123, 150; Great Britain, *China*, 1 (1901), 156 f.
25. Germany, *Die grosse Politik*, XVI, Nos. 5, 4615, 4617, 4641.
26. Great Britain, *China*, 1 (1901), No. 260, enclosure.
27. Germany, *Die grosse Politik*, XVI, No. 4692.
28. Great Britain, *China*, 1 (1901), No. 213.
29. *Ibid.*, No. 354; Germany, *Die grosse Politik*, XVI, No. 4549.
30. *Ibid.*, No. 4654.
31. *Ibid.*, No. 4641; France, *Documents Diplomatiques*, *Chine* (1899–1900), No. 256, Annexe Nos. 257, 263, 278; Great Britain, *China*, 7 (1901), No. 10.
32. Great Britain, *China*, 1 (1901), No. 79, enclosure; Great Britain, *China*, 6 (1901), No. 60.
33. Great Britain, *China*, 1 (1901), No. 85.
34. *Ibid.*, No. 315.

35. *Ibid.*, Nos. 358, 361, 363.

36. Great Britain, *China*, 6 (1901), No. 61.

37. Great Britain, *China*, 5 (1901), No. 264; Great Britain, *China*, 6 (1901), No. 84.

38. Germany, *Die grosse Politik*, XVI, 4692.

39. *Ibid.*, Nos. 4692, 4811; Great Britain, *China*, 6 (1901), No. 84.

40. France, *Documents Diplomatiques, Chine* (1899–1900), No. 256, Annexe; Germany, *Die grosse Politik*, XVI, Nos. 4617, 4658, 4659, 4661, 4679, 4698; Great Britain, *China*, 1 (1901), Nos. 249, 355, 361; Great Britain, *China*, 5 (1901), Nos. 174, 252; Great Britain, *China*, 6 (1901), No. 95.

41. Germany, *Die grosse Politik*, XVI, Nos. 4632, 4661, 4686, 4696, 4811.

42. *Ibid.*, Nos. 4617, 4695, 4811.

43. Great Britain, *China*, 1 (1901), No. 219.

44. *Ibid.*, No. 113, enclosure.

45. *Ibid.*, No. 78, enclosure.

46. France, *Documents Diplomatiques, Chine* (1899–1900), No. 169. "*Votre honorable nation a les rapports les plus cordiaux avec la Chine.*"

47. Waldersee, *op. cit.*, III, 86.

48. Germany, *Die grosse Politik*, XVI, No. 4575.

49. Great Britain, *China*, 3 (1900), No. 178.

50. France, *Documents Diplomatiques, Chine* (1899–1900), No. 167.

51. Germany, *Die grosse Politik*, XVI, No. 4557.

52. France, *Documents Diplomatiques, Chine* (1899–1900), No. 181. Italics supplied.

53. Great Britain, *China*, 3 (1900), Nos. 173–176.

54. Germany, *Die grosse Politik*, XVI, No. 4571.

55. *Ibid.*, No. 4553.

56. *Ibid.*, No. 4618.

57. *Ibid.*, No. 4625, marginal note 8. "Einen solchen Quatsch kriegt bei uns schon ein auf sich haltender Legationssekretär nicht mehr fertig."

58. *Ibid.*, No. 4625.

59. *Ibid.*, No. 4634.

60. *Rev. Stat.*, chap. v (1875).

61. *Cf. Hamilton* v. *McClaughry, Warden*, 136 Fed. 445 (1905).

62. "In short, the status of the country as to peace or war, is legally determined by the political and not the judicial department. When the decision is made the courts are concluded thereby, and bound to apply the legal rules which belong to that condition." *United States* v. *One Hundred and Twenty-nine Packages*, 27 Fed. Cas. 284, 289 (1862).

"The question, whether or not war, in its legal sense, exists, is to be determined alone by the political power of the government; and of this determination the courts must take judicial knowledge." *Sutton* v. *Tiller*, 98 Am. Dec. 471, 472 (1869).

63. *The Prize Cases*, 2 Black 635, 666 (1862).

64. Germany, Reichstag, *Denkschrift betr. die Expedition nach Ostasien*, p. 16.

65. *F.* v. *Reichsfiskus*, 58 Entscheidungen des Reichsgerichtes in Zivilsachen 328, 331 (1904).

66. Germany, Reichstag, *Bericht der Kommission für das Rechnungsjahr 1900*, p. 6. "Bei dieser Gelegenheit wurde auch die Frage erörtert, ob wir uns überhaupt mit China im Kriegszustand befänden oder nicht, worauf der Vertreter des Auswärtigen Amtes die Erklärung abgab, dass wir uns völkerrechtlich nicht im Kriege mit China befänden. . . ."

67. *Mr. Dooleys Says* (New York, 1910), pp. 212 f.

Section 3. German Military Operations against Italy, 1915–1916

1. United States, *Declarations of War, 1914–18*, pp. 39 ff.
2. Editorial, *La Nostra Dichiarazione di Guerra alla Germania*, p. 411.
3. *Ibid.*, p. 411.
4. Austria, *Österreich-Ungarns letzter Krieg*, II, 408.
5. *Bundesblatt der Schweizerischen Eidgenossenschaft*, 1916, III, 519.
6. Editorial, *La Nostra Dichiarazione di Guerra alla Germania*, p. 404.
7. *Verhandlungen des Reichstages*, CCCVII (1916), 1691.
8. Editorial, *La Nostra Dichiarazione di Guerra alla Germania*, p. 409. Italics supplied.
9. *Ibid.*, p. 422.

Chapter IV

Battles in "Peace"

Section 1. The Battle off Navarino, 1827, and Other Operations Accompanied by Protestations of Peace

1. Alison Phillips, "Greece and the Balkan Peninsula," *The Cambridge Modern History* (1907), X, 169–181, 189.
2. *Ibid.*, p. 182.
3. *Ibid.*, pp. 190 f.
4. *Brit. and For. State Papers* (1826–27), XV, 629–632.
5. *Ibid.*, pp. 1042–1048.
6. *Ibid.*, pp. 632–639.
7. *Ibid.* (1829–30), XVIII, 11–15.
8. *Ibid.*, pp. 10 f., 224–226, 231 f., 236 f., 238–240.
9. *Ibid.*, pp. 240–242.
10. Bourchier, *Life of Codrington*, I, 432, 469–472.
11. *Ibid.*, II, 6–7, 35.
12. *Ibid.*, II, 36–54.
13. *Ibid.*, II, 55–60.
14. Lane-Poole, *Life of Stratford Canning*, I, 449.
15. Bourchier, *op. cit.*, I, 461.
16. *Ibid.*, I, 362.
17. *Brit. and For. State Papers* (1826–27), XV, 1050 f.; Bourchier, *op. cit.*, II, 61 f.
18. Clowes, *The Royal Navy*, VI, 255.
19. Bourchier, *op. cit.*, II, 58, 70.
20. *Ibid.*, II, 71; Clowes, *The Royal Navy*, VI, 254–256.
21. *Ibid.*, VI, 256–260; Bourchier, *op. cit.*, II, 72.
22. Lane-Poole, *op. cit.*, I, 451.
23. *Ibid.*, pp. 306–308. Italics supplied.
24. *Ibid.*, pp. 312–314.
25. *Ibid.*, pp. 314 f. Italics supplied.
26. *Ibid.*, pp. 315 f.
27. *The Times*, Nov. 12, 1827, p. 2.
28. 18 *Parl. Deb.* (new ser., 1828), 70.
29. *Ibid.*, p. 67.
30. Bourchier, *op. cit.*, II, 139.

31. 18 *Parl. Deb.* (new ser., 1828), 59.
32. Clowes, *op. cit.*, VI, 261.
33. 18 *Parl. Deb.* (new ser., 1828), 3.
34. *Dictionary of National Biography*, XXVII, 47 f.
35. 18 *Parl. Deb.* (new ser., 1828), 387.
36. *Ibid.*, pp. 391–399, 410–419.
37. Bourchier, *op. cit.*, II, 245, 310–313.
38. 18 *Parl. Deb.* (new ser., 1828), 25 f.
39. Lane-Poole, *op. cit.*, I, 430.
40. *Ibid.*, pp. 451–453.
41. Gaillardin, *Histoire du Règne de Louis XIV*, III, 332–347.
42. Hearnshaw, "The European Revolution and After 1848–1854," p. 349.
43. United States, *Foreign Relations*, 1914, pp. 477, 479–481; United States, *Annual Reports of the Navy Department*, 1914, pp. 51, 141.
44. Baker, *Woodrow Wilson*, IV, 266, 293, 303, 324, 331, 333 f.; United States, *Foreign Relations*, 1914, pp. 476, 480, 482 f.
45. *Ibid.*, p. 476.
46. *N. Y. Times*, Aug. 27, 1941, p. 4.
47. Scott, *Hague Conventions*, p. 129.
48. *N. Y. Times*, Jan. 31, 1942, p. 7; *ibid.*, May 3, 1942, p. 1.
49. Calvo, *Le Droit International*, III, 539.
50. H. Remsen Whitehouse, *L'Effondrement du Royaume de Naples 1860* (Lausanne, 1910), p. 247.
51. W. F. Reddaway, J. H. Penson, O. Halecki, R. Dyboski, *The Cambridge History of Poland from August II to Pilsudski, 1697–1935* (Cambridge, 1941), pp. 530–534.
52. *N. Y. Times*, March 18, 1938, p. 1; *ibid.*, March 20, 1938, p. 1; *ibid.*, March 20, 1938, Sec. 4, p. 5.
53. League of Nations, *Official Journal*, 1928, pp. 149 ff., 154 f., 177.

Section 2. French Operations against Annam, 1882–1884, and against China, 1883–1885

1. Hardy, *Histoire de la Colonisation Française*, p. 212.
2. Bouinais et Paulus, *L'Indo-Chine Française*, II, 2, 63.
3. *Ibid.*, pp. 3, 66; Hardy, *op. cit.*, pp. 215 ff., 268 ff.
4. *Ibid.*, pp. 175–185; Chassigneux, "L'Indo-Chine," p. 408.
5. *Doc. Dipl.*, 1874–Décembre 1882, pp. 1–25, 118; Dupuis, *Le Tonkin de 1872 à 1886*, pp. 275–277, 295 ff.; Romanet du Caillaud, *Intervention Française au Tong-King*, pp. 265–267; Bouinais et Paulus, *op. cit.*, II, 49.
6. Dupuis, *op. cit.*, p. 40; de Lanessan, *L'Indo-Chine Française*, p. 629.
7. *Doc. Dipl.*, 1874–Décembre 1882, pp. 45, 49, 71, 195, 199.
8. *Ibid.*, p. 60.
9. *Ibid.*, pp. 85, 88, 90, 106, 116, 134, 139.
10. The Black Flags and their brothers, the Yellow Flags, were both remnants of the Taiping Revolution which had devastated the Chinese province of Kwangsi from 1849 to 1865. The Taiping revolutionaries were organized under four flags: black, yellow, red, and white, with the commission, respectively, to kill, to organize the conquered regions, to apply the torch, and to supply the army. The Black Flags and Yellow Flags numbered from 3,000 to 4,000 men. Some time after 1866 they were in possession of parts of the woodlands on the upper reaches of the Red River, and, as a law unto themselves, taxed the river traffic. Luu-vinh-phuoc, chief of the Black Flags, installed in Laokai, had been since 1875 a *con-*

dottiere in the pay of Annam, and head of an independent miniature state of his own. In 1882, at the latest, he was head of some sort of Annamite fief and commissioned to police the upper course of the Red River against the incursions of brigands. See Dupuis, *Le Tonkin de 1872 à 1886*, pp. 43–45; Chassigneux, *op. cit.*, p. 410; Diguet, *Annam et Indo-Chine Française*, p. 21; Gautier, *Les Français au Tonkin*, pp. 321 ff.; *Doc. Dipl.*, 1874–Décembre 1882, p. 223.

11. *Ibid.*, pp. 118, 131 ff., 140 ff., 173, 327.

12. *Annales du Sénat et de la Chambre des Députés, Documents Parlementaires*, 1881, I, 635–638; *Chambre, Débats*, 1881, II, 979–991; *Sénat, Débats*, 1881, II, 847.

13. *Doc. Dipl.*, 1874–Décembre 1882, pp. 190 ff., 208–211.

14. *Ibid.*, pp. 200 ff., 203 ff., 208 ff.

15. *Ibid.*, pp. 202, 217, 220–222; Bouinais et Paulus, *op. cit.*, pp. 97, 100; *Doc. Dipl.*, 1874–Décembre 1882, pp. 243, 247, 250.

16. *Doc. Dipl.*, 1874–Décembre 1882, pp. 259, 278, 292.

17. *Ibid.*, pp. 268, 273, 276; *Doc. Dipl.*, Décembre 1882–83, pp. 1–2, 11, 26, 29, 38, 46, 52, 57; *Chambre, Débats*, 1883, III, 580.

18. Rambaud, *Jules Ferry*, pp. 196, 201 ff.

19. *Chambre, Débats*, 1883, I, 406 ff.; *Sénat, Débats*, 1883, I, 207 ff. *"Messieurs, la politique extérieure de ce cabinet, comme celle de tous ses prédécesseurs depuis onze ans, ne peut être qu'une politique de paix. La paix est le premier besoin et l'instinct profond de toute grande démocratie. Mais une politique pacifique n'est pas nécessairement une politique inactive. Partout, dans toutes les questions où nos intérêts, ou notre honneur sont engagés, nous voulons, nous devons maintenir à la France le rang qui lui appartient."*

20. *Doc. Dipl.*, Décembre 1882–83, pp. 70, 72.

21. *Ibid.*, p. 13; *Chambre, Débats*, 1883, III, 711.

22. *Doc. Dipl.*, Décembre 1882–83, p. 83; *ibid.*, pp. 83–85.

23. *Ibid.*, pp. 88, 93, 117; Gautier, *op. cit.*, pp. 361–365.

24. *Doc. Dipl.*, Décembre 1882–83, pp. 93, 117, 120, 156, 158; *Chambre, Débats*, 1883, II, 450.

25. *Chambre, Documents*, 1883, I, 557 ff.; *Chambre, Débats*, 1883, II, 305, 311–313; *Sénat, Débats*, 1883, I, 326; *Doc. Dipl.*, Décembre 1882–83, pp. 93–97.

26. *Sénat, Débats*, 1883, II, 202, 208; *Chambre, Débats*, 1883, II, 315, 317, 451.

27. *Doc. Dipl.*, Décembre 1882–83, pp. 89 ff., 112, 122 ff., 126–129; *ibid.*, pp. 87, 117; *Chambre, Débats*, 1883, II, 1143.

28. Un Diplomate, *L'Affaire du Tonkin*, pp. 51, 55.

29. Dareste et Dareste, *Les Constitutions Modernes*, I, 11 ff. *"Le président de la République ne peut déclarer la guerre sans l'assentiment préalable des deux Chambres."*

30. Schuman, *War and Diplomacy in the French Republic*, pp. 57–77, 105–128.

31. *Chambre, Débats*, 1883, II, 1139, 1143, 1146, 1156.

32. *Sénat, Débats*, 1883, II, 662, 665 ff.

33. *Chambre, Débats*, 1883, III, 89; *Doc. Dipl.*, Décembre 1882–83, p. 204; Ministère des Affaires Étrangères, *op. cit.*, *supra*, p. 8.

34. *Doc. Dipl.*, Décembre 1882–83, pp. 119, 169, 229; Ministère des Affaires Étrangères, *op. cit.*, *supra*, p. 10; Bouinais et Paulus, *op. cit.*, II, 144; *Chambre, Débats*, 1883, III, 89.

35. Dupuis, *op. cit.*, pp. 440–443; Bouinais et Paulus, *op. cit.*, II, 145–154.

36. Bouinais et Paulus, *op. cit.*, II, pp. 136–143, 157–161; *Doc. Dipl.*, Décembre 1882–83, p. 169; Ministère des Affaires Étrangères, *op. cit.*, *supra*, pp. 12 ff.; *Chambre, Débats*, 1883, III, 90.

37. *Ibid.*, p. 121. *"Le principe, le voici: Quand le drapeau de la France, le drapeau de la République, flotte quelque part, sous peine de déchéance absolue,*

sous peine de ne plus compter pour rien dans ce monde, il doit être, par chacun de nous, depuis le premier jusqu'au dernier, quoi qu'il arrive et en toutes circonstances, soutenu, respecté, honoré quand même!"

38. *Ibid.*, pp. 113, 81–100, 102–123.

39. *Ibid.*, pp. 94, 189, 749, 860, 920; *Sénat, Débats*, 1883, III, 324 ff.

40. *Doc. Dipl.*, Décembre 1882–83, pp. 255–277; *Annales du Sénat et de la Chambre des Députés, Documents Parlementaires*, 1883, X, 532–534; *Chambre, Débats*, 1883, III, 705, 741.

41. *Ibid.*, pp. 717, 736 ff., 745, 920; Un Diplomate, *op. cit.*, p. 124; *Sénat, Débats*, 1883, III, 313.

42. *Chambre, Débats*, 1883, III, 749 ff.

43. Bouinais et Paulus, *op. cit.*, II, 181–193, 202–221.

44. *Doc. Dipl.*, 1884, p. 9. Un Diplomate, *op. cit.*, p. 157.

45. *Chambre, Documents*, 1884, IV, 355 ff.; Un Diplomate, *op. cit.*, pp. 163 ff.

46. *Doc. Dipl.*, 1884, pp. 5–7, 22; *Chambre, Débats*, 1884, II, 2010; *ibid.*, III, 463, 524; *Chambre, Documents*, 1884, IV, 356, 358.

47. *Ibid.*, p. 356; *Doc. Dipl.*, 1884, p. 13.

48. *Ibid.*, pp. 15, 17.

49. *Chambre, Documents*, 1884, IV, 356–358.

50. *Ibid.*, p. 349, Annexe No. 9.

51. *Doc. Dipl.*, 1884, pp. 16–18.

52. *Chambre, Débats*, 1884, II, 1092 f.

53. *Ibid.*, III, 491.

54. *Chambre, Documents*, 1884, IV, 344.

55. *Ibid.*, pp. 344 ff.

56. *Ibid.*, p. 346.

57. *Ibid.*, p. 348.

58. *Ibid.*, pp. 347, 358.

59. *Doc. Dipl.*, 1884, pp. 23, 37; *Chambre, Débats*, 1884, II, 1601 ff.; *Chambre, Documents*, 1884, IV, 347 ff.

60. *Doc. Dipl.*, 1884, pp. 19, 20, 22.

61. *Chambre, Documents*, 1884, IV, 351; *Chambre, Débats*, 1884, III, 510.

62. *Chambre, Débats*, 1884, III, 491; Un Diplomate, *op. cit.*, pp. 202 f.

63. *Ibid.*, pp. 197, 198, 228; *Chambre, Débats*, 1884, II, 1988, 2002; *Doc. Dipl.*, 1884, pp. 27, 39; *Chambre, Documents*, 1884, IV, 358.

64. *Doc. Dipl.*, 1884, pp. 38 ff., 42 ff.

65. *Chambre, Débats*, 1884, III, 467.

66. *Doc. Dipl.*, 1884–85, p. 5.

67. *Doc. Dipl.*, 1884, pp. 51, 52, 55, 57, 70 ff., 76.

68. *Chambre, Débats*, 1884, III, 524; *Sénat, Débats*, 1884, III, 1890.

69. *Doc. Dipl.*, 1885, p. 10.

70. *Ibid.*, pp. 27, 29, 34; Un Diplomate, *op. cit.*, pp. 216 ff.

71. *Chambre, Débats*, 1884, II, 1093; *Annales du Sénat et de la Chambre des Députés, Documents Parlementaires*, 1884, III, 289.

72. *Chambre, Débats*, 1884, II, 1988 ff.

73. *Ibid.*, p. 1992; *Doc. Dipl.*, 1884–85, p. 29.

74. *Chambre, Débats*, 1884, II, 1992, 2013; *Sénat, Débats*, 1884, II, 1476; *Doc. Dipl.*, 1885, p. 41.

75. *Ibid.*, pp. 14, 42, 47, 51; Un Diplomate, *op. cit.*, pp. 240, 315, 367.

76. Loir, *L'Escadre de l'Amiral Courbet*, p. 109.

77. Un Diplomate, *op. cit.*, pp. 205, 236 ff.; *Chambre, Débats*, 1884, II, 1992; *Doc. Dipl.*, Décembre 1882–83, p. 21; *Doc. Dipl.*, 1884, p. 42; *Doc. Dipl.*, 1884–85, p. 80; Loir, *op. cit.*, pp. 77, 103, 116–119, 359–368.

78. *Chambre, Débats,* 1884, III, 505; Un Diplomate, *op. cit.,* p. 251; Bouinais et Paulus, *op. cit.,* II, pp. 322, 304–327.

79. *Chambre, Documents,* 1884, IV, 342 ff., 352; *Doc. Dipl.,* 1884–85, pp. 42, 120, 122 ff.; Un Diplomate, *op. cit.,* p. 259; Bouinais et Paulus, *op. cit.,* pp. 331–335; Loir, *op. cit.,* pp. 169–189, 202–205.

80. *Doc. Dipl.,* 1884–85, pp. 126, 130; *Journal Officiel de la République Française,* jeudi 23 octobre, 1884, p. 5577; Un Diplomate, *op. cit.,* p. 272.

81. *Brit. and For. State Papers* (1884–85), LXXVI, p. 425. Waddington, French Ambassador to the Court of St. James's, to Earl Granville, Foreign Secretary, on or about November 5, 1884.

82. *Chambre, Débats,* 1884, III, 514.

83. *Doc. Dipl.,* 1884–85, p. 181.

84. Loir, *op. cit.,* p. 237.

85. *Chambre, Débats,* 1884, III, 517.

86. *Doc. Dipl.,* Décembre 1882–83, p. 142.

87. *Doc. Dipl.,* 1884–85, p. 93.

88. *Brit. and For. State Papers* (1884–85), LXXVI, p. 424.

89. *Doc. Dipl.,* 1884–85, p. 97; United States, *Foreign Relations,* 1884, p. 104.

90. Martens, *Nouveau Recueil Général de Traités* (1875), XX, 702.
"A neutral government is bound. . . .
"Secondly: Not to permit or suffer either belligerent to make use of its ports or waters as the base of naval operations against the other, or for the purpose of the renewal or augmentation of military supplies or arms, or the recruitment of men."

91. Un Diplomate, *op. cit.,* pp. 272 ff.; United States, *Foreign Relations,* 1884, p. 104.

92. *Chambre, Débats,* 1884, III, 513.

93. *Doc. Dipl.,* 1884–85, pp. 44, 87.

94. *Chambre, Documents,* 1884, IV, 4, 240; *Chambre Débats,* 1884, III, 517, 521 ff., 532, 536; *Sénat, Débats,* 1884, III, 1894.

95. *Chambre, Débats,* 1884, III, 9, 106, 373, 462–477, 482–500, 503–518, 521–539, 545 ff.

96. *Ibid.,* p. 498.

97. *Ibid.,* p. 513; *Sénat, Débats,* 1884, III, 1891.

98. Ragot, *Le Blocus de l'Ile de Formose,* pp. 70–78.

99. Hertslet, *The Map of Europe by Treaty,* II, 1282–84.

100. Malkin, "History of the Declaration of Paris," p. 34.

101. *Chambre, Documents,* 1884, IV, 352.

102. *Chambre, Débats,* 1884, III, 513; *Sénat, Débats,* 1884, III, 1891.

103. *Ibid.,* p. 132.

104. Falcke, *Blocus Pacifique,* pp. 91–96, 146–150, 166; Staudacher, "Die Friedensblockade," pp. 42 ff.

105. Falcke, *op. cit.,* pp. 85–91, 131–141.

106. Pistoye et Duverdy, *Traité des Prises Maritimes,* I, 372, 381.

107. Falcke, *op. cit.,* pp. 142–150.

108. *Ibid.,* pp. 96–100, 120–130.

109. *Ibid.,* pp. 115–120.

110. *Ibid.,* pp. 101–111, 112–118.

111. *Chambre, Débats,* 1884, III, 525; *Sénat, Débats,* 1884, III, 1886.

112. *Chambre, Débats,* 1884, III, 517, 539, 546.

113. *Doc. Dipl.,* 1884–85, pp. 5, 44, 89, 93, 112, 151.

114. Ragot, *op. cit.,* p. 24.

115. *Brit. and For. State Papers* (1884–85), LXXVI, 424 ff.

116. 294 *Parl. Deb.* (3d ser., 1884–85), 1009.

117. *Brit. and For. State Papers* (1884–85), LXXVI, 425.

118. *Ibid.*, pp. 426 ff., 429 ff.

119. *Ibid.*, p. 428.

120. 294 *Parl. Deb.* (3d ser., 1884–85), 1010.

121. 33 and 34 Vict. c. 90. *An Act to Regulate the Conduct of Her Majesty's Subjects during the Existence of Hostilities between Foreign States with Which Her Majesty Is at Peace.* [Aug. 9, 1870.]

122. Halleck, *International Law*, II, 205–207.

123. *Ibid.*, pp. 207–209. Letter addressed by Earl Derby, Foreign Secretary in Disraeli's Cabinet, on April 30, 1877, to the Treasury, the Home Office, the Colonial Office, the War Office, the Admiralty, and the India Office.

124. *Chambre, Documents*, 1884, IV, 361; Un Diplomate, *op. cit.*, pp. 248 ff.

125. Loir, *op. cit.*, p. 235; Geffcken, "La France en Chine," p. 147.

126. *Brit. and For. State Papers* (1884–85), LXXVI, 431, 434.

127. Loir, *op. cit.*, p. 235.

128. *Doc. Dipl., Affaires de Chine*, pp. 3, 5.

129. Hertslet, *op. cit.*, II, 1282 ff.

130. *Doc. Dipl., Affaires de Chine*, p. 3; *Brit. and For. State Papers* (1884–85), LXXVI, 435.

131. *Annuaire Diplomatique et Consulaire de la République Française*, 1884, p. 9.

132. Un Diplomate, *op. cit.*, pp. 248, 272. Italics supplied.

133. *Chambre, Débats*, 1885, I, 791 ff.

134. *Ibid.*, p. 783.

135. *Chambre, Débats*, 1884, III, 464.

136. *Chambre, Documents*, 1884, IV, 353, 360. This figure sheds doubts on Loir's report according to which 25,000 Chinese soldiers landed on Formosa from September, 1884, to January, 1885.

137. *Chambre, Débats*, 1885, I, 788.

138. *Chambre, Débats*, 1884, III, 507.

139. *Doc. Dipl.*, 1884–85, pp. 190, 260; Bouinais et Paulus, *op. cit.*, II, 340 ff.

140. *Ibid.*, pp. 349–353.

141. *Doc. Dipl.*, 1884–85, pp. 179, 192, 200, 217; Un Diplomate, *op. cit.*, pp. 294, 317.

142. Leyret, *Waldeck-Rousseau*, p. 416.

143. *Ibid.*, p. 417.

144. *Ibid.*, p. 418.

145. *Doc. Dipl., Affaires de Chine*, pp. 18–22; *Brit. and For. State Papers* (1884–85), LXXVI, 435–437, 442.

146. Chas. L. Nordon, "Blockade and Contraband: Law and Practice of Nations in Recent Times," *The Law Magazine and Review*, XXIX (1903–4), 192 ff.

147. Un Diplomate, *op. cit.*, p. 350; Brandt, *Dreiunddreissig Jahre in Ostasien*, III, 192.

148. *Doc. Dipl.*, 1884–85, pp. 183 ff., 196–200, 213 f.

149. *Doc. Dipl.*, 1884–85, pp. 224–226.

150. *Sénat, Débats*, 1885, II, 891.

151. *Doc. Dipl.*, 1884–85, pp. 224–226, Nos. 208, 209. Protocol, Art. 2; explanatory note, Pars. 1, 4.

152. *Ibid.*, explanatory note, Par. 5.

153. *Doc. Dipl.*, 1884–85, pp. 275, 283–286.

154. *Ibid.*, p. 281.

*Section 3. The Manchurian Conflict, 1931–1933, and the
Sino-Japanese "Incident," 1937–1941*

1. League of Nations, Doc. C. 663, M. 320, 1932, VII (hereafter quoted as
Lytton Report), 34, 37, 127.
2. *Ibid.*, pp. 65, 69–71, 89–111.
3. *Ibid.*, pp. 78, 80–83, 86.
4. *N. Y. Times*, July 7, 1942, p. 4; *ibid.*, July 8, 1942, p. 8.
5. United States, Dept. of State, *Bulletin*, Dec. 20, 1941, p. 559.
6. *N. Y. Times*, Jan. 19, 1938, p. 10; *ibid.*, Jan. 20, 1938, p. 6.
7. *Ibid.*, Aug. 26, 1937, p. 1; *ibid.*, Aug. 29, 1937, p. 1; United States, Dept. of
State, *Press Releases*, Sept. 11, 1937, pp. 235 ff.
8. Robert Levy, "French Neutrality during the Sino-Japanese Hostilities,"
Pacific Affairs, XI (1938), 442 f.
9. P. 18, above.
10. Levy, *op. cit., supra*, p. 442.
11. *N. Y. Times*, May 26, 1939, pp. 1, 10; *ibid.*, June 20, 1939, p. 8; *ibid.*, June
24, 1939, p. 2.
12. *Ibid.*, Oct. 19, 1941, pp. 1, 9.
13. *Ibid.*, Feb. 2, 1940, p. 22.
14. League of Nations, *Official Journal*, 1931, pp. 2265 ff., 2453 f.
15. *Ibid.*, pp. 2282, 2284, 2307.
16. *Ibid.*, pp. 2266, 2282.
17. League of Nations, *Official Journal*, Spec. Suppl., No. 101, p. 50. Italics supplied.
18. *Ibid.*, p. 75. Italics supplied.
19. *Ibid.*, p. 40.
20. *Ibid.*, p. 41.
21. *Basler Nachrichten*, March 5–6, 1932, p. 1.
22. League of Nations, *Official Journal*, 1931, pp. 2267, 2273.
23. See, for instance, Sato's speech in the meeting of the Council of Jan. 25,
1932, *ibid.*, 1932, p. 328.
24. League of Nations, Doc. C. 725, M. 330, 1931, VII, Geneva, Oct. 17, 1931,
Appeal of the Chinese Government in Virtue of Article 11 of the Covenant.
25. League of Nations, *Lytton Report*, pp. 81, 83, 109.
26. See, for instance, reply of Feb. 23, 1932, from the Japanese Government to
the appeal of the President of the Council of Feb. 16, 1932. League of Nations,
Official Journal, 1932, p. 385.
27. *Ibid.*, 1931, p. 2378.
28. League of Nations, *Lytton Report*, p. 126.
29. League of Nations, *Official Journal*, Spec. Suppl., No. 112, pp. 22, 73.
30. Eagleton, *The Attempt to Define War*, p. 254.
31. *Ibid.*, p. 254.
32. Hans Wehberg, "Hat Japan durch die Besetzung der Mandschurei das
Völkerrecht verletzt?" *Die Friedenswarte*, XXXII (1932), 1 f.
33. Eagleton, *op. cit.*, p. 257.
34. Guglielmo Ferrero, "L'Europe, l'Extrême Orient et la Société des Nations," *L'Esprit International*, 1932, p. 345.
35. 275 *H. C. Deb.* (5th ser., 1933), 59.
36. United States, Dept. of State, *Treaty for the Renunciation of War*, p. 45.
37. League of Nations, *Official Journal*, Spec. Suppl., No. 126, p. 33.
38. 50 *Stat.* 121 (1937); Deák and Jessup, *Neutrality Laws*, II, 1106 ff.
39. *Ibid.* (Loose-leaf ed.), II, pp. 1100 ff., 1105, 1106 ff., 1262 [1] ff.

40. Borchard and Lage, *Neutrality for the United States*, pp. 281 f., 314 f.

41. *N. Y. Times*, Aug. 15, 1937, p. 1; *ibid.*, Sept. 1, 1937, p. 3; *ibid.*, Sept. 12, 1937, p. 41.

42. *Ibid.*, Sept. 9, 1937, p. 3.

43. *Ibid.*, Oct. 6, 1937, pp. 1, 12; *ibid.*, Oct. 8, 1937, p. 3.

44. *Ibid.*, Aug. 23, 1937, p. 3.

45. *Ibid.*, July 29, 1937, p. 1.

46. *Ibid.*, Aug. 24, 1937, p. 3.

47. P. 22, above.

48. *Cong. Rec.*, LXXXII (1937), 92–93.

49. Raymond Leslie Buell, "American Policy in the Far East," *Foreign Policy Bulletin*, Aug. 27, 1937, pp. 1 f.

50. *N. Y. Times*, July 31, 1937, p. 14.

51. *Ibid.*, Sept. 8, 1937, p. 2.

52. *Ibid.*, Aug. 19, 1937, p. 3; *ibid.*, Oct. 7, 1937, p. 12.

53. *Ibid.*, Dec. 7, 1937, p. 11. Italics supplied.

54. *Ibid.*, April 7, 1939, p. 2.

55. Roosevelt, *Public Papers and Addresses* (1938), pp. 286 f.

56. Pp. 154–155, above.

Part II. Theoretical

CHAPTER V

Of Rules of Law on War

1. Scott, *Hague Conventions*, pp. 107–132.

2. Pp. 104–105, above.

3. Pp. 144–145, above.

4. Pp. 20–21, above.

5. *N. Y. Times*, June 27, 1945, p. 12. Italics supplied.

6. Pp. 39–41, above.

7. Martens, *La Paix et la Guerre*, p. 81.

8. Scott, *op. cit.*, pp. 96 ff., 100 ff., 133 ff., 209 ff.

9. Cf. von Gretschanino, *Politische Verträge*.

10. *Ibid.*, pp. 181, 195, 218, 230, 237, 269, 270, 277, 281, 302, 307, 357, 408, 460.

11. Miller, *Treaties*, II, 36.

12. 343 *H. C. Deb.* (5th ser., 1939), 625.

13. von Gretschanino, *op. cit.*, pp. 8, 12, 24, 35, 43, 47, 136, 227.

14. *N. Y. Times*, May 23, 1939, p. 8.

15. Hudson, *International Legislation*, III, 1670–1672.

16. *Ibid.*, V, 1–20.

17. *Ibid.*, V, 20–63.

18. *Ibid.*, VII, 490–492.

19. *Am. Jour. Int. Law.*, Suppl. III (1909), 179–220.

20. Giorgio Baladlore Pallieri, "La Forza Obligatoria della Consuetudine Internazionale," *Rivista di Diritto Internazionale*, XX (1928), 338–374; Maurice Bourquin, "Règles Générales du Droit de la Paix," *Académie de Droit International, Recueil des Cours*, 1 (1939), 61–67; Grégoire Gianni, *La Coutume en Droit International* (Paris, 1931).

21. *Publications of the Permanent Court of International Justice*, Series B, Collection of Advisory Opinions, Advisory Opinion No. 5 (Statute of Eastern Carelia), p. 27.

22. Anzilotti, *Lehrbuch*, pp. 53–56.

23. Von Waldkirch und von Vanselow, "Neutralitätsrecht," pp. 54, 318.

24. Oppenheim, "The Science of International Law," p. 334.

25. Huber, "Fortbildung des Völkerrechtes," p. 473.

26. United States, Senate, 61st Cong., 1st Sess. (1909–10), *Message from the President of the United States transmitting the Declaration signed by the Delegates of the United States to the International Naval Conference held at London, England, from December 4, 1908, to February 26, 1909*, pp. 4, 24.

27. T. E. Holland, *Letters to "The Times,"* pp. 90, 204.

28. Hammarskjöld, "La Neutralité en Général," pp. 74–76.

29. Huber, *Kriegsrechtliche Verträge und Kriegsräson*, p. 362.

30. P. 45, above.

31. P. 121, above.

32. P. 139, above.

33. Roscoe Pound, *The Formative Era of American Law* (Boston, 1938), pp. 13, 16.

34. Giuliano Enriques, "Considerazioni sulla Teoria della Guerra nel Diritto Internazionale," *Rivista di Diritto Internazionale*, XX (1928), 29. *"Anche oggi che quasi tutta la dottrina internazionalista si uniforma a quest' ultimo [moderno indirizzo positivo] non è poi tanto difficile trovare quà e là qualche infiltrazione gius naturalistica. . . ."*

35. Pp. 48–50, above.

36. P. 94, above; United States, *Foreign Relations*, 1914, pp. 481, 495 f.

37. Anzilotti, *Corso*, p. 189.

38. Oppenheim, *International Law*, II, 264.

39. Maurel, *Déclaration de Guerre*, pp. 247–251; Howard Lee McBain and Lindsay Rogers, *The New Constitutions of Europe* (New York, 1922), p. 150; B. Mirkine-Guétzevitch, "La Procédure Constitutionelle de Déclaration de Guerre," *Revue Politique et Parlementaire*, CXL (1929), 120 f.

40. Maurel, *op. cit.*, pp. 188–195, 219–235.

41. *N. Y. Times*, Oct. 1, 1946, p. 16; *ibid.*, Oct. 14, 1946, p. 1.

42. Adolphe Thiers, *Histoire du Consulat et de l'Empire* (Paris, 1874), XVII, 663, 673–675.

43. *Ibid.*, p. 673.

44. *Bulletin des Lois du Royaume de France*, 5e sér., I, 7–9.

45. According to Article 11, Paragraph 2 of the Constitution of the German Empire of April 16, 1871, the consent of the *Bundesrat* was required for a declaration of war by the Emperor, unless an attack was made upon the federal territory or its coasts. The Bundesrat consisted of representatives of the twenty-five members of the Confederation—Prussia, Bavaria, Saxony, Württemberg, and so forth. Dodd, *Modern Constitutions*, II, 328 f., 331.

46. Arthur Berriedale Keith, *The Government of the British Empire* (London, 1935), pp. 14, 293. Flournoy, *Parliament and War*, pp. 247 ff.

Chapter VI

"The" Legal Definition of War

1. P. 106, above.
2. For instance, P. Schoen, "Zur Lehre von den völkerrechtlichen nichtkriegerischen Mitteln der Selbsthilfe," *Zeitschrift für Völkerrecht*, XX (1936), 54. ". . . der in der Literatur und in der Praxis unbestritten feststehende Begriff Krieg."
3. P. 22, above.
4. Pp. 153–154, above.
5. P. 77, above.
6. P. 62, above.
7. P. 77, above.
8. Vattel, *Le Droit des Gens*, Liv. III, Secs. 1–4.
9. *Cong. Rec.*, LXIX (1928), 6929.
10. Oppenheim, *International Law* (2d ed. London, 1912), II, 60.
11. P. 153, above.
12. Paul Fauchille, *Traité de Droit International Public* (Paris, 1921), II, No. 996; Alberic Rolin, *Le Droit Moderne de la Guerre* (Bruxelles, 1920), I, 139.
13. Fritz Grob, *Seventy War Definitions Presented by International Lawyers in the Period from 1900 to 1940*. MS., Widener Library of Harvard University, Cambridge, Mass.; Library of Congress, Washington, D.C.; Swiss National Library, Bern.
14. P. 36, above.
15. Pp. 5, 149, above.
16. P. 78, above.
17. P. 359, above.
18. Walther Burckhardt, "La *Clausula Rebus sic Stantibus* en Droit International," *Revue de Droit International et de Législation Comparée*, XIV (1939), 23 ff.
19. Burckhardt, *Methode*, pp. 270 ff.
20. *Ibid.*, p. 278.
21. P. 161, above.
22. P. 166, above.
23. P. 144, above.
24. The Austrian delegate Hoffinger said on September 26, 1930, in the first Committee of the 11th Ordinary Session of the Assembly of the League of Nations: "It is very unlikely that public opinion will—or will even wish to—follow us in our subtle legal discussions. What it will gather from our debates is that even within the League itself no one really knows what the Pact of Paris is, what it prohibits and what it permits. The world will get the impression that all the talk which has been going on for the last two years about the Pact of Paris—which was to herald in the dawn of a new era—was perhaps very exaggerated, since it has been impossible even to agree on the meaning of the text and the manner in which that text can be embodied in the Covenant." League of Nations, *Official Journal*, Spec. Suppl., No. 85, p. 64.

International Law Association, *Briand-Kellogg Pact of Paris (August 27, 1928). Articles of Interpretation as Adopted by the Budapest Conference 1934* (London, 1934), p. 41. Mr. Grey: "We shall have no time unfortunately to go into the interpretation of some of the most important words in the Pact; for instance, what 'war' means and what an 'instrument of national policy' means."

25. Oppenheim, *International Law*, II, 172.

26. Oppenheim, "The Science of International Law," pp. 354 f.

27. Roland R. Foulke, *A Treatise on International Law* (Philadelphia, 1920), II, 130.

28. Jan de Louter, *Le Droit International Public Positif* (Oxford, 1920), II, 212.

29. John Westlake, *International Law* (2d ed. Cambridge, 1913), II, 1.

30. Henning Matzen, *Forlaesninger over den Positive Folkeret* (Köbenhavn, 1900), p. 259.

31. Leo Strisower, *Der Krieg und die Völkerrechtsordnung* (Wien, 1919), p. 4.

32. Marcel Moye, *Le Droit des Gens Moderne* (2me ed. Paris, 1928), p. 383.

33. Grotius, *De Jure Belli ac Pacis*, lib. I, cap. 1, sec. 2.

34. In his annotations Grotius quotes Servius, a Roman grammarian of the fourth century: "War is the whole period of time during which any preparation necessary for fighting is being made or in which fighting is carried on."

35. Alphonse Rivier, *Note sur la Littérature du Droit des Gens avant la Publication du Jus Belli ac Pacis de Grotius (1625)* (Bruxelles, 1883), pp. 3, 6.

36. P. 157, above.

37. P. 152, above.

38. *Cong. Rec.*, LXXXI, Appendix (1937), 1598.

39. P. 22, above. Italics supplied.

40. Charles H. Stockton, *Outlines of International Law* (New York, 1914), pp. 293 f.

41. Vattel, *op. cit.*, Liv. III, Secs. 1–4.

42. Ellery C. Stowell, *International Law* . . . (New York, 1931), pp. 490 f.

43. Luigi Olivi, *Diritto Internazionale Publico e Privato*, 3a ed. italiana, curata e accresciuta dal prof. Augosto Olivi (Milano, 1933), II, 446.

44. José Ramón de Orué, *Manual de Derecho Internacional Publico* (Madrid, 1934), p. 469.

45. Pp. 167–168, above.

46. Anzilotti, *Corso*, p. 183; Martens, *La Paix et la Guerre*, p. 23; Pillet, *La Guerre et le Droit*, p. 19; Rapisardi-Mirabelli, *Il Significato della Guerra*, pp. 49–52.

47. Saint Augustine, *De Civitate Dei*, lib. XIX, cap. VII. "*Iniquitas enim partis adversae justa bella ingerit gerenda sapienti.*"

48. Alfred Vanderpol, *La Doctrine Scolastique du Droit de la Guerre* (Paris, 1919), p. 28; Robert Regout, *La Doctrine de la Guerre Juste de Saint Augustin à nos Jours, d'après les Théologiens et les Canonistes Catholiques* (Paris, 1935), pp. 19, 299; Yves de la Brière, "Les Étapes de la Tradition Théologique concernant le Droit de juste Guerre," *Revue Générale de Droit International Public*, XLIV (1937), 129–161.

49. His Most Christian Majesty King Louis XIV of France seems to have known the teachings of his church none too well. He sets us wondering why he was not proclaiming a just war when in 1667 he invaded the Spanish Netherlands and fought against the Spanish Governor the so-called Queen's War in order to take what he said belonged to his Spanish consort Maria Theresa as of *right*. Instead he salved his qualms of conscience by the abstruse assertion that he was not breaking the peace. See p. 93, above.

50. *N. Y. Times*, Oct. 7, 1937, p. 12.

51. Wise words about the exercise of self-help in the family of nations have been written by Albert Gallatin, the Geneva aristocrat who was destined to become one of the most illustrious American statesmen. In 1835—when President Jackson was about to plunge the United States into a war with France because the French Chamber of Deputies temporarily refused to appropriate $25,000,000

which the government of King Louis Philippe had acknowledged as being due by France to the United States—Gallatin wrote to Edward Everett:

"The general position assumed by the President . . . and others, is, that whenever a nation has a claim clearly founded in justice, as that in question [against France] undoubtedly is, and justice is denied, resort must ultimately be had to war for redress of the injury sustained. This, as an abstract proposition, is wholly untenable, supported neither by the practice of nations nor by common sense. The denial of justice gives to the offended nation the right of resorting to arms, and such a war is just so far as it relates to the offending party. But to assert that a nation *must* in such a case, without attending either to the magnitude or nature of the injury, and without regard either to its own immediate interest or to political considerations of a higher order affecting perhaps its foreign and domestic concerns, inflict upon itself the calamities of war, under the penalty of incurring disgrace, is a doctrine which, if generally adopted, would keep the world in perpetual warfare, and sink the civilized nations of Christendom to a level with the savage tribes of our forests."

See Moore, *Digest,* VII, 122, 123–130.

52. *N. Y. Times,* Oct. 7, 1937, p. 12.

53. Johann Caspar Bluntschli, *Das moderne Völkerrecht der civilisierten Staaten als Rechtsbuch dargestellt,* 3. Aufl. (Nördlingen, 1878), p. 287.

54. Marqués Ramón de Dalmau y de Olivart, *Derecho Internacional Público* (5th ed. Madrid, 1906), p. 277.

55. Arnold D. McNair, "The Legal Meaning of War and the Relation of War to Reprisals," *Transactions of the Grotius Society,* XI (1926), 29–51.

56. *Ibid.,* p. 31.

57. *Ibid.,* p. 54.

58. *Ibid.,* p. 53.

59. *Ibid.,* p. 36.

60. P. 174, above.

61. P. 173, above.

62. P. 77, above.

63. P. 77, above.

64. P. 62, above.

Chapter VII

The Relativity of War and Peace

Section 1. General Considerations

1. P. 149, above.
2. P. 107, above.
3. P. 120, above.
4. P. 80, above.
5. Pp. 32–33, above.
6. Pp. 47–48, above.
7. P. 109, above.
8. P. 71, above.
9. P. 63, above.
10. Pp. 47, 63, above.
11. P. 72, above.

12. P. 143, above.

13. P. 144, above.

14. P. 151, above.

15. P. 153, above. In the case of *Kawasaki Kisen Kabushiki Kaisha of Kobe* v. *Bantham Steamship Company, Limited* [1939] 2 K. B. 544 the defendants, by a time chartership dated June 2, 1936, let a steamship to the plaintiffs as charterers. The chartership contained this clause: "Charterers and owners to have the liberty of cancelling the charter party if war breaks out involving Japan." On September 18, 1937, the defendants, by notice to the plaintiffs, withdrew the steamship and canceled the charter party on the ground that war had broken out involving Japan. The plaintiffs denied that this was so and claimed damages for breach of contract. The matter was referred to an umpire under an arbitration clause in the charter party. The umpire thought that the parties were using the word "war" and intended it to be construed as an ordinary businessman would understand it. He found, therefore, that war had broken out between China and Japan at the date in question and made an award in favor of the defendants. An appeal from the award to the King's Bench Division was dismissed. As against this it may be said that the parties in all probability used the word "war" with the intent and purpose of keeping the chartered ship out of the dangers as created through the establishment of blockades and the proclamation of contraband lists. There was no question here of contraband and running a blockade. The existence of war under the above clause, therefore, ought to have been denied and the award made in favor of the plaintiffs.

16. Hautefeuille, *Nations Neutres en Temps de Guerre Maritime*, I, 181.

17. Roosevelt, *Public Papers and Addresses* (1939), p. 156.

18. Pp. 47–48, above.

19. 1 *Stat.*, 716 (1799).

20. Pp. 20–22, above.

21. Pp. 49–50, 56–57, above.

22. P. 169, above.

23. Pp. 47–48, above.

24. P. 55, above.

25. Pp. 55–56, above.

26. P. 62, above.

27. Pp. 40–41, above.

28. P. 175, above.

29. P. 45, above.

30. P. 53, above.

31. P. 55, above.

32. P. 56, above.

33. *Ibid.*

34. Pp. 56–58, 77, above.

35. Pp. 56–57, above.

36. Pp. 74–75, above.

37. P. 75, above.

38. *Ibid.*

39. P. 17, above.

40. P. 78, above.

41. P. 171, above.

42. P. 7, above.

43. These prisoners of war are mentioned in the following paper: Great Britain, *Spain*, No. 1, pp. 19 f., 23, 26, 36 f.

44. Von Gretschanino, *Politische Verträge*, I, 274.

45. Franz Beyer, *Das deutsche Einschreiten in Finland 1918 als völkerrechts-mässige Intervention* (Braunschweig, 1927), pp. 32 ff., 74 f.

46. P. 57, above.

47. Pp. 24–29, above.

48. Falcke, "Die Friedensblockade," *Zeitschrift für internationales Privat- und öffentliches Recht*, XIX (1919), 120–126.

49. *Ibid.*, p. 125, n. 14. Italics supplied.

50. Pp. 60–62, above.

51. Johann Jacob Moser, *Grund-Sätze des Europäischen Völkerrechts in Kriegszeiten* . . . (Tübingen, 1752), p. 264; *idem, Versuch des neuesten Europäischen Völker-Rechts in Friedens- und Kriegszeiten* . . . (Frankfurt am Mayn, 1780), X, 2, p. 39.

52. United States, *Treaty Series*, No. 658.

53. Pp. 321–322, below.

54. P. 70, above.

55. *Drucksachen des Reichstages*, 10. Legislaturperiode, 2. Session 1900–1901, 2. Band, No. 132, p. 17.

56. Pp. 76–78, above.

57. P. 57, above.

58. P. 47, above.

59. P. 48, above.

60. Pp. 47–48, above.

61. Pp. 51, 58, above.

62. Rutherford, *Institutes of Natural Law*, II, 511.

63. P. 58, above.

64. Pp. 59–60, above.

65. Pp. 58–59, above.

66. P. 59, above.

67. P. 60, above.

68. P. 58, above.

69. P. 47, above.

70. P. 59, above.

71. P. 153, above.

72. P. 73, above.

73. Mérighnac, *Lois et Coutumes de la Guerre sur Terre* (Paris, 1903), p. 40.

74. P. 42, above.

75. P. 98, above.

76. Pp. 103, 124, above.

77. Pp. 57, 60, 62, above.

78. Something more than the restricted naval operations instituted through the Acts of May 28 and July 9, 1798, full-fledged naval operations perhaps, and operations on land must have been meant when several acts passed by the Congress in 1799 and 1800 referred to war not as actually existing, but only as a possible future contingency. See p. 49, above.

79. Chambre, *Documents*, 1884, IV, 352.

80. P. 140, above.

81. J. Shinobu, *International Law in the Shanghai Conflict* (Tokyo, 1933), II f.

82. *N. Y. Times*, Sept. 26, 1937, p. 35.

83. *Ibid.*, Jan. 9, 1938, p. 38.

84. Pp. 197–198, above.

85. Annex to Hague Conventions (II) of 1899 and (IV) of 1907, Arts. 23, al. a, b, c, e; 3. Scott, *Hague Conventions*, pp. 108, 116, 118.

86. Pp. 32–34, above.

87. Letter of the United States Attorney, Southern District of Texas, to the author, dated July 25, 1942, enclosing letter of State District Attorney, Laredo, Texas, to United States Attorney, Southern District of Texas, dated July 15, 1942.

88. *Rivista di Diritto Internazionale*, X (1916), 418.

89. Scott, *op. cit.*, p. 21.

90. *N. Y. Times*, July 4, 1940, p. 1.

91. Oppenheim, *International Law*, II, 375.

92. P. 72, above.

93. P. 71, above.

94. In his press conference of March 7, 1939, President Roosevelt—in a jocular vein, it is believed—gave a hint of the difficulties attending an attempt to legislate a war definition for the purpose of an amendment to the constitution requiring a referendum for a declaration of war by the United States. "In any constitutional amendment that goes into effect that uses the word 'war,' you will have to spend two pages in defining war; and if you define it, a situation would undoubtedly arise that would not come within the definition one way or the other." Roosevelt, *op. cit.*, p. 157.

95. Scott, *op. cit.*, p. 96.

96. Carnegie Endowment for International Peace, *Proceedings of the Hague Peace Conferences*, III, 169.

97. P. 36, above.

98. Pp. 201–203, above.

99. Pp. 16–17, above.

100. Scott, *op. cit.*, p. 96.

101. P. 17, above.

102. Pp. 17–18, above.

103. Cavaglieri, "Note Critiche," pp. 24, 31.

104. Examples of more recent studies on "measures short of war" are: Albert E. Hindmarsh, *Force in Peace. Force Short of War in International Relations* (Cambridge, Mass., 1933); Ludwig Keller, "Die nichtkriegerische militärische Gewaltmassnahme," *Völkerrechtliche Monographien*, Heft 11 (Berlin, 1934).

105. Pp. 18-19, above.

Section 2. Armed Intervention

1. Cavaglieri, "Note Critiche," p. 32.

2. Stowell, "Intervention," p. 92.

3. Pp. 166–168, above.

4. Pp. 164–166, above. This objection applies, for instance, to Lingelbach, "Doctrine and Practice of Intervention in Europe." This study is valuable, nevertheless, as a contribution to diplomatic history.

5. Oppenheim, "The Science of International Law," p. 346.

6. Malloy, *Treaties*, I, 362 ff.

7. Dareste et Dareste, *Les Constitutions Modernes*, IV, 155 f.

8. United States, *Treaty Series*, No. 866.

9. *Ibid.*, No. 881.

10. *Ibid.*, No. 923.

11. *Ibid.*, No. 881, p. 6. Italics supplied.

12. Cavaglieri, *L'Intervento*, p. 18; Fedozzi, *Saggio sul Intervento*, p. 47; Geffcken, *Das Recht der Intervention*, p. 3; Hettlage, "Intervention," p. 15; Hodges, *The Doctrine of Intervention*, p. 1; Lingelbach, *op. cit.*, p. 1; Strisower, "Inter-

vention," p. 582; and so forth, in particular, almost any textbook on international law.

13. Winfield, "The History of Intervention," p. 145; Potter, "L'Intervention en Droit International Moderne," pp. 610 f., 623.

14. *N. Y. Times*, Oct. 29, 1933, Sec. 4, p. 1.

15. *Brit. and For. State Papers* (1820–21), VIII, 1149–1151, 1811.

16. United States, *Messages and Papers of the Presidents*, II, 787–788.

17. *Ibid.*, XVI, 7789.

18. e.g., League of Nations, *Official Journal*, 1937, pp. 35, 262, 264, 572.

19. *Ibid.*, 1937, pp. 262, 264.

20. *N. Y. Times*, May 31, 1939, p. 13; *ibid.*, June 7, 1939, p. 1; *ibid.*, June 8, 1939, p. 12. Italics supplied.

21. *Ibid.*, June 6, 1939, p. 4. Italics supplied.

22. P. 228, above.

23. United States, *Messages and Papers of the Presidents*, XV, 7121; United States, *Foreign Relations*, 1906, p. 488.

24. United States, *Foreign Relations*, 1917, p. 712; United States, *Annual Reports of the Navy Department*, 1920, pp. 186 f., 222 f., 228, 235, 318 f.

25. United States, *Foreign Relations*, 1915, p. 438; *ibid.*, 1916, p. 319.

26. Pp. 225–226, above; United States, *Annual Reports of the War Department*, 1906, p. 24.

27. United States, *Annual Reports of the Navy Department*, 1920, pp. 321–324.

28. *Ibid.*, p. 311.

29. United States, *Foreign Relations*, 1915, p. 495. In 1916 Colonel Waller, commandant of the Marine Corps Brigade in Haiti, gave the following definition of a "Caco": "It must be explained that the Cacos have been the controlling element in all revolutions. They were purchased first by one candidate and then another. Finishing a contract with one man, they, having put him in power, would immediately sell their services to the next aspirant to unseat the first."

30. United States, *Foreign Relations*, 1916, pp. 226, 232; United States, *Annual Reports of the Navy Department*, 1917, p. 26; *ibid.*, 1920, p. 322.

31. United States, *Foreign Relations*, 1912, pp. 1032 f., 1043 f.; *ibid.*, 1915, p. 461; *ibid.*, 1916, pp. 317, 224; United States, *Annual Reports of the Navy Department*, 1920, p. 316.

32. Pp. 258–265, below.

33. Bemis, *Diplomatic History of the United States*, pp. 519 f.; *idem, Latin American Policy of the United States*, pp. 139 f., 142 ff., 165, 189 ff.; United States, *Foreign Relations*, 1916, pp. 222 f., 231, 317; United States, *Annual Reports of the Navy Department*, 1920, pp. 225, 247.

34. United States, *Foreign Relations*, 1915, pp. 479 f.; *ibid.*, 1916, pp. 231 f.; United States, *Annual Reports of the Navy Department*, 1920, p. 255.

35. United States, *Messages and Papers of the Presidents*, XIV, 6923 f. Italics supplied.

36. *N. Y. Times*, Sept. 18, 1920, p. 10.

37. United States, *Annual Reports of the War Department*, 1906, I, 492 ff.

38. Taft, *Our Chief Magistrate*, p. 96.

39. United States, *Right to Protect Citizens in Foreign Countries by Landing Forces, Memorandum of the Solicitor for the Department of State*, Oct. 5, 1912, 3d revised ed. with supplemental appendix up to 1933, Washington, 1934.

40. Article XIV of the treaty between the United States and Haiti relating to the finances, economic development, and tranquillity of Haiti, of Sept. 16, 1915, ratified in 1916, was a legal provision after the fashion of the Platt Amendment.

The word "intervention," though, was omitted. "The high contracting parties shall have authority to take such steps as may be necessary to insure the complete attainment of any of the objects comprehended in this treaty; and should the necessity occur, *the United States will lend an efficient aid for the preservation of Haitian independence and the maintenance of a government adequate for the protection of life, property and individual liberty.*" United States, *Foreign Relations*, 1915, p. 433; *ibid.*, 1916, p. 331. Italics supplied.

41. Compare, however, *Sen. Doc.*, No. 39, 70th Cong., 1st Sess. (1928).
42. Taft, *op. cit.*, p. 96.
43. United States, *Annual Reports of the Navy Department*, 1913, p. 38.
44. *Ibid.*, 1920, p. 305.
45. 35 *Stat.* 127 (1909).
46. 30 *Stat.* 364 (1898).
47. United States, *Annual Report of the Navy Department*, 1920, p. 268.
48. 39 *Stat.* 53 (1916).
49. United States, *Naval Digest*, 1916, p. 639.
50. *Rev. Stat.*, sec. 1624, art. 4 (1875).
51. *Amerikanische Schweizer Zeitung*, Mittwoch, den G. Juli 1949, p. 1.

Section 3. Armed Reprisals

1. The *Institut de Droit International* at its Paris session in 1934 considered a report made by Politis and adopted regulations concerning the use of reprisals "in time of peace." It recommended these regulations for adoption by the various governments. By "peace" is actually meant peace in relation to and in the meaning of treaties in which the contracting parties agree not to resort to war. Article 1 of the regulations gives a definition of the term "reprisals." There ought to be no blinking the fact that this definition is a *de lege ferenda* definition and valid only for the regulations concerned in the event of their adoption, *Annuaire de l'Institut de Droit International*, Sess. de Paris, Octobre 1934, pp. 3 ff., 629–646.
2. Vast, *Les Grands Traités*, II, 208.
3. Jessup and Deák, *The Origins* [of Neutrality], p. 13.
4. 2 *Stat.* 755 (1812).
5. 2 *Stat.* 759 (1812).
6. P. 355, n. 7, above.
7. Moore, *Digest*, VII, 123–130.
8. P. 50, above.
9. 2 *Stat.* 755 (1812).
10. P. 125, above.
11. Oppenheim, *International Law*, II, 118.
12. Pp. 197–198, above.
13. An Act of March 3, 1800, provided for salvage in case of recapture in reprisals. 2 *Stat.* 16 (1800).
14. 2 *Stat.* 45 (1800).
15. Rutherford, *Institutes*, II, 511; Burlamaqui, *Principles*, II, 258.
16. *N. Y. Times*, June 1, 1937, p. 1.
17. *Ibid.*, Sept. 26, 1940, p. 4.
18. *Ibid.*, Sept. 25, 1940, p. 2; *ibid.*, Sept. 26, 1940, p. 1.
19. *Ibid.*, Sept. 25, 1940, p. 2.
20. Anzilotti, *Corso*, p. 158.
21. P. 124, above.

22. *Annuaire de l'Institut de Droit International,* Sess. de Paris, Octobre 1934, p. 626.
23. P. 129, above.
24. Greece, *Doc. Dipl.,* Nos. 1, 3, 4, 5, 9, 10, 11, 12, 14, 23, 24.
25. *Ibid.,* No. 15.
26. League of Nations, *Official Journal,* 1923, p. 1306.
27. *Ibid.,* p. 1313. Italics supplied.
28. *Ibid.,* p. 1314.
29. United States, *Foreign Relations,* 1895, II, 1025–1034.
30. *Ibid.,* 1901, pp. 529 f.
31. League of Nations, *Official Journal,* 1923, p. 1352; *ibid.,* 1924, p. 523; *ibid.,* 1926, pp. 597–612.
32. Scott, *Hague Conventions,* pp. 157 ff.
33. *Ibid.,* pp. 161 f.; Hudson, "Present Status of the Hague Conventions," p. 116.
34. Greece, *Doc. Dipl.,* Nos. 22, 23, 24.

Section 4. Pacific Blockades

1. Hautefeuille, *Nations Neutres en Temps de Guerre Maritime,* III, 176.
2. Fauchille, *Du Blocus Maritime,* pp. 38–68; Söderquist, *Le Blocus Maritime,* pp. 132–139.
3. Albert Edmund Hogan, *Pacific Blockade* (Oxford, 1908); Hermann Staudacher, "Die Friedensblockade," *Staats- und völkerrechtliche Abhandlungen,* VII (1909), Heft 3; Horst P. Falcke whose writings are listed on p. 337, above.
4. League of Nations, Doc. A. 14. 1927. V., pp. 89–93.
5. Pp. 126–129, above.
6. Hautefeuille, *Nations Neutres en Temps de Guerre Maritime,* III, 176 ff.
7. P. 87, above.
8. It is indicative of the historical unreliability of this writer that, again without quoting any source, he also reports about a joint French-British blockade of the coasts of the Argentine Confederacy in the period from 1838 to 1848. Such a blockade likewise never occurred. Hautefeuille, writing around 1848, had no clear idea about the activities of the French and British Navies, not even for the decade that lay immediately behind him.
9. Pp. 89–90, above.
10. League of Nations, Doc. A. 1927. V., p. 89.
11. Falcke, "Friedensblockade" (1909), pp. 142–146.
12. Pp. 95–96, above.
13. For example, Fauchille, *Du Blocus Maritime,* pp. 38–68; J. Westlake, "Le Blocus Pacifique," *Revue de Droit International et de Législation Comparée,* XIV (1909), 203 ff.
14. Pp. 201–203, above.
15. F. Perels, "Le Blocus en Temps de Paix," *Revue de Droit International et de Législation Comparée,* XIX (1887), 244–252.
16. Söderquist, *Le Blocus Maritime,* p. 136.
17. Pp. 121–122, above.
18. Pp. 104–105, 133–134, above.
19. Falcke, *op. cit.,* p. 67.
20. *Ibid.,* 1920, pp. 116–119.
21. 116 *Parl. Deb.* (4th ser., 1902), 1490.
22. P. 143, above.
23. Pp. 193–194, above.

24. *Ibid.*
25. P. 158, above.
26. Fauchille, *op. cit.*, p. 46.
27. R. Pièdelièvre, *Précis de Droit International Public* (Paris, 1894), II, 97; Westlake, "Le Blocus Pacifique," p. 203; League of Nations, Doc. A. 14. 1927. V, p. 90.
28. United States, *Treaty Information Bulletin*, No. 47, August 1933, pp. 36 ff.
29. P. 251, above.
30. P. 125, above.
31. G. Fr. de Martens, *Nouveau Recueil Général de Traités* . . . (deuxième sér. Gottingue, 1876), I, 57 ff. This treaty provision, like many others, has been spoiled by the expression "state of war." It can make sense only if we read "war" instead of "state of war" (war in "the" legal sense).
32. Falcke, *op. cit.*, 1920, pp. 96, 101, 112, 118.
33. P. 24, above.
34. Falcke, *op. cit.*, pp. 61 ff.
35. *Ibid.*, pp. 70 ff.
36. *Ibid.*, pp. 75 ff.
37. *Ibid.*, pp. 94 ff.
38. United States, *Foreign Relations*, 1897, p. 255.
39. Falcke, *op. cit.*, p. 92.
40. *Ibid.*, pp. 85 f., 88.
41. Great Britain, *Venezuela*, Nos. 109, 136.
42. P. 368, n. 45, above.
43. Germany, *Die grosse Politik*, XVII, 241 f., 246, 254, 257 f.; United States, *Foreign Relations*, 1903, p. 454.
44. *Ibid.*, p. 259.
45. Great Britain, *Venezuela*, pp. 196, 206.
46. United States, *Foreign Relations*, 1903, pp. 422 f.
47. Great Britain, *Venezuela*, pp. 202–204.
48. United States, *Foreign Relations*, 1901, p. 196.
49. Pp. 256–257, above.
50. United States, *Foreign Relations*, 1903, p. 420.
51. *Ibid.*, p. 421.
52. *Ibid.*, p. 423.
53. Germany, *Die grosse Politik*, XVII, pp. 258, 273.
54. Basdevant, "L'Action Coercitive Anglo-Germano-Italienne," p. 415; 116 *Parl. Deb.* (4th ser., 1902), 1489.
55. United States, *Foreign Relations*, 1903, pp. 437, 476; Germany, *Die grosse Politik*, XVII, 290.
56. *Ibid.*, p. 275.
57. *Ibid.*, p. 274; Basdevant, *op. cit.*, p. 419.
58. 116 *Parl. Deb.* (4th ser., 1902), 1491. Italics supplied.
59. Great Britain, *Venezuela*, No. 234.
60. *Stenographischer Bericht des deutschen Reichstages*, X. Legislaturperiode, II. Sess., 1900–1903, VIII, 7511.
61. Basdevant, *op. cit.*, p. 425.
62. United States, *Messages and Papers of the Presidents*, suppl. covering the presidential terms of Theodore Roosevelt, p. 6665.
63. Great Britain, *Venezuela*, No. 138.
64. Dexter Perkins, *Hands Off*, pp. 220 f.
65. 116 *Parl. Deb.* (4th ser., 1902), 1252.
66. Dexter Perkins, *The Monroe Doctrine* (Baltimore, 1937), p. 382.

67. Germany, *Die grosse Politik*, XVII, 292.

68. Perkins, *Hands Off*, p. 218.

69. Turlington, *Neutrality*, p. 35.

70. Padelford, *Spanish Civil Strife*, pp. 9–13; Charles Rousseau, "La Non-intervention en Espagne," *Revue de Droit International et de Législation comparée*, XIX (1938), 528–537; *N. Y. Times*, March 9, 1939, p. 10.

71. Turlington, *op. cit.*, pp. 34–66.

Section 5. On the Parties to War

1. Scott, *Hague Conventions*, pp. 100 ff.

2. P. 169, above.

3. Art. 2 in either Convention.

4. Art. 2 of the Convention of 1907.

5. On April 1, 1945, the German radio announced that a "freedom movement" of "werewolves," including not only men, but women, boys, and girls, had been formed in areas already occupied by the Allies "to continue the fight against the hated enemy." The "werewolves" were ordered to conduct a suicidal campaign of death against every Allied soldier without regard to "the childish rules of so-called decent bourgeois warfare." Little, however, had been heard about the activities of the "werewolves," when Germany surrendered unconditionally five weeks later. See *N. Y. Times*, April 2, 1945, p. 7.

6. Meurer, *Die Haager Friedenskonferenz*, II, pp. 90–111.

7. *N. Y. Times*, Aug. 6, 1944, p. 23.

8. *Ibid.*, Nov. 16, 1941, p. 10.

9. *The Christian Science Monitor*, July 15, 1944, p. 9. On September 25, 1944, Lieut. Gen. Joseph-Pierre Koenig, commander of the FFI, said that "unworthy elements were very definitely intermingled among the FFI and these elements have committed acts contrary to military law by making false use of the title of the FFI." See *N. Y. Times*, Sept. 26, 1944, p. 4.

10. *Ibid.*, July 18, 1944, p. 3.

11. *Ibid.*, Oct. 21, 1941, p. 9.

12. *The Christian Science Monitor*, July 12, 1944, p. 1.

13. *N. Y. Herald Tribune*, Oct. 21, 1944, p. 1.

14. *N. Y. Times*, Aug. 10, 1940, p. 4; *ibid.*, June 18, 1944, p. 1.

15. Lawrence, *Documents*, pp. 280–285.

16. Deák and Jessup, *Neutrality Laws*, II, 990.

17. *Ibid.*, II, 999–1000, 1038–1047.

18. Padelford, *Spanish Civil Strife*, pp. 303, 367.

19. Pp. 235–236, above. In *Vashti LaRue v. Kansas Mutual Life Insurance Company*, 68 Kansas 539 (1904), the Supreme Court of Kansas recognized operations conducted in 1900 against the Army of the United States by insurrectos of the Moro tribe in the island of Mindanao, one of the Philippines, as war in the meaning of the war clause in a policy of life insurance.

20. *Chambre, Débats*, 1881, I, 741 f., 809, 811 f., 845 f., 854–857; *ibid.*, 1881, II, 2 f., 7 f., 64 f., 118–129, 399–401; *ibid.*, 1881, III, 98–115, 118–136, 160–183, 313–332. See Schuman, *War and Diplomacy in the French Republic*, pp. 65–72.

21. Pp. 104–105, above.

22. P. 147, above.

23. P. 144, above.

24. P. 193, above.

Section 6. Authorized and Unauthorized Operations

1. Pp. 84, 87–88, above.
2. Pp. 100–103, 106, 114–115, above.
3. *N. Y. Times*, June 29, 1946, p. 8.
4. P. 22, above.
5. P. 91, above.
6. Pp. 91–92, above.
7. Bourchier, *Life of Codrington*, II, 246; Phillips, *Greece and the Balkan Peninsula*, p. 201.
8. P. 169, above.
9. Pp. 32–33, above.
10. P. 218, above.
11. United States, *Foreign Relations*, 1916, pp. 593, 596.
12. P. 32, above.
13. The treatment of captives who wittingly have participated in unauthorized operations was a matter of great practical importance after the unconditional surrender of Germany in May, 1945. By Art. 1 of "An Act of Military Surrender," signed at Reims, France, on May 7, 1945 (*N. Y. Times*, May 9, 1945, p. 3), the German High Command surrendered unconditionally to the Supreme Commander, Allied Expeditionary Force, and simultaneously to the Soviet High Command, all forces on land, sea, and in the air which were at this date under German control. In Art. 2 the German High Command undertook to issue at once orders to all German military, naval, and air authorities and to all forces under German control to cease active operations at 23:01 hours Central European time on May 8 and to remain in the positions occupied at the time. In Art. 5 the Supreme Commander, Allied Expeditionary Force, and the Soviet High Command declared that they would take such punitive or other action as they deemed appropriate in the event of the German High Command or any of the forces under their control failing to act in accordance with the Act of Surrender. By the time of the dead line the German forces on land surrendered with the exception of the armies commanded by Field Marshal Ferdinand Schoerner. These German forces continued resistance against the Russians in Bohemia and in northern Austria for about five days with the aim to give up to the Western Allies rather than the Russians (*N. Y. Times*, May 11, 1945, p. 15; *ibid.*, May 13, 1945, p. 1). On May 11 Moscow dispatches reported that the Russians were employing "stern measures" with the Germans who had surrendered after having fought beyond the deadline of 11:01 P.M. on May 8 (*ibid.*, May 12, 1945, pp. 1, 5). It still remains to be learned from behind the "iron curtain" what these "stern measures" were.

Section 7. War and Diplomatic Relations

1. See, for instance, J. C. C. den Beer Portugael. *Oorlogs- en Neutraliteitsrecht op den Grondslag van de Conferentie van Genève in 1906 en de twee Haagsche Vredes Conferentien* ('s-Gravenhage, 1907), p. 84; Amédée Bonde, *Traité Élémentaire de Droit International Public* (Paris, 1926), p. 394; Alexander Hold-Ferneck, *Lehrbuch des Völkerrechtes* (Leipzig, 1932), p. 363.
2. P. 56, above.
3. P. 153, above.
4. P. 178, above.
5. *N. Y. Times*, Oct. 7, 1941, p. 1.

6. *Amerikanische Schweizer Zeitung,* Dec. 24, 1941; *ibid.,* Jan. 28, 1942.
7. G. B. Malleson, *Life of Metternich* (London, n.d.), p. 45.
8. Rousseau, "Conflit Italo-Éthiopien," pp. 681, 683 f.
9. *N. Y. Times,* Aug. 28, 1941, p. 6.
10. P. 169, above.
11. Rousseau, *op. cit.,* pp. 687, 698.
12. P. 216, above.
13. Pp. 142, 276, above.
14. Pp. 32–34, 218, above.
15. P. 216, above.
16. P. 142, above. There was in 1916 an American special agent with the de facto Government of Mexico of which General Carranza was the head. The de facto Government of Mexico, in turn, had a representative in Washington. See United States, *Foreign Relations,* 1916, pp. 465, 469 f.
17. P. 76, above.
18. *Ibid.*
19. P. 71, above.
20. P. 144, above.
21. League of Nations, *Official Journal,* Spec. Suppl., No. 138, pp. 113 f.
22. Deák and Jessup, *Neutrality Laws,* II, 1100.
23. *Ibid.,* p. 1107; p. 151, above.
24. Deák and Jessup, *op. cit.,* II, 1228–1230.
25. P. 158, above.
26. P. 153, above.

Section 8. War with and without Clash of Arms

1. Karl Strupp, "Ausgewählte Kapitel aus der Völkerrechtsgeschichte," *Zeitschrift für Völkerrecht,* VII (1913), 487–528.
2. Gabriel Hanotaux, *La Guerre des Balkans et l'Europe, 1912–1913* (Paris, 1914), p. 358.
3. *N. Y. Times,* April 11, 1940, p. 2.
4. Guglielmo Ferrero, *Peace and War* (London, 1933), pp. 5–7; *Pulcher tractatus de materia belli,* written in Italy by an anonymous author around 1300, is a remarkable manual of the finesses of unbloody victory. The author, a characteristic predecessor of Machiavelli, shows how fighting can be avoided by espionage, deception, bribery, treason, and clever propaganda among the enemy population and the enemy troops. See Alfred Pichler, "Der *Pulcher tractatus de materia belli,* ein Beitrag zur Kriegs- und Geistesgeschichte des Mittelalters," *Veröffentlichungen des historischen Seminars der Universität Graz,* IV (1927), 8, 18, 32–35.
5. Von Clausewitz, *Vom Kriege,* pp. 19–36, 626.
6. *Ibid.,* p. 29.
7. Lieut.-Col. G. F. R. Henderson, *Stonewall Jackson and the American Civil War* (London, New York, Bombay, 1898), I, 96, 517, II, 592.
8. Thomas Baty, *War, Its Conduct and Legal Results* (London, 1915), p. 397; Cavaglieri, "Note Critiche," p. 310; Strisower, *Krieg und Völkerrechtsordnung,* p. 10.
9. *Ibid.,* p. 9, n. 14; Franz Liszt, *Das Völkerrecht,* 12te Aufl. bearbeitet von Max Fleischmann (Berlin, 1925), p. 449.
10. Pp. 253–254, above.
11. Scott, *Hague Conventions,* pp. 100–132.
12. *Ibid.,* pp. 130 f.

13. P. 144, above.
14. League of Nations, Doc. A. 14. 1927, V, pp. 42 f.
15. 307 *H. C. Deb.* (5th ser., 1935), 347.
16. *N. Y. Times,* Dec. 11, 1945, p. 10.
17. *Ibid.,* Aug. 6, 1944, p. 27.
18. Webster's *New International Dictionary of the English Language* (2d ed.), II, 2871.
19. P. 22, above.

Section 9. On Declarations of War

1. Sir John Fischer Williams, *Some Aspects of the Covenant of the League of Nations* (London, 1934), pp. 159 f.
2. P. 148, above.
3. P. 153, above.
4. *N. Y. Times,* Jan. 19, 1938, p. 10.
5. *L'Europe Nouvelle,* 9 mars 1929, pp. 318–320.
6. Gemma, "Rassegna Criticha," p. 329; Cesare L. Gasca, *Le Leggi della Guerra* (Torino, 1914), p. 9.
7. *De verborum significatione Dig.,* 50, 16, 118. "*Hostes hi sunt, qui nobis aut quibus nos publice bellum decrevimus: ceteri 'latrones' aut 'praedones' sunt.*"
8. Hautefeuille, *Nations Neutres en Temps de Guerre Maritime,* I, 108.
9. Fauchille, *Blocus Maritime,* pp. 54 f.
10. Anzilotti, *Corso,* p. 236.
11. Gemma, *op. cit.,* p. 329.
12. Prosper Fedozzi, "Le Droit International et les Récentes Hostilités Italo-Abyssines," *Revue de Droit International et de Législation Comparée,* XXVII (1896), 586–589, 592.
13. William L. Langer, *An Encyclopaedia of World History* (Boston, 1940), p. 802.
14. Regarding the history of the declarations of war, see Holtzendorff, *Handbuch des Völkerrechtes,* IV, 334–341; Charles Dupuis, "La Déclaration de Guerre," *Revue Générale de Droit International Public,* XIII (1906), 731 f.
15. *Archives Diplomatiques,* 1871–72, pp. 189 f.
16. Westlake, *International Law,* II, 19; Baker and McKernan, *Selected Topics,* p. 31.
17. Scott, *Hague Conventions,* p. 96. Italics supplied.
18. G. G. Wilson, "War Declared and the Use of Force," *Proceedings of the American Society of International Law,* XXXII (1938), 110–111.
19. James Brown Scott, *Les Conventions et Déclarations de la Haye de 1899 et 1907,* Dotation Carnegie pour la Paix Internationale, Division de Droit International (New York, 1918), p. 96.
20. Scott, *Hague Conventions,* p. 96.
21. Bordwell, *The Laws of War,* II, 86.
22. Holland, *Letters,* pp. 43 f. Italics supplied; *Annuaire de l'Institut de Droit International,* XXI (1906), p. 292.
23. *Ibid.,* pp. 42, 274.
24. P. 253, above.
25. P. 218, above.
26. P. 216, above.
27. *Ibid.*
28. P. 164, above.

29. *Quinzième Conférence Internationale de la Croix-Rouge tenue à Tokio du 20 au 29 Octobre 1934, Compte Rendu,* p. 202.

30. P. 216, above.

31. P. 151, above.

32. Pp. 144, 193, above.

33. Deák and Jessup, *Neutrality Laws,* II, 1100, 1227–1230.

34. P. 144, above.

35. Carnegie Endowment for International Peace, *Proceedings of the Hague Peace Conferences,* p. 169.

36. It is beside the point to quote *The Eliza An,* 1 Dodson 244, 165 Reprint 1928 (1813), a prize court decision in which Sir William Scott (afterward Lord Stowell) commented about the significance of a declaration of war from the point of view of British prize law. This case has been quoted by William J. Ronan in his article on "English and American Courts and the Definition of War," *Amer. Jour. Int. Law,* XXXI (1937), p. 654.

37. On Nov. 14, 1885, Prince Alexander of Bulgaria, after having received the Serbian declaration of war, issued a proclamation in which he said: "While leaving to the Serbs and to their Government the responsibility for this war between brothers and for the disastrous consequences which it may have for both States, we announce to our beloved people that *we have accepted the war which has been declared by* Serbia. . . ." Adolf Koch, *Fürst Alexander von Bulgarien, Mitteilungen aus seinem Leben und seiner Regierung* (Darmstadt, 1887), pp. 243–245. Italics supplied.

38. United States, Dept. of State, *Bulletin,* Dec. 13, 1941, pp. 482 f.

39. *N. Y. Times,* June 3, 1942, p. 1.

40. United States, Dept. of State, *Bulletin,* June 6, 1942, p. 509.

41. *N. Y. Times,* Oct. 14, 1943, p. 6.

42. Eagleton, "The Form and Function of a Declaration of War," p. 22.

43. Pp. 283–284, above.

44. *Archives Diplomatiques* (Paris, 1871–72), pp. 189 f. Italics supplied.

45. United States, *Declarations of War,* pp. 11–73.

46. *Ibid.,* p. 40. Italics supplied.

47. *Ibid.,* p. 20. Italics supplied.

48. Besides the numerous declarations of war which follow the French pattern of 1870 there have been issued others with the wording of which there can be no quarrel. It is worth while to quote some of these declarations.

(1) The Imperial rescript issued at Tokio, Aug. 23, 1914: "We hereby *declare war* against Germany." [*Ibid.,* p. 50. Italics supplied.]

(2) The Italian Foreign Minister Count Ciano to the Ambassador of France, June 10, 1940: "Italy *considers herself to be at war* with France, beginning tomorrow, June 11." [United States, Dept. of State, *Bulletin,* Dec. 20, 1941, p. 553. Italics supplied.]

(3) The Hungarian Prime Minister to the American Minister at Budapest, Dec. 13, 1941: "Hungary *considers war to exist* between Hungary and the United States." [*Ibid.,* p. 561. Italics supplied.]

(4) The French Government to the Ambassador of the United States at Paris, in charge of Austro-Hungarian interests in France, Aug. 13, 1914: ". . . the Government of the Republic sees itself constrained to no longer recognize it [the Imperial and Royal Government of Austria-Hungary] as a neutral and *to consider it as an enemy* from the date of August 12, at midnight." [United States, *Declarations of War,* p. 25. Italics supplied.]

(5) Manifesto of the Sultan of the Ottoman Empire, proclaiming a Holy War

against France, Great Britain, and Russia, Nov. 12, 1914: ". . . we have been obliged *to break the peace* that we always wanted and to take arms to defend our legal interests in allying ourselves to Germany and Austria-Hungary." [*Ibid.*, p. 61. Italics supplied.]

(6) Proclamation by the Emperor of all the Russias, Oct. 19, 1915: "The Russian people regard with sorrow the treason of Bulgaria which was so near to it until these last few days, and, with bleeding heart, *it draws its sword against her*, leaving the fate of the betrayer of the Slav cause to the just punishment of God." [*Ibid.*, p. 58. Italics supplied.]

49. Compare declarations Nos. 2 and 3 in preceding footnote.

50. United States, Dept. of State, *Bulletin*, Dec. 13, 1941, pp. 491–496, 499 f.; *ibid.*, Dec. 20, 1941, p. 560.

51. *Ibid.*, Dec. 27, 1941, p. 584; *ibid.*, Feb. 7, 1942, p. 144.

52. United States, *Declarations of War*, pp. 21–23, 38, 39, 52–54. The wordings of the declarations made by Guatemala and Panama were unique. The National Legislative Assembly of the Republic of Guatemala decreed on April 20, 1918, that "in the present international conflict *Guatemala assumes the same belligerent attitude as the United States* toward the German Empire." [*Ibid.*, p. 38. Italics supplied.] The President of the Republic of Panama issued on April 7, 1917, a proclamation in which it was said "that the Panamanian nation will *lend its emphatic cooperation to the United States of America* against the enemies who may execute or attempt to execute hostile acts against the territory of Panama or against the Panama Canal, or which in any manner may affect or tend to affect the common interests of the two countries." [*Ibid.*, p. 54. Italics supplied.]

53. *Ibid.*, pp. 23, 52 f.

54. P. 253, above.

55. Italics supplied.

56. P. 135, above.

57. Great Britain, *Treaty Series*, No. 4 (1919), p. 1.

58. *Ibid.*, No. 11 (1919), p. 1.

59. Pp. 204–208, above.

60. Martin, *Latin America and the War*, pp. 508, 122 f., 498, 518, 503, 489.

61. *Ibid.*, p. 519.

62. *Ibid.*, pp. 115, 164.

63. Garner, *International Law and the World War*, I, 171.

64. Germany, Reichsamt des Innern, *Die Handelsverträge des deutschen Reiches* (Berlin, 1906), p. 492.

65. Garner, *op. cit.*, I, 56 f.

66. Scott, *Hague Conventions*, p. 141.

67. Regarding the controversial right of a *neutral* government to seize in an emergency, for public use and subject to compensation, merchant vessels of a belligerent that have taken refuge in its ports to avoid capture by the enemy, see Garner, *op. cit.*, I, 176–180.

68. P. 286, above.

69. United States, *Declarations of War*, pp. 23 f.

70. Martin, *op. cit.*, pp. 107–114.

71. *Ibid.*, pp. 505–510.

72. United States, *Declarations of War*, pp. 38 f.

73. Oppenheim, *International Law*, II, 270.

74. Martin, *op. cit.*, pp. 491–499.

75. *N. Y. Times*, Feb. 24, 1945, p. 1; *ibid.*, Feb. 28, 1945, p. 14; *ibid.*, March 6, 1945, p. 10.

76. United States, Dept. of State, *Bulletin,* 1945, pp. 231–233, 292–294, 373, 375, 538, 575.
77. *N. Y. Times,* Nov. 19, 1945, p. 3.
78. P. 79, above.
79. *N. Y. Times,* May 11, 1933, p. 1.
80. United States, Dept. of State, *Bulletin,* Dec. 20, 1941, p. 559.
81. P. 286, above.
82. *N. Y. Times,* April 11, 1933, p. 11.
83. Pp. 254, 262, above.
84. Pp. 263–265, above.
85. P. 194, above.

Section 10. On the Duration of War

1. *See New York Life Insurance Company* v. *Bennion, F.,* 158 (2d) 260; Edwin Borchard, "When Did the War Begin?" *Col. Law Rev.,* XLVII (1947), 742–748.
2. Pp. 32–34, above.
3. Scott, *Hague Conventions,* p. 108.
4. P. 218, above.
5. Scott, *op. cit.,* p. 133.
6. *Ibid.,* pp. 209–219.
7. *Ibid.,* p. 96.
8. Huber, "Fortbildung," p. 591.
9. P. 291, above.
10. United States, *Declarations of War,* p. 35.
11. e.g., George Grafton Wilson, *Handbook of International Law* (2d ed. St. Paul, Minn.), p. 239.
12. United States, Dept. of State, *Bulletin,* Dec. 20, 1941, p. 559. Italics supplied.
13. *N. Y. Times,* June 23, 1941, p. 5. Italics supplied.
14. United States, Dept. of State, *Bulletin,* Feb. 7, 1942, p. 144. Italics supplied.
15. *Ibid.,* June 6, 1942, p. 506. Italics supplied.
16. Ciano, *Diaries,* p. 370.
17. *N. Y. Times,* May 29, 1942, p. 1; United States, Dept. of State, *Bulletin,* June 6, 1942, p. 505.
18. United States, *Foreign Relations,* 1898, pp. 762 f.
19. *Ibid.,* pp. 766 f.
20. *Cong. Rec.,* XXXI (1898), 4244, 4252. Italics supplied.
21. *Ibid.*
22. United States, *Foreign Relations,* 1898, pp. 771 f.
23. Eagleton, "Form and Function of the Declaration of War," p. 30. "Why this date? Why not April 20th? Or, for that matter, January 1st?"
24. French Ensor Chadwick, *The Relations of the United States and Spain* (New York, 1911), I, 127, 130.
25. P. 236, above.
26. Chadwick, *op. cit., supra,* pp. 130–133.
27. *Ibid.,* pp. 201, 206, 212.
28. Italics supplied.
29. United States, *Opinions of the Attorney-General* (1897–99), XXII, 95–98.
30. 40 *Stat.* 411 (1917).
31. Scott, *op. cit.,* p. 152. Italics supplied.
32. A. Mérighnac, *Les Lois et Coutumes de la Guerre sur Terre* (Paris, 1903), p. 323.

33. Scott, *op. cit.*, p. 133.

34. *Am. Jour. Int. Law*, XIII (1919), Suppl., 97–108.

35. Von Waldkirch und Vanselow, "Neutralitätsrecht," p. 36.

36. A. Mérighnac et E. Lémonon, *Le Droit des Gens et la Guerre de 1914–1918* (Paris, 1921), II, 445.

37. P. 236, above; United States, *Naval Digest*, p. 181.

38. Miller, *Treaties*, II, 574–584.

39. *N. Y. Times*, March 14, 1940, p. 4.

40. Hudson, *International Legislation*, V, 20–63.

41. Scott, *op. cit.*, pp. 100–132.

42. See, for instance, Schuman, *War and Diplomacy in the French Republic*, pp. 125–127.

43. Rousseau, "Le Conflit Italo-Éthiopien" (1938), pp. 53–55.

44. *N. Y. Times*, Oct. 3, 1937, p. 1.

45. *Ibid.*, Oct. 8, 1937, p. 6.

46. League of Nations, *Official Journal*, 1938, pp. 333–347.

47. *Ibid.*, p. 334.

48. *Ibid.*, pp. 338 f.

49. Rousseau, *op. cit.*, pp. 74 f.

50. *N. Y. Times*, Feb. 23, 1937, p. 4.

51. Rousseau, *op. cit.*, p. 76.

52. Oswald Nostitz-Wallwitz, "Die Annexion Abessiniens und die Liquidation des abessinischen Konfliktes," *Zeitschrift für ausländisches öffentliches Recht und Völkerrecht*, VI (1937), 683.

53. The proclamations of May 24 and Sept. 1, 1900, by which Great Britain announced the annexation of the Orange Free State and of the South African Republic, respectively, were likewise premature, as is admitted on all hands. Neither republic was conquered until nearly two years later. It is only fair to say, however, that these proclamations were most strongly condemned in the British press and parliament, and that the Commander in Chief of the British forces, Field Marshal Lord Roberts, never resorted to the execution of captives. In a proclamation of Sept. 1, 1900, Lord Roberts declared that those burghers who had been continuously on commando since a time prior to the annexation of the Orange Free State should, if captured, be treated as prisoners of war. See Bordwell, *Law of War*, p. 146; Frantz Despagnet, *La Guerre Sudafricaine au Point de Vue du Droit International* (Paris, 1902), pp. 269–303, 329, 361; A. Mérighnac, *Les Pratiques Anglaises dans la Guerre Terrestre*, pp. 4–7, 10–11; Philippson, *Termination of War*, pp. 22–24; Spaight, *War Right on Land*, p. 64.

54. Pp. 125, 135, above.

55. P. 140, above.

56. In the armistice agreement of April 4, 1885, France consented to raise the blockade of Formosa immediately. See Un Diplomate, *L'Affaire du Tonkin*, pp. 394 f., 404 f.

57. Wehberg, "Das Seekriegsrecht," pp. 56 f.

58. *Archives Diplomatiques*, III (1873), p. 60.

59. *Annuaire de l'Institut de Droit International*, XXVI (1913), 641 f.

60. *N. Y. Times*, Sept. 21, 1944, p. 12.

61. The continuation of the allied "hunger blockade" against Germany beyond the date of Nov. 11, 1918 [Art. 26 of the Conditions of an Armistice with Germany, *Am. Jour. Int. Law*, Suppl. XIII (1919), p. 102] worked hardship not so much on the trade of third states as it did on the German civilian population. It ought to be pointed out, however, that Germany was caught in the meshes of its

own conception as to the significance of an armistice in relation to the right of maintaining a blockade. See von Waldkirch und Vanselow, *op. cit.*, p. 254.

62. Pp. 76–78, above.

63. P. 214, above.

64. *Hamilton* v. *McClaughry, Warden,* 136 Fed. 445 (1905).

65. *N. Y. Times*, Feb. 12, 1918, p. 1; Hyde, *International Law*, II, 821, italics supplied. On February 18 Germany resumed military operations and compelled the Soviet authorities to announce three days later that they were willing to accept the conditions dictated by the Central Powers. Negotiations were re-established, and led to the signature by both sides of the Treaty of Peace of Brest-Litovsk on March 3, 1918.

66. Oppenheim, *International Law*, II, 467.

67. United States, *Messages and Papers of the Presidents*, Suppl. 1921, pp. 8613–8619.

68. See, for instance, Treaty of Peace between Austria, France, Great Britain, Prussia, Russia, Sardinia, and the Ottoman Porte, signed at Paris, March 30, 1854, Article 1, and Treaty of Peace between Romania, Greece, Montenegro, Serbia, and Bulgaria, signed at Bucharest, July 20–August 10, 1913, Art. 1. Martens, *Nouveau Recueil Général de Traités* (1853–57), XV, 773; *ibid.*, 3me sér., VIII (1915), 61.

69. 40 *Stat.* 411 (1917). Italics supplied.

70. *N. Y. Times*, July 15, 1919, p. 1.

71. 41 *Stat.* 1359 (1921).

72. 42 *Stat.* 105 (1921).

73. *Cong. Rec.*, LXI (1921), 3247–3252, 3254–3262, 3276–3299.

74. P. 319, above.

75. Mr. Rogers in the House of Representatives on June 30, 1921: "I appeal to sixty democrats to cast aside partisan politics . . . and get behind this proposal to restore peace to a nation which is sick and tired of *technical war.*" Mr. La Follette in the Senate on July 1: "Mr. President, I hail with satisfaction the opportunity to vote to end the *technical state of war* which still exists between the United States and the Governments of Germany and Austria-Hungary [*sic*]." *Cong. Rec.*, LXI (1921), 3261, 3297.

76. *Ibid.*, p. 3290.

77. United States, *Declarations of War*, p. 68.

78. *N. Y. Times*, April 1, 1938, p. 10.

79. Peter Kaiser, *Geschichte des Fürstenthums Liechtenstein*, zweite, verbesserte Aufl. von Joh. Bapt. Büchel (Vaduz, 1923), pp. 576, 585 f.; Friedrich Umlauft, *Das Fürstenthum Liechtenstein* (Wien, Pest, Leipzig, 1891), pp. 21 f.

80. Pp. 290–292, above.

81. Martens, *op. cit.*, XVIII (1873), pp. 344–348.

82. *Ibid.*, pp. 331, 336, 366, 333, 352, 364, 363.

83. *Ibid.*, pp. 378, 386.

84. The above-mentioned dispatch to the *New York Times* suggests that this was due to an "oversight" on the part of Count von Bismarck. Liechtenstein, in other words, was forgotten. A perusal of the peace treaties which Prussia concluded with Württemberg, Bavaria, Saxony, and so forth, shows that there is no warrant for such a view. The reasons which prompted Prussia to negotiate these peace treaties simply were absent as far as Liechtenstein was concerned. There was, for instance, no Prussian army of occupation in Liechtenstein and the Prussian Army held no Liechtenstein prisoners of war. Büchel, one of Liechtenstein's recent historians, asserts (Kaiser, *op. cit.*, *supra*, p. 586) that Austria signed the Treaty of Peace of Prague of August 23, 1866, on behalf of both Austria and

Liechtenstein. Such assertion, however, is not borne out by the facts. On March 9, 1868, the Emperor of Austria, acting for himself and representing "the sovereign principality of Liechtenstein" did sign a commercial treaty with the King of Prussia, acting for himself and representing the North German Federation, Baden, Bavaria, Hesse, Württemberg, and Luxemburg. See Martens, *op. cit.*, XIX (1874), 336–421.

85. *N. Y. Times*, Oct. 5, 1936, p. 3.
86. *Ibid.*, Nov. 30, 1935, p. 8.
87. *Ibid.*, May 12, 1941, p. 1.

Section 11. *Observations Regarding War and Peace under the Charter of the United Nations*

1. United States, Dept. of State, *Dumbarton Oaks Documents on International Organization*, Conference Ser. 60, Publication 2223, Washington, 1944.
2. Art. 53, 77, and 107 refer specifically to World War II.
3. Italics supplied.
4. Italics supplied.
5. P. 187, above.
6. Eagleton, "The Attempt to Define War," p. 58.
7. United Nations, *Journal of the Security Council*, 1946, p. 76.
8. Italics supplied.
9. P. 325, above. Italics supplied.
10. Italics supplied.
11. United Nations Conference, San Francisco, 1945, *Documents*, XII, 341–343, 348 f., 505.
12. Italics supplied.
13. United States, *Charter of the United Nations, Report to the President*, p. 35.
14. Italics supplied.
15. Italics supplied.
16. *Am. Jour. Int. Law*, XXXV (1941), Suppl., pp. 191 f.
17. *N. Y. Times*, March 1, 1946, p. 10.
18. For an exception see p. 294, above.
19. Italics supplied.
20. Great Britain, *Commentary on the Charter*, p. 9.
21. *N. Y. Times*, June 20, 1945, p. 15.
22. Senate, 79th Cong., 1st Sess., Report No. 717.
23. *Ibid.*, p. 8.
24. Pp. 201–203, above.
25. Scott, *Hague Conventions*, pp. 100 ff.
26. Hudson, *International Legislation*, V, 20–63.
27. Public Law 264, 79th Cong. [Chapter 583, 1st Sess.]

Index of Authors

Allen, G. W., 356
Anzilotti, D., 284, 368, 370, 376, 382
Augustine, Saint, 184, 370

Baker, J. R., 382
Baker, R. St., 361
Basdevant, J., 263, 378
Baty, Th., 381
Beer Portugael, J. C. C. den, 380
Bemis, S. F., 375
Beyer, F., 373
Bluntschli, J. C., 185, 371
Bonde, A., 380
Borchard, E., 367, 385
Bordwell, P., 382, 386
Bouinais, A., 361–365
Bourchier, Lady J., 360–361, 380
Bourquin, M., 367
Brandt, M. A. S., 365
Brière, Y. de la, 370
Büchel, J. B., 387
Buell, R. L., 367
Burckhardt, W., 369
Burlamaqui, J. J., 376

Calvo, C., 96, 361
Cavaglieri, A., 223–224, 374, 381
Chadwick, F. E., 385
Chassigneux, E., 361–362
Ciano, Conte Galeazzo, 353, 385
Cicero, 180
Clausewitz, General von, 381
Clemens, P. H., 358
Clerq, A. J. H., 61, 357
Clowes, W. L., 360–361

Dareste, F. R., 362, 374
Dareste, P., 362, 374
Deák, F., 353, 366, 376, 379, 381–383
Despagnet, F., 386
Diguet, E., 362
Diplomate, Un, 362–365, 386
Dooley (F. P. Dunne), 359
Dupuis, Ch., 382
Dupuis, J., 361–362
Duverdy, Ch., 365
Dyboski, R., 361

Eagleton, C., 148–149, 187, 366, 383, 385, 388
Enriques, G., 368

Falcke, H. P., 247–248, 250–251, 354, 373, 377–378
Fauchille, P., 174, 284, 369, 377–378, 382
Fedozzi, P., 374, 382
Ferrero, G., 149, 366, 381
Fisher, A. H. L., 355
Fleischmann, M., 381
Flournoy, F., 368
Foulke, R. R., 178, 370

Gaillardin, C., 361
Garner, J. W., 384
Gasca, C. L., 382
Gautier, H., 362
Geffcken, F. H., 365, 374
Gemma, S., 284, 382
Gianni, G., 367
Gretschanino, G. von, 367, 372
Grob, F., 369
Grotius, H., 15, 179–182, 370
Guizot, F. P. G., 354

Halleck, H. W., 365
Hammarskjöld, H. J., 368
Hanotaux, G., 381
Hardy, G., 361
Hautefeuille, L. B., 195, 247–248, 284, 372, 377, 382
Hearnshaw, F. J. C., 361
Henderson, G. F. R., 381
Hertslet, Sir E., 364–365
Hettlage, K., 374
Hindmarsh, A. E., 374
Hodges, H. G., 374
Hogan, A. E., 377
Hold-Ferneck, A., 380
Holland, Sir T. E., 35, 355, 368, 382
Holtzendorff, F. von, 382
Huber, M., 368, 385
Hudson, M. O., 367, 377, 386
Hyde, Ch. C., 387

Jefferson, Th., 355
Jessup, Ph. C., 353, 366, 376, 379, 381, 383

Kaiser, P., 387
Keith, A. B., 368
Keller, L., 374
Koch, A., 383

Lage, W. P., 367
Lane-Pool, St., 360–361
Lanessan, J. L. de, 361
Langer, W. L., 382
Latané, J. H., 356
Latourette, K. S., 358
Lawrence, T. J., 379
Lémonon, E., 386
Levy, R., 366
Leyret, H., 365
Lingelbach, W. E., 374
Liszt, F., 381
Loir, M., 363–365
Louter, J. de, 178, 370

McBain, H. L., 368
McKernan, L. W., 382
McNair, A. D., 187, 371
MacNair, H. F., 358
Malkin, H. W., 365
Malleson, G. B., 381
Malloy, W. M., 374
Martens, F. de, 354, 364, 367, 370, 378, 387
Martin, P. A., 384
Matzen, H., 179, 370
Maurel, M., 368
Mérighnac, A., 373, 386
Meurer, Ch., 379
Miller, D. H., 355, 367, 386
Mirkine-Guétzevitch, B., 368
Moore, J. B., 355, 371, 376
Moser, J. J., 373
Moye, M., 370

Nordon, Ch. L., 365
Nostitz-Wallwitz, O., 386

Olivart, Marqués Ramón de Dalmau y de, 371
Olivi, L., 183, 370
Oppenheim, L., 178–179, 188, 275, 368–369, 370, 374, 376, 384, 387
Orué, J. R. de, 183, 370

Pallieri, G. B., 367
Paulus, A., 361–365
Penson, J. H., 361
Perels, F., 249, 377

Perkins, D., 256, 378–379
Philippson, C., 386
Philips, A., 360, 380
Pichler, A., 381
Piedèlièvre, R., 378
Pillet, A., 370
Pistoye, A., 365
Portiez, L., 357
Potter, P. B., 375
Pound, R., 368

Ragot, E., 365
Rambaud, A., 362
Rapisardi-Mirabelli, A., 370
Reddaway, W. F., 361
Regout, R., 370
Rivier, A., 370
Rogers, L., 368
Rolin, A., 174, 369
Romanet du Caillaud, F., 361
Ronan, W. J., 383
Roosevelt, F. D., 353–354, 358, 367, 372, 374
Rousseau, Ch., 381, 386
Rousset, C., 354
Rutherford, Th., 373, 376

Schoen, P., 369
Schuman, F. L., 362, 379, 386
Scott, J. B., 367, 373–374, 377, 381–382, 384–386
Shinobu, J., 373
Söderquist, N., 249, 377
Staudacher, H., 365, 377
Stockton, Ch. H., 183, 370
Stowell, E. C., 183, 224, 370, 374
Strisower, L., 179, 370, 381
Strupp, K., 381

Taft, W. H., 375–376
Thiers, A., 368
Thomson, H. C., 358

Umlauft, F., 387

Vanderpol, A., 370
Vanselow, E. von, 368, 386–387
Vast, H., 376

Wainhouse, D. W., 356
Waldersee, Graf A. von, 358–359
Waldkirch, E. von, 368, 386–387
Warren, Ch., 354

Wehberg, H., 149, 366, 386
Westlake, J., 179, 370, 377–378, 382
Wharton, F., 355

Williams, Sir J. F., 382
Wilson, G. G., 382, 385
Winfield, P. H., 375

Index of Other Persons

Aberdeen, Lord George Gordon, 16
Adams, John, 21, 46, 48, 51–53, 55, 61, 167, 199, 212
Aiken, George David, 64
Alexander, Prince of Bulgaria, 383
Alexander I, Czar of Russia, 83
Alexander III, Czar of Russia, 122
Annunzio, Gabriele d', 227
Archard, French deputy, 110
Arthur, Chester A., 54
Atherton, Ray, 4
Ayala, Eusebio, President of Paraguay, 301

Badens, Col. Pierre, 106, 190
Badoglio, Marshal Pietro, 290, 315
Balfour, Arthur James, 251, 254, 259, 262
Barkley, Alben William, 8
Barreaut, Captain, 50, 63
Baruch, Bernard M., 157, 182
Bas, John, 20
Benton, Thomas Hart, 54
Bethmann-Hollweg, Theobald von, 81
Billings, Josh, 177
Billot, Jean Baptiste, French diplomat, 135
Bingham, Hiram, 174
Bismarck, Prince Otto von, 104–105, 285, 387
Blokland, Beelaerts van, 146
Bonaparte, Joseph, 52, 58, 211
Bouët, Gen. Alexandre Eugène, 103, 106–107, 190
Bourée, Frédéric Albert, French diplomat, 101–102
Branting, Karl Hjalmar, 245
Brière de l'Isle, Gen. Louis Alexandre, 120, 122
Broadhead, James Overton, Congressman, 56
Broglie, Duke Jacques Victor Albert de, 106, 110, 129, 173, 244
Brown, Prentiss Marsh, 55
Bülow, Prince Bernhard von, 75

Burgoyne, Gen. John, 38–39
Brun, Charles Marie, French Minister of the Navy and of the Colonies, 107
Bryan, William J., 94
Byrnes, James F., 329
Byron, George Gordon, 91

Cabrera, Manuel Estrada, 299–300
Calhoun, John Caldwell, 54
Campenon, Jean Baptiste, French Minister of War, 108
Canning, George, 83, 87, 91–92
Canning, Sir Stratford, 28, 87, 89, 92
Caperton, William Banks, 299
Carnot, Sadi, 130
Carranza, Venustiano, 30–33, 274, 381
Case, Francis H., 156
Castro, Cipriano, 259
Catherine the Great, 83
Challemel-Lacour, Paul, French Minister of Foreign Affairs, 102–103, 109, 215
Chaffee, Gen. Adna R., 70
Chamberlain, Sir Austen, 150, 282
Chambers, Ezekial, U. S. Senator, 59, 212
Chang Hsüeh-liang, marshal, 142, 147
Chase, Samuel, 21–22
Chiang Kai-shek, 18, 223
Choate, Rufus, 54
Churchill, Winston, 7
Ciano, Count Galeazzo, 4, 11, 304–306, 383
Cicero, Marcus Tullius, 15, 180
Clarendon, Lord George William Frederick Villiers, 16, 202, 222
Clark, Champ, 8
Clark, D. Worth, U. S. Senator, 6
Clausewitz, Karl von, 280
Clayton, John M., 53
Clemenceau, Georges, 108–109, 116, 125, 129, 138, 147, 216, 244
Codrington, Sir Edward, 85–88, 90–91, 274
Connally, Tom, 331

Constantine I, King of the Hellenes, 256
Coolidge, Calvin, 55, 230
Cooper, Charley, 76
Cornwallis, Charles, 39
Courbet, Amédée A., French rear admiral, 106, 118–122, 125, 130–131, 134, 137, 190
Cullen, Thomas, U. S. Senator, 264
Cushing, Caleb, 27, 54

Daeniker, Armin, 288
Davie, William Richardson, 51, 58, 210
Davis, John, 55
Deane, Silas, 39
Delcassé, Théophile, 74
Derby, Edward Geoffrey Smith Stanley, Earl of, 17, 365
Dewey, George, 309
Duclerc, Eugène, 101
Dudley, Lord John William Ward, 87
Dugenne, Alphonse J., French lieutenant colonel, 114
Dumas, Charles W. F., 39
Dunne, Finley Peter, alias Mr. Dooley, 78

Eden, Anthony, 9
Eisenhower, Dwight D., 269–270
Ellsworth, Oliver, 51, 58, 210
Everett, Edward, 54, 59, 210, 371

Falkenhayn, Erich von, 80
Fallières, Armand, 101
Farrel, Edelmiro, 14
Ferry, Jules, 100–103, 105, 108–109, 111–113, 115–126, 130, 134–140, 147, 167, 171, 190–191, 215–216, 243–245, 248, 250, 259
Fish, Hamilton, 6, 153–154, 173, 188
Fletcher, Frank Friday, 94, 169
Fournier, Ernest F., 111–113, 115
Francis II, King of The Two Sicilies, 95–96, 127, 248–249
Franco, Francisco, 9, 12–13, 228, 242
Franklin, Benjamin, 38–39
Frederick the Great, 180

Gallatin, Albert, 370–371
Gambetta, Léon, 101
Garibaldi, Giuseppe, 95
Gates, Horatio, 38
Gaulle, Charles de, 270
Gavira, Gen. Gabriel, 31

George IV, King of Great Britain, 90
Gerry, Elbridge, 46, 51
Giers, Nicholas Karlovich de, 122
Gorelkin, Ivan, 305
Granet, Étienne, French deputy, 105, 108, 124, 136
Grant, Ulysses, 8
Granville, Earl Granville George Leveson-Gower, 131, 133, 135, 364
Grasse, François Joseph Paul de, 20, 39
Graziani, Marshal Rudolfo, 316
Grévy, Jules, 114
Grier, Robert Cooper, 77
Grotius, Hugo, 139, 167, 187
Guinazu, Enrique Ruiz, 10, 14
Guizot, François Pierre Guillaume, 23, 28–30

Hailie Selassie, Emperor of Ethiopia, 315–316
Halifax, Lord Edward Frederick Lindley Wood, 315
Halkett, Sir Peter, 28
Hamilton, Alexander, 46, 48
Hamilton, Fred, 76, 278
Hammarskjöld, Hjalmar, 166
Harding, Warren G., 232
Harmand, Jules, French diplomat, 104, 106–107, 190
Hay, John, 74, 260–261, 264
Healy, T. M., 262
Herbert, Sir Michael, 264
Heyden, Loquine, rear admiral, 86, 88
Hiep-Hoa, Emperor of Annam, 107
Hitler, Adolf, 10, 13, 229, 279, 290
Hoar, Sir Samuel, now Viscount Templewood, 12, 353
Hobhouse, John C., M. P., 91
Hoffinger, Max, Austrian delegate to League of Nations, 369
Holland, Sir Thomas Erskine, 35, 166, 287
Hoover, Herbert, 64, 230
Hötzendorf, Conrad von, 80
Houghton, Alanson Bigelow, 150
Huerta, Victoriano, 30, 94
Hughes, Charles Evans, 55
Hull, Cordell, 153, 157
Huskisson, William, 91

Ibrahim Pasha, 83, 85, 87
Inonu, Ismet, 9, 11

Jackson, Andrew, 239–240, 370

Jackson, Stonewall, 280
Jay, John, 43
Jefferson, Thomas, 42
Jones, Andrieus Aristieus, 321

Ketteler, Baron Clemens August von, 68
King, Ernest J., 49
Knapp, Harry Shepard, 230
Knox, Frank, 63
Koenig, Joseph-Pierre, 379
Kong, Prince, 99, 114, 123

Lafayette, Marie Joseph Paul Yves Roch Gilbert du Motier, 20
La Follette, Robert Marion, 387
Lamsdorff, Count Vladmir Nikolae-vitch, 74-75
Lansdowne, Henry Charles Keith Petty Fitzmaurice, Marquess of, 262
Lascelles, Sir Frank Cavendish, 75
Lavalle, General, 25, 28
Leblanc, Rear Admiral, 24, 26
Lee, Arthur, 39
Lespès, Adm. Sébastien N., 111, 113-114, 116-117
Liand, Chinese delegate to League of Nations, 150
Li-Fong-Pao, 118
Li Hung Chang, 101-102, 111-115, 123, 140
Livingston, Edward, 47, 59, 211-212
Lockroy, Edouard, French deputy, 136
Loir, Maurice, 119-120
Loubet, Émile François, 73, 208, 214
Louis XIV, King of France, 93, 238, 279, 370
Louis XVI, King of France, 38-41
Louis Philippe, King of the French, 24, 26, 98, 126, 239, 371
Luu-vinh-phuoc, 122, 361-362

MacDonald, Sir Claude, 68
Machiavelli, Nicolò, 381
Mackau, Adm. Ange René, 25
McKinley, William, 8, 73, 208, 307-308
Macnaghten, Sir Edward, 15
McReynolds, Sam D., 154, 156
Madison, James, 53
Maria Teresa, Spanish Infanta, 93, 370
Maria Theresa, German Empress, 180
Marshall, John, 46, 51, 53, 210

Mehemet Ali, Pasha of Egypt, 83
Melbourne, Lord William Lamb, 28-29
Metternich-Winneburg, Clemens Wenzel Lothar, 276
Mihailovic, Draza, 269
Miller, William J., Congressman, 6
Millot, Gen. Charles T., 110, 113-114, 137
Molé, Comte Louis Mathieu, 26, 29
Monroe, James, 45-46, 228
Montebello, Marquis Gustave de, 74
Moore, Alfred, 21
Münster, Prince Georg H., 74
Murray, William Vans, 51, 58, 210
Mussolini, Benito, 5, 10-11, 13, 227, 229, 306, 315-316

Napoleon I, 18, 52-53, 171, 228, 280
Napoleon III, 16, 104
Neditch, Milan, 269
Négrier, Gen. François, 138
Nicholas I, Czar of Russia, 15-16, 84, 93
Nicholas II, Czar of Russia, 69, 202
Nikita, King of Montenegro, 258
Normanby, Constantine Henry Phipps, Marquess of, 206

Oliver, James Churchill, 6

Peron, Juan Domingo, 14

Radolin, Prince Hugo, 74
Rheinart, French diplomat, 104
Ribbentrop, Joachim von, 241
Ribeaupierre, Gen. Alexandre, 92
Richthofen, Freiherr O. von, 262
Rigney, Rear Admiral Henri G. de, 86
Rivière, Henri L., 100, 102-104
Rivière, French deputy, 110
Roberts, Lord Frederick Sleigh Roberts, 386
Rochambeau, Jean Baptiste Donatien de Vimeur, 20, 39
Rogers, Edith Nourse, 6
Rogers, John Jacob, 387
Roosevelt, Franklin D., 5, 7-8, 19, 23, 37, 63-64, 95, 152-153, 156, 158, 173-174, 188, 191, 194-195, 212, 224, 226, 278, 283, 290
Roosevelt, Theodore, 184, 229-230, 232-234, 263-264, 374

Root, Elihu, 230
Rosas, Don Juan Manuel de, 23, 25–26, 206
Russel, Lord John Russel, 90

Salandra, Antonio, 245–246
Salisbury, Robert Arthur Talbot Gascoyne-Cecil, Marquess of, 74, 202
San Martin, Ramon Grau, 227
Saracoglu, Shukru, 9, 11
Sato, Naotaké, Japanese diplomat, 146, 366
Sawada, Renzo, 17
Schoerner, Ferdinand, 380
Scott, Sir William (later Lord Stowell), 17, 20–21, 23, 383
Semallé, French diplomat, 118
Seward, William H., 90
Seymour, Vice-Admiral, 65–67, 74, 202
Shanley, James Andrew, 182
Sherman, John, 307
Shinobu, Jumpi, 216
Short, Dewey, 6
Simon, Sir John, 150
Simovic, Dusan, 269
Smith, Congressman, 6
Soult, Nicolas Jean de Dieu, Duke of Dalmatia, 28
Spuller, French deputy, 130
Sternburg, Freiherr Speck von, 264
Stettinius, Edward R., Jr., 328
Stimson, Henry L., 7–8, 184, 202
Sumner, Charles, 54, 56, 200
Sze, Alfred, Chinese delegate to League of Nations, 146

Taft, Robert A., 64
Taft, William H., 55, 228–229, 231–235
Talleyrand-Périgord, Charles Maurice de, 46, 50, 58, 211
Tellini, Gen. Enrico, 244
Thomsen, Hans, 4
Ting, Colonel, 220, 289
Tingy, Thomas, 20
Tinoco, Federico, 298–299
Tinoco, Joaquim, 298–299
Tito, 269
Tojo, Eiki, 143
Treviño, Gen. Jacinto, 32
Trotzky, Leon, 318
Truxtun, Thomas, 50, 63
Tseng, Marquess, 101
Tu-Duc, Emperor of Annam, 99–100, 103, 106

Tung Fu Hsing, General, 66

Van Buren, Martin, 27
Vandenberg, Arthur H., 7, 203
Vattel, Emer de, 139, 167, 173, 197
Venizelos, Eleutherios, 256
Vergennes, Comte Charles Gravier de, 39
Victor Emmanuel II, King of Sardinia (later King of Italy), 95–96, 127, 249
Victor Emmanuel III, King of Italy, 315
Villa, Francisco, 30–32
Vishinsky, Andrei Y., 326
Voldemaras, Augustinas, Lithuanian statesman, 97

Waddington, William Henry, 131, 135, 364
Wadsworth, George, 4
Wakatsuki, Reijiro, 273
Waldeck-Rousseau, Pierre Marie, 138–139
Waldersee, Count Alfred von, 69–71
Waller, Col. Littleton W. T., 375
Walsh, David I., U. S. Senator, 55
Wang, Chengting T., 156
Washington, Bushrod, 21–22, 154, 173, 182, 188, 196, 273, 282
Washington, George, 21, 38–39, 42–43, 46, 48, 55, 167, 199, 214
Water, C. E. te, South African delegate to League of Nations, 146
Webster, Daniel, 54
Wellington, Arthur Wellesley, Duke of, 83, 91
Wheeler, Burton Kendall, 64
Wilhelm II, German Emperor, King of Prussia, 69, 73–74, 202, 208, 256, 264
William III, King of Great Britain, 238
Wilson, Woodrow, 30–32, 94, 151, 218, 230–232, 234, 298, 319, 321
Woodford, Steward Lynden, 307
Wright, Silas, 54

"XYZ," 46

Yen, W. W., Chinese delegate to League of Nations, 146
Yoshizawa, Kenkichi, Japanese delegate to League of Nations, 147

Young, John Russel, 123
Yung Lu, General, 68

Zapapa, Emiliano, 30
Zeligowski, Gen. Lucien, 96

Index of States

Afghanistan, 253
Annam, 82, 97–140, 190, 214–215, 362
Argentina, 9–10, 13–14, 23–28, 35, 127, 205, 255, 300–301, 377
Austria, 42, 65, 68, 83, 93, 125, 228, 276, 279, 295, 322–323, 380, 387
Austria-Hungary, 70, 79, 80, 104, 191, 218, 256, 258, 291, 298, 319–321, 383, 387

Baden, Grand Duchy of, 323
Bavaria, Kingdom of, 79, 323, 368, 387
Belgium, 6, 41–42, 68, 70, 93, 180, 370
Bolivia, 301, 327
Brazil, 126, 301
Bulgaria, 279–281, 290, 293, 319, 385, 387

Cambodia, Kingdom of, 97
Chile, 300–301
China, 17–18, 64–78, 82, 97–140, 141–158, 173–182, 190–192, 194, 198, 202, 208, 212–213, 215–216, 219, 223, 243, 250, 252–253, 266, 272, 275, 278, 282–283, 288, 291, 296, 301–302, 316–319, 324, 372
Colombia, 28, 127
Costa Rica, 293, 295, 298
Croatia, "Kingdom" of, 269
Cuba, 8, 225–227, 230–231, 293, 295–296, 298, 307
Czechoslovakia, 205, 279, 330

Denmark, 279, 285
Dominican Republic, 205, 230–232, 234, 237, 293

Ecuador, 300
Egypt, 84–86, 88, 92, 273
Eire, 300
El Salvador, 293
Esthonia, 253
Ethiopia, 170, 278, 289, 315

Finland, 205, 257, 313, 317, 373

France, 7, 11, 16–18, 20–30, 35, 37–64, 68, 70, 72–73, 82, 84, 92–93, 97–140, 143, 145, 149, 161–163, 165, 167, 169, 171, 173, 180, 190–191, 195–201, 203, 205–212, 214, 219, 223, 228, 238–248, 250–251, 255–256, 266, 269, 271–276, 284–285, 291–292, 297, 304, 311, 316–317, 370–371, 383–384, 387
Frankfurt-on-the-Main, Free City of, 323

Germany, 4–5, 10, 12–14, 35, 37, 63–68, 70, 76, 78–81, 83, 94–95, 104, 131, 142, 151, 165, 171, 180, 191–192, 203–205, 207–208, 214, 218–219, 228–229, 241–242, 256, 258, 260–265, 269–270, 276, 282, 285, 288, 290–291, 293, 295–296, 298–299, 300, 302, 304–306, 312, 319–321, 324, 379–380, 383–384, 386–387
Great Britain, 5–7, 11–12, 16, 20, 25, 27–29, 35, 40–43, 61, 64–70, 82, 84, 86, 88, 91, 93, 95, 123, 125–126, 130–135, 139, 149, 151, 163, 199, 201–203, 206, 210–211, 214, 219, 222, 238–239, 241–242, 245, 248, 250–251, 254–256, 258–265, 268, 273–274, 276, 285, 302, 304–305, 313, 324, 356, 385–387
Greece, 83–93, 126, 244–246, 248, 256–258, 266, 279, 282, 387
Guatemala, 293, 295, 299, 385

Haiti, 204, 229–232, 234–237, 271, 293, 295, 375–376
Hannover, Kingdom of, 323
Hanse Towns, 29, 127–128
Hesse-Cassel, Electorate of, 323
Hesse, Grand Duchy of, 323
Holy Roman Empire, 322
Honduras, 293, 295
Hungary, 290, 293, 383

Iceland, 63, 300
Iran, 95, 253, 277, 326
Italy, 4–5, 9–11, 12–14, 35, 37, 63–65, 68, 70, 80–81, 83, 95, 104–105, 142, 170,

Italy (*continued*)
191–192, 204, 218, 228–229, 242, 244–
246, 254, 256, 258, 261–265, 278, 284–
285, 288–291, 293, 302, 304–306, 312,
315, 323, 383

Japan, 9, 17–18, 64–65, 68, 70, 82, 123,
131, 139, 140–158, 173–174, 182, 192–
193, 212–213, 216–217, 223, 252–253,
266, 272, 275, 278, 282–283, 288, 291,
293, 301–302, 305, 366, 372, 383

Korea, 219

Laos, principalities of, 97
Latvia, 253
Lebanon, 300
Liechtenstein, 322–323, 387
Lithuania, 96–97
Luxemburg, 180

Madagascar, Kingdom of, 105
Manchukuo, 141
Mexico, 27, 29–35, 61, 94, 126–127, 169,
191, 218, 274, 303, 305–306, 311, 313,
381
Modena, Duchy of, 312
Montenegro, 256–258, 279, 387

Nassau, Duchy of, 323
The Netherlands, 6, 41–42, 68, 70, 126,
180, 291, 312
New Granada. *See* Colombia
Nicaragua, 174, 228, 230–237, 246–247,
293, 295–296
Norway, 6

Orange Free State, 386
Ottoman Empire, 82–93, 125, 133, 207,
246, 248, 256–257, 273, 279, 319, 324,
383, 387

Panama, 293, 295, 385
Paraguay, 300–301
Parma, Duchy of, 312
Peru, 301
Poland, 10, 96–97, 205, 253, 330
Portugal, 126
Prussia, 42, 93, 125, 228, 291, 297, 304,
322–323, 368, 387

Reuss elder line, Principality of, 323

Romania, 15–16, 253, 279–281, 290, 293,
387
Russia, 15–17, 64–68, 70, 74–75, 83–84,
86, 88, 92–93, 125–126, 133, 202–203,
228, 248, 256, 273, 318, 324, 385, 387.
See also Union of Soviet Socialist
Republics

San Marino, 324
Sardinia, Kingdom of, 42, 125–126, 312,
387
Saudi Arabia, 300
Saxe-Meiningen, Duchy of, 323
Saxony, Kingdom of, 323, 368, 387
Serbia, 279, 383, 387
Siam, 296
South African Republic, 386
Spain, 9–14, 126, 203–204, 228–229, 241–
242, 306–310, 313, 356, 372
Sweden, 285, 300, 312
Switzerland, 79–80, 123, 165, 268, 276,
300–301, 323
Syria, 300

Tunisia, Beyship of, 105–106, 271–272
Turkey, 9, 11, 14, 16, 253. *See also* Ot-
toman Empire
Tuscany, Grand Duchy of, 312
The Two Sicilies, Kingdom of, 126–
127, 312

Union of Soviet Socialist Republics, 4,
12–13, 95, 253, 257, 277, 282, 284, 290,
300, 305–306, 313, 317, 324, 326, 330,
387
United States of America, 10, 13, 17,
19–22, 27, 29–35, 37–65, 68, 70, 72–74,
76–77, 94, 123, 125, 130, 150–158, 162–
163, 169–171, 174–175, 191–192, 195–
202, 205–212, 214–215, 218, 223–227,
229–240, 254–258, 260–265, 270–271,
275–276, 278, 285, 290, 296, 298–299,
302–310, 313, 317–318, 320–321, 324,
328, 371, 375–376, 379, 381, 383, 387
Uruguay, 24, 28, 300

Venezuela, 35, 232, 256–265, 302

Württemberg, Kingdom of, 323, 368,
387

Yugoslavia, 269–270, 282, 305–306, 330

Index of Subjects

Act of war, 3, 5–8, 14, 36, 144, 161, *203*, *221*, 245–246

Aggression, 9, 19, 89–90, 98, 119, 148, 152, 157–158, 161–163, 193, 253, 278, 284, 292, 315, 325, 330; in relation to Article 1 of the Briand-Kellogg Pact, 253–254, 287; in relation to Article 39 of the Charter of the United Nations, 327–330

Alliances, 163–164

Allied and Associated Powers, 205, 312, 317, 319

Almeria, bombardment by German warships (1937), 241–242

American Society of International Law, 286

Armistices, 139, 207, 312, 317

Atlantic Charter, 7, 328

Attack, 163, 203, 259; "unprovoked attack" as *casus foederis*, 163–164

Authorized and unauthorized operations; 202, 273–274; unauthorized operations, 202, 273; war consisting of authorized operations only, 274; war consisting not necessarily of authorized operations, 274

Axis Powers, 12–14, 63, 163, 191, 300

Balkan Wars (1912–13), 256, 279

Bandits, 32–33, 69, 84, 147, 231, 236, 271–273, 284, 314, 316

"Bargain" of 1801, 53, 200

Beginning of war, declarations of war *antedating* the beginning of war, 305–310; *de lege* determination of legal beginning in relation to specific rules of law on war, 310; prejudiced determination in relation to certain rules of law on war, 310; various legal beginnings, 303–304; wording of declarations of war in general, 304–305

Belligerency, 4, 7–9, 14, 36, *221;* "demi-belligerency," 124, 215

Belligerents, 161, 268–270

Berwick-on-Tweed, 323–324

Black Flags, 99–101, 110, 122, 361–362

Blockade, 8, 24–30, 35, 43, 119, 121–122, 125, 132–133, 136–137, 143, 151, 153, 164, 167, 192–194, 205–206, 244, 253, 255, 302, 309, 316–317, 372, 387; long distance, 266; of the states of the Dey of Algiers by France (1827–30), 127; of Argentina by France (1838–40), 23–30, 127, 255; of Argentina by France and Great Britain (1845–48 and 1845–47, respectively), 127, 205–206; of China by Japan (1937–41), 143, 192, 252–253, 266; of Crete by the Concert of Europe (1897–98), 256–257, 261; of Foochow by France (1884), 119, 124; of Formosa by France (1884–85), 121–129, 131–133, 137, 167, 250; of Gaeta by Sardinia (1861), 127, 248–249; of Greece by France (1917), 256–258, 266; of Greece by Great Britain (1850), 126; of Mexico by France (1838), 127; of Montenegro and northern Albania by the Concert of Europe (1913), 256–258; of New Granada (Colombia) by Great Britain (1837), 28, 127; of Portugal by France (1831), 126; of Venezuela by Germany, Great Britain, and Italy (1902–3), 256–265, 302

Boer War (1899–1902), 14

Border incidents, 218, 303

"Boxers," 64–65, 67, 69

Briand-Kellogg Pact (August 27, 1928), 177, 253–254, 287, 294, 369

Brigands. *See* Bandits

"Cacos," 231, 236, 271, 375

Carnegie Endowment for International Peace, 187, 286, 326

Carrizal, "battle" of, 32, 191, 275

Casus belli, 122

Casus foederis, 163

Central Powers, 317, 387

Chaco conflict (1932–35), 301

Chetniks, 269–270

Circuit Court for the District of Kansas, 76, 173, 208, 317

Circuit Court for the District of Pennsylvania, 21

Civil war, 8–9, 25, 203–204, 270–271, 329

Collective security, 282
Combat operations. *See* Operations
Concert of Europe, 256–258
"Condor Legion," 204, 228–229
Confederate States of America, 239
Congress of Laibach (1821), 228
Congress of Troppau (1820), 228
Constitutional law and war, in general, 170–171; in France, 104–106, 109–110, 117–118, 124, 129, 136–137, 161, 171, 190, 208, 214, 243–245, 271–272; in Germany, 171, 203, 208, 214, 259, 368, n. 45; in Great Britain, 172; in the United States, 6, 60, 64, 94, 170–171, 197–198, 201, 203, 206, 208, 214, 217, 224, 232–234, 237, 240, 285, 332
Contraband of war, 8, 40–41, 43, 122–123, 130, 135, 139–140, 143, 151, 153, 164, 167, 192–194, 244, 253–255, 294, 302, 310, 316–317, 372
Contracts with war clauses, 170; insurance policy, 379, n. 19; time chartership, 372, n. 15
Corfu, bombardment by Italy (1923), 244–246
Court of Claims of the United States, 23, 54–62, 73, 173, 188, 197–202, 207, 209–212, 215
Court of Criminal Appeals of the state of Texas, 33, 218, 274
Crimean Conference (1945), 300
Crimean War (1853–56), 15, 222, 324
Cuban Army of Pacification (1906–9), 230, 234
Customs of war, 169

Dakar, Free French and British sea attack on (1940), 241
Declaration of a paper war. *See* Paper war
Declaration of war, 4–5, 17, 20, 47, 51, 58, 60, 63, 71, 74–75, 80–81, 105, 109–110, 117–118, 125, 129–130, 136, 142, 148–149, 153–154, 161–162, 170–172, 184, 197–198, 203, 208, 210, 212, 215, 217, 220, 222, 232–234, 239–240, 259, 262, 271–272, 322–323, 374; discountenance and rejection of, as political demonstration, 289–290; made in the midst of operations but meaning nothing in terms of *additional* operations, 301–302; no evidence for legal existence of war, 290–302; no requisite for legal existence of war,

284–289; not an offer or challenge requiring acceptance, 289; *see also* Paper war
De facto war, 4–5, 14, 36, *221*
Definition of war, 5, 22, 34, 62–64, 77, 110, 153–154, 189–190, 196, 226, 246, 249–250, 267, 273, 275, 282–283, 326, 374, 383; *de lege* definitions, 219–220; difference in latitudes of relative definitions: the "laws and customs" of war on land and at sea, 217–218, rules on neutrality, 218–219; great variety of book definitions, 173–175; infeasibility of book definition, 175–177; monographs on, 186–187; reality behind book definitions: belief, 182–183, common meaning of "war," 178–182, common meaning of **"war"** or belief or both and natural law (mixed definitions), 182–186, etymology of "war," 186; summary, 188
"De jure war," 4–5, 14, 36, *221*
"Demi-belligerency," *see* Belligerency
Diplomatic documents with references to operations, 58, 71, 73–74, 204, *210–215*
Diplomatic relations, 16, 46, 56, 71, 79, 95, 104, 118–119, 142, 153–154, 260, 275–278; severance of, no requisite for legal existence of war, 277–278
District Court of Pennsylvania, 20–21
Dumbarton Oaks, proposals of, 324
Duration of war, 170, 303, 320; *see also* Beginning of war, End of war
Duty to wage war, 184

Emergency legislation, 170, 320
End of war, 140; conspicuously late legal endings, 317–318; futility of decreeing "the" legal end of war, 318–322; "perpetual" wars, 322–324; premature annexations, 314–316; various legal endings: with conclusion of general armistice, 312, with signature or ratification of a treaty of peace, 312–313, subsequent to the coming in force of a treaty of peace, 313
Enemy, 21–22, 49, 62, 73, 106–107, 109, 120, 122–123, 125, 161, 169–170, 190, *196*, 200, 209, 213, 235–236, 254, 293, 383
Essence of war, 189; in relation to Ar-

ticle 39 of the Charter of the United Nations, 328–329

Estado de guerra, 181

État de guerre, 181

Expeditions, 31, 69, 73, 78–79, 103–105, 108–109, 192, 202, 213, 215; Boxer Expedition (1900–1), 37, 64–79, 188, 191, 198, 203, 208, 213–214, 219–220, 278, 317–318; "China Relief Expedition" of the United States (1900), 70–71, 78; Pershing Expedition into Mexico (1916–17), 31–33; Seymour Expedition (1900), 65–67, 74

F.F.I. (French Forces of the Interior), 269–270, 379

Foochow, battle of, 118–120, 136

"Footing of hostility," 103, 215

Franco-Prussian War (1870–71), 297

Franctireurs, 270

Freedom of the seas, 25, 151, 194, 254, 263, 265, 294, 317

French Legion of General de Gaulle, 241, 270

French spoliations, 20, 43–53, 167, 356

French spoliation claims, 45–46, 51–62, 198–200, 210

Friendship pacts, 163

Gas and bacteriological methods of warfare, 164

"General" international law, 168

German Confederation (1815–66), 322–323

Gibraltar, bombardment by France (1940), 241–242

"Good Neighbor" policy, 226

Greco-Turkish War (1897), 256

Grotius Society of London, 187

Guarantee pacts, 163–164

Hague Academy of International Law, 224

Hague Peace Conferences (1899 and 1907), 166, 220, 268, 285, 289

Holy Alliance, 228

Hostilities, 73, 84–85, 146–147, 192, 213, 222; *see also* "State of hostilities"

Imperfect war, 15, 19–23, 30, 35–36, 196, *221*, 357

"Incident," Sino-Japanese (1937–41), 17, 142–144, 150–158, 188, 192, 194, 216, 275, 277–278, 283, 288, 301–302

Incomplete war, 15, 19, 29–30, 35–36, *221*

Indians, 31

Indirect rules of law on war, 161–163, 326

"Indivisibility" of war and peace, 195

Institut de Droit International, 185, 243, 287–288, 317, 376

Insurrectos, 379, n. 19

Intent and purpose of rules of law on war, 21, 189, 193–195, 197–200, 204, 217, 220–221, 226, 236, 253, 267, 272, 277, 289, 303, 311, 325, 372

Interference, 228

"Intermediate state," 15, 17, 36, 119, 203, *222*

Internal customary law and war, 165, 167–170

International customary rules of law on war, 164–166, 168–169, 225, 296

Interposition, 228

Interpretation of rules of law, 175–177, 199, 204

Intervention, 18, 36, 73, 213–214, 311, 376; *de lege* definition of, 226–227; legal definition of, 226; rules of law on, 225–226; term inofficially applied to operations, 228; term officially applied to operations by United States, 228–230: as an expression of common parlance, 230–231, in relation to Platt amendment, 230, with a *legal* design, 232–234, with a *political* design, 231–232; textbook definitions of, 227; "time of war" in relation to the Articles for the Government of the Navy, 236; "time of war" in relation to the general principle of law in accordance with which the United States makes reparation for injurious acts committed by its armed forces to another state in time of peace, 236; war pensions for certain officers and men of the Marine Corps who participated in intervention in Haiti (1915), 235–236

Italo-Ethiopian War (1895–96), 285, 314–316

Italo-Ethiopian War (1935–36), 276–278, 289

Jus ad bellum, 161, 184

Jus in bello, 161, 184–185
Just and unjust war, 184–186, 370–371

Kelung, occupation by France (1884–85), 121
Knox-Porter resolution (1921), 208, 321–323
Kriegszustand, 181
Kroumirs, 271–272

"Laws and customs of war," 56–57, 72, 161–162, 196–197, 209–210, 216–218, 244, 267–269, 274, 277, 280, 285–286, 288, 294, 309, 314, 379; explanation of this expression, 169
League of Nations, 97, 144–150, 161, 177, 193, 216, 220, 244–247, 272, 278, 281–283, 289, 315, 325
Levée en masse, in enemy-occupied territory, 268; in territory not occupied by the enemy, 267–268
Limited war, 15, 19–23, 30, 35–36, 196, *221,* 357
Logistic Operations. *See* Operations
London Naval Conference (1908–9), 166
Lytton Report (1932), 148, 283, 288

Manchurian Conflict, 140–150, 272–274, 277, 282–283, 288
"Measures short of war," 15, 18–19, 36, *223–224,* 241, 247, 374
Memel, annexation by Germany (1939), 279
"Merchants of death," 151, 193–194, 252, 278, 289
Militia and volunteer corps, 64, 267–268
Monroe Doctrine, 228, 232, 263, 265

Naming of operations. *See* Operations
"Natural" international law, 166–169, 183, 197, 201, 207, 210, 225, 368
Natural-law school of thought, 167–168, 183–186, 201
Navarino, battle off (1827), 88–89, 248, 273–274
Neutrality, 4, 7–14, 18, 40, 42–45, 72, 80, 123, 130–136, 143, 149–158, 161–165, 173, 193–195, 199–200, 214, 217–219, 255, 260, 263, 270–271, 286, 301, 303–304, 312, 364, 385
Neutrality acts, 8, 170; Great Britain, 250, 365; United States, 4, 150–158,

173, 188, 193–195, 212–213, 252–253, 270–271, 275, 278, 283, 288–289, 302
Neutrality pacts, 163
Nonaggression pacts, 163
Nonbelligerency, in general, 10, 14; of Argentina, 9–10, 13; of Italy, 9–11; of Spain, 9, 11–13; of Turkey, 9, 11
Nonintervention, 227

Office of Naval Records and Library, United States Navy, 23
"Open war," 106
Operations, all-out, 20, 190, 193–194, 196, 198, 210, 242, 293; combat operations, 180–181; geographically limited, 20, 47–48, 63, 71, 74, 191, 193, 196–197, 217; logistic, 180–181; military, without corresponding naval operations, 72, 142, 191–193, 217, 219; naming of, by governments, 143–144, 156, 192, by historians, 192; official namelessness, 192, 229–230, 247; naval, not supplemented by operations on land, 191, 196–197; qualification of, by governments or members of parliaments, 59–60, 204, *210–215;* with restricted objectives, 191, 196; of short duration, 218–219; "short of war," 15–19, 35–36, *221–224;* with small number of combatants, 190, 193, 217; *see also* Authorized and unauthorized operations
Oran, battle off (1940), 219

"Pacification," 69, 314
Pacific blockade, 18, 36, 125–129, 132–136, 224; long-distance blockades, 266; objections in point of fact, 248–249; objections in point of law, 249–251; origin of the term, 247; pacific, i.e., illegal, blockades in relation to Declaration of Paris, 254–265; practical significance of term, 251–254; summary, 265–266
Pacifism, 184
Pact of Paris. *See* Briand-Kellogg Pact
Panama policy of the United States, 232, 234
Paper blockade, 122
Paper war, declarations of, 293–295; enemy aliens in, 295–297; enemy merchant ships in, 297–298; followed by "treaty of peace," 295; private

enemy property in, 295–297; why declared, 298–300

Partial war, 15, 19–23, 30, 35–36, 196, 221, 357

Parties to war, 189; under many rules of law on war a state against another state, 267–270; under other rules of law on war not necessarily two states, 270–272; political exploitation of prejudice that states only are parties: with regard to Article 9 of the French Constitutional Law of July 16, 1875, 271–272, with regard to Article 16 of the Covenant of the League of Nations, 272–273; *see also* Bandits, Brigands, "Cacos," Insurrectos, Pirates

Partisans of Marshal Tito, 269–270

Pay of officers and men, 77–78, 204, 235, 309, 332

Peace, breach of, 161–162, 325–327, 385; common meaning of word, 194; definition of, 189; "in the legal sense," 221, 319; threat to, 162, 325–327; *see also* "State of peace," Treaties of peace

Peking, siege of the legations (1900), 68–69

Penal law and war, 76–77, 170, 236, 277–278, 309, 312–313, 317–318

Permanent Court of International Justice, 368

"Phony war," 180

Pirates, 44, 98–100, 271

Platt amendment (1901), 225–226, 230, 233–234, 375

Positive law, 225

Positivist conception of international law, 166, 168, 185, 368

Prisoners of war, 49–50, 56–57, 72, 140, 164, 169, 185, 197, 201, 204, 207, 209, 216–218, 242, 267, 274, 276–277, 281, 288, 294, 303, 314, 320, 372, 380, 387

Privateers, 20, 40–41, 43–45, 47, 50, 195, 355, n. 7; *see also* Reprisals

Prize courts, 45, 47, 167, 170, 310

Protection of American lives and property in foreign parts by landing forces, 65, 208, 232–234

Puerto Cabello, bombardment of forts by Germany and Great Britain (1902), 260

Qualification of operations by government or members of parliaments. *See* Operations

Quasi war, 15, 23, 30, 36, 63, 221

Queen's War, The (1667), 93, 370

Red Flags, 361, n. 10

Reichsgericht, 78, 175

Reprisals, 18, 36, 224; British "general reprisals," 239–240; *general* "letters of marque and reprisals": "letter of marque and reprisals" and "letter of marque" or "privateer," 238–239; legal definition of, the expression "state of reprisals," 237–238; operations officially styled as "reprisals," 240–241: to camouflage illegitimate operations, 243–246, to indicate some limited operation for the purpose of retaliation, 241–242, to proclaim that operation is serving just cause, 242–243; relation of "letters of marque and reprisals" under Article I, Section 8, Paragraph 11 of the Constitution of the United States to war in the sense of some rules of law on war, 240; rules of law on, 237; *special* "letters of marque and reprisals," 238; summary, 246–247

Risorgimento, 95

Rules of law on peace, 3, 188, 325

Rules of law on war, 3, 188–189, 254, 303, 311, 325; in general, 161–162; international, 162–169; municipal, 170–172

Russo-Japanese War (1904–5), 297

Russo-Turkish War (1877), 133

San Carlos, bombardment of fort by Germany (1903), 262

San Francisco World Security Conference (1945), 300, 324, 328

San Ignazio, "battle" of (1916), 32–34, 191, 218, 275, 277, 303

Schaffhausen, bombardment by A.A.F. (1945), 237, 376, n. 51

Self-defense, 7, 103, 148, 330

Self-help, 184, 238

Seven Weeks' War (1866), 322–323

Seventh International Conference of American States at Montevideo (1933), 226–227

Shanghai, battle of (1932), 142, 146

"Shoot-on-sight" order, issued by President Roosevelt (September 11, 1941), 37, 63–64, 191
Sino-Japanese War (1894), 297
Spanish-American War (1898), 297, 307–310
Spanish Civil War (1936–39), 228–229, 241, 242, 266, 271, 372
State District Court of Webb County, Texas, 33
"State of hostilities," 15, 17–18, 20–21, 23, 36, *222–223*
"State of hostility," 124, 215
"State of peace," 3–4, 6, 14–15, 36, 133, *221–222*, 319
"State of reprisals," 124–125, 128–129, 131, 134–136, 215, *237*, 243–244
"State of war," 3–5, 14–17, 26, 36, 47, 58–59, 74–75, 78–80, 89, 96–97, 136, 151–154, 156–158, 161, 174, *181–182*, 188, 193–194, 202–203, 208, 211–213, 221–222, 237, 252–253, 255, 261–263, 275, 278, 283–284, 291–292, 295, 303–306, 311, 318–319, 321, 323–324, 378; *de facto* "state of war," 73, 213; imperfect "state of war," 30, 36, *221*; incomplete "state of war," 30, 33–36, *221*; limited "state of war," 30, 36, *221*; partial "state of war," 30, 36, *221*; quasi "state of war," 30, 36, *221*
"State of war" theory, 187–188, 223
Statutes and decrees referring to war, 170
Submarine warfare, 164, 266
Supreme Court of the state of Kansas, 379
Supreme Court of the United States, 21, 23, 29, 34, 57, 77, 173, 175, 182, 188, 196, 200, 282

Tampico incident (1914), 94
Tientsin, battle of (1900), 67
Titles of statutes concerning operations, 204, 208–210
Trading-with-the-enemy acts, 170, 320
Treaties of peace, 57, 60–62, 70, 140, *204–208*, *295*, 312–314, 316–317, 319, 323–324, 387
Treaties referring to war, 162–164

United Nations, 300, 317; an antiwar agency through rules of law on peace, 325–327; difficulty in interpreting Charter, 324–325; relation of enforcement action under Articles 42 and 43 of the Charter to rules of law on war, 330–332; violations of Article 39, 330; war in relation to Article 39 of the Charter, essence of, 328–329, parties to, 329, use of force by members consistent with Article 39
Universal compulsory service, 280
Unrelated assertions, questions and answers as to legal existence or non-existence of war, *201–203*, 221, 249, 251

Vera Cruz, occupation by United States Navy (1914), 94, 169
Vilna, capture by "rebel" General Zeligowski (1920), 96–97
Volunteer armies, 142

War, common meaning of word, *178–181*, 185–187, 190, 213, 218, 224, 275–277; as an instrument of justice, 183–186; as an instrument of policy, 177, 184–185; "in the sense of international law," 5, 78, 106, 149, 175–176, 359; "in the legal sense," 5, 148–149, 175, *176–177*, 181–183, 187–189, 195, 200, 213, 221–223, 237, 284, 292, 304–305, 311, 319, 321, 323; "in the material sense," 179; part way, 15, 19–36, *221*; "*sub modo*," 35–36; "in the technical sense," 5, 387; threat of, 145, 161; *see also* Imperfect war, Incomplete war, Limited war, Partial war, Quasi war, War with and without fighting
War Crimes Tribunals, Nuremberg, 282; Tokio, 273
War with and without fighting, historical considerations, 279–280; legal existence of war without fighting, 280–281; fighting a requisite for legal existence of war, 281–282; summary, 282–283
"Werewolves," 379, n. 5
White Flags, n. 10
World War I, 37, 79, 105, 144, 151, 157, 163–165, 171, 179–180, 205, 227, 266, 269, 276, 293, 299, 318
World War II, 9, 95, 157, 163–164, 180, 224, 255, 257, 266, 269, 276, 293, 300
Wounded and sick, 162, 164

Yellow Flags, 99, 361, n. 10